Clogh Oughter Castle, Co. Cavan:
archaeology, history and architecture

ARCHAEOLOGICAL MONOGRAPH SERIES: 8

Frontispiece—View of Clogh Oughter by William Ashford. (Donated by the McCarthy family to the Irish Heritage Trust and on display in Fota House, Cork. © Irish Heritage Trust.)

Clogh Oughter Castle, Co. Cavan: archaeology, history and architecture

CONLETH MANNING

With specialist contributions by

Karl Brady, Laureen Buckley, Heather Gimson, Elizabeth Heckett, Susan Lyons, Rosanne Meenan, Paul Mullarkey, Joseph Norton, Sara Pavia, Siobhán Scully, Damian Shiels, Richard Unitt and Joanna Wren

And

artefact drawings by Patricia Johnson, other publication drawings by Martin Halpin and photography by Con Brogan

Price: €30

Department of Arts, Heritage and the Gaeltacht

Archaeological Monograph Series

GENERAL EDITORS—ANN LYNCH AND CONLETH MANNING

1 Excavations at Roscrea Castle (Conleth Manning, ed.)
2 St Audoen's Church, Cornmarket, Dublin: archaeology and architecture (Mary McMahon)
3 Kells Priory, Co. Kilkenny: archaeological excavations by T. Fanning and M. Clyne (Miriam Clyne)
4 The history and archaeology of Glanworth Castle, Co. Cork: excavations 1982–4 (Conleth Manning)
5 Tintern Abbey, Co. Wexford: Cistercians and Colcloughs. Excavations 1982–2007 (Ann Lynch)
6 Trim Castle, Co. Meath: excavations 1995–8 (Alan R. Hayden)
7 Parke's Castle, Co. Leitrim: archaeology, history and architecture (Claire Foley and Colm Donnelly)

These monographs are subject to international peer review.

BAILE ÁTHA CLIATH
ARNA FHOILSIÚ AG OIFIG AN tSOLÁTHAIR
Le ceannach díreach ó
FOILSEACHÁIN RIALTAIS,
52 FAICHE STIABHNA, BAILE ÁTHA CLIATH 2
(Teil: 01 – 6476834 nó 1890 213434; Fax 01 – 6476843)
nó trí aon díoltóir leabhar.

DUBLIN
PUBLISHED BY THE STATIONERY OFFICE
To be purchased from
GOVERNMENT PUBLICATIONS,
52 ST STEPHEN'S GREEN, DUBLIN 2.
(Tel: 01 – 6476834 or 1890 213434; Fax: 01 – 6476843)
or through any bookseller.

ISBN: 978-1-4064-2777-6

Designed and typeset by Environmental Publications
Cover design by Design for Market
Copy-edited by Emer Condit, Wordwell Ltd
Printed by Castle Print (Galway) Ltd

Contents

Acknowledgements

The author would like to thank the following: Ruairí Ó Baoill, the senior supervisor on the excavation; Michael Ward, Kenneth Wiggins, Caroline Donaghy, Audrey Gahan and Franc Myles, archaeological assistants; Angela Dolan, Bernadette Dolan, Cathal Fleming, John Joe Carmichael, Stephen Hartung and Tom Connolly, who also worked on the excavation; Bríd and Walter Myles for much assistance during the excavation; all involved in the conservation work, especially Paul McMahon, senior architect, P.J. Dolan, Senior Clerk of Works, and Charlie Fleming, foreman, and the other workers on the conservation team; John O'Brien (OPW) for the floor plans of the castle and for photographs taken during the conservation work in 1986; Kevin O'Brien (OPW) for supplementary survey work and for arranging a boat in 2012; Con Brogan (DAHG) for his superb site photographs, the artefact photographs and the wonderful aerial photographs taken in March 2011; Tony Roche and Patricia Keenan for scanning the old photographs (unattributed photographs are by the author); Muiris de Buitléir for a survey of the island in 1987; Martin Halpin for the versions of the maps, plans and sections for publication, apart from Figs 2.2 and 2.4, which were done by Abigail Walsh and rescued from her computer by Gareth John; Patricia Johnson for her wonderful artefact drawings and for research on the decorated copper-alloy gun fragment; Sadhb Moddel for the drawings of the copper-alloy spurs; Phelim Manning for the reconstruction illustrations of the castle; Karl Brady for arranging, carrying out and writing up the underwater survey; the authors of the specialist reports and appendices; Joseph Norton for conservation work on most of the copper-alloy artefacts; Susannah Kelly, UCD, for conservation work on the large collection of iron artefacts and a few copper-alloy objects; Raghnall Ó Floinn, National Museum of Ireland, for advice on the copper-alloy objects, and Paul Mullarkey, NMI, for metal analysis; Brian Scott for advice on the iron artefacts; Kenneth Wiggins for supplying the photograph of the portrait of Henry Jones; Raymond Refaussé of the Representative Church Body Library for supplying the image of Bishop Bedell and for permission to reproduce it and the painting of Henry Jones; Kevin Baird of the Irish Heritage Trust for supplying an image of William Ashford's painting of Clogh Oughter and for giving permission to reproduce it; Neil Armstrong, the owner of the site of the Culme house in Inishconnell townland, for permission to carry out the geophysical survey of the house site; Paddy O'Donovan for informing me about the tower on Port Island; Caroline Donaghy for informing me of the old finds from Clogh Oughter in the National Museum; Michael Fewer, Umberto Pascali and Bernardo Carfagna for information on Dionisio Massari; the staff of the following libraries for their help with the historical research: Cavan County Library, the National Library of Ireland, the Russel Library, Maynooth College, the Royal Irish Academy (especially Siobhán Fitzpatrick and Bernadette Cunningham), Trinity College Library, the National Archives of Ireland (especially Aideen Ireland) and the Royal Society of Antiquaries of Ireland (especially Siobhán de hÓir); Brendan Scott for reading over and commenting on the history section and for other assistance; my colleagues in the National Monuments Service, especially Brian Duffy, Chief Archaeologist, Ann Lynch for support and encouragement, and Paul Walsh for carefully reading over and providing very useful comments on a draft of the text.

Introduction

The castle of Clogh Oughter is a large, circular tower on a tiny island in Lough Oughter, Co. Cavan. It is a national monument in State care (No. 602) and is listed in the statutory Record of Monuments and Places (CV020-060). Archaeological excavation, associated with conservation work on the structure, was directed by the present writer over a six-week period in 1987. The excavation, along with building analysis and historical research, has thrown much new light on the history of the castle and how it was used over the centuries. Virtually all of the finds from the excavation relate to the last half-century of its use up to the siege, surrender and destruction of the castle in 1653. It was built originally by the de Lacys about 1220 on a mostly man-made island but soon ended up in Irish hands and was held by the O'Reillys, the local chiefs, for most of the rest of the medieval period until around 1600. Around the time of the Plantation of Ulster (1610) the building was adapted to serve as a government stronghold and prison under its constable, Hugh Culme. The Culme family lived in a house on the southern shore of the lake and were subsequently granted the castle and its associated lands outright. At the outbreak of the 1641 rebellion the house and castle were captured by the insurgents and remained in their hands until surrendered to Cromwellian forces after a siege and artillery bombardment in 1653. The excavation and underwater investigations have thrown considerable light on the siege and four burials found are likely to relate to it. There are many first-hand accounts of the castle during the 1640s, especially relating to important prisoners who were held here, such as Bishop Bedell, Arthur Culme and Viscount Montgomery of Ards. The great Irish commander Owen Roe O'Neill died at Clogh Oughter in 1649.

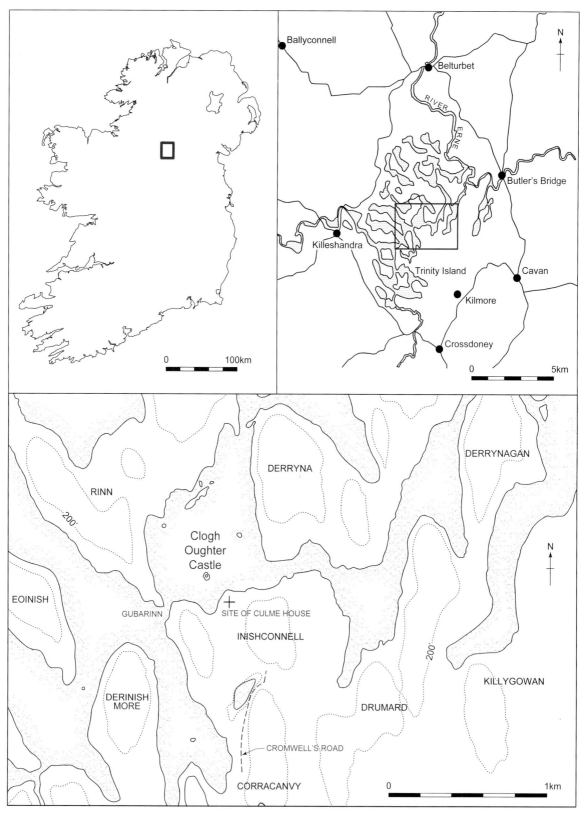

Fig. 1.1—Location map.

1. THE SETTING OF THE CASTLE

Lough Oughter is the uppermost major lake on the River Erne system—hence its name in Irish, *Loch Uachtair* (the upper lake). Downriver from it are the other two major lakes of the system, Upper Lough Erne and Lower Lough Erne, both in County Fermanagh. All three lakes were known as Lough Erne in early medieval times (Ó Mórdha 2002b). Unlike its sister lakes, Lough Oughter is not a wide expanse of water but rather a maze of interconnected smaller bodies of water interspersed with islands, former islands and promontories—in effect a drowned drumlin landscape. The section of lake in which Clogh Oughter stands is one of the larger open areas of water, measuring 1km long on the north/south axis and 700m wide (Fig. 1.1). The tiny island on which the castle stands (Irish Grid ref. 235783, 307847; ITM ref. 635726, 807858) is in the southern part of this open water, some 160m from the southern shore, which is part of the townland

of Inishconnell. As the townlands around the lake, as marked on the Ordnance Survey six-inch maps, only extend to the lake shore, Clogh Oughter is not officially in any townland. The townland of Inishconnell is in the parish of Kilmore, barony of Upper Loughtee, Co. Cavan (OS 6in. sheet 20).

The strategic importance of Clogh Oughter stems from the fact that it commands a narrow point in the lake called Gubarinn, some 300m to the south-west between the townlands of Rinn and Inishconnell. Gubarinn (*Gob an rinn*) could be translated as 'the mouth of or at the promontory'. All the water of the river system flows through this narrow point; any boats going up or down the lake now or in the past, when water levels were higher, have or had to go through Gubarinn and pass within sight of Clogh Oughter (Pl. 1.1). The castle in wintertime was described as follows in the seventeenth century: 'There was of old a little

Pl. 1.1—Aerial view of Clogh Oughter and Gubarinn in March 2011 (Con Brogan).

1

island about it, but it was worn all away to the bare stone walls, and not one foot of ground was to be seen, only a tall, round tower, like a pigeon house, standing in the midst of the waters' (Shuckburgh 1902, 189–90). Possibly more accurately, the owner in 1641, Arthur Culme, referred to 'there being not four yards of ground about it' (Gilbert 1879–80, I, 412).

The underlying bedrock in the area is limestone, and flat, fissured limestone bedrock can be seen at the northern end of the island when water levels in the lake are low. Above this the island consists mainly of loose stones piled up by man. At its greatest extent during low water levels the island on which the castle stands measures up to 70m north–south by 40m east–west. There are a number of other possible crannogs in this small section of the lake, and a few more, including some certain ones, within 2km of the castle (O'Donovan 1995, 175–90). The castle is overlooked by drumlin hills on the neighbouring shores in the townlands of Rinn to the west, Derryna to the east and Inishconnell to the south. Prior to drainage works on the river system, carried out between 1849 and 1859 (Lohan 1994, 242–3), the water levels were higher, with the result that present-day high winter levels are probably roughly equivalent to pre-drainage summer levels. Low summer levels today are lower than the lake ever was in medieval or early modern times. The present level of the lake around Clogh Oughter, as recorded under normal summer conditions by the Ordnance Survey, is 45m above sea level. As the townland boundaries followed the lake shore prior to drainage, there is now a narrow strip of land all around the lake and islands that is not officially within any townland.

2. THE HISTORY OF CLOGH OUGHTER

THE MEDIEVAL PERIOD AND THE SIXTEENTH CENTURY

The early history of Bréifne and the Uí Raghallaigh

The kingdom of Bréifne, corresponding roughly with the modern counties of Leitrim and Cavan (Fig. 2.1), has always been a border territory between the provinces of Ulster, Mide and Connacht. It has long been accepted that a branch of the Uí Briúin dynasty of Connacht, later known as Uí Briúin Bréifne, conquered this territory in the eighth century (Byrne 1973, 84, 232). It has recently been argued, however, that the connection between the Uí Briúin of Connacht and the so-called Uí Briúin Bréifne may be a fiction and that these kings of Bréifne were part of a powerful local dynasty who, for political reasons, fabricated a connec-

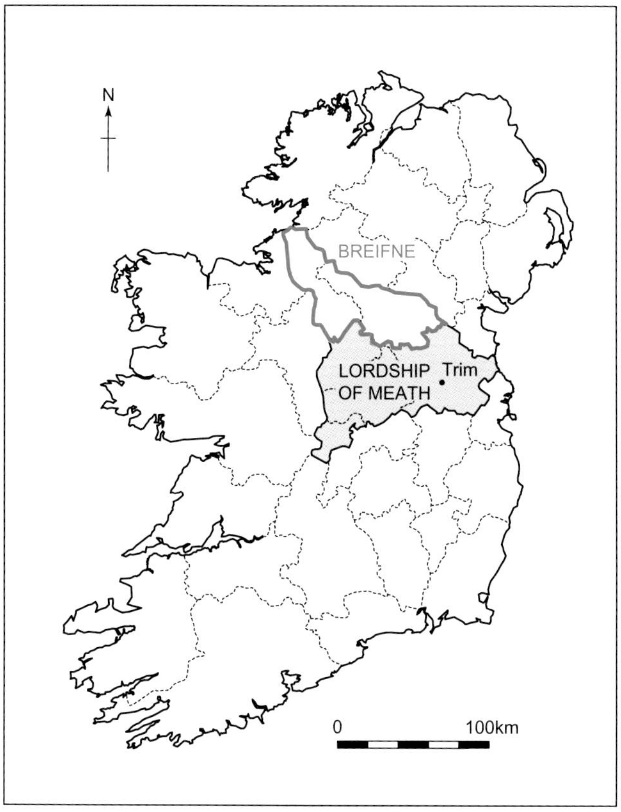

Fig. 2.1—Map showing Bréifne and the lordship of Meath.

tion with the Uí Briúin (Ó Mórdha 2002a). Be that as it may, Bréifne was subsequently considered part of Connacht and from the late tenth century up to the early twelfth century four kings of Connacht were of the Uí Briúin Bréifne. The dynasty adopted the surname Ó Ruairc (O'Rourke) after Ruarc, a ninth-century king of Bréifne, and by the mid-twelfth century Bréifne was a significantly powerful border kingdom under its ruler Tigernán Ó Ruairc.

The Uí Raghallaigh (O'Reillys) or Muintir Maoilmórdha, a branch of the Uí Briúin Bréifne (Table 2.1), were the kings of Machaire Gaileang in the eastern part of Bréifne, the area around Lough Ramor in present-day County Cavan. Under that surname they made their first appearance in the annals in 1128, when Cathal Ó Raghallaigh, fighting with his overlord, Tigernán Ó Ruairc, was killed by Conchobhair Mac Lochlainn. The Uí Raghallaigh had designs on the kingship of Bréifne, however, and rebelled against Tigernán Ó Ruairc in 1153; as a result their chief, Geofraidh, was banished to Connacht. He was back in Bréifne in 1155, opposing Tigernán until he and his son were assassinated at Kells in 1161 by Tigernán's son Maelsechlainn (Mac an Ghallóglaigh 1988, 539–40). With the arrival of the Anglo-Normans in 1169, the Uí Raghallaigh saw an opportunity to throw off the yoke of Ó Ruairc overlordship and allied themselves with the invaders. As early as 1171 Ó Raghallaigh was with Strongbow, defending Dublin against the high king, Ruaidhri Ó Conchobhair, and Tigernán Ó Ruairc, king of Bréifne (K. Simms 1979, 305–6; Parker 1995, 38). The high king and his allies were defeated, and when Tigernán died in 1172 East Bréifne became a semi-autonomous lordship under the Uí Raghallaigh. The new threat they were now facing came from the de Lacy lordship of Meath (Fig. 2.1), a lordship that in theory encompassed both Bréifne and Airghialla (Oriel).

The de Lacys, Bréifne and Clogh Oughter

It is uncertain how early the de Lacys[1] began moving into Bréifne but they had acquired rights to the area by 1196 (Parker 1991, 157) and de Lacy's vassal Gilbert de

---

[1] For the family background of the de Lacys see Wightman 1966.

3

Table 2.1—A simplified and selected genealogy of Uí Briúin Bréifne to AD 1330.

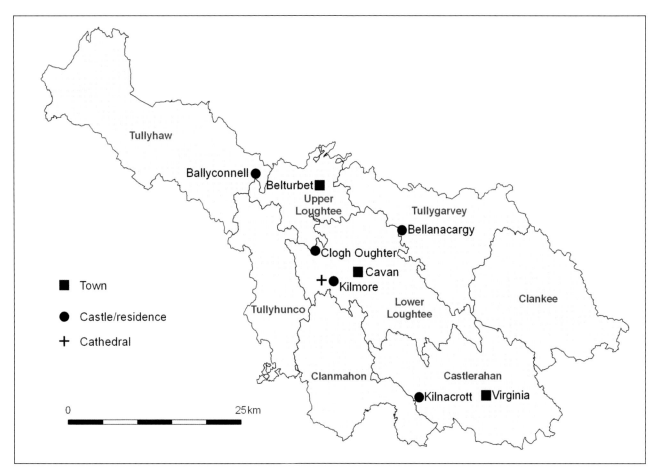

Fig. 2.2—A map of County Cavan, showing the modern baronies and some of the places mentioned in the text.

Nangle appears to have had a foothold in Bréifne by that time (Orpen 1920, vol. 3, 32). It is possible that some of the motte-castles in County Cavan were constructed around this time but the earliest references we have to any of them date from 1211–12, when the lordship of Meath was being administered by the king because of his mistrust of the powerful de Lacys (Davies and Quinn 1941, 25, 37–41). The mottes referred to in this source were those at Kilmore, the important church site and diocesan centre only three miles from Clogh Oughter, and Belturbet, further north on the River Erne (Fig. 2.2). These were important links in the chain of communication with Clones, where a castle was built in an attempt to conquer central Ulster. This campaign was unsuccessful and Clones was burnt by Ó Néill in 1212 (*AFM*). By then the cooperation between the Uí Raghallaigh and the Anglo-Normans had broken down, for while Ó Ruairc was peacefully paying rent to the seneschal of Meath, Ó Raghallaigh was being held prisoner (Davies and Quinn 1941, 37, 45).

In 1215 Walter, son of Hugh de Lacy, was reinstated in the lordship of Meath, and the castle of Kilmore was restored to him along with his other possessions (Orpen 1920, vol. 3, 32–3). He soon set about expanding his influence in Bréifne. In 1220, according to the *Annals of Loch Cé*, he 'performed a great hosting to the crannog of Ó Raighilligh. He went upon it and obtained hostages and great power' (*ALC*, I, 261–3; Orpen 1920, vol. 3, 33; K. Simms 1979, 307). In 1221 de Lacy granted the kingdom of Bréifne to his vassal Philip de Angulo (Nangle) and agreed that his half-brother, William Gorm de Lacy,[2] would 'build three stone castles for the use of de Angulo' in Bréifne (Orpen 1920, vol. 3, 34–5; Morrin 1862, 197). Even if previously begun by the de Lacys, Clogh Oughter may possibly have been one of these three castles.

---

[2] William Gorm was a son of the original Hugh de Lacy, who was killed in 1186, the offspring of his second marriage to a daughter of Ruaidhri Ó Conchobhair, the last high king of Ireland (Scott and Martin 1978, 338, n. 352). She subsequently married an Anglo-Norman called Blund, by whom she had the sons mentioned here, Henry and Thomas. For an account of the career of William Gorm de Lacy see Veach and Verstraten Veach 2013. There is uncertainty about the first name of William Gorm's mother, for only one source, an unreliable one, gives it as Rose (Veach and Verstraten Veach 2013, 63–4).

By 1224 William Gorm appears to have made considerable progress in Bréifne, for in that year the king of Connacht, Cathal Croibhdhearg Ó Conchobhair, complained to Henry III that Bréifne had been taken by William (Shirley 1862, 223–4),[3] who may have been hoping to hold it for himself rather than de Nangle. In the same year the de Lacys fell out of favour with Henry III because of their attempt to seize the earldom of Ulster. In June William Marshal the younger, earl of Pembroke and lord of Leinster, was sent to Ireland as justiciar with an army to subdue the rebellion of the de Lacys. He defeated William Gorm in battle (K. Simms 1979, 307). 'The same day an Irishman named O'Reilly, powerful in his country, who had come to the King's peace after the Earl had come to the office of justiciary, rode over to a castle called Cronoc Orauly (Crannog O'Reilly); sat down in an island and besieged the castle, praying succour of the Earl. The latter sent knights and soldiers to him, who took the castle' (Sweetman 1875, 183; Shirley 1862, 500–1). The knights who assisted Ó Raghallaigh in besieging the castle were Walter de Riddlesford and Richard de Tuit (Sweetman 1875, 184). In the castle at the time of its capture on 28 July were William Gorm's mother, who was the daughter of Ruaidhri Ó Conchobhair, William's wife Gwenllian,[4] who was the daughter of Llywelyn ab Iorwerth (Llywelyn the Great), prince of Wales, and the wife of his half-brother, Thomas Blund (Orpen 1920, vol. 3, 43). The following day the castle of Kilmore was besieged and surrendered along with William's half-brother Henry Blund and a clerk called Hugh. An unnamed brother of William Gorm and Henry Blund was killed in this campaign and his head was presented to William Marshal. Marshal used the threat of imprisoning William's mother as a means of bringing the new king of Connacht, Aedh Ó Conchobhair,[5] to the king's peace. The castle of Cronoc Orauly (Crannog O'Reilly) is in all likelihood Clogh Oughter.

In 1225, after the de Lacys had come to terms with the Crown, certain castles were returned to them, including Kilmore (Orpen 1920, vol. 3, 46). As there is no mention of the castle of Crannog O'Reilly or Clogh Oughter, it may have been left in Uí Raghallaigh hands. In 1226 (*AFM*) in a daring move Cathal Ó Raghallaigh attacked and demolished Kilmore Castle and presum-

ably drove the de Lacys out of Bréifne. William Gorm de Lacy made a last attempt to regain control of Bréifne in 1233 by leading a large army of Irish and Anglo-Normans into the territory. He was decisively beaten by Ó Raghallaigh at the battle of Móin Crandchain (probably the townland of Creighan, immediately south of Cavan town), was wounded in the battle and died soon afterwards (K. Simms 1979, 311). This brought an end to the realisation of de Lacy ambitions in Bréifne.

The Uí Raghallaigh from 1233 to the early sixteenth century

For the rest of the medieval period East Bréifne remained a border territory, between the Anglo-Norman lordship of Meath to the south and the powerful semi-independent Gaelic lordships of Ó Néill (O'Neill) and Ó Domhnaill (O'Donnell) of Ulster to the north. The leaders of the Uí Raghallaigh formed various alliances from time to time with neighbouring Gaelic lords, such as Mac Mathghamhna (MacMahon) to the east in Monaghan, Mág Uidhir (Maguire) in Fermanagh and their former overlords the Uí Ruairc in West Bréifne (present-day County Leitrim). At times these neighbouring Gaelic lords took sides in internal dynastic disputes among the Uí Raghallaigh or simply raided the Uí Raghallaigh territory. Ó Raghallaigh would have engaged in similar activities in their territories, as well as occasionally raiding the lordship of Meath.

In the immediate aftermath of the defeat of the de Lacys, the Uí Raghallaigh had ambitions to control all of Bréifne and formed various alliances to achieve this end. Ó Ruairc and Ó Conchobhair invaded East Bréifne in 1255 and set up Conchobhar Ó Raghallaigh, son of Cathal (Table 2.1), as a puppet leader. The following year they defeated Cathal Ó Raghallaigh in battle and Cathal himself was killed (Parker 1995, 39–40). For a time after this battle Ó Ruairc controlled all of Bréifne, with Conchobhair Ó Raghallaigh ruling East Bréifne under his overlordship. The earliest reference to Clogh Oughter castle under the original form of its present name dates from this period. It is the death notice of Conchobhar Ó Raghallaigh, who died at Clogh Oughter in 1257, and it occurs only in a late compilation of annals of Bréifne interest (de hÓir 1970,

---

[3] William Gorm was the grand-nephew of Cathal Croibhdhearg.
[4] While Llywelyn did marry Joan, the daughter of King John, there is evidence to suggest that his son Gruffudd and daughter Gwenllian (Lloyd 1919) had a different mother, Tangwystyl. Marshal's letter specifies that William de Lacy's wife was the sister of Gruffudd by both mother and father (*de patre et matre*) (Shirley 1862, 502). William Marshal the younger was married to another daughter of King John, so he may have been distancing himself and the king (King John's son) from Gwenllian by specifying the relationship.
[5] Cathal Croibhdhearg died in 1224. William Gorm's mother was Aedh's first cousin.

64). The name used in this source and other later annalistic references is *Cloch Locha hUachtair*, or sometimes *Caisleán Locha hUachtair*. *Cloch* in the former version, which basically means a stone or rock, can also mean a construction of stone, especially a fortress, stronghold or castle (*DIL*). In more recent times the name became shortened from *Cloch Locha hUachtair*—the castle of Loch Uachtair or the upper lake (of the Erne river system)—to Clogh Oughter.

The next reference to Clogh Oughter is in a legendary story from a text in Irish of *c.* 1700 about the O'Reillys (Carney 1959). The text explains how the Uí Sirideán (Sheridans) came to Bréifne sometime after the death of Cathal na Beithighe Ó Raghallaigh (1256) and probably when Fearghal an Tóchair Ó Raghallaigh was chief (1285–93). Ó Ruairc apparently still had possession of Clogh Oughter and Ó Sirideán and his sons, who had recently fled from Connacht, were promised land by Ó Raghallaigh if they could take the castle. They watched the castle from the shore of the lake until servants were sent out in cots (logboats) to cut firewood on the shore. The Uí Sirideán slew the servants, put on their clothes of animal skins and were admitted to the castle by the unsuspecting soldiers of Ó Ruairc, whom they promptly slew. In this way Ó Raghallaigh regained Clogh Oughter and as a reward the Uí Sirideán got some of the best land in East Bréifne (Carney 1959, 116–17).

From the 1280s for over a century a peripatetic branch of the Uí Conchobhair of Connacht called the Clann Muircheartaigh (Simms 2001) were involved in Bréifne, allying themselves against the Uí Raghallaigh, sometimes with Mac Ciarnán, sometimes with Ó Ruairc. They were heavily defeated by Ó Raghallaigh in 1317 but returned to fight later in the century. The first mention of Clogh Oughter in the main collections of Irish annals occurs under the date 1327, when it is stated that *Cloch Locha hUachtair* was burnt by Cathal Ó Ruairc (*AFM*).[6] This is succeeded by a confusing second reference under the same date that *Caislén Locha hUachtair* was taken by Ó Ruairc by cunning, for twenty cows (*AFM*).[7]

The next reference to Clogh Oughter occurs in a time of serious internal strife among the Uí Raghallaigh. A strong chief of the Uí Raghallaigh,

Giolla Iosa Ruadh, who held the chieftainship from 1293 to 1315, had thirteen sons; after he retired to end his days in the Franciscan friary in Cavan, the chieftainship passed to different sons—firstly Maelseachlainn, who died in 1327, then to Risdeard, who died in 1349, then to Cú Connacht, who retired to the friary in 1365, and then to Pilib (Table 2.2). Pilib appears to have tried to advance his own immediate family to the exclusion of the families of his brothers. He got embroiled in a dispute between the archbishop of Armagh, Milo Sweetman, and Riocard Ó Raghallaigh, the bishop of Tir Brun (Kilmore), who happened to be his nephew, a son of his brother Maelseachlainn (Table 2.2). There had been complaints about Bishop Riocard concerning his harsh treatment of diocesan clergy and his incestuous relationship with his first cousin, who had been married to a Mág Uidhir of Fermanagh. The archbishop sought Pilib's help in dealing with the problem and Pilib used this excuse to misappropriate the lands of the bishop of Kilmore for his own benefit (Smith 1996, 54–5, 67–8, 100). Riocard died in 1369. In the same year Maghnus Ó Raghallaigh, a son of Pilib's immediate predecessor, Cú Connacht, led a rebellion against Pilib and incarcerated him in Clogh Oughter, severely bound and fettered (Parker 1991, 161–2; *AFM*). Maghnus then assumed the lordship, but Pilib's faction, with the help of Mac Mathghamhna and the chiefs of Oriel, defeated Maghnus at the battle of Bléine an Chupa (Bleancup townland, two miles south of Clogh Oughter). Pilib Mág Uidhir, lord of Fermanagh, brought vessels to Lough Oughter, took the castle and liberated Pilib, who then reassumed the lordship. In the following year Maghnus Ó Raghallaigh was taken prisoner and confined to Clogh Oughter, where he remained until 1380. In that year he was released during a campaign by Ó Néill and Mág Aonghusa and his brother gave undertakings on his behalf (de hÓir 1970, 66). The imprisonment of Pilib at Clogh Oughter is also referred to in *A genealogical history of the O'Reillys*, where it is related that 'he had no allowance save a sheaf of oats for day and night, and a cup of water, so that he was compelled to drink his own urine' (Carney 1959, 105–6). The Clann Muircheartaigh of the Uí Conchobhair invaded East Bréifne in 1370 and in 1391, but after being defeated in the latter invasion they never again involved them-

---

[6] The Irish text here uses the word *loscadh*, meaning 'burning', though O'Donovan mistakenly translated it as 'taken'.

[7] The early seventeenth-century compilers of the *Annals of the Four Masters* must have got these two entries from different sources, and possibly did not realise that they referred to the same place and presumably event. As the event is not recorded in any other surviving set of annals it is difficult to work out what exactly happened. Connellan, in his translation of the *Annals of the Four Masters*, paraphrased the two entries as follows: 'The Castle of Lough Oughter was taken by O'Rourke, but he delivered it up again for 20 cows' (Kirker 1890–1, 296).

Table 2.2—A simplified and selected genealogy of the O'Reilly chiefs from the early fourteenth century, with those who served as chief in bold.

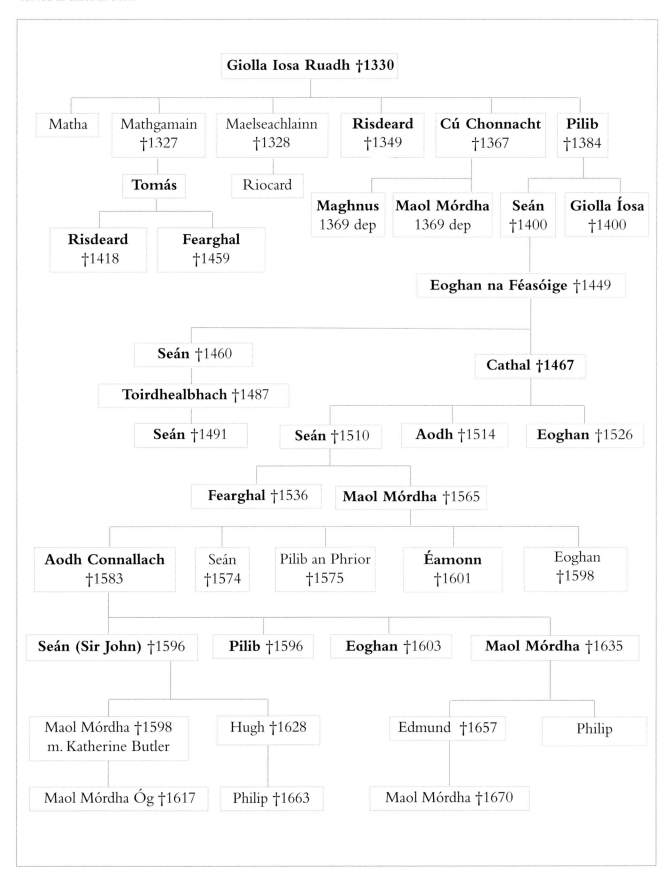

selves in Bréifne (Parker 1995, 41). In 1390 Maghnus Ó Ruairc, who was being held as a prisoner in Clogh Oughter, escaped from the castle and went to the castle of Lough Scur, but he was betrayed by the Clann Muircheartaigh 'and they killed him as he stepped out of his skiff' (*AC*).

From at least the fourteenth century Ó Raghallaigh appears to have set up his main residence at Tullymongan, on the edge of the present-day town of Cavan. Seán Ó Raghallaigh died in his bed at Tulach Mongáin in 1400 (*AFM*) and a later chief, Toirdhealbhach, is described as dying 'in his castle of Tullymongan' in 1487 (*AFM*). An early fifteenth-century Ó Raghallaigh, Eoghan na Féasóige ('of the beard'), set up a market near his castle at Cavan (Tullymongan) and encouraged trading links with the Anglo-Normans of Meath and the Pale. He may also have been responsible for the minting of 'O'Reillie's money', counterfeited English groats, the use of which was outlawed in 1456 (Parker 1995, 45–6). By this stage East Bréifne's connections with Connacht were very much in the past and its links were more with Ulster to the north and the descendants of the Anglo-Normans to the south. From the 1490s the earls of Kildare began interfering in the politics of East Bréifne and made a number of raids into the territory to impose their will. After the suppression of the Kildare rebellion, the new chief, Maol Mórdha, elected in 1536, initiated a period of close cooperation with the Dublin government.

THE SIXTEENTH CENTURY

Maol Mórdha forged alliances with the Old English families of the Pale and some of his sons and one daughter married into the Nugent, Barnewall and Plunkett families. On his death in 1565, his eldest son, Aodh Connallach Ó Raghallaigh, followed him as chief and was also cooperative with the Dublin government. He expressed himself amenable to the process of surrender and regrant but the detail was never worked out. He allowed Lord Deputy Henry Sidney to take his son Seán (John) to meet the queen and formally surrendered the lordship (Brady 1985, 240). Seán remained at court or in Dublin for up to eight years and was given a good education in the English language and law, as well as a knighthood (*ibid.*, 254). East Bréifne was designated as the county of Cavan in 1579 and a sheriff and other officials were appointed (Cunningham 1995, 61; Maginn 2009). Aodh Connallach was knighted in the same year and was subsequently known to the English as Sir Hugh O'Reilly. When he died in 1583 the succession was by

no means a foregone conclusion: while Seán Ruadh (Sir John), the eldest son, was favoured by the Dublin government, his younger brother Pilib was better regarded locally, having defended the territory against the O'Neills while John was away. In addition, under the Irish system a number of brothers and uncles, especially Éamonn (Table 2.2), who had been *tánaiste* under Aodh, would have been equally eligible.

As matters transpired, Éamonn and Pilib agreed with the Dublin government that Sir John would be appointed O'Reilly or captain of his nation. Agreement on surrender and regrant was eventually achieved in 1584, whereby Sir John agreed to surrender his claims to the overlordship of all of Cavan and was granted the lordship of the baronies of Cavan (equivalent to the present baronies of Lower and Upper Loughtee) and Tullygarvey in fee simple and retained seigneurial rights in Clonballykernan (Tullyhunco) and Tullyhaw baronies (Fig. 2.2). His uncle, Éamonn, was to be granted the barony of Castlerahan in fee simple, while Clanmahon barony was to be divided between his uncle Cathaoir Gearr and the sons of his uncle Pilib an Phrior. Clankee barony was to be granted to his brother Pilib (Brewer and Bullen 1868, 391; Brady 1985, 246–7; Cunningham 1995, 66).

The new system ran into problems almost immediately, mainly because it favoured Sir John too much and as a result was seen by the other O'Reillys as unfair (Brady 2004, 182–3). Possibly because of difficulties he had with the settlement, Sir John's brother Pilib was arrested and imprisoned in Dublin Castle late in 1585 and was not released until 1592. The property division of 1584 remained in place, however. Eventually it was the rebellion in Ulster that proved disastrous for the O'Reillys. In 1593 Hugh Maguire of Fermanagh went into rebellion, and early in 1594 an attack on his castle of Enniskillen was launched from Cavan with the cooperation of the O'Reillys. In retaliation Maguire plundered and burnt Cavan town and much of the county in 1595, by which time Pilib and some of the other O'Reillys had defected to the rebels (Brady 2004, 182–5). Without the support of all the O'Reillys, Sir John was no longer strong enough to effectively oppose Hugh O'Neill, earl of Tyrone, and the other Ulster rebels. Also, the Dublin government was not in a position to guarantee him protection from O'Neill, nor to curb the activities of their captains in County Cavan. Sir John was left with little option but to submit to O'Neill. This he did with his brother Pilib and others on their knees in the market-place in Dundalk (Carney 1950, 183). He died soon afterwards in 1596, 'in rebellion'. O'Neill appointed Sir John's brother Pilib as O'Reilly but he was killed by O'Neill's followers that same year. O'Neill then appointed Sir John's elderly uncle Éamonn as O'Reilly (Wood 1933, 147).

Sir John's eldest son, Maol Mórdha, who was married to Katherine Butler,[8] a niece of Thomas, the 10th earl of Ormond, remained loyal to the Crown. The new lord deputy, Sir Thomas Burgh, and Maol Mórdha recaptured the ruined Cavan town in 1597, and Maol Mórdha was appointed military commander of the county (Brady 2004, 186). O'Neill reported that by 1598 Maol Mórdha had banished Éamonn out of Bréifne and was holding his uncles Eóghan and Maol Mórdha as prisoners (Cunningham 1995, 71). That same year he was killed fighting with Bagenal on the English side at the Battle of the Yellow Ford in County Armagh. According to Philip O'Sullivan Beare he had a 'singularly fine figure and wonderfully handsome countenance', from which he was named the 'fair'. At the battle he did his best to rally the government troops but died fighting valiantly (Byrne 1903, 106, 111–12). He was survived by his widow, Katherine Butler, and their son Maol Mórdha Óg,[9] who fled to the protection of Dublin soon after the battle, while his uncles Hugh and John went to fight for the queen in Munster. Hugh O'Neill usurped the lordship himself in 1599 and appointed Turlough Mac Shane O'Reilly as *tánaiste*. In 1600 Lord Mountjoy raided Cavan and had Turlough Mac Shane publicly executed (Brady 2004, 187). Katherine Butler, Maol Mórdha's widow, may have been reinstated in her properties, because lists of government forts in 1600–1 name her as the warden of Clogh Oughter and Bellanacargy castles (Fig. 2.2), where she commanded six men (*CSPI* 1601–3, 16, 347). Éamonn died in 1601 and the leadership passed to Sir John's brother Eóghan, who with the help of Sir John's sons Hugh and John first declared for O'Neill, when he was on the way to Kinsale, and then sought a pardon from the government after the defeat of O'Neill at the battle of Kinsale. When Eóghan died in 1603 Cavan was devastated by war and its people demoralised. The leadership passed to Eóghan's brother Maol Mórdha, who lived on until 1635.

A map of Ulster dating from about 1590 in the National Maritime Museum, London, shows Clogh Oughter as a dot on a small island on the River Erne, as well as showing Cavan town and Belturbet (Margey 2009, 107, pl. 3). Another map of around the same period, from the National Archives, London, shows the entire River Erne system schematically; while it does not show Clogh Oughter, it gives a bird's-eye view of the town of Cavan (Swift 1999, 45; Margey 2009, 106–7, pl. 1). Tullymongan Castle is shown on a hill above the town with the caption 'Aurelies castle on the hill over the Cavan'. This was presumably the main residence of Sir John O'Reilly. In 1584 he is referred to as 'of the Cavan', which is probably a reference to this residence.[10] Clogh Oughter, which along with Cavan town is in the barony of Upper Loughtee, was probably not used as a high-status residence since at least the fourteenth century, though it was under the control of the O'Reilly chief and was used mainly as a prison and stronghold. Some official sources give an indication of where other members of the O'Reillys were living. For example, Sir John's brother Pilib is described as of Bellanacargy, in the barony of Tullygarvey, in 1584 (*Irish Fiants*: Elizabeth no. 4534; Ó Mórdha 1981, 52), though he probably had to hand this over to Sir John and move to Clankee barony as a result of the land division of that year. Bellanacargy is certainly found later in the hands of members of Sir John's family. Sir John's uncle Éamonn is described as of Kilnacrott (Fig. 2.2), in the barony of Castlerahan, in 1582 (*Irish Fiants*: Elizabeth no. 3914), and this appears to have continued as his residence after 1584.

THE SEVENTEENTH CENTURY

The episode of the baron of Delvin

Sir Christopher St Lawrence, baron of Howth, reported to the lord deputy, Sir Arthur Chichester, in the summer of 1607 that when in Flanders he learned of a conspir-

---

[8] Katherine Butler was a daughter of John Butler of Kilcash, Co. Tipperary, and therefore a sister of Walter of the Rosaries, who later became the 11th earl of Ormond (*CSPI* Eliz., vol. 7, 422; NLI MS 12,024, p. 5). According to Jackson (1975–6, 482), sometime after the death of Maol Mórdha she married Sir Énri Óg O'Neill, a second cousin and enemy of Hugh O'Neill and grandfather of Sir Phelim O'Neill, who was one of the leaders of the 1641 rebellion. Sir Énri and his son Turlough Óg died fighting on the English side in 1608 during the rebellion of Sir Cahir O'Doherty. This information on her second marriage is confirmed by a letter of Sir Arthur Chichester of 1612 (Edwards 1938, 28). She was back in Cavan in 1610 to take up, with her son Maol Mórdha Óg, the estate he was granted under the Plantation of Ulster, with a right to 1,000 acres for her life of the 3,000 acres he was granted (Moody 1938, 202).
[9] Maol Mórdha Óg had a praise poem written in Irish in his honour but died young in 1617 (Carney 1950, 121–7, 228).
[10] It is not recorded whether it was badly damaged in Maguire's raid of 1595. It was certainly in ruin by the later seventeenth century, when a poem was written about the ruined castle, listing all of the O'Reillys who lived in it (Carney 1950, 114–21). Unfortunately, nothing survives today of the castle (O'Donovan 1995, 233).

acy against the government, and he named Sir Richard Nugent,[11] baron of Delvin, as one of the conspirators (Ó Muraíle 2007, 505–6). Whatever truth was in this supposed conspiracy, the earls of Tyrone and Tyrconnell and Maguire and their families took ship for the Continent in September 1607 in what has become known as 'the Flight of the Earls'. Delvin was arrested and imprisoned in Dublin Castle on suspicion of high treason. With the help of a rope that was brought in to him, he escaped from Dublin Castle and fled first to his castle at Finnea, Co. Westmeath, and later to Clogh Oughter, 'a strong castle . . . which standeth in the middle of a great lough' (Wood 1933, 184). He owned land in Cavan and had family connections with the O'Reillys, and on this occasion some of the O'Reillys joined with him (Carney 1959, 28, 37). On 23 November 1607 he wrote a letter from Clogh Oughter to Sir Arthur Chichester, the lord deputy (Pl. 2.1), seeking a pardon, but when the possibility of a pardon was suggested he did not reply (*CSPI* 1606–8, 337–8). At this time Chichester described Clogh Oughter as 'an old castle without a roof, standing in a lough in the county of Cavan, which he meant to take into the King's hands and make fit to contain a store of munition and victuals to supply that country upon occasion it being passable by boat, with a little help over a ford or two, almost to Balashanan' (*ibid.*, 336). Chichester sent Sir Garret Moore with some troops to Cavan in pursuit. When Delvin sent out some of his men from the castle to snatch cows and sheep locally for food, they were attacked by Sir Garret Moore's men; after a few were killed, the rest got back across the lake to the castle in their 'cottes' (logboats) (*ibid.*, 352). After Fergal Óg O'Reilly deserted him, Delvin left Clogh Oughter and his infant son in the hands of some of his followers (*ibid.*, 356). In the meantime, Sir Richard Wingfield, high marshall of Ireland, was sent after him with 200 foot and a troop of horse, and on reaching Clogh Oughter laid siege to it from the mainland (Wood 1933, 184–5). They captured the castle along with Delvin's son, while Delvin himself had taken to the woods dressed as a 'woodkerne in mantle and trouses' (*CSPI* 1606–8, 362). Delvin submitted to the government in May 1608 and was granted a pardon by the king.[12] The government continued to hold Clogh Oughter.

Pl. 2.1—Sir Arthur Chichester (after an eighteenth-century print reproduced in McCavitt 1998).

The Plantation of Ulster and associated surveys

In the aftermath of the treaty of Mellifont between Hugh O'Neill and the government in 1603, the approach to dealing with County Cavan was to be a refinement of the settlement of 1584 that would be fairer to all concerned (Brady 2004, 178). Katherine Butler had been claiming the whole county in right of her late husband Maol Mórdha, son of Sir John O'Reilly. Sir George Carey, during his term as lord deputy in 1603–4, assigned to her one third of the profit of the county and the custody of her son, while entrusting the land of the county to Sir John's brother, Maol Mórdha (Table 2.2) during the king's pleasure (Morley 1890, 350). The attorney general, Sir John Davies, visited Cavan with the lord deputy in 1606 to initiate survey work with a settlement such as that of 1584 in mind (*ibid.*, 343–80; Hayes-McCoy 1960, 181; McCavitt 1998, 95–6). They pitched their tents on the south side of 'this poor Irish town' and set up commissions to enquire into what lands in the county were escheated to the Crown (Morley 1890, 374–6). The commission found that the entire county was forfeited to the Crown and Lord

---

[11] Nugent, born in 1583, was the 15th baron of Delvin. He succeeded to the title on his father's death in 1602 and was knighted by Lord Deputy Mountjoy in Dublin in 1603 in the same ceremony in which Rory O'Donnell was made earl of Tyrconnell (Ó Muraíle 2007, 506).

[12] He was made earl of Westmeath in 1621 and died in 1642 after rough treatment by the rebels when he was trying to make his way to Dublin, having refused to join the rebellion (Manning 1997).

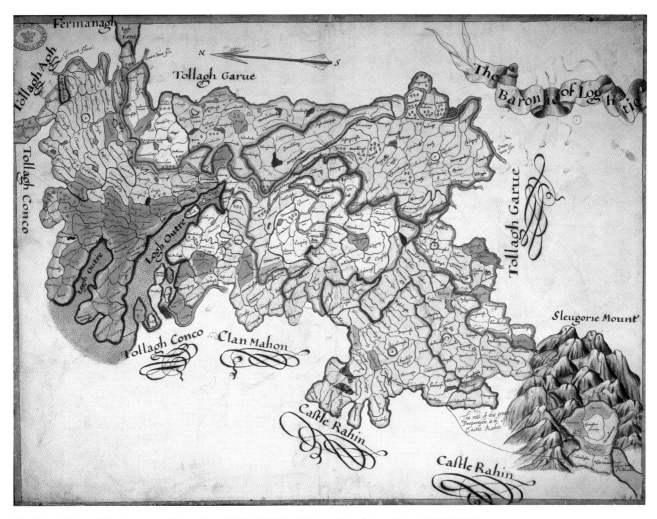

Pl. 2.2—Map of the barony of Loughtee, 1609. (© The National Archives, Kew. MPF1/52.)

Deputy Chichester deferred any decisions until he returned to Dublin. The political situation in Ulster changed completely with the Flight of the Earls in 1607 and a new plantation was mooted for the lands of O'Neill, O'Donnell and Maguire. Though County Cavan was not part of these lands, it was added to the five other counties and the scheme became known as the Plantation of Ulster. The argument of the government was that the last few O'Reilly chiefs had died in rebellion and that therefore the territory reverted to the Crown (Brady 2004, 175).

A descriptive survey of the six escheated counties was completed in 1608 by order of the king (MacNéill and Hogan 1931). That for County Cavan is dated 6 September 1608 and gives the names of all the 'ballybetaghs' into which each barony was divided, as well as the number of 'polls' (roughly equivalent to townlands)[13] in each ballybetagh. Ecclesiastical lands were also listed, along with fairs and fisheries (*ibid.*, 204–13). This survey was followed by a mapped survey of each barony in the

six counties, carried out between July and October 1609 (Andrews 1974, 142). Original copies of these maps for four of the six counties survive in London, including those of all seven Cavan baronies (Andrews 1974; Margey 2009, 108–11, pls 5–7). The maps were produced under the supervision of Josias Bodley and, while they purport to show all of the townlands in the baronies, are not accurate cartographic surveys. The map of the barony of Loughtee (Pl. 2.2) shows 'Clogh Outre' as a castellated tower on a small island in 'Logh Outre', which is very inaccurately depicted (Margey 2009, pl. 5; Swift 1999, 60).

When Chichester and Davies returned to Cavan in 1610 they had their minds made up as to how the plantation would be carried out. Once see and glebe lands were reserved for the church, the remainder of the county was to be divided among English and Scottish undertakers, servitors (those who had served in the army or administration in Ireland) and natives. Strict rules were laid down that undertakers had to

---

[13] All such local land measures ('polls' in Cavan, 'tates' in Monaghan and 'ballybetaghs') are discussed in McErlean 1983, 316–26.

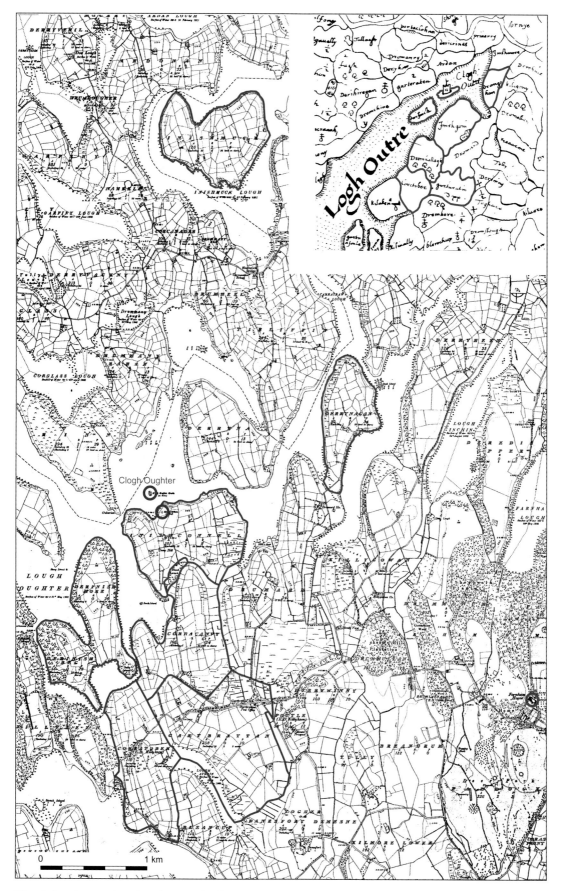

Fig. 2.3—A map showing the townlands assigned to Clogh Oughter Castle under the Plantation of Ulster. (© Ordnance Survey Ireland. All rights reserved. Licence no. EN0059212.) Clogh Oughter, the site of the Culme house and Farnham House are also highlighted. A detail of the Bodley map of 1609 (see Pl. 2.2) with the lands attached to Clogh Oughter highlighted is shown in the top right-hand corner.

Pl. 2.3—Detail of a map of the escheated counties of Ulster *c.* 1610, showing the county of Cavan. (© The British Library Board. Cotton MS Augustus I.ii.44.)

settle people from Britain on their lands and could not lease to native Irish. Native grantees were to share baronies with servitors, who could lease to native Irish, whereas the undertakers were in theory to colonise entire baronies. The barony of Loughtee was designated for English undertakers (Hunter 1973–5, 471–3), and the baronies of Clankee and Tullyhunco were reserved for Scottish undertakers (Perceval-Maxwell 1999, 97). Thirty polls were to be allotted to the three corporate

towns: Cavan, Belturbet and another to be developed halfway between Kells and Cavan (Virginia). Ten townlands were to be allotted to the castle of Cavan, six to the castle of Clogh Oughter and fourteen for a free school to be founded in Cavan (Hill 1877, 113–14; Moody 1938, 294–5).

The first mention of the Culme family in connection with Clogh Oughter dates from 1608, when Captain Hugh Culme[14] carried out repairs to the castle

---

[14] He was a younger son of Hugh Culme of Canonleigh in Devon and a brother of Benjamin Culme, dean of St Patrick's Cathedral, Dublin (Table 2.3). Richard Culme, probably his eldest brother, inherited Canonleigh, while another brother, Philip, became a merchant tailor in London (Ainsworth 1948, 26). Two of Hugh's uncles, John and Robert, had already settled in Dublin (Trevelyan and Trevelyan 1872, pedigree of Culme family). Hugh came to Ireland as a soldier in 1606 and got the army post of saymaster for testing leather. He served as sheriff of County Cavan in 1607, 1611 and 1612. He was elected as MP for Cavan borough in 1613 but was unseated because of electoral irregularities. He was knighted in 1623. He had four sons and three daughters by his wife, Mary Emerson of Derbyshire, who after his death at Clogh Oughter in 1630 married General Michael Jones (*DIB*, II, 1079).

Pl. 2.4—Detail of a map of the escheated counties of Ulster *c.* 1610, showing Cavan town and Clogh Oughter. (© The British Library Board.)

costing £10 harps (Irish) and was reimbursed for it (*CSPI* 1608–10, 80). Under the Plantation of Ulster, Culme was made 'constable of the king's castle of Cloughoughter'. The following lands allotted to the castle were leased to him for 21 years at a yearly rent of one pound Irish on 16 November 1610: the islands of Cloughowter, Derry-Inishe (Derinish More and Derinish Beg), Derrinegan (Derrynagan), as well as the following lands near the castle: Inishgonine (Inishconnell), Dromhallagh (probably Corracanvy townland), Gorturahine (Gortbratten), Carrowtubber (Corratubber) and Inishmuckane (Inishmuck) (Griffith 1966, 182; *CSPI* 1611–14, 141; Manning 1989–90, 28) (Fig. 2.3). Culme was given a force of ten wardens and was appointed provost-marshal of the county (Hill 1877, 338, n. 257). He was also granted lands as a servitor in the barony of Tullyhaw (Hill 1877, 338).

A large proportion of the barony of Loughtee was granted to English undertakers. The largest grants of land were given to Stephen Butler (Cluosey, near Belturbet, which was notionally 2,000 acres but in fact was over 13,500 acres), John Fishe (Drummany, west of Drumlane, notionally 2,000 acres, in fact 8,800 acres), Richard Waldron (Dromhill and Dromellan, later known as Farnham, notionally 2,000 acres, in fact 7,000 acres) and Sir Nicholas Lusher (Lisreagh, notionally 2,000 acres, in fact 6,600 acres) (Hunter 1973–5, 476). Three other un-dertakers got 1,500 acres. Scots undertakers were granted most of the baronies of Tullyhunco and Clankee. Of these, Tullyhunco barony is closest to Clogh Oughter and of most relevance to its subsequent history. The Scots land grants in Tullyhunco were 2,000 acres to Sir Alexander Hamilton and 1,000 each to Sir Claud Hamilton, Alexander Achmutie, John Achmutie and John Browne (Roulston 2009, 123). The names by which these grants were known are sometimes difficult to identify today; over the first few decades of the plan-tation, land grants were sold or inherited and some were amalgamated to make larger holdings (*ibid.*, 121–6). By 1631 the two Hamilton grants in Tullyhunco had been amalgamated as the manor of Castlekaylaghe and were in the hands of the young Sir Francis Hamilton, the grandson of one of the original grantees (*ibid.*, 124). The Hamiltons had built a 'strong Castle, and a Bawn of Lime and Stone thoroughly finished' by 1619 (*ibid.*, 127). This is now the townland of Keelagh (Fig. 2.4) and the demesne of Castle Hamilton immediately east of

Killeshandra and some altered remains of a courtyard of the period survive (O'Donovan 1995, 231, 245). The grants of the Achmutie brothers were acquired by Sir James Craig, who built a 'strong bawne of lime and stone, 75 feet square, 16 feet high, and four round towers to flank the wall. He hath also a strong and large castle of the length of the bawn, 20 feet broad within the walls, and five storeys high' (Roulston 2009, 127). This is the castle known in 1641 as Croaghan (Fig. 2.4). Nothing survives of it apart from the possible remains of a corner tower in the townland of Coolnashinny or Croaghan to the north-west of Killeshandra (O'Donovan 1995, 237).

The natives who received the largest allocations of land were Maol Mórdha Óg O'Reilly (Table 2.2), who got 3,000 acres situated around Bellanacargy Castle in the barony of Tullygarvey (Ó Mórdha 1981), and his grand-uncle, the last O'Reilly chief, Maol Mórdha, son of Aodh Connallach, who got 2,000 acres situated around Lismore (Fig. 2.4) in Kilmore parish and mostly in Clanmahon barony (Hill 1877, 342, 347). Others who got large allocations were Hugh, son of Sir John O'Reilly (1,000 acres around Lisgannon (Fig. 2.4) in Tullygarvey barony), Maol Mórdha, son of Pilib, son of Aodh Connallach (1,000 acres in Tullygarvey barony), and his brother Seán (900 acres in Castlerahan barony) (*ibid.*, 345, 347–8). Other members of the O'Reilly and other Gaelic families got allocations of between 30 and 500 acres (Moody 1938, 202–4).

An anonymous map of the escheated counties of Ulster in the British Library (Cotton MS Augustus I.ii.44)[15] shows the estates allocated to the different un-dertakers in 1610 and the church and other lands (Pl. 2.3) (Margey 2009, pl. 8; Moody 1938, fold-out be-tween pp 289 and 290).[16] Though we do not know the cartographer, it is more accurate than Bodley's maps, es-pecially in relation to rivers and lakes; it also shows castles and churches, and even a small bird's-eye view of the town of Cavan (Pl. 2.4). Clogh Oughter is depicted with a conventional castle symbol on a small island in 'Loughowter'. The castle is captioned 'Cloghowter' and the land allocated with it is misnamed 'towneland', whereas it should have been named 'castle land'. The lands allocated with the towns of Cavan and Belturbet are correctly captioned 'towneland'. Bellanacargy Castle, captioned 'Ballinecarrig', in Tullaghgarvey barony, is also shown.

Further surveys were carried out in 1613, 1619 and

---

[15] This was formerly wrongly attributed to John Norden (Margey 2009, 111–12 (n. 30)).

[16] The detail on this map can best be seen, if only in black and white, in Moody 1938. The colour version in Margey 2009 is reproduced at too small a scale to see most of the detail.

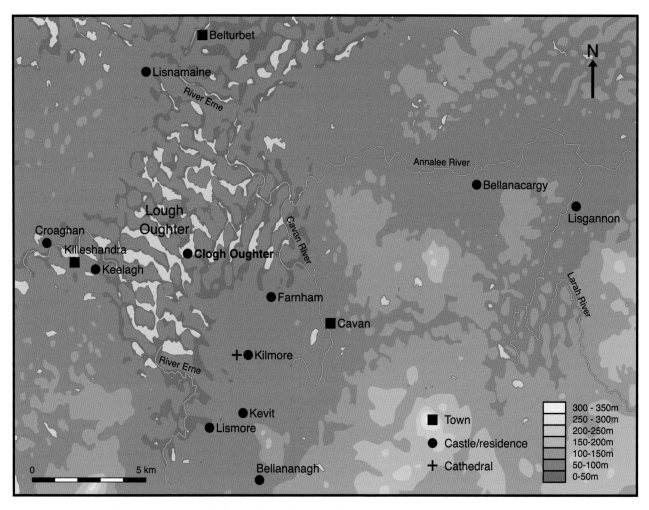

Fig. 2.4—A map of the area around Clogh Oughter, showing places mentioned in connection with the 1641 rebellion.

1622 to document whether undertakers were resident, whether they had built defensible houses and bawns, and whether they had settled people from Britain on their lands. Clogh Oughter, being a royal castle, was not covered by these surveys. Bodley's survey of 1613 includes interesting information on some of the natives who were allocated land. At Bellanacargy Maol Mórdha Óg 'hath near his house a strong pile or castle within a large bawn of earth and sod, of competent thickness and height and well ditched', while Maol Mórdha, son of Pilib, 'hath begun a bawn of sod about a great Irish house, with two flanks at opposite angles', and 'Capt Rely' (Hugh, son of Sir John) at Lisgannon 'hath a bawn or sconce of good strength on the top of a hill, which was sometimes a Dane's fort, being round and about 120 feet in diameter, double ditched and trenched, the rampier of sufficient height and breadth, with the parapet accordingly' (Bickley 1947, 161). This fort at Lisgannon[17] (written 'Liscannon' at the time) is referred to as new in 1600, when the baron of Dunsany based himself there when spoiling the surrounding countryside (Brady 2004, 187). Bodley reported that Waldron was behind in his endeavours but had achieved a certain amount, Fishe had built a brick house within a 'rath or Danish fort',[18] Mr Butler's house and bawn were under construction, with the town of Belturbet progressing well, while Lusher's grant showed little progress (Bickley 1947, 162–3). Bodley reported in 1613 that Captain Hugh Culme was busy with Archy Moore at Tullaghfin (Tullyvin) in Tullygarvey barony, building a house and

---

[17] This interesting earthwork was levelled sometime between 1968 and 1990 (O'Donovan 1995, 117–18).

[18] By July 1611 John Fishe had made 140,000 bricks and 200 barrels of lime for this building project. He had two boats on the River Erne, in which he probably brought timber from County Fermanagh for the building. Bodley described the completed building as 'being 36 feet square and with defence from spikes [gun loops] and battlements at the top'. The 1622 survey states that 'within the bawn there is a strong and handsome house of brick and lime, 34 feet square and four stories high'. The bawn wall was made of stone and lime, 8ft high, following the bank of the ringfort, with a chamber and drawbridge at the gate (O'Reilly 1985, 265–6).

bawn, and also in Tullyhaw barony, at Ballyconnell (Fig. 2.2), with Walter Talbot, where they had built '3 or 4 handsome Irish houses' and were planning the building of a castle (*ibid.*, 160–1, 165).

By the time of Pynnar's survey of 1619 Hugh Culme had also taken on Captain Ridgeway's 1,000 acres, called the manor of Chichester, on the shores of Lough Ramor in Castlerahan barony. A bawn was reported as having been built here and a house was under construction. Culme was also to build the town of Virginia (Fig. 2.2), where he had already built eight houses and settled eight English tenants in them. The house at Tullyvin was almost completed in 1619, while at Ballyconnell Culme and Talbot had completed a strong bawn and castle (Hill 1877, 458–9, 473).

The 1622 commission reported that Culme had completed the house within the bawn at Lough Ramor 'of stone and lime, slated, 71 foot long and 26 foot broad and 28 foot high, being 3 storeys, and a cockloft . . . Captain Culme himself was in England but his wife, children and family are resident . . .'. The development of the town of Virginia, which was Culme's responsibility since 1613, was not very satisfactory, with only five houses completed and two being built and the poor settlers complaining (Treadwell 2006, 513). Tullyvin was strongly built, but Archibald Moore had recently died and his widow and children were not able to maintain the house and bawn, which was partly Culme's responsibility (*ibid.*, 513–14). Culme and Talbot's castle at Ballyconnell was lived in by Talbot and his family, who with all their tenants were described as recusants (*ibid.*, 522–3). Captain Hugh O'Reilly was living at Lisgannon in his 'Irish house' within a bawn of sods. Maol Mórdha Óg O'Reilly had died 'and an uncle of his hath so much of the land as he sold not in his lifetime. There is a bawn of sods and an old castle in it, called Ballynecarghy, repaired, wherein the lady Rely[19] dwells' (*ibid.*, 514).

By 1622 Sir Richard Waldron at Drumhill and Dromellan (now called Farnham (Figs 2.3 and 2.4)) was dead; he was succeeded by his son, Sir Thomas Waldron, who was living in England. There was here a fair house or castle of stone, brick and lime and a large sod bawn with corner bastions and a smaller bawn of stone and lime, unfinished (Treadwell 2006, 515). Sir Stephen Butler at Cluosey was living in his fair house and bawn and was high sheriff of the county. His town of Belturbet had 34 houses with British tenants (*ibid.*, 517–18). Maol Mórdha MacHugh O'Reilly, the brother of

Sir John, was still alive and resident in 1622 on his allocation of 2,000 acres at 'Comett' (now Kevit (Fig. 2.4)) in Clanmahon barony, 'upon which is built a strong house of stone and lime, 3 storeys high, 40 foot long and 20 foot broad' (*ibid.*, 520).

Hugh Culme was given a new grant of Clogh Oughter and the associated lands for 21 years on 8 February 1620 (Griffith 1966, 461). In the same year the castle was described as follows in an inventory of Crown fortifications:

> 'Cloghowter, in Co. Cavan, Capt. Hugh Culme holds this castle and the island and certain lands . . . by his lease he is tied to reparation . . . This fort was made choice of for keeping priests, and £200 sterling allowed for reparation and fitting the lodging there, which money is disbursed and the place ready to be employed' (*CSPI* 1615–25, 284).

Later that same year the inland forts of Connacht and Ulster were granted outright by the king to those in possession, including Clogh Oughter, provided they were kept in repair (*CSPI* 1615–25, 292; Griffith 1966, 484–5). Considering the £200 spent on it before 1620, it is surprising to find it listed with other Ulster forts in 1623 as needing repairs (*CSPI* 1615–25, 430). The formal grant of Clogh Oughter and its lands to Sir Hugh Culme in 1625 specified that he was 'to keep the castle in repair, with a sufficient number of men, horse and foot, well armed and victualled; to assist the Lord Deputy at any disturbances etc' (Griffith 1966, 586–7).

The Culme family had a house on the shore of the lake in Inishconnell townland (Pl. 2.5), which may have been built in the years after 1620, when Clogh Oughter and its lands were granted outright to Culme. On 4 December 1621 he borrowed £600 from his brother Philip (Table 2.3), a London merchant (Ohlmeyer and Ó Ciardha 1998, 85, 200), and at least some of this money may have been for the building of the house. By 1626 he was in a position to loan £330 to Sir Archibald Acheson of Clancarny, Co. Armagh (*ibid.*, 85, 164), although, as is clear from his will below, he may not have repaid all of the debt to his brother Philip. On 6 May 1630, eight days before he drew up his will, he borrowed £600 from his brother Benjamin (Table 2.3), the dean of St Patrick's, Dublin (*ibid.*, 85, 200). He must have been seriously ill at the time and short of ready funds

---

[19] Presumably Katherine Butler, the widow of Maol Mórdha, son of Sir John O'Reilly, and the mother of Maol Mórdha Óg, who was now also dead.

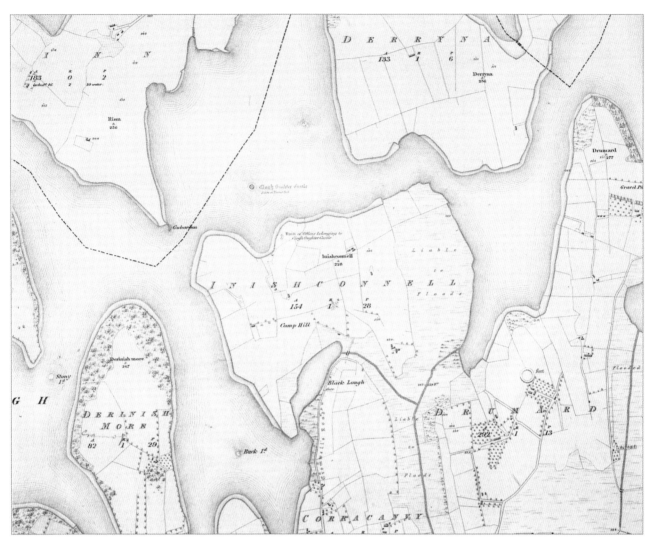

Pl. 2.5—Extract from the first-edition OS map, showing Clogh Oughter. (© Ordnance Survey Ireland. All rights reserved. Licence no. EN0059212.)

to make the bequests he wished to make. Hugh Culme died at Clogh Oughter in 1630; in his will, drawn up on 14 May 1630, he bequeathed the castle and lands of Clogh Oughter, fourteen townlands at Tullyvin and the lease of Mr Waldron's land (Farnham) to his eldest son Arthur (O'Reilly 1985, 270). The leases and houses of Clogh Oughter were left to his wife, Dame Mary Culme, for her life, £40 yearly out of the lands of Tullevin and three horses, 50 ewes, 50 lambs and a ram. The lands leased from the bishop of Clogher[20] were left to Arthur Culme, provided that he repay within seven years the £300 owed to Hugh's brother Philip. His sons Hugh and Philip were left £500 each, while his youngest son Amery was left the eight polls of land in Tullyhaw and two polls in Lurgan, which he held from the bishop of Kilmore (NAI MS T.4861).

Arthur Culme's wife, Mary, was a daughter of Sir Faithful Fortescue (TCD MS 833, f. 209), who was born in Devon, was a nephew of Sir Arthur Chichester and in 1606 was appointed constable for life of Carrickfergus Castle. In 1637 Arthur Culme inherited £1,000 from his uncle Philip, who had been a merchant tailor in London. He also forgave Arthur the £300 that was still owing to him (Ainsworth 1948, 26). In 1638 a large proportion of the land in the parish of Drumlane that had been granted to John Fishe under the Plantation of Ulster, and on his death to his son Edward Fishe in 1629, was granted to Arthur Culme of Clogh Oughter and his uncle, Benjamin Culme, the dean of St Patrick's in Dublin. As a result, Arthur Culme and his uncle now owned the mansion house of Lisnamaine (Fig. 2.4). Fishe's lands were confiscated because he had

---

[20] These lands were referred to in Arthur Culme's deposition of May 1642 as '35 tates of land which this deponent holds from the bishop of Clogher in the county of Monaghan, for which lease this deponent refused several times £1,000' (Gilbert 1879–80, I, 413).

Table 2.3—A simplified and selected genealogy of the Culme family.

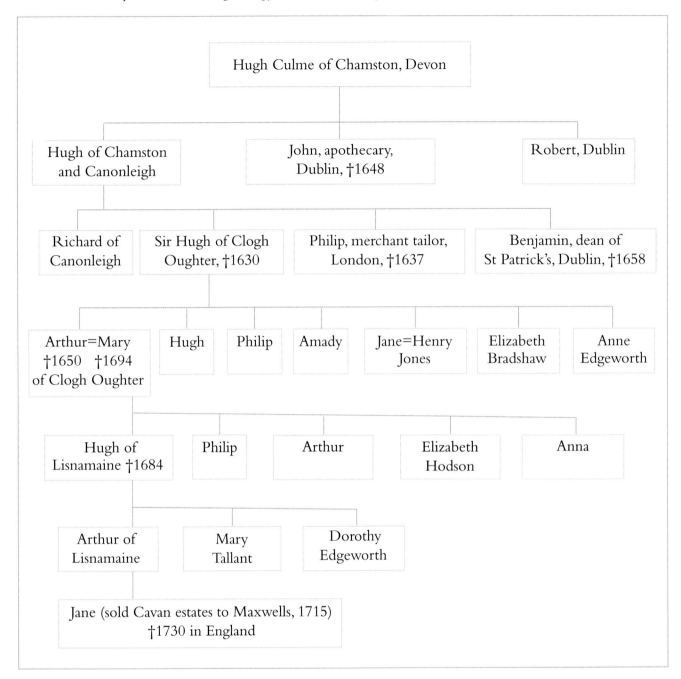

let them to tenants who did not take the Oath of Supremacy (O'Reilly 1985, 268–9). Later copies, dating from 1784, of the letters patent of May 1639 confirming Arthur Culme's ownership of Clogh Oughter and other lands and of September 1639 confirming the grant of Lisnamaine and other lands to Arthur Culme and his uncle, Benjamin Culme, survive among the Farnham papers (NLI MS 41,123/1).[21] By this time Arthur Culme seems to have been relatively wealthy, for in July 1639 he gave Thomas Burnett of Ballinaleck, Co. Monaghan,[22] a loan of £2,000 (Ohlmeyer and Ó Ciardha 1998, 85, 185).

---

[21] In the NLI Collection List on the Farnham Papers (No. 95) (2004–5) these have been wrongly assigned to the reign of Charles II and the date 1673.

[22] John Burnett purchased a large estate in County Monaghan, which county was not part of the plantation of Ulster, from a number of Irish families and settled at Ballyleck in 1609 (Livingstone 1980, 122). His son, Thomas Burnett, was married to Ellenor Fortescue, a sister of Arthur Culme's wife. According to his deposition of May 1642, Arthur Culme had bought twelve tates and a quarter of land in the barony of Trough, Co. Monaghan, for £800 from Thomas Burnett (Gilbert 1879–80, I, 413). Arthur's brother Hugh was, according to his deposition, living at Leitrim, Co. Monaghan, in 1641 and leasing land from Burnett.

Pl. 2.6—Portrait of Bishop Bedell. (© Representative Church Body.)

The 1641 rebellion

The principal individuals in County Cavan who played a part in the events surrounding the 1641 rebellion, especially in relation to Clogh Oughter, were as follows: Arthur Culme, who was in control of Clogh Oughter on the eve of the rebellion and was resident in the house on the shore; William Bedell,[23] who was Protestant bishop of Kilmore (Pl. 2.6) and lived in a house beside the old cathedral; Henry Jones,[24] dean of Kilmore (Pl. 2.7), who lived in a castle at Bellananagh (Fig. 2.4); Richard Castledine, an Englishman, owner of the Farnham estate;[25] the Scottish undertakers Sir Francis Hamilton and Sir James Craig at their castles Keilagh and Croaghan, both situated close to Killeshandra;[26] Edmund, son of Maol Mórdha (Mulmore) O'Reilly, who was regarded by the Irish as the O'Reilly and was living at Kevitt in the parish of Kilmore; his son Maol Mórdha (Mulmore or Myles), also of Kevitt (Fig. 2.4), high sheriff of the county, who was married to a sister of Owen Roe O'Neill[27] (Walsh 1960, 173; Gilbert 1879–80, vol. 2, 23); Edmund's brother Philip, resident at Lismore (Fig. 2.4) in the parish of Kilmore; and Philip Mac Hugh O'Reilly, who appears to have inherited both Lisgannon and Bellanacargy after the death of his

---

[23] William Bedell was born in Essex on 29 September 1571 (Shuckburgh 1902, 1), studied at Cambridge and was ordained in 1597. Before becoming rector of Horningsheath, he served for three years as chaplain to the English ambassador to Venice. In 1627 he was appointed provost of Trinity College, Dublin, and in 1629 bishop of Kilmore and Ardagh. He resigned Ardagh in 1633 but retained Kilmore until his death (*DNB*, vol. 4, 765–8). From his time as provost of Trinity he took an interest in the Irish language and once appointed bishop was anxious to ensure that ministers appointed to Irish-speaking districts should have a knowledge of the language. He is best known today for his work on the translation of the Old Testament into Irish. He employed two Irish scholars, Murtagh King and James Nangle, to do the actual translation and, by this time having acquired a knowledge of Irish, checked the translation himself. The manuscript was completed prior to the outbreak of the 1641 rebellion and luckily survived the turmoil of those years, to be published for the first time in 1685 (Williams 1986, 43–55, 80–94). The manuscript is preserved today in Marsh's Library, Dublin. A biography of Bedell, written by Bishop Gilbert Burnet, was published in London in 1685 and in Dublin in 1736. Bedell was an honest and fair-minded man and made himself unpopular in the established church by his attempts to stamp out abuses. He was much respected by the native Irish, and although upon his death in 1642 the Catholic bishop did not want him buried in Kilmore churchyard, as was specified in his will (Jones 1872, 192–5), the O'Reilly leaders overruled him and turned up at the funeral to show their respect (Shuckburgh 1902, 73–4, 204–6).

[24] Henry Jones (1605–82) was the eldest son of Lewis Jones, bishop of Killaloe, and his wife Mabel Ussher. He was made dean of Kilmore in 1637 and his first wife was Jane, daughter of Sir Hugh Culme of Clogh Oughter. His brother, General Michael Jones, married Mary, the widow of Hugh Culme, in 1646/7 and died in 1649. Another brother, Sir Theophilus Jones, was in charge of the siege of Clogh Oughter Castle in 1653 (*DNB*, vol. 30, 511–13; *DIB*, vol. 4, 1025–7, 1034, 1039–40). Henry Jones was appointed bishop of Clogher in 1645 but subsequently joined the Cromwellian forces as scoutmaster general. He was appointed bishop of Meath in 1661 and was responsible for having the Book of Kells and the Book of Durrow deposited in Trinity College Library.

[25] Richard Castledine came to Ireland as a carpenter to work on Sir Richard Waldron's building projects at Farnham. In time he bought out his master's castle and lands at Farnham and Waldron returned to England. Castledine and his wife had no sons but had two daughters; one of these married Waldron's youngest son John, and Farnham was to be left to them (Shuckburgh 1902, 191–2; TCD MS 832, 144r). The latter reference and other references to the 1641 Depositions in manuscript here have been accessed through the 1641 Depositions Project, on-line transcript December 2009 [http://1641.eneclann.ie].

[26] It is noteworthy that in a muster roll of about 1630 the men of these two estates were proportionately among the best armed in the county, having between them 40 of the 166 swords listed for the county among eighteen estates, 40 of the 100 pikes, twelve of the seventeen muskets, one of the eight calivers, nine of the 46 snaphaunces and one of the three halberds (Gilbert 1879–80, I, 332; Hunter and Perceval-Maxwell 1977).

[27] Owen Roe O'Neill was also related to the O'Reillys. It has been argued that his mother was an O'Reilly, probably a daughter of Hugh Connallach (Casway 1984, 10, 274), which would have made him a first cousin once removed of both Philip Mac Hugh O'Reilly and Mulmore Mac Edmond O'Reilly, the sheriff.

Pl. 2.7—Portrait of Henry Jones. (© Representative Church Body.)

father Hugh in 1628, though Katherine Butler, widow of Maol Mórdha, son of Sir John O'Reilly, continued to live at Bellanacargy until her death in 1640 (Vicars 1897, 66). Philip Mac Hugh O'Reilly had served in the French army, was commissioner of the peace in 1625, high sheriff of the county in 1629, member of parliament for the county in 1640 and was married to Rose, a daughter of Sir Turlough O'Neill of the Fews. She is mentioned in the Depositions (Scott 2007, 29; TCD MS 832, 80r, 213v). Philip's father Hugh was a first cousin of Edmund Mac Mulmore O'Reilly of Kevitt, and Philip was a second cousin of the high sheriff, Maol Mórdha (Mulmore Mac Edmund) (Table 2.2).

On Saturday 23 October 1641, the second day of the rebellion, Mulmore Mac Edmund O'Reilly, the high sheriff for the county, having already obtained arms at Farnham (Manning 1989–90, 58–60), surprised the unsuspecting Arthur Culme at his house at Clogh Oughter on the shore to the south of the castle and got the keys of the castle. Owen O'Reilly was made constable of the castle and Arthur Culme was put into his charge as a prisoner. Arthur Culme's own account of these happenings, as given in his deposition on 9 May 1642, is worth quoting in full:

'Arthur Culme, Esq., of Cloughutur in the county of Cavan, who being duly sworn and examined, deposed and said: that on Saturday the twenty-third of October last, between the

hours of seven and eight o'clock in the evening, one Thomas Pallat, an Englishman, repaired to this deponent from Cavan town and told him that there were several rebels with some Scotch forces, which had taken Clounis in the county of Fermanagh, and killed Mr Arthur Champion at his house at Shanocke, and that Mr Edward Aldridge with others had fled for their lives and were in Cavan, where Capt. Baily was, as he said, preparing to resist the rebels and that Mulmore Mc Edmund Rely, the then high sheriff of that county, with divers others in his company, had repaired to Farnham Castle to seize on such arms as were there to arm men for the prosecution of the said rebels, as also for the defence of the country, for in that castle there was, as this deponent had been credibly informed, complete arms and armour for forty men at least, it being a castle belonging to the heir of Sir Thomas Waldrum, who is an undertaker in the county of Cavan. The said Pallat had scantly done his relation, when the high sheriff of that county, Mulmore Mc Edmund Relie, with divers in his company, knocked at the deponent's door and required entrance and conference with this deponent, and [for] the speedy advancement he had for some service to his majesty, this deponent, nothing suspecting him, opened his doors, and immediately there rushed in divers men with skeans, swords, pistols and pikes and told this deponent that he must yield himself and his arms and ammunition unto their hands, for they had a commission from his majesty, to disarm all the British. Being by the deponent demanded the reason of it, they said the intention of his majesty was by their means to bring into subjection the Puritan faction of the parliament of England and that they would right the queen's majesty for aspersions laid on the royal progeny too bold for to speak of or without modesty to be related. Having thus with naked weapons at the breast of this deponent seized him, they told him if there were resistance made by any that their commission was to kill their wives and children before their faces, to burn their houses and afterwards to kill the parties resisting, and on this they demanded the key of the castle of Clowater, which was a strong tower situate in the midst of a lough some musket shot from this deponent's house; which this deponent refusing to do, because it had the name of a fort without maintenance or allowance they were ready to have murdered this deponent until one Anthony Culme, a kinsman of the deponent, who then had the key of the castle in his custody, desired them to hold their hands and he would deliver them the key, which accordingly he did. Immediately upon this Mulmore Mc Edmond Relie, the then high sheriff, and Edmond Mc Mulmore Relie, the said sheriff's father, called for a bible and charged this deponent on peril of his life to depose what powder, arms or other ammunition he had in his house. Unto which I replied I would hide nothing from them, and bade them to search, which accordingly they did. Immediately they told me that I must forthwith be carried to that inhabited and comfortless castle of Clowater, there to remain with a strong guard till they had subdued the whole kingdom, and their pleasures were further known. The deponent's poor afflicted wife, who was but lately before delivered of a child, with tears did solicit their favour that the deponent might stay in his house till the next morning with a safe guard, but in that rebellious route neither words nor tears would avail, but away both she and I were carried that night to the castle, where we were left with a strong guard about us, and one Owen Mc Turlagh Rely was left captain or chief commander of that guard, who for aught that ever I could perceive was a mighty civil man, much troubled at these distempers, and, under God, during my imprisonment, which was for six months, a continual preserver of his life'[28] (Gilbert 1879–80, vol. 1, 408–9).

Other accounts are in agreement that Culme was taken by surprise at Clogh Oughter. Henry Jones (Pl. 2.7), Culme's brother-in-law, recounted that the sheriff gained access to Culme's house 'under colour of accustomed friendship' (Jones 1642; Gilbert 1879–80, vol. 1, 478), while Clogie in his biography of Bishop Bedell refers to the episode in language that is less favourable to Culme:

'. . . Mr Arthur Cullum . . . whose father Sir Hugh being a captain under the q[ueen] in Tyrone's wars, had that fort committed to his trust, for the keeping of which he had a large proportion of lands given to him; but his son,

that knew nothing of the wars of the Lord, neglected the place so much, where the magazine ought to have been kept for the defence of the country against sudden insurrections, that though he said, *he had in his house* (when he was taken prisoner) *ten pounds worth of sugar and plums, yet he had not one pound of powder, nor one fixed musket for the defence of it*' (Shuckburgh 1902, 190).

The progress of the rebellion in Cavan over the following months was recounted in detail by Henry Jones in a pamphlet published in London in 1642 and reprinted by Gilbert (Jones 1642; Gilbert 1879–80, vol. 1, 476–97). The most populous and heavily planted town in the county, Belturbet, was taken by Philip Mac Hugh O'Reilly by persuasion and agreement on 24 October, and the small government garrison under Captain Ryves travelled on to Cavan town and from there to Ardbraccan, Co. Meath. The small garrison under Captain Bayly in Cavan town positioned themselves in the county gaol, the place of greatest strength in the town, and were there surrounded by the rebels on 25 October. They surrendered two days later on condition that the arms be kept by Captain Bayly at his own house near Cavan and that the soldiers were not to join with Sir Francis Hamilton or Sir James Craig at their castles near Killeshandra. Jones's own castle at Bellananagh (Fig. 2.4) was surrendered and garrisoned on 29 October, while he and his family were committed to the charge of Philip Mac Mulmore O'Reilly of Lismore, the sheriff's uncle. Within a week of the start of the rebellion the entire county was in the rebels' hands, apart from Sir Francis Hamilton's castle at Keilagh and Sir James Craig's castle at Croaghan, both situated near Killeshandra (Fig. 2.4) (Gilbert 1879–80, vol. 1, 478–80).

While the leaders of the rebellion in Ulster generally promised protection to the British settlers, they could not control their followers; many of the settlers were robbed and some were killed (Canny 2001, 469–92). William Bedell, the bishop of Kilmore, and his family were initially allowed to remain at their house in Kilmore and gave shelter and food to many refugee settlers from other parts of the county. The leaders of the rebellion in County Cavan, in seeking to explain their actions to the Dublin government and in looking for redress for their grievances, put together a document called 'An Humble Remonstrance' and persuaded the dean of Kilmore, Henry Jones, to present it to the lords

---

[28] As with all quotations here, the spelling has been modernised apart from names.

justices and council in Dublin. He, along with John Waldron of Farnham, delivered the document, which was signed by nine members of the O'Reilly family, to the lords justices in Dublin on 6 November and, having spent ten days in Dublin, returned with a written answer from them dated 10 November. The reply pointed out that, though those involved claimed that they had royal sanction for their actions, they had in fact no such sanction and no authority to take up arms, assemble forces and seize forts. They undertook to pass on the petition to the king only on condition that those who signed the petition returned peaceably to their homes and made restitution to those who had been robbed of their lands, goods and chattels (Gilbert 1879–80, vol. 1, 364–7, 481–2).

An attack on the castle of Croaghan by the rebels was repulsed by Sir James Craig and during it Laghlyn O'Rourke and Brian O'Rourke, leaders of the Leitrim rebels, were captured. In a later engagement Sir Francis Hamilton killed a number of the rebels and captured Owen O'Rourke and Philip O'Reilly, an uncle of Philip Mac Hugh O'Reilly (Gilbert 1879–80, vol. 1, 487–8). As a bargaining point to get the rebel prisoners released, the O'Reilly leaders decided to imprison Bishop Bedell in Clogh Oughter Castle. The bishop's house was taken over by the rebels on 18 December and the bishop, his sons, William[29] and Ambrose, and his stepson-in-law, Alexander Clogie,[30] were brought to Clogh Oughter. The women of the family were allowed to stay with an Irish minister, Denis O'Sheridan. Both William Bedell junior and Alexander Clogie wrote biographies of the bishop and these texts (Shuckburgh 1902, 1–75, 78–213) are therefore eyewitness accounts of these events, though written in a hagiographical style with copious quotations from the Bible.

The prisoners were brought out to the castle in a logboat 'made of one piece of timber', and Clogie described the castle thus: 'There was of old a little island about it, but it was worn all away to the bare stone walls, and not one foot of ground was to be seen, only a tall, round tower, like a pigeon house, standing in the midst of the waters, and above a musket shot from it to each shore' (*ibid.*, 189–90). They were held on the first floor of the castle and the young men were often shackled in

irons, though the constable of the castle treated them all as humanely as possible. The castle appears to have been in a poor state of repair, 'where no son of man had lodged in 40 years before' (*ibid.*, 192), and, it being midwinter, the poor state of the castle added greatly to their discomfort:

'In this pit there was neither door nor window of glass or wood to keep out snow or rain, and the boards of the floors so rotten and broken with rain, that it seemed not very safe to walk upon them: but God's providence in this mount of extremity was marvellously seen towards them; else they might have perished with cold in the height of the winter and in the midst of the waters in that desolate place. For the rebels had brought one Mr Richard Castledine prisoner, who had been a carpenter, but for many years before had not touched a tool, being become one of the wealthiest men in those parts. But now he was not ashamed to return to his old trade: he procured some tools and boards, and made shuts for the large windows, that were very dangerous to them and himself' (*ibid.*, 191).

The prisoners appear to have had a fireplace and had to cook for themselves, as their jailors

'brought him flesh and bread enough, and bid him and the other five prisoners with him to dress it as they would, for they were no cooks, but keepers; nor would they allow any of his servants to attend him in this extremity. So they got a pot and boiled some, and upon the coals roasted or broiled some part, as in the camp or leaguer soldiers are glad to do' (*ibid.*, 192).

Much of the effort of the rebels was directed towards a siege of Drogheda and, while they were successful in attacking a force sent from Dublin to assist the defenders of Drogheda, the siege itself was making no progress. The prisoners heard news of the siege of Drogheda, as documented by William Bedell junior in his biography of his father:

---

[29] William Bedell junior was minister in the parish of Kinawley in 1641 and subsequently was minister at Rattlesden in Suffolk (Shuckburgh 1902, 194, 213).
[30] Alexander Clogie (1614–98) was born in Scotland. He married Leah Mawe, a daughter of William Bedell's wife by a previous marriage, who died soon after. In 1641 he was the minister in Cavan town. From internal evidence in the text he appears to have written the biography of Bishop Bedell over some years in the 1660s and 1670s. From 1647 until his death he was minister of Wigmore in Herefordshire (*DNB*, vol. 12, 181).

Pl. 2.8—The small medieval cathedral of Kilmore, now used as a parish hall, with its western tower.

'But it happened that in the castle where the bishop was prisoner, one night a soldier, newly come from Droghedagh, was entertained by some of the guards, who kept their court in the lowest rooms. In the night late some of the guard questioned the soldier, *what news there was from Droghedagh*. One of the English prisoners that understood Irish, being just over their heads, laid his ear to a clift in the plancher and listened to their discourse. The soldier told them plainly that *the siege was broken up*, and showed them his own hands and arms, all scratched and rent with thorns and briars, while he was in a hasty retreat from an assault they had made upon the city. He told them also that *the bullets poured down as thick from the walls as if one should take a fire-pan full of coals and pour them down upon the hearth*; which he acted before them, sitting all together at the fire. And for his own part, he said, *he would be hanged before he would go forth again upon such a piece of service*. He that listened soon communicated this good news to his fellow-prisoners; whereby it pleased God to revive

their spirits not a little; but they were fain with all diligence to keep the matter to themselves' (*ibid.*, 68–9).

The exchange of prisoners with the Scots was agreed after Christmas, and the bishop, his two sons and son-in-law were released on 7 January 1642, having spent just three weeks in Clogh Oughter. Because, in the meantime, the bishop's house and cathedral at Kilmore (Pl. 2.8) had been taken over by the Catholic bishop, Eugene Sweeney, an Irish Protestant minister, Denis O'Sheridan, took the bishop and his family into his own house, probably at Drumcor in the parish of Kilmore (Jones 1872, 207). There was an outbreak of fever among other displaced settlers who sought refuge at O'Sheridan's house, and Bishop Bedell, possibly weakened by his imprisonment at Clogh Oughter, contracted fever and died on 7 February 1642, aged 70 years (Shuckburgh 1902, 73, 202).

The issue of his burial now presented a problem, because the Catholic bishop did not want the body of what he regarded as a heretic buried in the graveyard at Kilmore. But Edmund Mac Mulmore O'Reilly over-

Pl. 2.9—The tomb of William Bedell at Kilmore.

Pl. 2.10—Print of the slab on William Bedell's tomb (from Mant 1840).

ruled Bishop Sweeney in this and Bishop Bedell was buried in the same grave as his wife Leah and son John, who had predeceased him, in accordance with his last will and testament (Jones 1872, 192–5), which also specified that the following inscription be placed on the tomb: 'GULIELMI QUONDAM KILMORENSIS EPISCOPI DEPOSITUM'. He was not in favour of burial within the church itself, a common practice at the time, and had picked a remote part of the graveyard as the burial place for himself and his family (Shuckburgh 1902, 73–4). The tomb with the inscribed slab on top of it survives to this day (Pls 2.9 and 2.10). Edmund O'Reilly and his son (the sheriff) attended the funeral, offered their condolences to the family, accompanied the bishop to his grave and ordered the firing of a volley over it as a mark of respect (*ibid.*, 174–5, 204–6).

Richard Castledine was released at the same time as the bishop and his family but Arthur Culme continued as a prisoner at Clogh Oughter. Their depositions are also informative about the conditions of their imprisonment and about the castle itself.[31] Attempts were made to get Culme to convert to Catholicism, and he claimed to have been

'continually threatened with several deaths, as hanging, stabbing, and sometimes to be knocked in the head with stones from an upper loft when I was asleep, for fear I should resist them, never being suffered all the while I was there to go off the island where the castle stood, there being not four yards of ground about it, and most times locked close in my chamber; and

they many times bolted both his legs, and so he lay night and day; but praised be God for it, he had favour in the eyes of the captain of the castle, who many times, contrary to the command of the sheriff, whose prisoner he was, eased me of my bolts, and did him many other favours, for which he prayeth God to requite him' (Gilbert 1879–80, vol. 1, 412).

Castledine's deposition is even more informative in many ways and was clearly intended to be of assistance to government forces attempting to take the castle:

'And this deponent further says that he well knows the castle of Clowater and that it is a very strong hold hardly to be won, but that they have no wood for firing nearer than a musket shot from the castle at least, but the stairs and floors and that the chain that makes fast the two grates goes through a piece of timber that lies in the wall; which may be burned by building a strong boat and a frame carried over in the said boat roofed over with ribs of iron to defend the men from stones, which they may throw down from the top of the castle: And he further says that Mulmore McEdmund the sheriff and his father and others have carried in very great store of all sorts of corn since May; And that the great[est]

---

[31] Ambrose Bedell also made a deposition but, in relation to Clogh Oughter, it adds nothing to the other accounts (Hickson 1884, vol. 1, 218–20).

wealth of the whole county is carried in there and into Mr Arthur Culme's house upon [the] shore. And that they have begun to build a very strong fort, between the wood and the lough, to preserve [and] defend the said house. And that they gave warning to many in the county to give their help and assistance thereto' (TCD MS 833, f. 114; Manning 1989–90, 40).

His account of conditions in the castle accords well with the other descriptions:

'the deponent was committed prisoner with the Lord Bishop of Kilmore and three of his sons to Clowater Castle, it being a fortnight before Christmas Day or thereabouts and remained there close prisoner contained with bolts. But the captain of the castle was strictly commanded to keep them in bolts continually night and day. But he took some pity of them lest they should perish with cold, the place being raw, windy and wet in the midst of a lough, and the windows of the castle all open to wind and weather. But after a month's stay we were released by some exchange of prisoners with Sir James Craig, knight, hard taken. And the deponent had a chamber appointed in his own house at Farnham and a guard set and appointed to look after him. And Luke Dillon, Esq., Philip McMulmore Rely, Esq., Mr Denis Sheridan, minister, became bound for the deponent that he should be a true prisoner there, for he was very weak with sickness when being in the castle of Clowater' (Manning 1989–90, 60).

Arthur Culme was eventually released from Clogh Oughter in April 1642, when 'by the providence of God and favour of my lord Moore, he was with his wife and eldest boy exchanged to Drogheda for other prisoners, about the twenty third of April' (Gilbert 1879–80, vol. 1, 412). By this time the Scots holding out at the castles of Croaghan and Keilagh had given up all hope of being relieved by government forces from Dublin, had run out of food supplies and many had died of fever. On 8 April Sir James Craig died and his wife had fallen sick with fever. Eventually, on 4 June articles of agreement for sur-

Pl. 2.11—Portrait of Owen Roe O'Neill (from Gilbert 1879–80).

render were drawn up and signed between Philip Mac Hugh O'Reilly and Sir Francis Hamilton, and these were published by Henry Jones in his account of the rebellion in Cavan (*ibid.*, 494–6). The garrisons and other persons in both castles were to have protected safe passage to Drogheda, along with any other settlers who wished to join them from the county, all departing on 15 June. Some 1,340 people in all, including the Bedell and Castledine families, made their way under guard to Drogheda, which they reached on 22 June. Some stayed in Drogheda, some took passage to England and about 1,000 continued on to Dublin (*ibid.*, 491–6; Shuckburgh 1902, 211–13). With the number of refugees flocking to Dublin, food shortages and fever were rife and may have contributed to the deaths of Richard and Rebecca Castledine there later in 1642 (Vicars 1897, 81).

The wars of the 1640s and the Cromwellian reconquest

Owen Roe O'Neill (Pl. 2.11)[32] landed at Doe Castle, Co. Donegal, about 8 July 1642 on his way from Flanders to take part in the rebellion. He was soon made

---

[32] Owen Roe O'Neill was a nephew of Hugh O'Neill, earl of Tyrone, who, as part of the Flight of the Earls, left Ireland in 1607 and died in Rome in 1616. Owen Roe fought for many years in the Spanish army, especially in the Netherlands, and was a gifted and very experienced military leader. This image of Owen Roe O'Neill is a lithograph that first appeared in the 1856 edition of the *Ulster Journal of Archaeology*. The original on which it was based cannot now be found. A painting of Owen Roe O'Neill, now in private ownership in Portugal, is likely to have been based on the lithograph (Morgan 2010, 24–5).

lord general of the Ulster rebel army, while Sir Phelim O'Neill, one of the chief leaders of the rebellion in Ulster and a member of a rival branch of the O'Neills, was named lord president of Ulster (Casway 1984, 62–3). By this time the native Irish rebels of Ulster and the Old English mainly of the Pale had found common cause in seeking freedom to practise the Catholic religion. They set up the Catholic Confederation, based in Kilkenny, and their parliament sat for the first time on 24 October 1642. In the meantime, as a result of an agreement between the English and Scottish parliaments a Scottish army landed in Ulster under the command of Major General Robert Monro. By the end of 1642, therefore, the Scots had control of much of east and north Ulster, the government controlled areas around Dublin and Cork, and most of the rest of the country was loosely under Confederate control. In October 1645 the papal nuncio Cardinal Rinuccini arrived in Ireland. He advocated a strongly Catholic line in the Confederation of Kilkenny and advised against any compromise with Ormond and the royalists.

After Owen Roe O'Neill's victory over the army of Robert Monro at the battle of Benburb in 1646, Clogh Oughter was again used as a prison to hold some of the officers who were captured. The most prominent of these was Viscount Montgomery of Ards (Gilbert 1879–80, vol. 1, 139). King Charles wrote to Owen Roe O'Neill, requesting that Montgomery be released; O'Neill replied, politely declining to do so and pointing out that Montgomery was an enemy of the king (Meehan 1870, 499).[33] Monsignor Dionisio Massari,[34] dean of Fermo in Italy, who accompanied Cardinal Rinuccini on his mission to Ireland, was sent by Rinuccini to meet Owen Roe O'Neill in Ulster in 1646. O'Neill regularly rested his army in County Cavan, where the O'Reilly leaders were related to him and Myles the sheriff was married to his sister (Casway 2006). When Massari caught up with him, his army was encamped close to Lismore, near Kilmore, Co. Cavan. Massari visited Clogh Oughter in July 1646, as he recorded in his memoirs. He described the castle as

> 'an impregnable fortress in the middle of a large lake. It was a first rate position, possessed a lofty tower, was surrounded by a thick wall, and by such great depth of water that it was unapproachable except by boat, and could easily be held by a small garrison of 100 men' (Massari 1917, 181).

Quarters were prepared for Massari in Culme's house on the shore of the lake and, with the permission of the constable of the castle, he was rowed over to Clogh Oughter to visit Montgomery.[35]

> 'On my arrival, I found him in a room almost at the top of the tower, with two other Colonels, prisoners. He came to the door to meet me and, with a profound bow, said jokingly that the Constable was the cause of his not having advanced further to meet me, but that I must pardon him. He spoke in Italian, welcoming me as well as he could in that language. I replied that I should prefer to find His Lordship in other circumstances the first time it was my good fortune to see him; but since God had so ordained, I was there to place my services entirely at his disposal, out of regard for his great merit, valour and nobility. He warmly thanked me, remarking that such were the fortunes of war, and requested us all to be seated. He then talked for a while on various topics, and especially on the charms of Italy, concerning which he displayed an amount of information that led me to think that he had actually seen and enjoyed these, but he added that he had never

---

[33] Hugh Montgomery (*c*. 1625–63), 3rd Viscount Montgomery of the Ards and later first earl of Mount Alexander, belonged to a Scottish family that had settled in County Down in 1605 on part of the lands of the Clandeboy O'Neills and founded the town of Newtownards (*DNB*, vol. 38, 851–2). Monro's Scottish army was allied with the parliament in England and therefore against the king, as well as being opposed to the Irish rebels. Montgomery may have been swayed in his support of the Scottish army by the fact that Monro had married his widowed mother. He was by inclination a royalist, however, and long before the restoration of Charles II in 1660 he had reverted to support of the monarchy and was rewarded with an earldom thereafter (Ohlmeyer 2012, 122–3, 181, 273).

[34] Dionisio Massari was born in Ortezzano near Fermo in 1597 and died in Fermo in 1664. After his return to Italy from Ireland in 1649 he was appointed secretary to the Congregation for the Propagation of the Faith, a position he held until 1657. He retired to Fermo in 1660 (Bernardo Carfagna, pers. comm.).

[35] Montgomery was only 21 at this time and, in all, appears to have spent over a year and a half in prison at Clogh Oughter. As a result of a childhood accident he had a large open space in his chest, which was covered with a metal plate, and this wound had to be washed by his manservant every day. He had been given a liberal education at home and in other countries; he was proficient in French and, as is clear from this account, had some knowledge of Italian, having travelled on the Continent in 1641–2 (Ohlmeyer 2012, 443; *DIB*, vol. 6, 592–4).

been there. Eventually I took my leave of him, and as I was departing he made me a present of a watch of elaborate contrivance, which indicated the hours, the days, the month, and the phases of the moon, and which he pressed on me with much courtesy. After some protests, I took it, and thanking him, I asked him to grant me one favour, without, however, expressing what it was; and when he had at once replied he was my servant, and would do whatever I might command, I requested him to agree to this arrangement, that whilst the ownership of his beautiful present belonged to me, he would oblige me by having the use of it until such time as he was free, since it was not right that in addition to the troubles and inconveniences of prison life he should also be deprived of the knowledge of the hours, and thus be unable to make a satisfactory distribution of the short time I hoped he would be detained in the tower. He laughed at this, showing that he appreciated the polite fiction and the kindness with which I expressed it, and in deference to my wishes he consented to take back the watch. Parting from him in the same position in which he was when I entered, I descended to the bottom of the tower, and then took boat back to my lodgings' (Massari 1917, 182).

The following day Massari received a letter from Montgomery, pleading with him to make representations for his release as part of an exchange of prisoners or in some other way. Massari replied that he would use whatever influence he had to that end.

After representations from the parliament of Scotland, the London parliament resolved on 30 December 1647 'that Colonel [Michael] Jones be written unto, and that he shall exchange Colonel Birne and the Earl of Westmeath, for the Lord of Airdes and Colonel Theophilus Jones, if he can get none else . . .' (Gilbert 1879–80, vol. 1, 806). Montgomery was released in an exchange of prisoners in February 1648 (Kavanagh 1936, 688–9; *DIB*, vol. 6, 592–4).

Owen Roe O'Neill and the Irish of Ulster backed Rinuccini in his dealings with the Confederation of Kilkenny. Rinuccini pressed a strongly Catholic line and was opposed to compromises with James Butler, the earl of Ormond, who served for periods as lord lieutenant and was commander of the royalist army in Ireland. This led to major divisions within the Confederation. After an unsuccessful Confederate campaign to capture

Dublin in 1647, Ormond handed the city over to English parliamentary forces under Colonel Michael Jones rather than see it fall to the Confederate Catholics. In May 1648 the Confederation agreed a cessation of arms with Lord Inchiquin, who had initially been on the parliamentary side but had now joined with the royalists. Rinuccini condemned the cessation; Owen Roe O'Neill supported him and was consequently deprived of his military command by the Confederation and later declared a traitor. O'Neill's Ulster army stuck by him and he avoided an engagement with Confederate forces (Casway 1984, 215–36).

In January 1649 Charles I was executed and Rinuccini returned to Italy. These developments left Owen Roe O'Neill politically isolated and he began negotiations with Ormond and the royalists on the one hand, and on the other with the parliamentary side— Colonel Michael Jones in Dublin, Sir Charles Coote in Derry and General George Monck in Dundalk. He agreed a cessation of hostilities with Monck in May, and in July Coote sought his help because he was being besieged in Derry by royalists and Scots Covenanters under the command of Viscount Montgomery of Ards. O'Neill moved towards Derry and the besiegers retreated; in return, Coote gave him ammunition and supplies that he needed. In August 1649 Oliver Cromwell brought his parliamentary army ashore in Dublin and soon afterwards captured Drogheda. O'Neill and Ormond now began serious negotiations so that they could unite against the common enemy, Cromwell, and O'Neill began moving southwards from Derry. During this time O'Neill was becoming increasingly ill, apparently with tetanus, and by the time he had reached Ballyhaise, Co. Cavan, on 9 October he was being carried in a horse litter (Casway 1984, 237–61). Soon afterwards he signed articles of agreement with Ormond, after which the army of Ulster was fighting on the royalist side. By the end of October he had been brought to Clogh Oughter, and in one of his last letters to Ormond, dated 1 November at Clogh Oughter, he wrote of being 'on my deathbed, without any hope of my recovery' (Casway 1980, 246). It is most likely that he spent his last days in the house of the Culme family on the Inishconnell shore at Clogh Oughter rather than in the castle itself, which was only fit to be a prison. He died on 6 November 1649 with his personal physician, Owen O'Shiel, in attendance, and with his son Henry, Philip Mac Hugh O'Reilly, Archbishop Hugh O'Reilly of Armagh and the bishop of Kilmore present. He was buried at the Franciscan friary in Cavan town (Gilbert 1979–80, vol. 3, 212; Casway 1984, 262).

The Catholic archbishop of Armagh, Hugh O'Reilly,[36] was living somewhere near Clogh Oughter in 1646 and came to visit and dine with Massari when the latter was staying at the Culme house (Massari 1917, 246–7). He appears to have taken up residence at Clogh Oughter, probably again at Culme's house on the shore of the lake, from at least 1650, for a letter on behalf of the Ulster bishops was signed by him there in August of that year (Gilbert 1879–80, vol. 3, 173). He also held a council of the bishops of the province of Armagh at Clogh Oughter (*apud Petram Superiorem*) on 27 July 1651, the proceedings of which survive (*ibid.*, vol. 2, 179–87; Kavanagh 1941, 579–88). The archbishop continued to write letters from Clogh Oughter, as evidenced by one dated 3 October 1651, and according to one source he died there on 9 January 1652 (Giblin 1958, 83; Walsh 1960, 127).

The Cromwellian forces made good headway in late 1649 and early 1650 in regaining most of Leinster and parts of Munster; Cromwell himself returned to England early in 1650, leaving the army under the control of his generals to complete the reconquest. At this time Philip Mac Hugh O'Reilly, who held the rank of colonel, was in charge of a regiment of seventeen companies in the combined royalist/Confederate army (Gilbert 1879–80, vol. 2, 503–4). Letters of May 1650 from Ormond to Colonel Philip Mac Hugh O'Reilly and to his second cousin Colonel Myles O'Reilly concern a change of mind on his part as to which of them should control Clogh Oughter Castle, with Philip winning out (*ibid.*, 487–8). In June 1650 the Ulster Catholic army, under the command of Ever MacMahon, the Catholic bishop of Clogher, was heavily defeated by Sir Charles Coote at Scariffhollis, Co. Donegal; captured officers, including Owen Roe O'Neill's son Henry, were executed (Casway 1984, 266). As early as 1651 the Cromwellians were making inroads into Cavan, and in September of that year Philip Mac Hugh's own house and castle at Bellanacargy were attacked by Colonel

Venables, who, however, retreated again (Gilbert 1879–80, vol. 2, 200–1). Venables returned in 1652, repaired Bellanacargy Castle and left a garrison in it. By early 1653 most of Ireland was under the control of the Cromwellians, and the last sea connection was broken with the surrender of Inishbofin off the Galway coast on 14 February 1653. Thereafter only small pockets of resistance remained, especially the remnants of the Ulster army in and around the lake country of Fermanagh and Cavan, though they were increasingly surrounded on all sides. One of their leaders, Colonel Philip Mac Hugh O'Reilly, held out at Clogh Oughter.

Colonel J. Jones[37] in a letter to Major Scott dated 1 March 1652 (new style 1653) from Dublin throws some light on the start of the siege, when he reported that

'this day we have intelligence from Colonel Barrow that Trinity Island, in the county of Cavan (as I take it), and some other island thereabouts, are delivered up unto him, and that he is now before Cloughwater Castle, and hath by a fiery float burnt their boats or cottes (as he hopes), and with sluges hath burnt their corne, and hopes in a short tyme it will be rendered or quitted. This is their most confideing garrison in Ulster. God hath brought them very low, both in spirit and number in the north' (Gilbert 1879–80, vol. 3, 371).

'Sluges' in this case are probably mortar bombs (see account of military artefacts, pp 140ff). A second letter from Jones to a Morgan Lloyd reported that same year that Colonel Barrow[38] was in the hands of 'cruel bloody men' demanding £2,000 ransom (*ibid.*, 372). It is not clear whether this was before, during or after the siege but, whatever the outcome, Barrow survived. The siege of the castle ended in surrender and the only other record of the siege that survives is the surrender agreement, which was signed on 27 April 1653. Clogh

[36] Archbishop Hugh O'Reilly was born about 1581. He was connected to the main branch of the O'Reillys but was the grandson of a first cousin of Aodh Connallach, who was also called Aodh (Hugh), a son of Fearghal (Table 2.2), who died in 1536 (Ó Mórdha 1970, 9). After studying for the priesthood in Ireland, he studied philosophy in Rouen *c.* 1618 and theology in Paris; he also studied in Rome (*ibid.*, 14). He was appointed bishop of Kilmore in 1625 and archbishop of Armagh in 1628. John Colgan's *Acta sanctorum Hiberniae* of 1645 was dedicated to him. He was active in reorganising the Catholic archdiocese and played a prominent part in the Confederation of Kilkenny (Ó Mórdha 1972, 352). While archbishop of Armagh he resided mostly in the parish of Kilmore, Co. Cavan, a fact that is adverted to by Bishop Bedell in one of his letters (Shuckburgh 1902, 300).

[37] Colonel John Jones, a Welshman, served from 1650 to 1654 as one of the parliamentary commissioners who ruled Ireland (Barnard 1975, 14), while his correspondent seems to have been Thomas Scott, who was in charge of intelligence in England at this time. Both were regicides, having, with 59 others, signed the death warrant of Charles I, for which both were executed in 1660 (*DNB*, vol. 30, 546–8; vol. 49, 479–81).

[38] Colonel Robert Barrow came to Ireland with Cromwell's army as a lieutenant colonel in Colonel Venables's regiment. He was subsequently promoted and was still active in Ireland at least up to 1659 (Dunlop 1913, 40–1, 68, 641).

Oughter was the last important fortified position to hold out in Ireland against the Cromwellians and, presumably because they realised that further resistance was pointless, the garrison surrendered on relatively good terms to Colonel Theophilus Jones, who was coincidentally a brother of Henry Jones. The articles of the surrender are as follows (*ibid.*, 374–5):

'Articles of agreement between Colonel Theophilus Jones and Phillip Reily, on behalf of himself and his party, and the Lord Eniskillin, Colonel Miles Reily, Colonel Mac Mahonne, Colonel Hugh McGueer, Colonel Conn O'Neil, Colonel Dannell O Cann, and such others of the Ulster party as shall accept thereof by the 18th of May next, or before ensuing the date hereof.

1. Pardon of life and indemnity of all things done by his party, except murder and robbery at the beginning, or any murder since and violation of protection.

2. Liberty of transportation and that the benefit of any agreement which they can make with the Spanish Agent, or any other in amity with the State, and protection to such as desire to remain in the nation.

3. Leave to make sale of their goods before their departure, and the enjoyment of their personal estates by such of them as desire to live in the nation.

4. Satisfaction for their horses at reasonable prices.

5. Priests or any other in Popish orders to go away within one month: Provided during their stay they exercise not their function during their stay, and had no hand in murders, massacres and robberies.

6. Such as are transported to have fourteen days free quarter after their laying down arms and throughfare to the waterside.

7. That Colonel Reily with the party now with him on the west side of Loughern lay down their arms, and deliver such forts in the islands, with all the ammunition and provision therein and is in his power, at or before the 18 of May next, at Crohan, and Colonel Hugh Mc Guier's regiment to lay down their arms the 18 of May next, at Belcowe fort, in the county of Fermanagh, and all others of his party included in these articles are to lay down their arms in the several counties where their quarters are, in such places as the Governors of the several counties shall appoint.

8. That such colonels of Colonel Relie's party as shall at any time before the day of their laying down arms, declare to the Governors of the respective counties or garrisons there, being included in these articles, by giving in an hostage for each of their performances to the said Governors, that then the said Governors, are to give to the respective colonels and their companies, passes to secure them from the violence of the soldiers until the day of their laying down arms, they acting nothing prejudicial to the Commonwealth of England to their armies or garrisons.

9. That the respective officers have liberty to dispose of their horses for their best advantage to any of the Parliament's party, as likewise liberty to wear their travelling arms.

10. That Major Charles Reily remain as hostage, at the garrison of Lismore, for the performance of the laying down arms of Colonel Phillip Reilly's regiments both of horse and foot, at the time and place aforesaid, as also for the delivering of all such forts, in islands, with all the ammunition, provision, and other utensils of war, in any of the said forts that is now under his command; by provision is meant, that which is laid in for the public store.

11. That in case the Lord General Fleetwood and the Commissioners of Parliament assent not to the confirmation of the above articles, at or before Wednesday next, being the fourth day of May, that then these articles are to be void and of none effect, and Major Charles Reilly is thereupon to be returned safe unto Colonel Phillip Reilly, who is likewise to be freed from any engagement by the above said articles. In witness of all which, we have hereunto interchangeably set our hands and seals this 27 of April, 1653.

Phillip Reily.

Witness present,
Phi. Reily
Will. Thurnhill.

I do hereby engage and promise that upon notice given unto me, by Colonel Jones of the Lord General Fleetwood and Commissioners of Parliament's confirmation of the articles concluded between the said Colonel Jones and myself, bearing date this day, to deliver the Castle of Cloughwater, with all the arms, ammunition, provision, goods, and whatever else is in the said

Pl. 2.12—View of Clogh Oughter by Revd Samuel Wynne (Roger Stalley).

Castle, to Colonel Jones, or to whom he shall appoint, for the use of the Commonwealth of England, as witness my hand, this 27 of April, 1653.

Phillip Reily.

The explanation of the article concerning murder given to Colonel Phillip Reilly himself is as follows: He is not esteemed guilty of murder, except he had actually a hand in a particular murder, or did command the same, or except he was present or had commanded when a particular murder was committed by persons under his command by his order—provided he had no knowledge thereof before it was done, nor is it thereby intended that any killed in fight in the open field at any time since the beginning of the Rebellion, be decreed and adjudged murder. Dated 27 April.

Signed: Theo. Jones.'

The terms of the surrender appear to have been honoured and, while there is no specific reference to the

castle's being slighted, the lack of any subsequent reference to it and the present state of the building indicate that it was in all likelihood blown up with gunpowder soon after the surrender.

The leaders of the O'Reillys in Cavan all lost their estates in the Cromwellian confiscations. In May 1653 Philip Mac Hugh O'Reilly travelled from Waterford with 1,000 men to Galicia in Spain, where they joined the Spanish army. He served in Dunkirk and Flanders, and the Franciscan historian John Colgan dedicated his treatise on Johannes Scotus Eriugena, which was published in Antwerp in 1655, to him (Gilbert 1879–80, vol. 3, xxix; Colgan 1655). He was arrested in 1660 for corresponding with the Cromwellians in the hope of being able to return to Ireland. He was still alive in 1664, when he got a pension from the king of Spain (*DIB*, vol. 7, 866–7). Col. Myles (Mulmore) O'Reilly, the former sheriff, also joined the Spanish forces in 1653. He was based in Flanders in 1670, when he took ill and died at an Irish Capuchin friary called Charleville (Walsh 1960, 171–3).

Arthur Culme joined the Cromwellian army and was killed at the siege of Clonmel in 1650. In his will, drawn up in March 1650, he left to his wife Mary his interest in Sir Henry Talbot's lands at Templeogue, Co. Dublin, and other property for her life. His son Hugh was to get the estates in County Cavan. His other children, Elizabeth, Philip, Arthur and Anna, were to get money on coming of age, and his mother, his uncle Benjamin and his brother Amedas were also mentioned. He added a codicil to the will on 12 May 1650 'at the camp before Clonmel', two days after the end of the siege. It is possible that he was dying from wounds received in the siege. The codicil details some debts that he owed and specified that his brother Amedas was to get his pistols. He also left 'his wife and children to the care of the Parliament of England and the Lord General Cromwell to whom he had been a faithful servant' (NAI MS T.4861).[39]

The Culme estates were restored to the family in the Cromwellian settlement, but the family resided from then on at Lisnamaine Castle, to the north of the lake near Drumlane (O'Reilly 1985, 273). The house at Clogh Oughter was probably abandoned, while the castle appears to have been slighted with gunpowder after the siege. The estates passed first to Arthur's son Hugh and then in turn to Hugh's son Arthur and Arthur's daughter Jane (*ibid.*, 273–4) (Table 2.3). Bishop Bedell's[40] successor, Robert Maxwell, who, though appointed in November 1642, would not have been able to take up his post until sometime after 1653, bought the Farnham estate from the Waldrons in 1664. In 1715 the Maxwells, later earls of Farnham, acquired the Culme estates in Cavan from Jane Culme, the last of the family to reside at Lisnamaine (*ibid.*, 274; NLI MS 41,123/9).

Pl. 2.13—Engravings of the castle as published by Mant (1840).

THE CASTLE SINCE THE SEVENTEENTH CENTURY

Antiquarian illustrations and previous research

One of the earliest antiquarian illustrations that we have of Clogh Oughter is by Revd Samuel Wynne and dates from around 1770–90 (Pl. 2.12). A number of Wynne's drawings were used in the making of prints for Francis Grose's *Antiquities of Ireland* (Strickland 1913, vol. 2, 566). This pencil and watercolour illustration of the castle from the east is quite accurate, particularly in showing clearly the projecting bonding stones for the removed stair turret on the north side. It has been claimed that a watercolour by Gabriel Beranger of a lake scene with a castle is a picture of Clogh Oughter (Harbison 2012, 62, 148), but the circular tower shown in this picture, which is described as an imaginary landscape, is part of a larger castle (Crookshank and the Knight of Glynn 1994, 39, pl. 37) and therefore could not be Clogh Oughter. Probably late eighteenth-century in date is William Ashford's beautiful oil painting, usually described as a group of tourists visiting Clogh Oughter Castle (Frontispiece). This shows the ruined and ivy-clad castle from the south, with two boats moored at

---

[39] Arthur's widow, Mary, daughter of Sir Faithful Fortescue, died in 1694 at Coolkenna, Co. Wicklow, at the house of her daughter, Elizabeth Hodson (NAI MS T.4861).

[40] The only member of the Bedell family to return to Cavan was the bishop's son Ambrose, who died at his estate at Carne, Co. Cavan, in 1683 (Vicars 1897, 29).

Pl. 2.14—Photograph of Clogh Oughter with ladies in a boat *c.* 1890. (Reproduced by permission of the Royal Society of Antiquaries of Ireland ©.)

the shore and a group of five adults, a child and a dog beginning to explore the ruin, while two servants are unloading baskets for a picnic. This painting was in Lord Farnham's collection until it was sold in Dublin in 1827[41] (Strickland 1913, vol. 1, 11). It is likely to date from sometime between 1774 and 1800, when Ashford was most active in Ireland (*ibid.*, 7–8; Crookshank 1995).

Two prints of the castle (Pl. 2.13) were published in 1840 in a history of the Church of Ireland (Mant 1840). Both show the castle from the south, but in the upper one the engraver has wrongly depicted openings in the north wall as if they were in the south wall, thus giving a totally inaccurate impression of the ruin. The castle is marked on the first edition of the Ordnance Survey six-inch map (surveyed in 1835), as are the remnants of Culme's house on the shore of the lake to the

south-south-west in Inishconnell townland (Pl. 2.5). The latter is depicted as an L-shaped structure and is labelled 'ruin of offices belonging to Clogh Oughter Castle'. It must have been largely demolished prior to the 1909 edition of the map, which marks it merely as 'Castle Offices (site of)'. The first edition and subsequent editions also mark the small road leading into Inishconnell townland from the south as 'Cromwell's Road', and an area 350m south of Culme's house as 'Camp Hill', presumably where the Cromwellians camped during the siege.

Two photographs of the castle from about the 1890s in the collections of the Royal Society of Antiquaries of Ireland may be connected with Kirker's researches on the castle (Kirker 1890–1). Kirker himself was a photographer and may have taken both photographs. One shows three ladies in a boat at the shore of

---

[41] It was for many years in the Wood Collection and on display at Fota House, Co. Cork. It was recently acquired by the Irish Heritage Trust, having been donated to the trust by the McCarthy family, and is now once more on display at Fota House. Jane Fenlon (pers. comm.) is of the opinion that the clothes indicate a date in the 1780s and that the occasion might have been a visit by a number of antiquarians, including possibly a Protestant clergyman. The figures do not appear to be posed in a manner grand enough to be the owners of the estate, Lord and Lady Farnham.

Pl. 2.15—Photograph of Clogh Oughter and nearby islet *c.* 1890. (Reproduced by permission of the Royal Society of Antiquaries of Ireland ©.)

Inishconnell townland close to the site of the Culme house, with the castle on its island in the background (Pl. 2.14). The other was taken from higher ground also in Inishconnell townland, further to the west above Gubarinn, and as well as the castle it shows a possible crannog to the north-east (Pl. 2.15). That the Maxwells of Farnham continued to take an interest in Clogh Oughter into the twentieth century is shown by the inclusion of photographs of the castle from about 1930 in their photographic collection (Scott 2010, 66).

The earliest detailed account of the castle is that by Kirker, published in 1890–1. This consists of a reasonably accurate description of the castle illustrated by sketch-plans, one dated 1888, and a section of the building. He noted the gap in the parapet on the north side and the projecting masonry beneath it but made the understandable error of interpreting it as the remains of a machicolation (Kirker 1890–1, 294). This also led him to believe that the principal entrance was on the north side. He noted that two original cut stones of the first-floor window on the east side survived, as they do today, and that the windows of the upper storeys were wider than those below and had flat heads (*ibid.*, 295). In

Inishconnell townland, where 'Castle offices (site of)' is marked on the modern OS six-inch map, he noted that the remains of walls survived and were roughly roofed over as a cattle shed. These have been completely levelled in the intervening period. Of particular interest are his observations regarding the make-up of the island on which the castle stands. It was formed of loose stones, but at low water he observed that 'stakes or small piles are visible all round its margin, and even some of the horizontal timbers are exposed to view. The piles are of native timber, from 4 to 6 inches in diameter, and pointed at the lower ends; while the horizontal beams are larger, being about 9 to 12 inches in diameter' (*ibid.*, 295). These observations are of particular interest, having been made within a few decades of the drainage work, which lowered the level of the lake and would have exposed timbers to view that were hitherto submerged.

He also quoted interesting local traditions about the castle, and in particular the siege, which were in fact lifted verbatim, without acknowledgement, from an Ordnance Survey Letter written by John O'Donovan from Cavan on 30 May 1836:

Pl. 2.16—Photograph by Oliver Davies in the early 1940s of the exterior on the eastern side, showing first- and second-floor openings.

'The traditions connected with this curious fortress are wild, indistinct, and various; some say it was built in the sixth century, and before the *Cloctheach* (Round Tower) of Drumlane; others, that it was built by a Danish prince whose name is not now remembered; and a third part heard that it was built by the Sheridans! All, however, agree that it was dismantled by the great and wicked warrior Cromwell; but they do not agree on the manner in which he *tossed* it. According to some Oliver first planted his *devilish engine* on the hill of Drumany, and (to use Moryson's phrase) beat against the cloch from the north, and after having let fly some bolts from that side he found that it was invulnerable there. He then removed his cannon to Gub-a-rann [Gubarinn] and played upon the Rock of *Loch Uachtair* from the west, but he found the cloch invulnerable there also. It is said that he then removed, by the advice of some Irish betrayer, to Inish-gonnell [Inishconnell], and then having planted his culverins on the hill, since called Gub-a campa, (i.e. point of the camp) from this circumstance, he commenced battering the south face of the castle, but in vain, until a false woman, who was inside, hung out a white cloth opposite the spot where the wall was weak: at this spot he directed all his shots until he made a breach which exposed the warders inside to the fury of his firing. Others say that the Rock of Lough Oughter was so strong that Cromwell was not able to effect a breach in any part of it until he landed a body of his soldiers and sappers on the stony island, who set a sap to the foundations, and then tumbled them on that part of the circle. The blasted wall was precipitated partly into the water and partly on the small island, whereon large pieces of it are still to be seen most admirably cemented. A small old road leading to this castle through the townland of Corraconwy [Corracanvy] and Inish-gonnell, is still called Cromwell's road, and is said to have been made by him for the purpose of drawing his cannon to destroy the castle' (Herity 2012, 357; Kirker 1890–1, 295–6).

These traditions, while clearly mistaken in placing Cromwell himself at the 1653 siege, are interesting in showing the impact of these events on the local popular memory in the pre-Famine period and may contain some grains of truth.

The reporting of a number of finds from Clogh Oughter Castle between the 1850s and the 1880s would suggest that some digging/treasure-hunting was taking place there around that time, possibly encouraged or initiated by Lord Farnham, who presented a number of the finds to the Royal Irish Academy. These include two iron swivel guns, listed in the National Museum Register for 1865, which are probably the same items as those listed in the Wakeman Catalogue as 1851 Wk 134 (gun barrel, length 6 feet) and 1852 Wk 135 (gun barrel, 5 feet, 6 inches), all having come from Clogh Oughter. Unfortunately, these cannot now be located. In 1887 Lord Farnham presented a musket mechanism to the Royal Irish Academy (1887 Wk 169). This has been located in the National Museum of Ireland, which holds the Royal Irish Academy's collection of antiquities, and is described and illustrated below in the report on military artefacts under its present catalogue number, NMIHA1995:1174. Another object, comprising 'portions of an ancient cast-iron powder-horn, having a loop at the neck for suspension', which was found 'amongst the ruins of Cloughoughter Castle', was presented to the Kilkenny and South-East of Ireland Archaeological Society in 1857 by Piers Butler of Woodstock Cottage, Inistioge, Co. Kilkenny (*JRSAI* **4** (1856–7), 358).

Kirker (1890–1, 296–7) quoted the fourteenth-century annalistic references to the castle but was inclined to follow Petrie (1972, 228) in dating it to the pre-Norman period. He favoured the supposition that it was built by the O'Reillys in the eleventh century. The first scholar to claim that it was built by the Anglo-Normans was Goddard Orpen (1920, 33–5) and he associated its building with documented attempts by the de Lacys to conquer Bréifne in the early thirteenth century. He identified the Castle of Crannog O'Reilly, mentioned in 1224, as Clogh Oughter (Orpen 1920, 43–4).

The next significant description and discussion of Clogh Oughter was by Oliver Davies, published in 1947 as part of an article on the castles of County Cavan. This included a reasonably accurate plan of the first floor, showing the joist holes and floorboard slots (Davies 1947, 84, fig. IV).[42] He was adamant in claiming that the tower had a slight batter, but in fact this is so slight as to be imperceptible except through measurement, the walls being only 0.1–0.15m narrower at the top than at the base. He mistook the opening in the parapet and the projecting masonry below it on the north side as a machicolation and accordingly claimed that the main entrance was on the north side (*ibid.*, 85). He correctly noted that the second floor was an insertion because it cut across the tops of openings on the first floor. He also observed that 'along the flat sandy beach on the northeast are traces of piles and beams, the remains of defensive outworks or quays' (*ibid.*, 83). These were not visible at the time of the excavation. Davies was of the opinion that Clogh Oughter was built by the Irish in the early fourteenth century (*ibid.*, 82–3, 85–6). A number of Davies's photographs from the early 1940s are preserved in the Topographical Files, National Monuments Service Archive Unit, Department of Arts, Heritage and the Gaeltacht. An external view of the east side shows the condition of the first- and second-floor windows (Pl. 2.16), while an internal view shows the poor state of the first- and second-floor openings on the north side (Pl. 2.17).

No further significant research was carried out on the castle prior to the excavation in 1987. A preliminary report on the work and associated historical research was published soon after the excavation (Manning 1989–90) and an Archaeology Ireland Heritage Guide on the castle was subsequently produced (Manning 1999). An article on the method of flooring circular towers of the thirteenth century in Ireland and Wales

Pl. 2.17—Photograph by Oliver Davies in the early 1940s, showing the poor state of the first- and second-floor openings on the northern side from the interior.

was published by McNeill, but unfortunately the plan was transposed with that of Inchiquin Castle, Co. Cork, the floor beams are shown with the wrong orientation and the location of the first-floor openings is completely muddled (McNeill 2003a, 100, fig. 2). In a second article the identification of the plan was corrected but the problems with it remained (McNeill 2003b, 314, fig. 3). More recently an article placing the tower in the context of other thirteenth-century circular towers in Ireland was published (Manning 2012).

The political symbolism of the castle

In the nineteenth century Clogh Oughter was revered by both sides of the political/religious divide as, on the one hand, the place where the great nationalist hero Owen Roe O'Neill died and, on the other, as the place of imprisonment and quasi-martyrdom of the Protestant bishop of Kilmore, William Bedell. The following verse from Thomas Davis's poem, 'Lament for the death of Eoghan Ruadh O'Neill', illustrates the interest of Clogh Oughter for nationalists:

> 'Though it break my heart to hear, say again the
> bitter words.'
> 'From Derry against Cromwell, he marched to
> measure swords;
> But the weapon of the Sacsanach met him on
> his way,
> And he died at Cloch Uachtar upon St
> Leonard's Day.'

---

[42] The late Henry Wheeler accompanied Davies on his inspection and survey of Clogh Oughter in the early 1940s and assisted him with measurements (Henry Wheeler, pers. comm.). A memo by Henry Wheeler in the OPW Semi-official files, which are in the care of the National Monuments Section, Office of Public Works, gives the date when he was on the island with Davies as 1941.

A major commemoration of Owen Roe O'Neill was held in Cavan town on the tercentenary of his death in October 1949 and a souvenir programme was produced for the occasion (Anon. 1949). This includes a short account of Clogh Oughter Castle accompanied by a photograph (*ibid.*, 39), as well as longer pieces on Owen Roe O'Neill, the Battle of Benburb and Bréifne and its chieftains. There are also messages from John D'Alton, the Catholic archbishop of Armagh, Minister for Defence T.F. O'Higgins and L. Archer, the chief of staff of the army (*ibid.*, 17–19). The commemoration included an exhibition, a military tattoo and historical pageant, high Mass, the unveiling of a plaque at the traditional site of his grave, and a review and march-past to be attended by the president of Ireland.

The story of Bishop Bedell became better known in Ireland and Britain as a result of a short published account of him by Nicholas Bernard (1659) and a subsequent fuller published biography by Bishop Burnet (Burnet 1685; 1736). The latter was based to a large extent on the manuscript biography written by Bedell's stepson-in-law, Alexander Clogie. It is probably no accident that this work first appeared in the same year as the first published edition of Bedell's translation of the Old Testament (Bedell 1685). There was a revival of interest among Protestants and unionists in Bedell in the nineteenth century. A new biography was published in 1843 (Monck Mason 1843) and Alexander Clogie's manuscript was published for the first time in 1862 (Clogie 1862). Different editions of the life by his son William were published in 1871 and 1872 (Bedell 1871; Jones 1872). In addition, the new cathedral in Kilmore, begun in 1858, was built in his memory. Finally, the biographies by Clogie and by his son William were published together in a more academic edition in 1902 (Shuckburgh 1902). Because of his great work of translation, Irish-language scholars, nationalists and historians began to take an interest in Bedell in the twentieth century (Breathnach 1971; Williams 1986; Clarke 1989; Bottigheimer 1998; McCaughey 2001; McCafferty 2009), so that he can be seen today as someone who in some ways straddles the divide between unionism and nationalism.

3. DESCRIPTION OF THE CASTLE

The castle of Clogh Oughter consists of a massive circular tower, 10.57m in internal diameter and 15.57m in external diameter. It stands 18.35m high from present external ground level to the top of the parapet (Pls 3.1 and 3.2). There is a very slight batter in the walls, whereby they narrow from 2.5m in thickness above the slight projecting plinths at the base to between 2.35m and 2.4m at the roof level. The original main entrance to the tower was at first-floor level, facing south-south-west. There were two other doorways through the

Pl. 3.1—An aerial view of the castle in March 2011 from the south-south-east. Note the north-western side of the original first-floor entrance on the left (Photographic Unit, NMS).

Pl. 3.2—An aerial view of the castle from the north in March 2011 (Photographic Unit, NMS).

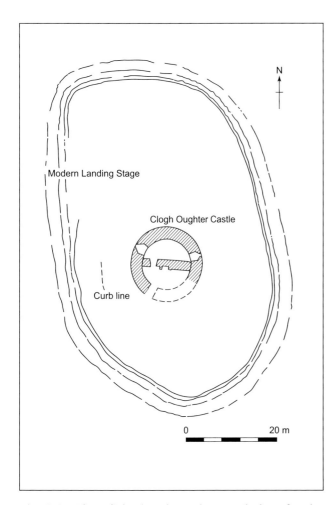

Fig. 3.1—Plan of island, with simple ground-plan of castle.

thickness of the wall at this level; that to the north led to an attached stair turret that no longer survives, while the purpose of that to the south-east is uncertain. A later doorway was broken through the wall at ground-floor level on the south-south-west side. Almost one third of the circumference of the castle on the south side is missing from about 1m above floor level to the top, presumably as a result of its deliberate slighting by the Cromwellians after the siege of 1653. The description below includes details uncovered during the excavation and is based for the most part on descriptions written and measurements taken of parts of the building that were accessible during the course of the excavation in 1987. This is supplemented by information from photographs taken by the author at an early stage of the works in 1985, photographs taken by John O'Brien during conservation works in 1986 and some additional survey work carried out by the author and Kevin O'Brien in 2012.

The walls of the tower are of roughly coursed random rubble limestone masonry. Limestone is the local bedrock and the stone for the building was presumably quarried in the neighbourhood of the lake or somewhere close to the banks of the Erne as it flows northwards to Belturbet. Limestone was quarried in a number of places in the county for particular building projects in the nineteenth century, as for example at Keadew, just north of Cavan town, where stone was quarried close by for the building of the workhouse (Hegarty, forthcoming). Wherever the stone was quarried, once it was close to the lake or the river it could have been easily carried on water to Clogh Oughter. The bedrock to the west of the lake is sandstone, and the dressed stone for the original windows and doorways may have been sourced in that area.

THE ISLAND

The island in its present form is oval, with its long axis north–south. Under normal summer lake levels it measures about 68m long by 43m wide (Fig. 3.1; Pl. 3.3). It rises from the lake on all sides to a berm about 3m wide around the tower itself, which is at the highest point closer to the southern end of the island (Fig. 3.2). The make-up of the island on all sides appears to be piled-up rocks sitting on limestone bedrock, which is generally visible at the northern end of the island during low summer lake levels. The ground-floor level within the castle is some 5m above normal summer lake level. In winter, however, the lake can rise by about 2m, which gives a better idea of summer levels prior to nineteenth-

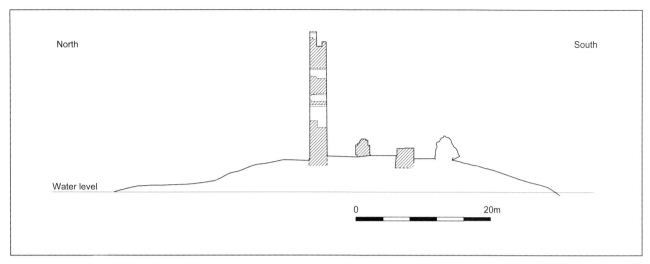

Fig. 3.2—North–south section through island and castle.

century drainage works. During high winter lake levels prior to drainage the waters of the lake could presumably have lapped almost up to the base of the tower, as some of the seventeenth-century accounts state: 'There was of old a little island about it, but it was worn all away to the bare stone walls, and not one foot of ground was to be seen, only a tall, round tower, like a pigeon house, standing in the midst of the waters' (Shuckburgh 1902, 192).

THE GROUND FLOOR

Below ground-floor level in the interior there was a slight widening of the wall for the foundation, which was found to extend to a depth of 1.6m below this level. The widening or plinth was 0.1m wide on the southern side and was immediately below the original ground-floor level. A similar plinth on the exterior of the wall (Pl. 3.4) varies from 0.07m to 0.27m in width and is

Pl. 3.3—An aerial view of the castle and its island from the north-west in March 2011 (Photographic Unit, NMS).

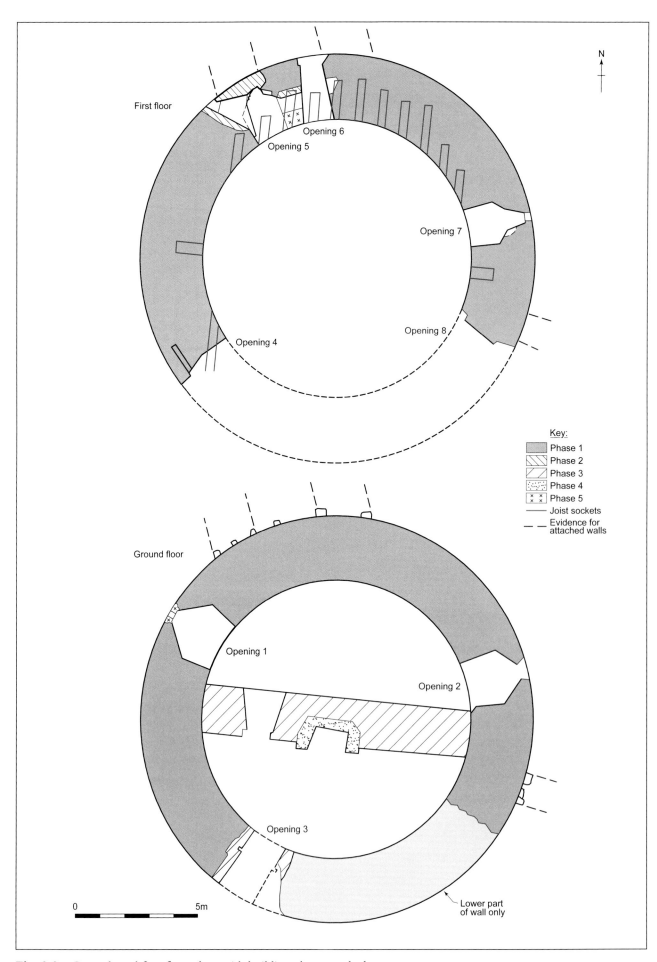

Fig. 3.3—Ground- and first-floor plans with building phases marked.

Pl. 3.4—The external plinth on the north-western side.

0.3m lower than the internal plinth. Ground level externally was lower still, with the seventeenth-century cobbled level on the northern side being up to 0.3m lower than the plinth. At a couple of points the external plinth narrows until it is flush with the wall.

Ground-floor openings

There are three openings in the wall at ground-floor level but only two of these—both embrasures—are original features (Fig. 3.3).

Opening 1

This embrasure faces roughly north-west and is 2m wide at the inner wall face. Its sides initially follow the line of radii of the circle defined by the tower. Because of this the width of the embrasure actually increases, so that at a point 1.25m in from the inner face it is 2.53m wide. At this point the side walls turn inwards at an obtuse angle towards the opening in the exterior face. This opening was damaged and survived only as a ragged hole, up to 0.7m wide, with none of its original dressed stones. The arch of the embrasure is a flat segmental arch, which rose only 0.28m at the centre above the springing at the sides. The soffit of the arch shows impressions of the planks used for the centring (Pl. 3.5) and there are five nib holes at each side for securing the centring. The side walls of the embrasure were only 1.05m high, with the quoin stones of punch-dressed sandstone being quite complete on the right side. The original floor of the embrasure had been broken through to a depth of 0.35–0.45m.

Opening 2

This embrasure faces east (Pl. 3.6) and is only 1.63m wide at the inner face of the wall. Like its counterpart on the north-western side, its side walls initially follow radii of the circle formed by the tower, so that it in-

Pl. 3.5—The head of the north-western embrasure (Opening 1) on the ground floor, showing the impressions of plank centring (Photographic Unit, NMS).

Pl. 3.6—The east-facing embrasure (Opening 2) on the ground floor before conservation (Photographic Unit, NMS).

Pl. 3.7—The western side of the late ground-floor entrance (Opening 3) as uncovered in 1986 during conservation works (John O'Brien).

creases to a width of 2.1m about 1.5m from the interior. At this point the side walls turn at an obtuse angle towards the opening in the outer face of the wall. The embrasure was originally only 1.15m high, the height of its inner jambs. Its head is a flat segmental arch, which rises only 0.3m at the centre. Impressions of plank centring are visible in the soffit of the arch. These show that

Pl. 3.8—The interior during excavation, from above, showing the remains of the internal wall (Photographic Unit, NMS).

Pl. 3.9—The southern face of the eastern half of the internal cross-wall, showing the slot at the base where the foundation beam had been (Photographic Unit, NMS).

planks 0.18–0.2m wide and 0.025m thick were used on the northern side, while more rounded planks, 0.18–0.25m wide, were used on the southern side, eleven planks in all. The funnel-shaped outer portion of the arch shows impressions of ten smaller tapered planks. The outer opening survived as a ragged hole, 0.66–1m wide and up to 1.5m high, with none of its dressed stones. The floor of the embrasure was broken through to a depth of 0.95m at the centre.

Opening 3
The only other surviving feature at ground-floor level in the tower wall was the late ground-level entrance facing roughly south-west. This is situated at the western side of the major breach in the tower, and its upper part and most of its south-eastern side were destroyed when that breach was made after the siege of 1653. The north-western side had already been conserved, partly rebuilt and repointed by the conservation team prior to its examination and description during the excavation, but a photograph from 1986 showed its western side as uncovered by the conservation team (Pl. 3.7). The doorway is 1.45m wide at the inner face of the tower wall and only a short length (0.7m) of the south-eastern side survived here at the base. The only feature visible in the north-western side was a vertical groove in the side,

0.92m from the inner face. This was 0.13–0.15m wide and 0.1m deep on the inner side but 0.18m deep on the outer side. This may have been a portcullis groove at a point where the opening widened slightly towards the inside. This feature did not survive at all on the other side of the doorway. None of the original jamb stones survived in place at the outer part of the doorway but one was found on the ground outside during the excavation, and this showed that the doorway had an outer iron grill or yett. Another similar jamb stone was subsequently found by the conservation team.

Cross-wall

The other feature of the ground floor was the cross-wall, which divided the interior area into two roughly equal parts (Pl. 3.8). This is a late feature and is not bonded into the side walls. It is 1.75m wide, had a doorway near its western end and a fireplace close to the middle of its southern side. It was built directly on the original floor of the castle, with a substantial timber frame acting as a foundation. This timber frame had rotted away completely, leaving only the voids where the timbers had been at the base of both wall faces (Pls 3.9 and 3.10) and at a number of points running through the wall. The void for the beam along the southern face

Pl. 3.10—The northern side of the internal cross-wall, showing the slot for the foundation beam (Photographic Unit, NMS).

Pl. 3.11—The interior of the castle from the south during excavation, showing the beam holes for the first floor and the conserved northern first- and second-floor openings (Photographic Unit, NMS).

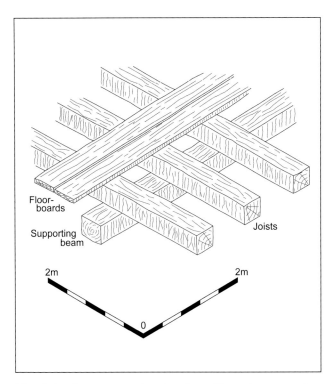

Fig. 3.4—A reconstruction drawing of how the supporting beam, joists and floorboards were arranged.

is 0.3m wide and 0.2m high, while that along the northern face is 0.25m wide and high. The existence of these beams has meant that the wall face does not reach floor level and, with the timbers gone, the weight of the wall was supported by its core. Further voids at the base of the wall indicate that there were four cross-beams connecting the two long beams. These were all of similar dimensions to the main beams and were noted at points 1.5m, 3.8m, 6.2m and 8.6m respectively from the western end of the wall.

The doorway opening in the cross-wall was constructed with its jamb stones, where the door was hung, on the southern side of the wall, with splayed sides widening to 1.7m on the northern side. The jamb stones only survived on the eastern side, where three stones without a chamfer reached a height of 1.05m (Pl. 3.11). If the jamb stones had survived on the western side, the width between them would have been 0.85m. There is a large threshold stone, 1.1m by 0.58m, beneath the level of the jamb stones, and it appears that the foundation beam stopped at the edge of the doorway at each side. On the northern side of the doorway, the fact that cobbling in the floor of the doorway stopped at a line 0.25m from the line of the wall face indicates that the foundation beam continued across the doorway and served as part of its surface. Part of what looked like a drawbar socket survived in the western jamb at a height of 0.85m above the threshold level. It was 0.16m high, 0.18m wide and 0.8m deep. No corresponding hole was

found in the eastern jamb but it is possible that it was blocked up when the fireplace was inserted. No evidence survived for the head of this doorway opening.

The cross-wall survived to a maximum height of 3.25m at its southern face some 2m from its eastern end. The maximum height of the northern face in the same area was only 1.9m. West of the doorway the wall survived to a maximum height of 1.75m.

There was apparently no fireplace at ground-floor level in this wall as it was originally built, and the present fireplace in the southern face is a secondary feature (Pl. 3.11). The back of the fireplace was recessed into the pre-existing wall, and the sides were carried forward as two projecting pilasters to provide sufficient depth for the hearth. The western pilaster is 0.45m wide and projects 0.24m from the wall face. The corresponding pilaster on the east is 0.52m wide and projects 0.24–0.26m from the face of the wall. The fireplace is 1.37m wide at the back, 1.44m wide at the front, 0.7m deep on the eastern side and 0.82m deep and splayed on the western side. The stones used in the jambs were undressed but were covered with plaster. The jambs survive to a height of 1.25m above the contemporary floor level and there is evidence of a narrowing of the flue at the rear above this level. Part of the impression of what appeared to have been a wooden lintel, some 0.19m deep from the face of the jamb, survived at the top of the eastern jamb. A small section of a contemporary cobbled floor survived in front of the fireplace but no good surface for the hearth itself was found. There must have been a fireproof surface or stone in place, as it appeared that the foundation beam was still in place beneath the hearth when the fireplace was in use.

THE FIRST FLOOR

Joist holes for the first floor

A number of holes in the circular wall of the tower show that the original first floor was supported on eleven large joists aligned north–south, which were in turn supported in the middle by a large cross-beam aligned east–west (Figs 3.3 and 3.4; Pl. 3.11). Floorboards had been laid on these joists and these were set into the curving wall of the tower in the area to the east and west of the last joist at each side. The resulting groove is still clearly in evidence. This entire timber floor was an original feature of the thirteenth-century castle and was put in place during the building of the tower, when the walls had reached this height. Whatever survived of this floor was probably removed when the

Pl. 3.12—The surviving western side of the main first-floor entrance, showing the drawbar hole and the slot for a beam beneath the threshold. Note also the bar holes in the lower part of the jamb from the later use of the lower part of the doorway as a window (Photographic Unit, NMS).

Table 3.1—The dimensions of the main joist holes for the first floor.

Joist hole (north side)	width	height	depth
1	0.35m	0.35m	1.45m
2	0.35m	0.34m	1m
3	0.32m	0.30m	1.50m
4	0.35m	0.37m	1.10m
5	0.32m	0.36m	1.50m
6	0.33m	0.39m	1.65m
7	0.30m	0.38m	1.36m
8	0.40m	0.35m	1.33m
9	0.31m	0.35m	1.85m
10	0.32m	0.35m	1m
11	0.31m	0.42m	1m
Joist hole (south side)			
1	0.30m	0.35m	1.2m+

cross-wall was built in the seventeenth century, though it is possible that some parts were retained and the cross-wall built around them.

The hole for the supporting cross-beam on the western side (Pl. 3.10) is 0.44m wide by 0.37m high and 0.84m deep, while that on the east side is 0.42m wide by 0.37m high and 1m deep. The holes for the main floor joists are here numbered 1–11 from west to east. All eleven holes survive on the northern side, though some on the western side were already partly rebuilt at the wall face prior to recording during the excavation. The inner ends of them are, however, all original. Because of the great breach in the tower on the southern side only one joist hole survived here, the most westerly one (Pl. 3.10), though its original depth is unknown, as its end was lost in the breach. Evidence for two other joist holes on the southern side was recorded in a displaced chunk of masonry. The measurements of the joist holes are presented in Table 3.1, the depth,

when the holes penetrate the wall at an angle, being measured at the centre point.

These joists seldom held their square or rectangular shape to their ends, to judge from the surviving sockets. For example, the first joist became more rounded at its southern end, while the second beam narrowed to 0.2m square over its last 0.3m. Five joist holes held their shape to the end, indicating well-squared timbers that did not taper. The tops of the joist holes were at a relatively even level, the same as that of the base of the floorboard slots in the eastern and western walls. This was about 0.28m above the top of the hole for the supporting cross-beam on the western side and 0.3m above the corresponding hole on the eastern side. Any discrepancies in the heights of the main joists could have been accommodated by cutting a slot either in the top of the cross-beam or in the underside of the joists.

Where best preserved, the slots for the floorboards in the eastern and western walls (Pl. 3.10) give accurate shapes and dimensions of the ends of these boards. They averaged 0.06m in thickness and most varied between 0.4m and 0.47m in width, especially on the eastern side. On the western side two boards were 0.25m wide while one was 0.66m wide. They penetrated to various depths into the wall, averaging about 0.33m; while most had squared ends, one was pointed.

Pl. 3.13—The interior, looking north, in 1986, before the first- and second-floor northern openings were conserved. Note that the blocked window to the left (Opening 5) had a pointed head (John O'Brien).

First-floor openings

There is evidence for three doorways and two windows, one altered and realigned, at first-floor level (Fig. 3.3). These are described here in a clockwise order, starting with the thirteenth-century main entrance at the south-west.

Opening 4

Only the western side of this original main entrance survives, because it is at the edge of the large breach on the southern side of the tower (Pl. 3.12). The jamb of the doorway is 1.87m high to the springing of the arch. Initially the inner side of the opening is on the line of a radius of the circle formed by the tower for a depth of 1.14m from the inner face of the tower. The side then splays inwards for 0.82m to the door position, beyond which the outer jamb projects 0.14m for a distance of 0.54m until it reaches the outer face of the tower. At a height of 1m above threshold level there is a drawbar

hole, 1.35m deep and 0.23m wide and high. Part of a beam hole (0.35m high and at least 0.76m deep in the wall), under the jamb and 0.13m below the threshold level (Pl. 3.12), indicates that originally there may have been a cantilevered timber platform in front of the doorway, which would have been accessed on the outside by either a timber stair or ladder. It is impossible to know for certain whether the head of the doorway was circular or pointed. A strange feature of the floor or threshold of the doorway is that it is about 1.4m above the level of the first floor inside the tower.

There are nib holes at the springing of the arch for the outer jamb and the rear arch of the embrasure. There are also three holes cut into the outer jamb, which appear to be secondary and connected with the secondary conversion of the lower part of the doorway into a window (Pl. 3.12). Two of these, 0.1m from the outer corner and 0.3m and 0.7m respectively above the threshold, appear to be bar holes for this window. They average 30mm square and 20mm deep. The third hole, 1.2m above the threshold, is 70mm high, 40mm wide and 170mm deep. It is 170mm back from the outer face and may be connected with the use of a wooden shutter against the bars of the window.

Opening 5

The next opening (going clockwise) is one of two openings facing roughly northwards. This was originally a straightforward window but in a secondary phase of work was blocked and a smaller light opened to one side at an angle. It appears that the building of an attached stair turret necessitated the blocking of the window and the realignment of the opening to one side.

Like the openings in the ground floor and the main entrance on the first floor, the inner sides of this opening are radii of a circle defined by the tower, though very little of the sides survived. On the eastern side the point at which the side turned in at an obtuse angle survives, 1.08m from the inner face of the tower, with dressed stones defining the angle. Much of the rest of this side was damaged by a passage cut into it, which connects with the adjacent doorway. The western side of the embrasure was considerably disturbed by the realignment of the window opening. The outer part of the opening is completely blocked with masonry, mainly of small stones. The western side of the embrasure was 1.7m high from the original floor to the springing of the arch. The floor of the embrasure has been cut down by over 1m. The springing, where it survives, indicates that the arch was originally pointed, and photographs taken prior to conservation in 1985 show the remains of an internal pointed arch (Pl. 3.13). This

Pl . 3.14—A view of the tower from the north in 1985, showing the openings on the northern side before conservation and large voids in the masonry. The northern doorway appears to have had a pointed head.

was reconstructed as a roughly round arch in the course of the conservation works. The western side of the embrasure has a secondary facing of small stones running straight from the inner corner of the embrasure to the blocking and continuing down 1.35m lower than the original floor of the embrasure. The realigned opening has been cut through the wall of the tower on the western side of the embrasure. This angled opening has sides 1m high at each side, its head being merely quarried through the wall. The outer opening here is rectangular, 0.4m wide and 0.55m high. There are two bar holes in the top and bottom but none in the sides. The sill of this opening is about 0.8m higher than the likely level of the sill of the blocked opening. The passage in the eastern side of this embrasure is a secondary feature and is cut to a level of over 1m below the original floor of the embrasure. Its northern side has been partly refaced with small stones and is 1.25m from the inner face of the tower. The pillar of masonry on the southern side of the passage, which divides the door and window embrasures on the inside, was entirely built during the conservation works to strengthen this part of the tower. Prior to conservation this feature was open to the interior of the tower and may have been so in the later phases of use of the castle.

Pl. 3.15—An internal view of the east window at first-floor level (Opening 7) prior to conservation, with the second-floor east window (Opening 10) above it (Photographic Unit, NMS).

Pl. 3.16—The surviving dressed sandstone jamb and partial head of the first-floor east window (Opening 7).

Opening 6

The adjacent opening to the east is a doorway and has—and always had—straight, evenly tapered sides, wider (1.2m) on the inside. The outer jamb stones are missing, but at a point 0.3m from the outer face the opening is 0.9m wide. Only a small portion of the original arch of the embrasure survives, with one nib hole on the eastern side. The side of the embrasure was originally 2m high to the springing of the arch. Its floor was originally 1.37m above the first-floor level but its inner portion

only had been reduced by about 1m in a secondary phase of use. Prior to conservation, part of the external arch survived on the eastern side (Pl. 3.14) and this suggests that the arch was pointed. The drawbar hole for the doorway survives on the eastern side, 0.3m from the outer face. It measures 0.12m by 0.12m and 1.26m deep. The corresponding socket on the western side is 0.1m by 0.09m and 0.14m deep. There was also a ragged hole in the eastern side about midway along its length. Only one original jamb stone survived at the inside.

Opening 7

Continuing clockwise, the next opening is a window (Pl. 3.15). Again the inner sides of the embrasure followed the line of radii of a circle defined by the tower. Where best preserved on the southern side, this radial inner portion is 1.15m long to the point where it narrows in sharply for 0.54m to another angle, beyond which it splays evenly to the exterior. The original southern inner jamb (1.6m high) has its original five quoins, badly spalled. The pointed arch of the embrasure reached a height of 0.7m above the springing. The original floor of the embrasure was 1.72m above the surface of the first floor. Both the embrasure and the outer opening had been enlarged on the northern side in a

Pl. 3.17—A view of the interior, looking north, during the conservation works in 1986. Note the lines of ragged holes in the wall indicating the location of the second, third and fourth floors (John O'Brien).

Pl. 3.18—A view of the north-western segment of the inner face of the wall in 1986, after removal of ivy but before repointing. Note the ragged holes for joists for the second and third floors and the large beam hole at the top which is not directly connected with any floor (John O'Brien).

secondary phase of work. Luckily, however, two dressed stones of the original window survived on the southern side. These were both of sandstone and formed one half of the pointed window head and the jamb stone immediately beneath it (Pl. 3.16). These stones were 0.22m deep, with a plain chamfer on the outside. They were rebated on the inside to a depth of 0.05–0.06m for a wooden shutter. A small drawbar hole to hold this shutter measures 0.075m by 0.08m and 0.55m deep. Beneath the two carved stones there are ghost impressions of four other jamb stones and the impression of another stone, probably the sill. It is possible that the window head was originally a single stone, as its edge above the point of the window is a broken one. In this broken edge can be seen a section of a socket for a vertical iron window bar or stanchion (40mm deep and 30mm wide) and it is possible that in rusting the pressure of the expanding bar cracked the stone. In the lower stone there is a hole for a horizontal iron window bar (saddlebar) just below the joint, 25mm by 25mm and 40mm deep. All of this evidence indicates that this original window was 1.7m high and 0.25m wide externally, with a pointed head.

The enlarged embrasure was between 1.76m and 1.84m wide and had been refaced on the northern side but the upper part of the original northern side survived. The outer opening had been enlarged towards the north for a larger light, which could have been up to 0.8m wide. At the time of the excavation the opening was ragged. The inner part of the floor of the embrasure was cut into to a depth of 1.4m and faced on both sides. There was a step of 0.8m up to the sill level of the secondary enlarged opening.

Opening 8
At the ragged end of the wall caused by the huge breach on the south-eastern side there is evidence for another doorway. Like the northern doorway, it has a straight side, though the outer and inner jambs are missing. The surviving northern side of the doorway is about 2m high. Between the doorway and the window some 1.25m above first-floor level there is a large beam hole of uncertain purpose in the wall. It is 0.44m wide and 0.34m high and may have been connected with a wooden stair giving access to the roof/parapets during the initial building phase (Phase 1).

SECOND FLOOR

The second floor was clearly a secondary feature, as it cuts across the top of the tall openings on the ground

Pl. 3.19—A view of the interior in 1987, with some of the filled-in holes and the floor levels they represent marked. The approximate position of Opening 12 is also marked.

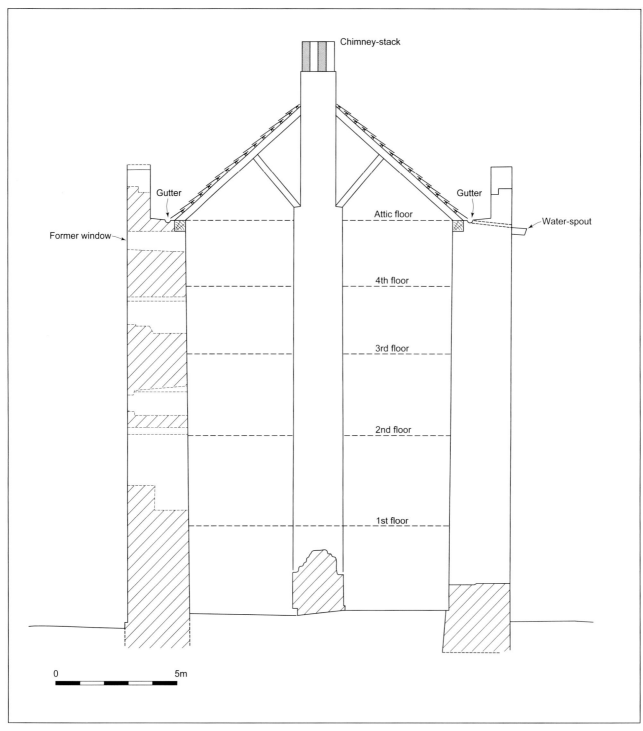

Fig. 3.5—A reconstructed north–south section of the Phase 3 tower, showing the approximate levels of the different floors, the cross-wall, chimney and roof.

floor. Apart from the first floor, with its large joist sockets, there is no evidence for any other original (Phase 1 or Phase 2) floors in the tower. Even the evidence for how these upper Phase 3 wooden floors were supported is not clear in the tower as conserved, but there were some roughly quarried-out holes in the inner face of the tower (Pls 3.17–3.19), the infilling of which was marked with a damp-proof course during the conservation work. These holes must have held Phase 3 joists, the other ends of which could have been supported by

the cross-wall, which, with fireplaces in it, is likely to have continued up to the roof (Fig. 3.5). Kirker's (1890–1, 294) section drawing of the tower indicates evidence in the form of joist holes for a second, third and even a fourth floor, but this drawing is schematic and the holes for the second to fourth floors were not at all as regular or clearly defined as those on the first floor.

Only two openings survived at second-floor level (Fig. 3.6), one facing north and one facing east; both are secondary features broken through the wall.

Pl. 3.21—The second-floor east window prior to conservation (Opening 10).

Pl. 3.20—The northern side of the tower, showing the toothing for the attached turret extending up to the top and the doorway from the turret to the parapet (Photographic Unit, NMS).

Opening 9

Before conservation the floor of the opening facing north had long since fallen away, and on the inside it formed one large, ragged hole with the doorway below it (Pl. 3.13). There had been a large chasm in the wall running through these two openings and by the time of the excavation the opening had already been restored, with a segmental arch on the inside and a modern rectangular opening externally (0.69m high by 0.5m wide) (Pl. 3.20). Enough of the original sides survived to show that the opening was 1.9m wide on the inside and tapered evenly to a width of 0.93m at a point 0.43m from the outer face. The sides of the embrasure were 0.96m high and, as restored, it now rises to 1.15m at the centre. No evidence survives for how the head of this secondary opening was finished. It is possible that it was left as quarried through the wall.

Opening 10

When described, the opening facing east had not yet been conserved (Pl. 3.15). It too is a secondary opening

that was quarried through the wall. The embrasure is evenly splayed from a width of 1.5m at the inside to 0.76m just before the outer jamb stones. There was a gap at the top of the secondary side walls, which may have held timber lintels originally. Above this was the soffit of the opening as quarried through the wall. Close to the outside the embrasure was only 0.8m high but there were some large steps down to the interior. At a point 0.7m from the outer face of the tower the floor of the embrasure dropped 0.2m, then sloped slightly for 0.8m, after which there was a rough drop of 0.6m. All this was best preserved on the northern side. On the southern side it was partly damaged, especially where it cut into the head of the first-floor window embrasure below (Opening 7).

Externally the window itself was rectangular, but only its southern jamb and lintel survived (Pl. 3.21). These indicate that the opening was 0.8m high by 0.64m wide. The jamb stones are 0.2–0.25m deep, with no chamfer. There is a rebate of 0.06m between the inner corner of the jamb and the side wall of the embrasure but no evidence of shutter fittings. There were three bar holes in the lintel and two in the jamb, all 30–40mm square and 20mm deep.

THE THIRD AND FOURTH FLOORS

Third-floor window

There was only one surviving opening at this level (Opening 11). This too was secondary and quarried through the wall (Fig. 3.6). It is wider than those on the second floor and has two lights. The sides of the embrasure, only 0.92m high, are almost parallel and narrow slightly from a width of 1.78m at the inside to 1.72m

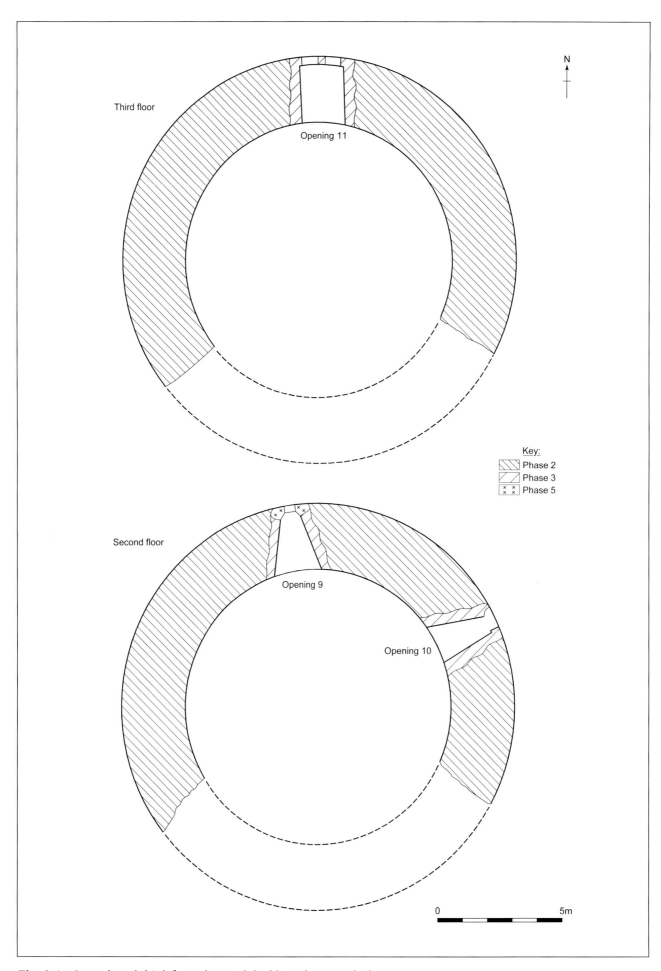

Fig. 3.6—Second- and third-floor plans with building phases marked.

Pl. 3.22—The western jamb of the third-floor window prior to conservation (Opening 11).

Pl. 3.23—The eastern jamb of the third-floor window prior to conservation (Opening 11).

short of the window stones. No evidence survived for how the embrasure had been roofed; the present flat arch was inserted in the course of conservation work. The two window openings are 0.66m wide and 0.77m high. The window stones are 0.24m deep. Both the mullion and the two lintel stones were recovered on the ground by the conservation team and replaced, while the jambs at each side survived intact (Pls 3.22 and 3.23). There was evidence for three horizontal and two vertical bar holes in each light.

Large cross-beam

On the western side of the tower is a rectangular, parallel-sided hole running through the wall (Pls 3.18 and 3.24). Its base is roughly level with the head of the third-floor opening. The hole is 0.75m high and about 0.5m wide, and there was a corresponding hole in line with it in the eastern wall. Before conservation one side of the latter hole could be seen in the broken edge of the tower, and the other half of the hole survived in one of the chunks of masonry on the ground. It is evident that

Pl. 3.24—A view of the castle from the south-east, showing the holes for a large beam above third-floor level (Photographic Unit, NMS).

57

Pl. 3.25—A view from the south-east of the fourth-floor window (Opening 12) during conservation work in 1986, showing the surviving face of the western side of the embrasure (John O'Brien).

Pl. 3.26—A view of the fourth-floor window (Opening 12) in 1986, showing the line of the western face of the embrasure (John O'Brien).

these holes held a massive beam of timber, which un-doubtedly was put in place when the wall of the tower reached this height. The beam spanned the interior and extended to—or possibly even beyond—the outer faces of the tower. The function of this massive beam is un-clear. Perhaps it provided support for the Phase 2 roof. It is certainly an original feature of the upper part of the tower, in fact the only surviving one between the first-floor openings and the parapets.

The fourth floor

It was only at a very late stage in the preparation of this report that clear evidence for the existence of a fourth floor came to hand in the form of photographs taken by John O'Brien during the course of conservation works in 1986. These photographs show rough holes for joists in the northern inner face of the wall (Pls 3.17 and 3.18) and a large, mostly ragged, north-facing open-ing in the wall immediately below the parapet walk

(Opening 12) (Pls 3.25 and 3.26), which was filled soon afterwards with masonry as part of the conservation work and is now indistinguishable from ground level. This opening can be seen in old photographs (Pls 2.14 and 2.15) and again in 1985 after the removal of ivy and other growth (Pl. 3.14). Like the openings on the sec-ond and third floors, it appears to have been quarried through the wall in Phase 3. Some of the facing of the embrasure survived on the western side (Pls 3.25 and 3.26) but otherwise the opening was mostly ragged, without any external jamb stones surviving. The former head of the opening, presumably stone or timber lintels, must also have served as the surface of the parapet walk. The embrasure appears to have been quite narrow and low and probably not unlike Openings 9 and 10 on the second floor.

Pl. 3.27—A projecting step leading to the doorway in the parapet on the northern side, from below, prior to conservation.

ROOF LEVEL AND PARAPETS

The parapets and parapet walk

The parapet wall around the top of the tower was already mostly conserved at the time of the excavation, when the present record was made. It is 0.95m thick and up to 1.9m high above the level of the wall walk. The gaps or crenels in it are unevenly spaced but mostly they were 2.2–2.54m apart. Of an estimated original twelve gaps in the parapet there is now evidence for only eight in the remaining portion of the tower. One of those facing north is different from all the others and is in fact a doorway that provided access from the stair turret (Pls 3.1 and 3.2). It extends down to the level of the wall walk; it is 0.63m wide on the inside and widens to 0.8m wide on the outside, where there are traces of walling continuing out up to 0.4m and 0.5m wide on the western side and 0.68m wide on the eastern side in the lower half of the opening (Pl. 3.27). This doorway is 1.9m high on the inside and there are steps down from this towards the outside, each 0.25m high. Eighteenth- and early nineteenth-century illustrations (Frontispiece; Pl. 2.13) indicate that the lintel of this doorway was still extant at that time.

The openings or crenels in the parapet, for the most part, are 0.85m wide on the inside and 0.68m wide on the outside. The openings are mostly 1m high on the inside, with a step up of 0.28m at a point 0.48m from the inside. The last two openings to the west are narrower than the others, being only 0.55 wide externally, 0.74m wide internally and with bases only 0.5m above the wall walk on the inside.

Approximately two thirds of the tower had been conserved when this record was made during the excavation; only the last section to the east remained to be conserved. About midway across the remaining portion of the wall inside the parapet there was a gutter running concentrically with the wall (Pls 3.28 and 3.29). On the inner side of the gutter, where conservation had not yet been carried out, there was a ragged hollow, possibly the location for a wall beam supporting the base of the roof. It was filled with plant growth and it was not possible to examine it closely. Where conservation had been carried out, a low wall was built up here to hold a modern timber railing. This was erected to make the wall walk safe for visitors (Pl. 3.30).

The gutter was made of sandstone and formed a continuous channel running some 0.55–0.65m from the inner face of the wall. The channel was 0.12m wide and

Pl. 3.28—A view of the north-eastern segment of the top of the tower during conservation in 1986, showing the parapet prior to conservation and a small part of the gutter on the right (John O'Brien).

0.02–0.025m deep in the centre. The stones of the gutter were well set in mortar and were about 0.25m wide and 0.12–0.18m thick. It probably drained out through three water-spouts, of which evidence for two survived, facing west and north-east. These had been restored as part of the conservation work. In the portion not conserved there was evidence for sandstone flags sloping from the parapet to the gutter and overlapping the flat part of the stone (Pls 3.28 and 3.29). Such flags being held in place with mortar along with roof tiles mortared into place on the roof would explain traces of mortar on the gutter stones on each side of the channel.

Attic floor

While no evidence for an attic floor survived, it is quite likely that there was one supported off the wooden wall-plate or ring-beam that also held the roof. There must also have been a wooden doorway at this level, built in the style of a dormer window, to give access from the interior on to the parapet walk. Access between the floors and up to this level in Phases 3 and 4 was by wooden stairs.

EVIDENCE FOR FORMER ATTACHED WALLS

A number of bonding stones project from the exterior of the wall 0.4m north of the eastern doorway (Opening 8), indicating that there was originally a wall attached to the tower here. A possible explanation is that these are

Pl. 3.29—The unconserved wall walk on the eastern side, with the curving stone gutter and grass-grown inner edge, in 1987.

the bonding stones of a curtain wall or intended curtain wall for a small attached enclosure (Fig. 3.3; Pl. 3.31). They indicate a wall 1.17m wide and at least 2.8m high. There was an angled beam hole in the wall of the tower here, 1m north of these bonding stones, which may be angled to be parallel with the missing wall. It was level with the floors of the adjacent doorway and window. It was 0.4m high, 0.3–0.4m wide and about 1m deep. If there was a curtain wall here the doorway may have given access from the tower to its wall walk, while the hole could have held a beam supporting a timber hoarding on the curtain wall.

On the northern side of the tower numerous bonding stones project from the wall over its entire height— evidence of a former attached stair turret, which may also have contained a garderobe. Most of these projecting

stones are in vertical lines, indicating the outer and inner faces of the walls of this turret (Pl. 3.32). These indicate that the eastern wall was 1.84m wide, while that on the western side was 1.75m wide (Fig. 3.3). The overall width of the turret was about 6m. It appears likely that the eastern wall belonged to Phase 1 and was part of the attached enclosure, with a widening close to the tower to accommodate a garderobe. The western wall must have belonged to Phase 2, as it necessitated the blocking of a Phase 1 window. At the top of this wall is a doorway leading to the parapet walk of the main tower (Pl. 3.20), and it appears likely that this wall contained a spiral stair leading from first-floor level up to this doorway. This hypothesis is supported by the fact that two newel stones from a spiral stair were found on the island (see p. 138). Two of the bonding stones indicate a slight projection to the west at the level of the first floor just below the skewed Phase 2 window. These, however, were sockets before conservation (Pl. 3.14) and could have held timbers. The plan of this former turret is unfortunately unknown, and the very limited excavations carried out here only confirmed the existence of foundations but did not reveal their overall shape or form.

THE PHASES OF THE BUILDING

Phase 1

This initial phase in the building of the circular tower, which is undoubtedly of early thirteenth-century date, consisted of the ground and first floors and possibly a small attached area enclosed with a curtain wall. The main entrance was at first-floor level and the two other doorways may have given access to the wall walk of the curtain wall, that to the north possibly being wider to accommodate a garderobe (Fig. 3.3). The first floor was lit by at least two windows. The missing portion of the tower could have had either another window or a fireplace at first-floor level. A series of eleven large beams held the timber first floor. Access to the ground floor can only have been by a wooden stair or ladder between two of these beams. There are two surviving embrasures with narrow loops at ground-floor level and the missing portion of the tower may have had another. No evidence was noted, or indeed seemed to survive, for what type of parapet or roof system was used at this stage.

Phase 2

In this phase the height of the tower was doubled and a stair turret attached on the northern side. This also appears to be of thirteenth-century date and probably followed soon after Phase 1. Adding the stair turret necessitated blocking up the first-floor window facing north and breaking out a smaller light from its embrasure towards the west to avoid the new structure. The shape of the turret is unknown; it may have been square, rectangular or D-shaped. As its width against the wall of the main tower was 6m, it may have contained a garderobe as well as a stair. The turret rose the full height of the heightened tower and gave access to the parapets through the surviving doorway in the parapet wall. There is no evidence for any original openings or floors in the

Pl. 3.31—A view of the tower from the south-east, showing (on the right) the toothing in the wall for a possible curtain wall and one side of the first-floor south-eastern doorway above (Photographic Unit, NMS).

Pl. 3.32—The toothing in the wall on the northern side for the attached turret (Photographic Unit, NMS).

upper part of the tower, which was built during this phase (Fig. 3.6). The parapets would appear to be original to this phase but whether there was a roof at this level in Phase 2 or at a much lower level within the tower is unknown. No clear evidence for a lower roof and its necessary water outlets was noted, but much of the tower was already conserved at the time of the excavation and the remainder was mostly covered with ivy. There is a difference in the masonry between Phases 1 and 2. In Phase 1 more use was made of quarried stone, with many of the stones having good, well-squared faces and a brownish tinge (Pl. 3.33), whereas in Phase 2 more weathered stones were used, possibly field stones or stones sourced on the lake shore. A clear line can be seen between the two phases on the western side about 0.8m above the head of the original entrance (Pl. 3.33).

Phase 3

This would appear to be the historically recorded work carried out between 1610 and 1620, when the castle was adapted to serve as a prison for priests and as a fortress if required. The main elements of this work consisted of the demolition of the stair turret on the northern side and all other attached walls or structures, the opening of a new ground-floor doorway facing southwest, the insertion of a cross-wall within the building, the insertion of new wooden floors and stairs within

the building, and the making of new window openings to serve the new second, third and fourth floors (Figs 3.3–3.6). It would also have involved the erection of a new conical roof at the top of the tower, with presumably a central chimney to serve fireplaces in the new cross-wall. There was probably also an attic floor and a doorway from the attic, within a timber structure similar to a dormer window, giving access to the battlements.

Phase 4

This phase involved some minor alterations to the building probably carried out in the 1640s, when it was being used as a prison. The ground-floor fireplace and associated cobbled floor appear to belong to this phase (Fig. 3.3).

THE SITE OF THE CULME HOUSE IN INISHCONNELL

This site is located on the shore of the lake to the south of the castle (Fig. 1.1; Pl. 1.1). Though marked as an L-shaped structure on the first edition of the OS map, there is no trace visible on the ground today. A geophysical survey of the area carried out in 2011 is described in Appendix 1. Part of the ruin had been adapted as a cattle shelter by the 1890s (Kirker 1890–1, 295). Oliver Davies (Topographical Files, Archaeological Archive Unit, National Monuments Service) recorded some traces still visible in the early 1940s and some traditions about the place:

> 'All along the top of the bank, which slopes gently northwards, is black earth containing many fragments of mortar, and many stones and bones have been found, among them cup-marked stones which may have been door-post sockets. Only one ruin can now be seen, a rectangular building of mortared masonry with traces of brick fragments, now partly sunk in the ground. The walls are 2'10" [0.9m] thick, internal diameter 26' x 17½' [8m by 5.4m]. In the same field is a lone bush, which it is regarded as best not to interfere with. It used to be said that one should not leave animals in this field at night, or they would disappear before morning. 30 yards north-east of the ruin, at the edge of the steep bank is a paved hole, which is believed to be the entrance of an underwater tunnel to Clogh Oughter Castle. The whole field is

Pl. 3.33—A view of the tower from the west, showing a clear distinction in the colour and nature of the stone between Phase 1 and Phase 2.

known as the Plum Orchard,[1] suggesting English settlement; there are no fruit trees in it now.

The second field to the south-west of the Plum Orchard is a small triangular patch, rather curiously cut off from the neighbouring fields. It is believed to be the field in which bullocks were kept at the time that Clogh Oughter Castle was in use.'

---

[1] This reference to plums is interesting in the light of Clogie's sarcastic account of Arthur Culme having sugar and plums in his house in 1641 but no gunpowder (see above, p. 23).

4. THE CONSERVATION OF CLOGH OUGHTER

Representations by interested local people to have Clogh Oughter taken into State care can be traced back as far as 1959 (National Monuments Service file F94/1151/1, p. 2). While there was recognition that Clogh Oughter was a national monument under the meaning of the Act, and an important and interesting one at that, the opportunity to take it into care did not arise until the 1980s because of other commitments. European Economic Community funding for approved projects in counties along the border with Northern Ireland was availed of in 1985 to carry out a conservation project on the castle. The fact that the castle and its tiny island had no registered owner since the breakup of the Farnham estate made the acquisition of it by the State problematic. This was overcome by placing a Preservation Order on it on 7 March 1985 under Section 8 (1) of the National Monuments Act, 1930, and then taking it into guardianship by order under the seal of the Commissioners of Public Works in Ireland on 25 April 1985 under Section 9 (2) of the National Monuments Act, 1930.

Clogh Oughter had lain in a ruined state from the time of its slighting in the seventeenth century until conservation work commenced in 1985. While Lord Farnham appears to have done some digging at the castle in the nineteenth century, when two swivel guns from there and part of a musket were presented to the Royal Irish Academy (see pp 151–2 below), there is no evidence or suggestion that he or anyone else carried out any conservation or other works on the walls, apart possibly from some removal of ivy. In fact, the general condition of the building does not seem to have changed much since it was first illustrated in the late eighteenth century. By 1985 the island itself was densely overgrown and the walls of the tower were heavily covered with ivy (Pls 4.1 and 4.2). There was a large crack in the wall of the tower on the northern side, with voids in the masonry extending through the doorway at first-floor level to the windows above it on the same side and continuing to the top.

The aim of the project was to conserve the building as a ruin and ensure its continued survival into the future. Soon after the monument was taken into guardianship the National Monuments Section of the Office of Public Works commenced work at the site.

Pl. 4.1—Clogh Oughter from the south during the early stages of the work in 1985.

Pl. 4.2—The interior of the tower from the south in 1985, showing the loss of masonry around openings on the northern side.

Pl. 4.3—Charlie Fleming, foreman.

Pl. 4.4—The northern part of the island during the excavations in 1987, when the water level in the lake was low. Note the tea hut of the conservation team on the right.

Pl. 4.5—The same tea hut during high winter lake levels in 1989 and after some of the trees behind had been cut back.

The work was carried out for most of its duration under the direction of Paul McMahon, Senior Architect, who was succeeded towards the end of the project by Willie Cumming, Architect. Directing the work from start to finish was P.J. Dolan, Senior Clerk of Works at the Trim National Monuments depot, who, as a Cavan man, took a special interest in the project. Most of the conservation team were recruited locally for the job and included Charlie Fleming, foreman (Pl. 4.3), Eddie Brady, Seamus Cunningham, Hugh Fitzpatrick and Paddy Hoey.

A small temporary depot was set up and enclosed with a fence at Gubarinn, known locally as Rann Point, and a small concrete jetty was constructed for boats. Another small concrete jetty was constructed on the north-western side of the island, and huts were erected on the island for shelter, materials and equipment (Pls 4.4 and 4.5).

During the course of the work the entire tower was scaffolded in sequence, starting on the western side. All ivy and other growth were removed and masonry joints cleaned out as necessary and repointed (Pls 4.6 and 4.7). New work, such as filling in ragged holes in the masonry, was marked with a damp-proof course (DPC). New masonry cappings and additional masonry to re-pair jambs and heads of openings were marked in the same way.

The main structural issue that had to be tackled was the major crack through the wall on the northern side. This ran through and had severely damaged a number of openings. Engineering advice was sought, and reinforced concrete pins were built into the structure across the crack to help hold the two halves of the building together. A substantial amount of new masonry was inserted to fill the voids associated with the crack and to strengthen the openings through which it ran (Pls 4.2, 4.7 and 4.8).

Pl. 4.6—The tower under scaffolding with conservation work in progress in 1987 (Photographic Unit, NMS).

Pl. 4.7—The interior of the tower, looking north, during the excavation (1987), when the eastern part had not yet been conserved (Photographic Unit, NMS).

Pl. 4.8—A view of the tower from the north in 2012, showing clearly the restored second-floor window above the first-floor northern doorway (Photographic Unit, NMS).

Pl. 4.9—A view of the tower from the east in 2012, showing the various openings and the restored large beam hole at the top left (Photographic Unit, NMS).

Pl. 4.10—An exterior view of the first-floor eastern window as restored. Note the two original stones *in situ* at the top left (Photographic Unit, NMS).

Generally the inner jambs, floors and heads of embrasures were restored to their original form. At ground-floor level not a single cut stone of the two arrow loops survived. These were presented as narrow cut-stone openings (Pl. 4.9) but are not intended to replicate what was or might have been there. It was only possible to repair the western side of the seventeenth-century ground-floor door opening. Only the inner corner survived on the eastern side and the remainder was left ragged. The voids at the base of the cross-wall, where a frame of timber beams had formed its foundation, were infilled with concrete to replicate the timber beams and to give support to the wall faces above them.

At first-floor level a considerable amount of re-building was carried out on the northern side in repairing first-floor joist holes and the inner part of the doorway and former window embrasure (Pl. 4.7). All of this work was undertaken to strengthen the new connection between the two halves of the building. Both openings were given new circular heads internally. The eastern window was the only thirteenth-century open-

ing with any fine original cut stone surviving. This was therefore fully restored with modern sandstone (Pls 4.9 and 4.10).

The seventeenth-century openings at second- and third-floor levels were restored using all new stones for the second-floor northern window (Pl. 4.8) but only one new jamb in the case of the eastern window (Pl. 4.9). The mullion and two lintels of the third-floor two-light window were found on the ground and put back in place (Pl. 4.8). All were given segmental arched heads on the inside (Pl. 4.7), though originally they may have had timber lintels. The seventeenth-century window opening at fourth-floor level was very ragged, with part of the parapet wall surviving precariously above it (Pls 3.25 and 3.26). This was completely blocked up with masonry.

Masonry was added to the ragged wall-end on the eastern side and, in the process, the beam hole at about fourth-floor level had its missing southern side restored (Pl. 4.9). At parapet level the merlons were repaired and capped, and iron railings set between them for safety if the public were ever to get access to the top. The low, ragged inner face of the tower wall at the top was built up to a level higher than the wall walk and a timber railing was set into it (Pls 4.8, 4.9, 4.11 and 4.12).

From the outset of the project it had been hoped that it would be possible for members of the public to access the top of the tower, so that the view could be enjoyed. The difficulties of achieving this objective safely gradually became apparent, however. A system of wooden platforms was installed which allows access to the top, with the addition of ladders, for maintenance and cleaning works. The first of these platforms is a partial reconstruction of the original first floor in the north-eastern segment of the tower, using the four easternmost joist holes. The internal cross-wall was built up to this level to support the southern ends of these beams, and floorboards were laid on the beams. Three more timber platforms, supported off the inner face of the wall, were erected so that ladders can be used by a maintenance team to gain access to the top of the tower (Pls 4.11 and 4.12).

Loose architectural stones recovered from the site were firmly set and displayed around the fireplace on the ground floor, where the cobbling found in the course of the excavation was replicated. Pebbles were laid over the rest of the floor and on a strip around the walls. Stepped mortared-stone terraces were laid on the southern side of the island, especially around the large displaced chunks of masonry from the southern wall. Although many trees on the island were cut as part of

Pl. 4.11—A view of the interior of the tower in 2012, showing the timber platforms that were erected on the interior of the wall to facilitate ladder access to the top (Photographic Unit, NMS).

Pl. 4.12—An aerial view of the tower from the south in March 2011 (Photographic Unit, NMS).

Pl. 4.13—A view of the island, looking east, from the lake in 2012 (Photographic Unit, NMS).

the conservation works, trees have grown again on the margins of the island in the intervening years (Pl. 4.13).

While the conservation project was carried out in the hope that the monument could be easily accessible, no boat service to the island was ever established and, in consequence, very few people wishing to see the castle actually get to set foot on the island. Most have to content themselves with a fine view of the castle from the shore at Gubarinn. Some of those who do land on the island by boat have lit campfires within the castle and, unfortunately, this has damaged some of the carved stones on display. . The castle is subject to ongoing maintenance by staff from the National Monuments Service of the Office of Public Works, who are ensuring that this important piece of Cavan's built heritage will survive into the future.

5. THE EXCAVATION

INTRODUCTION

After Clogh Oughter was taken into State guardianship in April 1985, conservation work was started without delay on the building but without any archaeological input or advice. By the time I was informed of the situation and got to inspect the site on 6 September 1985, a large amount of rubble had been excavated in and around the circular tower without archaeological supervision (Pls 5.1 and 5.2) and animal bones and seventeenth-century pottery were being recovered. Unsupervised excavation continued, and a few weeks later human remains were uncovered in the rubble on the south-western side of the castle. I inspected the find on 4 October and excavated and lifted what was left of the skeleton. It was agreed at this stage that an archaeological excavation would be carried out and that until then only the upper levels of rubble would be removed without archaeological supervision.

The excavation was carried out over a six-week period from 15 June until 24 July 1987 under my direction with a team of archaeologists and other workers (Pl. 5.3). The work was undertaken to facilitate the conservation and presentation of the monument. The aim of the excavation was to reduce the interior and part of the exterior of the tower to original floor levels and to record all information relating to the history of the castle in the process. Scaffolding was in place and conservation work was continuing on the northern half of the castle, and this partly determined where excavation

Pl. 5.1—The northern half of the tower in September 1985, showing removal of rubble prior to archaeological excavation. The depth of rubble being dug out can be judged by the soil mark on the wall.

Pl. 5.2—The northern half of the tower from the west in September 1985, showing removal of rubble prior to archaeological excavation. The soil mark on the wall shows that the rubble had been lower around the eastern embrasure.

could take place (Pls 5.4 and 5.5). After two weeks the scaffolding against the interior face of the northern wall was removed, allowing excavation to take place in the northern half of the interior (Area B).

The excavation licence number for the site is E409. For the purposes of this report the areas excavated (Fig. 5.1) have been relabelled as follows: Area A, the southern half of the interior, including the late external ground-floor doorway; Area B, the northern half of the interior, including the doorway in the internal dividing wall; Area C, the area immediately outside the late doorway on the south side; Area D, an area that was only superficially excavated close to the tower on the northern side; Area E, the area immediately outside the eastern first-floor doorway; and Area F, a small area 25m northwest of the tower at the modern boat jetty built by the conservation team. In the account below the layers will be described starting with the earliest.

At the outset of the excavation only about 0.3m and less of deposits survived above floor level in Area B, while up to 1m survived over most of Area A apart from the area between the two doorways, which was almost at floor level. The two doorways and the area between had been mostly cleared to threshold level (Pls 5.4 and 5.5). Outside the wall of the tower and close to it on the southern side up to 1.5m of rubble remained over the old surface except in the immediate area of the sec-

Pl. 5.3—Members of the excavation team beside the compound at Gubarinn, packing finds for transport to Dublin. From left to right: Caroline Donaghy, Ruairí Ó Baoill, Audrey Gahan, Mick Ward and Stephen Hartung.

Pl. 5.4—The surface level in Area A on the first day of the archaeological excavation in 1987.

Pl. 5.5—The surface in Area A at the start of the archaeological excavation, showing the lower level between the two doorways.

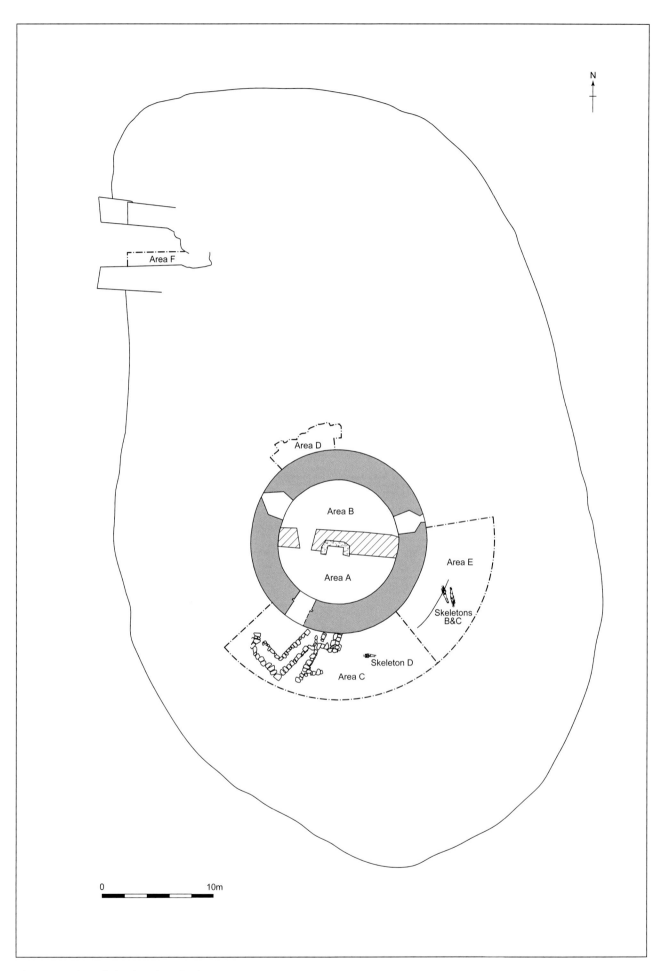

Fig 5.1—Plan of island and castle, showing excavation areas.

Pl. 5.6—Ruairí Ó Baoill and Kenny Wiggins starting to dig Sondage 2 in Area A.

ondary entrance, where the wall of a structure was partly uncovered. The depth of rubble tapered off towards the shore of the island.

AREA A

The earliest layer encountered here was the layer of stones thrown down to make up the island, F106. The cutting beneath the floor of the castle, Sondage 2, was dug to a depth of 2m beneath the floor but had to be abandoned for safety reasons at that stage, despite the use of shuttering (Fig. 5.2; Pls 5.6 and 5.7). The only finds recovered from this layer were two iron nails. The stones forming F106 continued below the limit of excavation. The base of the foundation of the wall of the tower was found at a depth of 1.6m below floor level and the stones in F106 were of larger size beneath the foundation. It appeared that while the lowest 1.6m of the tower wall was being built, the stones of F106 continued to be thrown down until floor level was reached. Alternatively, it is possible that a foundation trench was dug through the already piled-up stones of F106 and backfilled with the stones as the wall was built. Such a

Pl. 5.7—The foundation of the tower wall in Sondage 2. The 2m ranging rod is calibrated in 200mm sections.

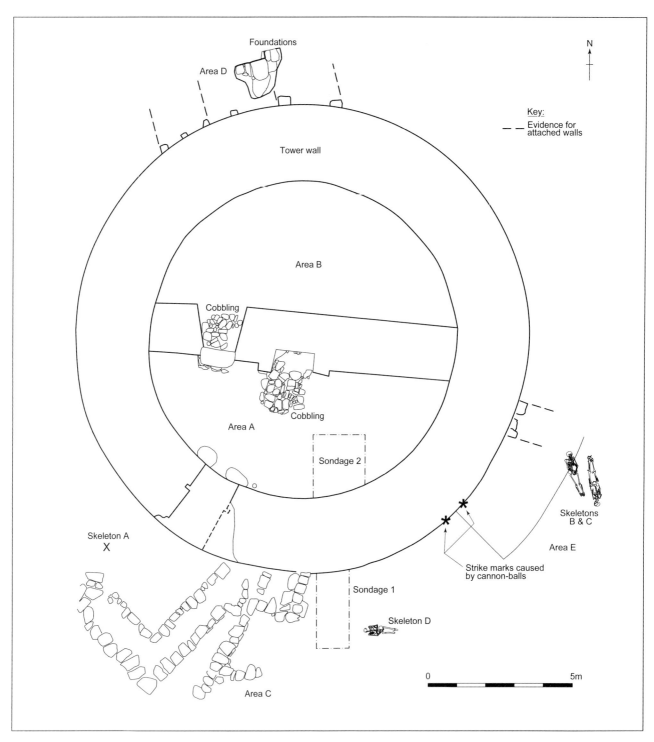

Fig. 5.2—General plan of tower and Areas A to E, with most significant detail of walls, cobbling and burials.

foundation trench would be difficult to recognise in loose stones, even if more extensive deep excavation had been carried out. Just below the original floor level the wall of the tower widened by 0.1m in a narrow plinth, and the wall face below was of much rougher construction than that above (Pl. 5.7).

On top of F106 was the earliest floor surface in the castle, F76. This was a rather lumpy, stony, discontinuous and worn mortar surface, and there were small holes in it opening into voids among the stones of F106. It var-

ied in thickness from 20mm to 60mm. Directly overlying this mortar layer was the roughly east–west cross-wall (F17), which has already been described in some detail in the description of the castle (Fig. 5.3). It had an original doorway (F14) and a later fireplace (F13) and was built on a frame of heavy timbers, which had rotted away completely to leave voids under the face at each side and where a number of cross-timbers had been. Part of one of these slots (F79), between the doorway and the fireplace, produced faunal remains. To the

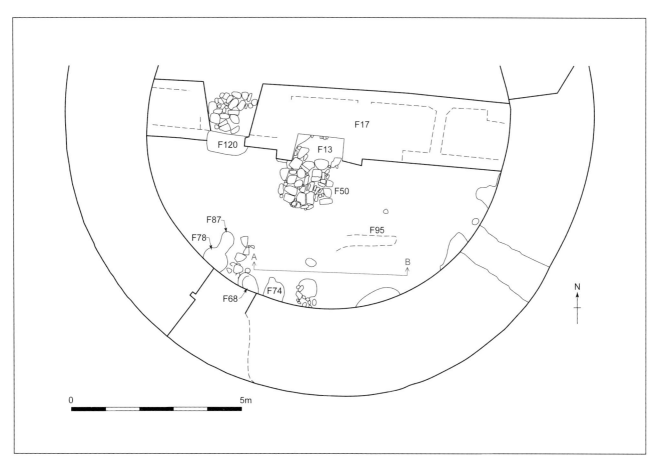

Fig. 5.3—Plan of Area A with excavation detail of floor.

Pl. 5.8—The early seventeenth-century mortar floor (F28) in Area A after the removal of the cobbling (F50) in front of the fireplace. Note the post-holes in front of the late doorway (Photographic Unit, NMS).

Pl. 5.9—The cobbling (F50) in front of the fireplace in Area A.

south of the doorway in the cross-wall was a well-set threshold stone (F120), which measured 1.12m by 0.6m. Covering most of the floor above mortar floor F76 was a creamy yellow fine, sandy material up to 0.1m thick (F54), which was interpreted as a leveller for the laying of the second mortar floor (F28) (Pl. 5.8). Some animal bones, one iron fragment and part of a late medieval/early modern copper-alloy cheek-piece (814) were found in this sandy layer (F54). Within this layer and between the two doorways was a rough line of stones bonded together with mortar (F67). It could have formed part of a rough ramp from the late door-way, which was in use during the Phase 2 construction work. The second or upper mortar floor (F28) was better preserved than the earlier one (F76). It was a yellowy colour and up to 50mm thick. Forming an east–west channel in the surface of this mortar floor was F95 (Fig. 5.3; Pl. 5.8). It was 1.3m long by 0.25m wide and 0.07–0.1m deep. It may have been where a plank or beam of wood was set into the floor for some structural purpose or as a base for a piece of furniture, stairs or partition.

There were a number of features in front of the late entrance doorway, which seemed to be associated with it (Fig. 5.3; Pl. 5.8). The earliest of these appeared to be

two post-pits (F74 and F78). The more easterly post-pit (F74) had its packing stones still in place and was situated against the inner face of the tower wall, 0.25m east of the eastern jamb of the late doorway. It measured at the lip some 0.5m by 0.6m and narrowed to a diameter of 0.1m at the base, where it was 0.35m deep. The *in situ* packing stones indicated a squared timber upright about 0.15m square. It was cut through the secondary mortar floor (F28). The fill consisted of dark sandy soil with some mortar and produced two sherds of Medieval Ulster Coarse Pottery (607–8), four nails and two other pieces of iron. The more westerly post-pit (F78) was located against the inner face of the tower at the western jamb of the late doorway. It measured 0.7m by 0.5m and was 0.4m deep. Its fill of dark soil produced three fragments of roof tile (537) and the bones of two juvenile jackdaws. It appeared to cut a shallower pit (F87), which adjoined it to the north. This was 0.3m wide by 0.6m long and 0.11m deep.

Another post-pit (F68), which could have been a replacement for F74, was situated at the eastern jamb of the doorway and encroaching slightly into the opening. It was 0.3m in diameter and 0.4m deep. It appeared to have been cut through F32, the layer above the second-ary mortar floor (F28). Its fill (F69) was a dark soil

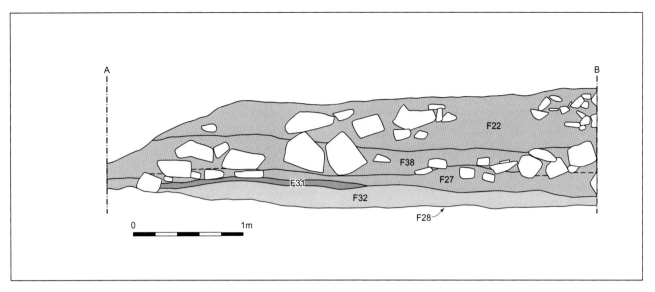

Fig. 5.4—Section A–B in Area A as shown on Fig. 5.3.

flecked with mortar and charcoal and produced three pottery sherds (tin-glazed earthenware (569), Frechen (570) and glazed red earthenware (571)) and an iron buckle (574).

Above the secondary mortar floor (F28) was a gravelly mortar layer with some rubble and small stones (F32), which underlay the surviving portion of flagged floor (F50) in front of the fireplace (Figs 5.3 and 5.4; Pl. 5.9). The laying down of this layer was contemporary with the insertion of the fireplace (F13) into the southern face of the cross-wall. This layer had the appearance of hardcore in places and appears to have been a levelling-up and foundation layer for the latest floor laid in the tower. It varied in depth between 0.05m and 0.2m. This layer produced a number of finds, including fragments of iron (a pot handle (454), padlock fragments (316, 415) and nails and fragments of cannon-balls), a piece of tin-glazed earthenware (312), a piece of Medieval Ulster Coarse Pottery (438), two lead musket-balls (441, 882), a fragment of a clay pipe stem (53), a fragment of a roof tile and part of a small copper-alloy vessel (320).

An area of well-laid stone flags (F50), some 1.5m square, survived in front of the fireplace. Some of the flags were up to 0.4m in maximum dimension and one was a reused brick with mortar adhering to it. It is possible that all or most of Area A was at one time covered with a similar paving but that it was robbed for potential use as missiles during the siege, as there seemed to be no proper floor surface at this level over the remainder of the room. The paving (F50) did not extend right into the fireplace itself, where there was a mixture of ash, loose brown soil, bones and small stones. The existence of mortar bedding around the edges indicated that there

had been a mortared stone base for the fire but it did not survive, possibly because of heat damage and repeated shovelling out of ash from the fire.

In an area where the flagged floor (F50) did not survive in the western part of Area A there was a spread (F31), some 2m across and 0.04–0.08m deep, of burnt clay with charcoal and bone. Many pieces of iron, including fragments of cannon-balls, a hinge (52b) and a hammer head (452), a piece of copper-alloy piping (382), a fragment of a clay pipe stem and fragments of tin-glazed earthenware, roof tile and a fragment of a drinking glass (308) were found in this layer. Above this in parts was a brown silty clay with small stones and charcoal, 0.1m deep (F53). A possible iron handle with copper-alloy plating (1102) and a fragment of a drinking glass (408) were found here. Above these layers (F50, F31 and F53) were layers of rubble that related to the destruction of the castle (Fig. 5.4). The lowest of these consisted of mortar and stones with a relatively high soil content (F27). It was up to 0.2m thick and produced a large collection of finds, including a variety of pottery sherds (blackware, Westerwald, tin-glazed earthenware, glazed red earthenware and crude coarse pottery), roof tiles, clay pipe stems and glass, iron keys (63, 91, 263, 402), buckles (105, 405), knives (70, 370a), nails and many fragments of cannon-balls, fragments of a cast-iron cooking pot (367 etc.), a plumb bob (106), a pair of dividers (69), a staple hasp (268), a handle (403), a plain iron spur (64), one with copper-alloy inlay (104) and a very finely decorated copper-alloy rowel spur (242), a book clasp (407) and the bottom stone of a rotary quern (818). This is likely to have been the debris layer caused by the slighting of the castle after the siege, when debris from upper floors must have collapsed

Pl. 5.10—Cannon-ball strikes on the wall of the tower. There is a rounded hollow in the centre of the one to the left, with a larger area of shatter damage around it. The sections of the ranging rod are 200mm.

down to the ground floor. This layer was overlain by a mottled soil and sand mixed with yellow clay and mortar, about 0.16–0.3m thick (F38). Fragments of cannonballs and other iron objects, including a buckle (229) and part of a jew's harp (232), and fragments of blackware, crude coarse pottery and roof tiles were found in this layer. Above this was another layer of rubble (F22), the upper parts of which had been removed by the conservation workers. It survived to a depth of 0.05m at the west and to 0.53m on the east and contained large stones with mortar attached, loose mortar, sand, shells and some brown soil. It contained a wide variety of finds, including blackware, tin-glazed earthenware, glazed red earthenware and crude coarse pottery, a fragment of a clay pipe stem, fragments of roof tiles and can-

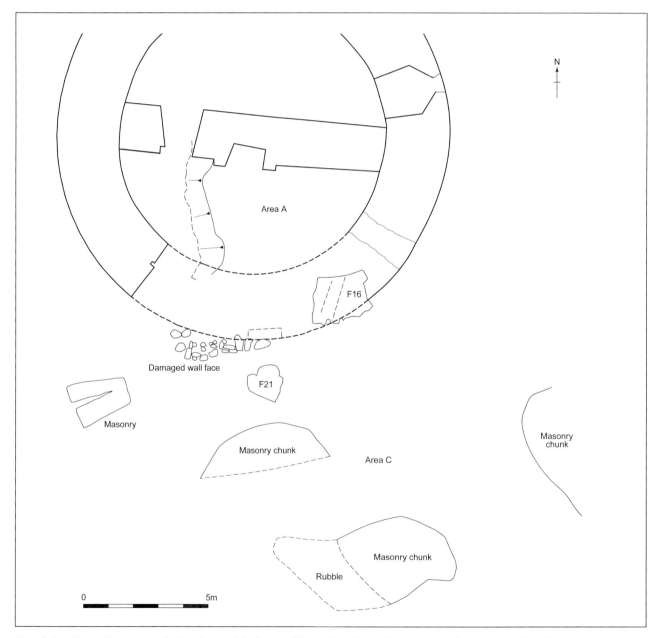

Fig. 5.5—Plan of Areas A and C at the initial phases of the archaeological excavation, showing chunks of masonry and damaged outer edge of tower wall.

non-balls, parts of a cast-iron cooking pot (29a etc.), an iron buckle (30a), a key (89), a lock bolt (30c), a loop hasp (29b), a staple hasp (30b), hinges (30d, 113), part of the mechanism of a matchlock musket (30a) and a piece of copper-alloy piping (277). This layer may have been caused by a secondary collapse some time after the original slighting when further collapse of badly damaged walls may have occurred, or the remains of timber floors may have fallen with associated debris.

The western end of Area A, especially the area between the two doorways, had been reduced almost to floor level by the conservation team. The layers here were partly disturbed and difficult to interpret. A layer of redeposited modern soil (F62) associated with the conservation work produced a mixture of seventeenth-century and modern finds, including an eyepiece of glass (525) and the base of a wine bottle (618).

The remains of the late entrance doorway (F15) are described under the description of the castle. It had already been dug out to threshold level by the conservation team and its western side had been conserved and pointed with mortar. One pocket of loose silty soil (F105) survived in the floor of the doorway and it produced a few pieces of iron, a piece of pottery and roof tile, and two fragments of textile, probably silver lace (1119).

The remains of the southern wall of the tower as uncovered during the excavation are described here. Below floor level, as seen in Sondage 2, the construction was rough and poorly finished. Above floor level it was well finished and built of good blocks of limestone with natural quarried faces. Only the lower part of the tower wall survived at the breach and this rose from a height of 0.65m and less at the eastern jamb of the late entrance doorway to 1.5m at the other or eastern side of the breach. Close to this last point, and facing 30 degrees east of south, two indentations caused by the impact of cannon-balls were noted, 0.6m apart and 1.15m and 1.25m above the late external cobbling (Fig. 5.2; Pl. 5.10). The larger of these was a hollow 0.15m in diameter and 0.08m deep with a shattered area 0.32m in diameter around it. The other was a hollow 0.14m in diameter and only 0.04m deep. There was further cannon damage higher up to the east, probably caused by glancing blows. For a distance of about 3m east of the late entrance the low surviving upper part of the wall of the tower was badly shattered. The upper course of facing stones was displaced and overhanging the face of the wall (Fig. 5.5; Pls 5.11 and 5.12). This appeared to be the result of a major explosion that is thought to have caused the huge breach in the wall. If this was the case, the charge must have been placed in the wall in this

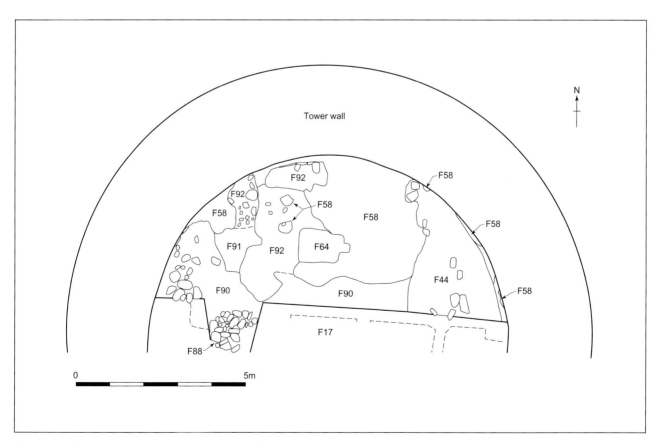

Fig. 5.6—Plan of Area B with excavation detail.

Pl. 5.11—A displaced section of the face of the tower close to the late doorway. This was probably caused by the explosion that destroyed the southern wall.

Pl. 5.12—A partly displaced section of the southern wall of the tower, which was numbered for rebuilding.

area, where one would expect to find a third original embrasure at ground-floor level.

A large piece of dislodged masonry (F16) sat partly on the remains of the wall and partly on rubble outside it at the eastern half of the breach (Fig. 5.5; Pl. 5.13). It measured 1.22m high by 1.72m wide and up to 2.5m in thickness. It had the remains of two beam slots in it from the first floor (Pl. 5.14), the better preserved of these being 0.65m wide by 0.45m high and up to

1.68m deep. After recording, this masonry was broken up to allow the excavation to proceed safely.

AREA B

This area had been reduced to a level about 0.25m above the original floor by the conservation team prior to the archaeological excavation (Pls 5.1 and 5.2). Part

Pl. 5.13—A view from above of Areas A, B and C at the start of the archaeological excavation. Note the large chunk of dislodged masonry (F16), with remains of beam-holes in it, beside the diggers on the left.

Pl. 5.14—The chunk of displaced masonry (F16), showing one of the beam-holes.

Pl. 5.15—The floor of Area B. Note the loose, disturbed soil in the foreground, which is probably the result of nineteenth-century digging (Photographic Unit, NMS).

of the area in the eastern corner showed evidence of old digging (F44), probably from the nineteenth century, when finds were recovered from Clogh Oughter (Fig. 5.6; Pl. 5.15). At the commencement of the excavation the surface of Area B consisted of debris from the conservation work—a mixture of soil and vegetable matter cleaned from the wall and mortar slobber from the repointing and other conservation works.

As with Area A, the earliest layer here was the layer of stones thrown down to build up the island (F106). This was not cut into in this area as part of the excavation but was visible where old digging cut into it at the eastern corner and in voids beneath the floor. The earliest floor here survived mainly in the western half of the room and consisted of three contemporary and contiguous layers, F90, F91 and F92 (Fig. 5.6). F90 was a layer of smaller stones in loose brown soil inside the doorway, extending into the western corner and along the northern face of the cross-wall immediately above the basal layer of stones (F106). F91 was a patch of yellowish clay adjoining F90, while F92 was a couple of patches of hard-packed stony clay. These surfaces were left in place and no finds were recovered from them. Partly overlying these layers was the remains of a mortar surface (F58). This would appear to be the equivalent of the second mortar floor in Area A (F28) and survived in an area some 3.5m square in the centre of the room. It was badly worn and broken through in places. Above it in a patch in the centre of the room was a layer of burnt clay (F64) that produced some sherds of Frechen pottery, three clay pipe stem fragments and iron fragments.

Above the mortar floor (F58) and the burnt clay (F64) was a layer of purplish-brown loose soil with

stones (F57). This layer produced a large collection of finds, including roof tiles, a wide range of pottery (Raeren, Frechen, Westerwald, Fulham, tin-glazed earthenware and some sherds of a later date that must be intrusive), quernstone fragments (514, 517, 1009), fragments of window glass and drinking glasses, clay pipe stem fragments, iron nails, an iron key (664), one cannon-ball fragment, three fragments of snaphaunce musket (662, 663a, 663b), a copper-alloy spur (811) and a harp peg (812). Above this layer (F57) was a loose brown soil (F56) which again produced a wide selection of finds, including pottery (Frechen and sherds of a later date that must be intrusive), two cannon-ball fragments, roof tiles and part of a drinking glass (492), which is thought to be of eighteenth-century date, an iron clench bolt (495) and quernstone fragments (515–17, 1008). Faunal remains from the surface of F58 and from F56, F57 and F64 were analysed as a group (see p. 188) and among them were a rat bone and a horse bone with butchering marks. In the doorway (F14) there was a cobbled surface of rounded stones (F88). This stopped in a straight line on the northern side, where the foundation beam under the northern side of the cross-wall must have originally served as part of the surface in the doorway (Fig. 5.6; Pl. 5.16). The cobbles were set in a loose brown soil, referred to as F56 in the feature sheets and site notes but which, apart from being similar to F56 in the room, is unlikely to have been exactly contemporary with it. A dug feature in the eastern end of area B was a treasure-hunting pit (F44) from the nineteenth century, which appears to have dislodged some of the face of the cross-wall near its eastern end. It was partly filled with soft brown soil, stones and modern finds, and penetrated beneath the original floor level

Pl. 5.16—Areas A and B from above. Note the straight northern edge to the cobbling in the doorway in the cross-wall, where one of the foundation timbers ran (Photographic Unit, NMS).

and partly into the basal layer of stones thrown down to form the island (F106).

Directly above F56 and F57 in the northern room was the modern conservation debris (F44), which itself produced a number of disturbed finds. The rubble layers in Area B had been removed as part of the conservation works (Pls 5.1 and 5.2).

AREA C

The deeper cutting outside the wall of the tower (Sondage 1) was only dug to a depth of about 1m (Figs 5.2, 5.7 and 5.8; Pl. 5.17). Here a stony surface (F111) set in sand was found and a decision was taken not to dig any deeper in this narrow cutting. This abutted the wall of the tower and presumably overlay the stones thrown down to build up the island (F106), though there may be intervening layers. Overlying this stony surface was a sandy grey-brown clay with flecks of mor-

tar and stones of different sizes (F108). This layer was between 0.5m and 0.6m thick; it contained a few nails and a fragment of a cannon-ball. Above this again was a black loamy soil (F107), which produced tin-glazed earthenware, a sherd of Frechen and a sherd of Medieval Ulster Coarse Pottery, clay pipe fragments, a silver penny of James I (815), a copper-alloy pestle (1105), a lace-chape (1068), iron nails (1067e and f), a hinge (1106a) and a door lock (1106b). Both F107 and F108 produced faunal remains. Above this was a loose yellow/red clay (F84) that produced nails (380, 629), pottery and a clay pipe stem fragment. Above this were three roughly contemporary and partly overlapping layers over a wider area: F83, a light brown sandy grey soil; F85, what appeared to be a mix of F40 and F84; and F86, a brown/grey fine sandy soil. The only finds from these layers were a few nails. Above these layers was a fine brown sandy soil (F40), which immediately underlay the rubble collapse (F30) and produced faunal remains and a large collection of finds, including roof tiles, a wall

Pl. 5.17—Sondage 1 in Area C, showing some of the foundation courses of the tower.

Pl. 5.18—A carved jamb stone from the seventeenth-century entrance doorway, which was found in the excavation. It was found very close to its original position in the doorway and displays a rebate for a yett.

tile fragment (716), blackware, Fulham ware, North Devon ware and Medieval Ulster Coarse Pottery, clay pipe fragments including a spurred bowl (485), a small fragment of window glass and a piece of bottle glass, a bone button (487), two cannon-ball fragments, nails, an iron pot leg (805) and door lock (321), and half a leaden papal seal (816).

The rubble collapse (F30) in this area produced one of the biggest collections of finds from any layer on the site, including the largest number of cannon-ball fragments. Immediately south of the castle and to the east of the walls (F46), outside the late entrance, it was relatively undisturbed and survived to a height of up to 1.7m (Figs 5.8 and 5.9). As well as faunal remains, roof tiles, a piece of bottle glass, a wide range of pottery (blackware, Westerwald, Frechen, tin-glazed earthenware, glazed red earthenware and stoneware mineral bottle sherds), clay pipe fragments including a bowl with a flat spur and the maker's initials AL (739) and the base stone of a quern (200), it also contained a wide range of iron objects, including a decorated and a plain iron spur (1121, 354), curry-comb fragments (301, 302a), candle-holders (302, 303), a large fireback (199), buckles (164, 652, 957), keys (150, 420), portions of a number of mounted locks (153, 156, 296) and padlocks/fetters (155b, 240), knives (152, 454, 837, 838), the head of a hammer (218), part of a saw (952), scissors (286), a hinge (781), a loop hasp (220), a leg and sherds from a cast-iron pot (426 etc.), nails (155a etc.), the cock of a snaphaunce musket with a piece of flint still in place (217) and a jew's harp (1122). Copper-alloy objects found included a cooking pot (183), a buckle (655), an attachment for a cheek-piece (654) and two brass candlesticks (188, 216).

In places where the upper part of the rubble (F30) had not been disturbed during the conservation works, it was overlain by a brown organic topsoil and sod (F25) with stones and the roots of plants and trees. This produced a wide range of finds, including two decorated copper-alloy book mounts (119, 158), roof tiles, clay

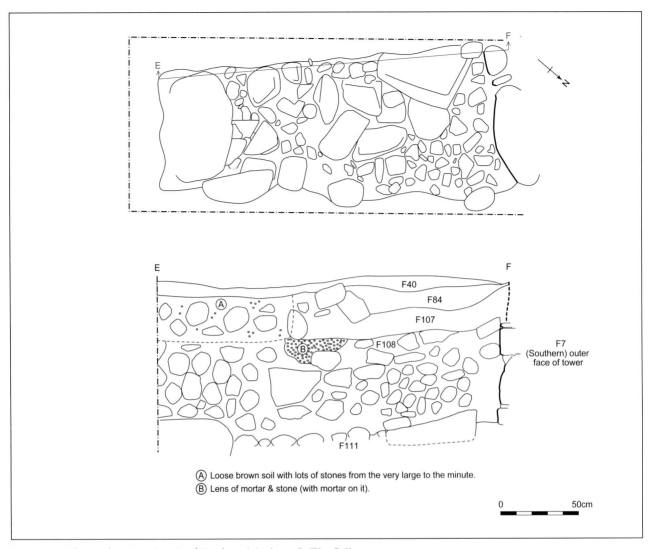

Ⓐ Loose brown soil with lots of stones from the very large to the minute.
Ⓑ Lens of mortar & stone (with mortar on it).

0   50cm

Fig. 5.7—Plan and section (E–F) of Sondage 1 in Area C (Fig. 5.8).

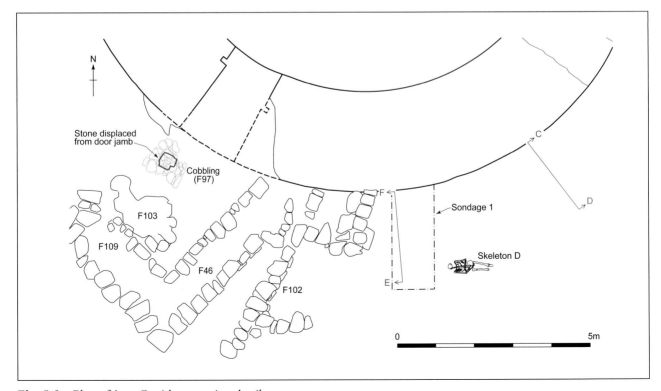

Fig. 5.8—Plan of Area C with excavation detail.

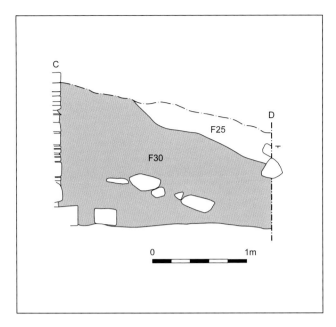

Fig. 5.9—Section C–D in Area C, as shown in Fig. 5.8.

pipes, pottery, bottle glass and iron objects, including keys (73, 1095), a hasp (1005), a hinge (786), the sear of a snaphaunce musket (843a) and a spherical padlock (167). Most of the finds were of seventeenth-century date but some of the pottery (especially transfer-printed ware), glass and metal objects were of more recent date.

An L-shaped wall (F46) outside the late entrance doorway on the south-western side of the castle (Fig. 5.8) was uncovered by the conservation team prior to the archaeological excavation. Further excavation was carried out here in the area immediately in front of the doorway and around the wall to uncover more of it. In its interior, in front of the doorway, the earliest layer excavated was a dark burnt clay (F49), which contained much charcoal and faunal remains and abutted the L-shaped wall (F46). A lot of Medieval Ulster Coarse Pottery was found in this layer (F49), as well as clay pipe fragments, quern fragments (859, 891), a musket-ball (972) and iron finds, including a key (712) and a nail (971a). Above this were the remnants of a rough stony surface (F100), and at a slightly higher level and probably replacing a damaged section of this surface (F100) was a section of cobbling about 1m by 1m (F97) in front of the doorway. Some iron objects, including a large section of a cast-iron cooking pot (817), a mounted lock (867), a key (1089) and a handle (834b), a copper-alloy harp peg (813), two pieces of gold lace textile (1120), two lead musket-balls (1091c (A, B)) and two casting headers for lead shot (1100), a quern fragment (964) and a sherd of blackware were uncovered in and around this cobbling. Partly overlying this patch of cobbling (F97), a carved limestone jamb stone from the late doorway

was found (Fig. 5.8; Pl. 5.18). It had a rebate in it for an outer iron gate or yett. A little further out from the doorway was a thin lump of rubble collapse (F103), rising 0.3m higher than the cobbling (F97). Above these features were remnants of the general rubble collapse of stone and mortar (F30).

The L-shaped wall (F46) in front of the late entrance (Fig. 5.8; Pl. 5.19) had at least two phases of construction in it and additional faces to the east that were difficult to interpret. The most westerly section (F109) had its inner or western face at the eastern jamb of the late doorway and was about 1m wide; 2m out from the doorway it turned at a right angle to the west and continued for about 1.7m, to a point where evidence of it ran out. No evidence for a western side to this structure was found. It was built mostly of dry stone, with larger stones forming the faces. The inner face of this wall was called F77 and the outer face F101. Abutting this wall to the east was an added section of wall (F102), some 0.8–1m wide. East of this again was a small platform of stone about 1.2m square at the angle between F102 and the wall of the circular tower (Fig. 5.8; Pl. 5.20), while near the southern end of F102 a short line of stones extended towards the east. These features are difficult to interpret but may have formed part of some form of jetty for boats at the entrance when lake levels were higher, as we know they were in the seventeenth century. Among the stones of the inner face (F77) was a green-yellow clay (F48), which produced a bowl of a flat-heeled clay pipe bowl (465) and a stem fragment, an openwork copper-alloy mount (479), an iron hinge (467), part of an axe (469) and the handle of a pot (475). What remained of the old surface in this area in front of the entrance was a brown silty sandy clay (F45). A copper-alloy spur (304) was found in it.

Around the point where the western section (F109) of the L-shaped feature (F46) peters out and some 2m from the wall of the tower is where Skeleton A was found by the conservation team in October 1985 (Fig. 5.2); this was excavated and lifted by the present writer. It was under the layer of rubble collapse (F30), which sloped steeply from a height of 0.9m to 0.6m above the remains. The remains were in a contorted position, with leg bones overlying the skull (Pl. 5.21). This is dealt with in more detail in the section on the burials.

In 1989, during the final site works subsequent to the excavation, a further burial, Skeleton D, was encountered some 5m east of the L-shaped structure (F46) and about 2m from the wall of the tower (Fig. 5.8). The lower leg bones had been disturbed by the conservation team but the remainder was excavated and lifted by the present writer. Only a small part of the skull, which had

Pl. 5.19—The L-shaped wall (F46) outside the seventeenth-century entrance.

Pl. 5.20—The area in front of the seventeenth-century entrance in Area C as it initially appeared.

Pl. 5.21—Skeleton A as originally exposed

Pl. 5.22—*In situ* masonry remains (F33) in Area D.

not suffered any post-interment disturbance, survived, indicating that the cause of death was a horrific head injury. This interment is described in more detail in the section on the burials.

AREA D

A small area on the north side of the tower was cleaned back and partially excavated to examine wall remains visible on the surface beneath the scaffolding (Figs 5.1 and 5.10). The upper layers, probably just topsoil and a

thin layer of collapsed stone, had been removed by the conservation team prior to erecting the scaffolding. This area lay just outside the wall of the tower, where a doorway at first-floor level gave access in Phase 2 to an attached stair turret, which was removed in Phase 3. The excavation here could only be partial because the scaffolding was still in use for ongoing conservation work on the walls.

The earliest excavated feature here was an *in situ* fragment of wall (F33). It was not possible to excavate enough of this feature to get a full plan but it was certainly the remains of a mortared wall. The only faces

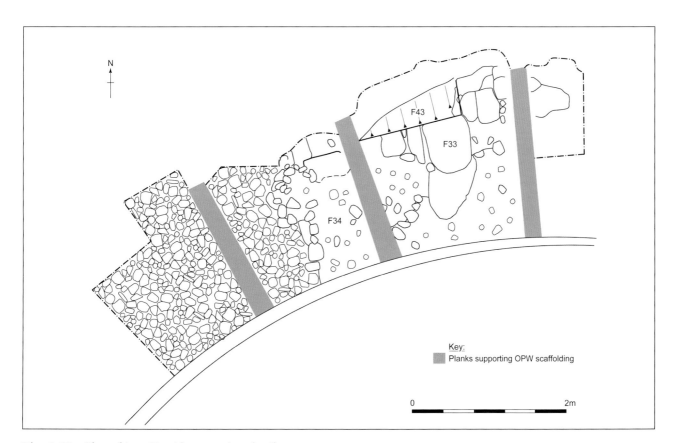

Fig. 5.10—Plan of Area D with excavation detail.

identified appeared to form an internal right angle (Fig. 5.10; Pl. 5.22). The lowest layer encountered here was a sandy deposit (F43) abutting the remains of the wall (F33). Above this again was a silty brown organic clay with flecks of charcoal some 0.1m thick (F35), into which a cobbling of small stones (F34) was set. This cobbled surface ran up to the higher bits of the wall (F33), which served as part of this surface. This surface was 0.2m below the level of the external plinth of the tower. A sherd of tin-glazed earthenware (161) was found in the clay layer (F35). Above the cobbling (F34) a hard-packed stony mortar layer (F36) survived in places, and where the cobbling ran out, some 2m out from the tower, there was a thick mortar layer (F37) sloping away to the lake. Above all of these was modern debris from the conservation work, including some hardened mortar (F39). Some pottery sherds and a fragment of an iron lock bolt (94) were recovered from this layer (F39).

AREA E

This area was excavated along the outer wall of the tower on the eastern side (Figs 5.1 and 5.11), where there were the remains of a first-floor doorway and some bonding stones projecting from the wall, indicating that there had been an attached wall or that such a wall was to be built.

The earliest layer encountered in this area was a brown gritty and silty loose soil with charcoal and mortar flecks (F98/F104). This layer produced animal bones, iron fragments including nails and pieces of cannonballs, clay pipe stem fragments, two pieces of window glass and two sherds of glazed red earthenware. It underlay a stony platform (F99) that projected 2m out from the base of the wall of the tower. This was revetted by a kerb of large stones, some mortared in place (F112) and set concentric with the tower (Fig. 5.11; Pl. 5.23). Its southern end was roughly marked with a kerb (F116), while at the northern end the platform continued beyond the limit of excavation and possibly joined up with the area of cobbling (F34) in Area D. The sur-

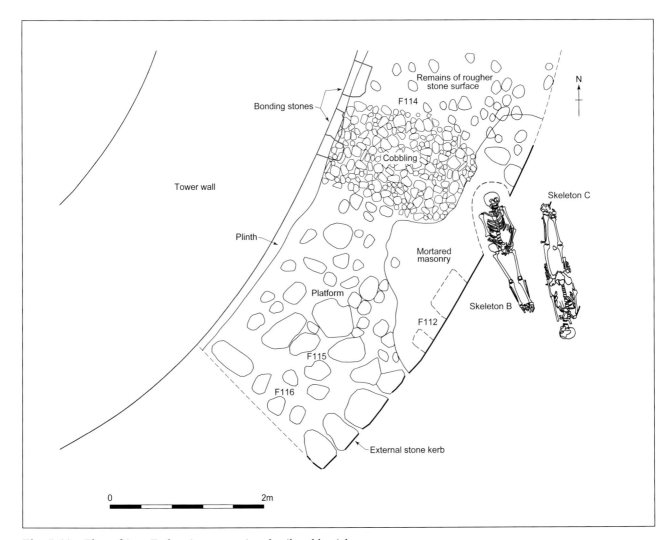

Fig. 5.11—Plan of Area E, showing excavation detail and burials.

Pl. 5.23—The platform (F99) in Area E.

face treatment of the platform varied over its length, with the remains of a small-stone cobbling (F114), like that (F34) in Area D, at its northern end and a surface of larger stones (F115) in the remainder of the platform. Overlying the larger stones (F115) near its northern edge was a deposit of burnt clay. Two burials were discovered at this point (Skeletons B and C) (Figs 5.11 and 5.12) cut into the soil (F98), and the first of them also cut into the kerb of the platform (F112) (Pl. 5.24). These are described in detail in the section on the burials. Finds from F98/F104 included an iron hinge (1077) and part of a cast-iron cooking pot (1084).

Above these features were remnants of the collapsed rubble layer (F30), which tailed off to nothing at the northern limit of the excavation area.

AREA F

This was located just over 20m north-west of the tower at the present summer shoreline. To ensure easy access to the island, the conservation team had built a small jetty of mortared stone for their boat. During the course of the excavation they wanted to deepen the area between the two walls of the jetty, and to facilitate this a

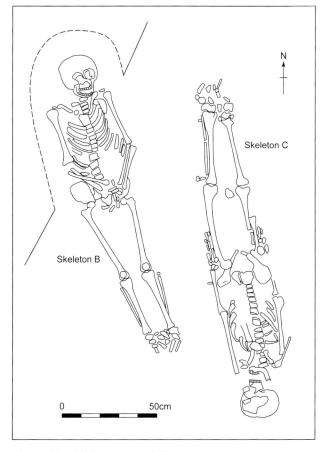

Fig. 5.12—Skeletons B and C.

Pl. 5.24—Skeleton B in Area E. The upper part of the grave was cut into the platform (F99).

Pl. 5.25—Area F, the cutting at the jetty.

small cutting was excavated in this area (Fig. 5.1; Pl. 5.25). It was hoped that this work might also reveal something of the make-up of the northern part of the island.

The earliest layer encountered appeared to be a natural deposit consisting of a blue-grey clay with some roots and stones (F96). Overlying this was a thick layer of building stones (F93) with mortar attached to many of them and some blue-grey soil between and beneath a similar layer of rubble (F94) with dark soil between the stones (Pl. 5.26). One sherd of Frechen was recovered from F93. The surface of the jetty area, which had a skim of recent mortar on it, overlay the rubble. This rubble, being on the northern side of the island, could not have been derived from the slighting of the castle after the siege of 1653. It seems likely, however, that it was derived from the demolition of the stair turret on the northern side of the castle, which was carried out in Phase 3. The discovery of a couple of newel stones from a spiral stone stair on the surface of the northern side of the island by the conservation team would tend to support the suggestion that the demolition rubble from the stair turret was spread in this area.

Pl. 5.26—Stones with mortar attached in Area F.

THE BURIALS

Skeleton A (Pls 5.21 and 5.27)
This was not a formal burial, as the skeleton was in a contorted position and may have been partly dismembered. It was found at the old ground level beneath the rubble collapse (F30) in October 1985 prior to the ar-

chaeological excavation. The remains were not in any sort of noticeable pit, though it is possible that they could have been placed in a very shallow pit in the old topsoil. On the other hand, it is possible that, in the confusion of the siege, the remains may have continued to lie where the person fell and, having become covered with debris, were never retrieved for more formal burial. These remains were excavated under inclement weather conditions and time constraints which did not permit a plan to be made of them, although photographs were taken before and during their excavation. The remains were found about 2m from the wall of the tower a short distance west of the seventeenth-century ground-floor entrance. Part of the remains had been dug away by the conservation team prior to recording and removal.

Skeleton B (Figs 5.11 and 5.12; Pls 5.28 and 5.29)
This burial was found during the excavation in Area E in a shallow grave cut into the soil F98, the earliest layer excavated in this area. The grave was also cut partially into the cobbled platform F112, which projected 2m from the base of the tower at this point. The alignment of the burial was roughly north-north-west/south-south-east, with the head at the northern end. There was no evidence that the body had been placed in a cof-

Pl. 5.27—Articulated arm bones and skull of Skeleton A.

fin and no artefacts were found in association with it. The remains were carefully deposited with both hands over the pelvic area.

Skeleton C (Figs 5.11 and 5.12; Pl. 5.30)
This burial was immediately east of Skeleton B and was aligned in the opposite direction, with the head at the southern end. The presence of four nails evenly spaced around the body indicates that it was buried in some form of wooden coffin, of which nothing else survived.

Pl. 5.28—Burial B in Area E.

Pl. 5.29—A close-up of Burial B.

Pl. 5.30—Burial C in Area E. Note the broken right femur.

Pl. 5.31—Burial D, excavated in 1989 after the main archaeological excavation. Note that only a small part of the skull was present despite the fact that the area of the head had not been disturbed. The lower part of the legs had been disturbed in the course of conservation works.

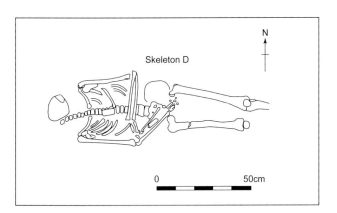

Fig. 5.13—Skeleton D.

The hands were positioned by the side. The right femur was clearly broken and this injury is likely to have been the cause of death.

Skeleton D (Figs 5.8 and 5.13; Pl. 5.31)

This burial was found during final site works by the conservation team in 1989 and was subsequently exca-vated and recorded by the writer. It was found in Area C to the east of the entrance area and some 8m to the west of the other two burials (Skeletons B and C). It was aligned east–west with the head to the west in the usual Christian manner. The left arm was flexed at a

right angle across the abdomen, while the right hand lay on the pelvic area. A fragmentary copper-alloy wire bracelet (E409:1123) was found on the wrist of the right arm and this has left a green stain on the right ulna. The lower part of the legs had been dug away by the conservation team but the remaining elements of the skeleton—in particular the area of the head—had not been disturbed after burial. The fact that most of the skull was missing is indicative of a horrific injury; this was the cause of death.

For further details of skeletal remains see the report by Laureen Buckley (pp 179–85).

6. FINDS AND SPECIALIST REPORTS

The finds are described below under the different materials from which they are made or the categories to which they belong. They are referred to under their original catalogue numbers, without the National Museum prefix for the excavation—E409. The original catalogue has 1,123 entries, mostly covering individual finds but sometimes covering a number of similar pieces found together, such as nails, pipe stems or what appeared at the time to be undiagnostic iron fragments. Where necessary, some of these have been divided into sub-numbers, with the addition of a, b, c, etc., for particular finds. The vast bulk of the finds belong to the first half of the seventeenth century up to the siege and destruction of the castle in 1653. The following abbreviations are used: L for length/long, W for width/wide, D for diameter and T for thickness/thick. The context of the find is indicated in every case by the feature number (F1, etc.), accompanied at times by a short description of the context in the case of the more significant finds.

SILVER, LEAD AND PEWTER OBJECTS

Coin

815. An English silver penny of James I dating from 1603–4. Very worn, with a small punched perforation near the centre. Found in a layer (F107) beneath the old surface sealed by the destruction rubble in Area C.

Lead and pewter objects

816. Half a papal *bulla* or seal of one of the popes called Clement, probably Clement VIII, who was in office from 1592 to 1605 (Fig. 6.1). Found in the old surface layer (F40) beneath the destruction rubble in Area C, to the south-west of the entrance.

The design of these leaden papal seals remained constant over many centuries, with Saints Peter and Paul on one side and the name and number of the pope on the other. The seal was attached to the letter by a ribbon, which ran lengthways through the seal from top to bot-

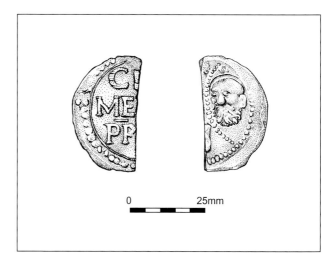

Fig. 6.1—The two sides of the fragmentary papal seal (no. 816).

tom. This created a weakness in the seal, causing it on occasion to crack along this line, as in the case of a seal of Innocent III (1198–1216) from Kells Priory, Co. Kilkenny (Clyne 2007, 390–1), or to break in two, as in this case.

1100. Two flat strips of lead with cylindrical protrusions on one side. These are casting headers—waste from the making of lead shot. A: L 30mm; W 4mm. It has three unevenly spaced cylindrical protrusions, 2.5–3mm in diameter, which project up to 3mm from one side. B: L 27mm; W 5mm. It has four unevenly spaced cylindrical projections, as in A. The ends of all the projections show evidence of having been roughly cut. From a layer (F97) beneath the destruction rubble in front of the entrance in Area C. For further discussion on these objects see pp 147–8 below.

96. A roughly flat, shapeless piece of lead. L 57mm; W 15–21mm; T 2–5mm. From F39 in Area D, a modern disturbed layer.

360. A fragmentary small pewter vessel, like an eggcup, with a hollow cylindrical stem. What is probably the upper part is broken off at the stem. What appears to be the lower part of the foot has been cut away and the sides have been partly flattened. There is a slight shoulder below the stem, beyond which the sides flared out-

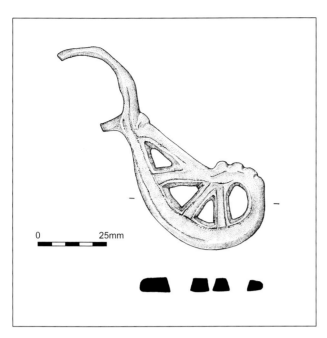

Fig. 6.2—Fragment of a cheek-piece (no. 814).

COPPER-ALLOY OBJECTS

Cheek-piece

814. Part of a late medieval or early modern horse harness cheek-piece of a distinctively Gaelic type with openwork decoration (Fig. 6.2). It is broken and wrenched out of shape at the point where it would have connected with the bit and also shows evidence of considerable wear. Present L 95mm; max. W 32mm; max. T 5mm. Found in F54 (a layer on the medieval mortar floor) in Area A. A number of these objects have been found in Ireland (Armstrong 1917–18). In a short note on one from Clontuskert Priory, Co. Galway, Rynne suggested a sixteenth- or seventeenth-century date for it (Fanning 1976, 124–6). The example from Clogh Oughter is similar in design to two found still attached to an iron horse-bit from Doohatty townland, Co. Monaghan (Anon. 1968, 149–50), though the design on the Doohatty cheek-pieces is more accomplished and well finished (Fig. 6.3).

wards. The hollow base opens into the hollow stem. D of stem 17mm; H 15mm. Shoulder W 6mm. Maximum surviving L of one side of foot beyond shoulder 22mm. Found in destruction rubble (F30) in Area C.

Pieces of lead shot (musket-balls) are described below (pp 146–8) in the section on military artefacts.

654. Looped attachment or strap-staple for connecting a rein to a cheek-piece, with decoration on one side and on the loop (Fig. 6.4). There are two rivet holes in each of the flat pieces that connected to the rein and remnants of an iron rivet in one of these holes. L 73mm; W of flat pieces 11mm; inner D of loop 14mm; outer D of loop 27mm. From the destruction rubble (F30) in Area C.

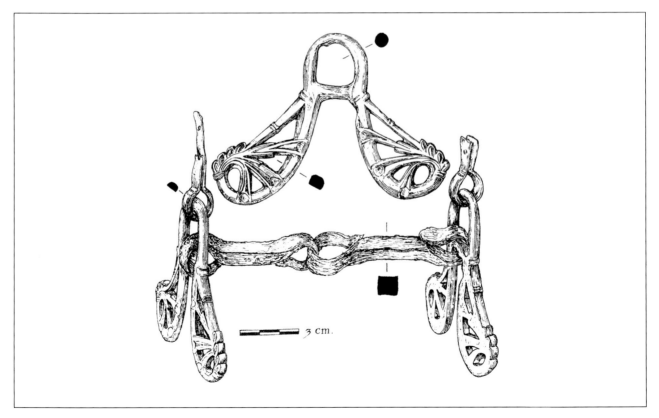

Fig. 6.3—An iron horse-bit with copper-alloy cheek-pieces and strap-staples still attached, from Doohatty, Co. Monaghan (National Museum of Ireland).

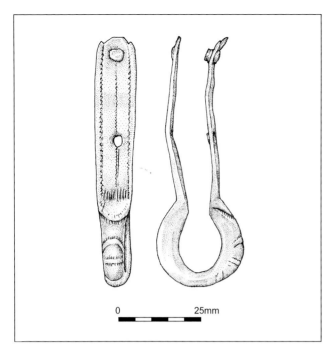

Fig. 6.4—A strap-staple for a cheek-piece (no. 654).

This is probably of much the same date as the cheek-piece above, and the cheek-pieces from Doohatty, Co. Monaghan, still had a strap-staple attached to each (Fig. 6.3) (Anon. 1968, 149–50). What was referred to as a binding strip from Montgomery Castle is rather similar (Knight 1993, 200–1).

Spurs

242. A very finely decorated rowel spur with a seven-pointed rowel (Fig. 6.5; Pl. 6.1). There is incised decoration all over the object, with lines, circles, flower motifs, dots and short strokes. Part of one of the figure-of-eight terminals is broken. The loops at the terminal show little or no sign of wear. The sides drop at the centre to accommodate the ankle, and a greater drop on the left side would indicate that it is a spur for the left foot. The neck (L 32mm) is curved downwards sharply. W (across the sides) 83mm; L (not including rowel) 97mm; D of rowel 31mm. Corrosion product, which did not survive conservation, indicated that the pin that held the rowel and an attachment in one of the terminals were of iron. Found in destruction rubble (F27) in Area A.

304. Finely made rowel spur with rowel missing (Fig. 6.6). The neck is long (46mm) and elaborate, with criss-cross incised decoration at the top of a flat-ended projection. Both figure-of-eight terminals are complete and show hardly any signs of wear. W (across the sides) 65mm; L 117mm. The sides are plano-convex in section, with a slight drop towards the centre. Found in a layer beneath the destruction rubble (F45) in Area C.

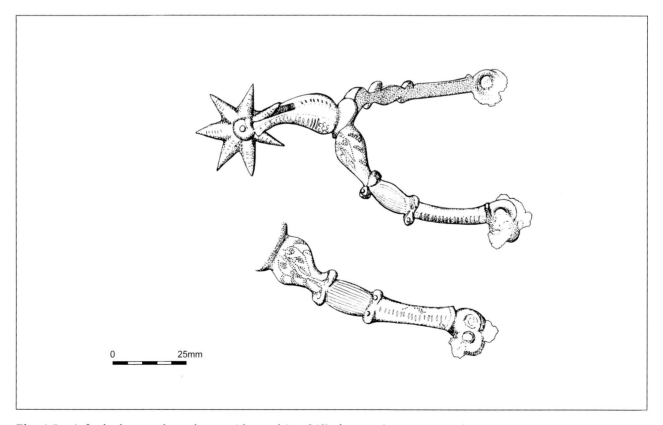

Fig. 6.5—A finely decorated rowel spur with rowel (no. 242), drawn prior to conservation.

Pl. 6.1—The finely decorated rowel spur (no. 242) after conservation (Photographic Unit, NMS).

811. A plainer rowel spur with rowel missing (Fig. 6.6). The neck is short (31mm) with simple baluster moulding. The figure-of-eight terminals show considerable signs of wear and a part of one is missing. The sides are plano-convex in section, with no drop in the middle for the ankle. W (across the sides) 80mm; L 95mm. From a partly disturbed floor layer (F57) in Area B.

Metal analysis shows that the three spurs are made of brass, without any evidence of gilding (see Appendix 3). According to Blanche Ellis (pers. comm.), no. 242 is a fine example of a decorated spur of the early seventeenth century, and the decoration, with its punched circles and scroll and foliage patterns made up of tiny dotted lines, is typical. Spurs were at that time almost a form of masculine jewellery and it was fashionable to go booted and spurred all the time, even indoors. English examples with somewhat similar decoration include a gilded copper-alloy example from Hinton-in-the Hedges, Northamptonshire, and a fragmentary example from the Roach Smith Collection in the British Museum (Blanche Ellis, pers. comm.). An example from Ireland with somewhat similar decoration was described and illustrated by Wilde (1861, 601–2, fig. 501). 'A brass spur, of elegant workmanship, richly adorned', which was found in a bog, possibly in County Cavan, in the late eighteenth century, was illustrated by

Daniel Grose (Stalley 1991, 133–5). While its decoration appears to be more three-dimensional than that on the Clogh Oughter example, its rowel is quite similar. Both copper-alloy and iron spurs of this period were found in excavations at Parke's Castle, Co. Leitrim (Foley and Donnelly 2012, 84). The two plainer spurs are also of early seventeenth-century date.

Harp tuning pegs

812. A large harp tuning peg (Fig. 6.7). It is mostly circular in cross-section but changes to a square cross-section at the end to fit the key used for tuning. This end is decorated with simple incised lines. The other end is perforated to hold the wire string. L 108mm; D at perforated end 6.5mm; D at square-sectioned end 7mm. Found in a partly disturbed floor layer (F57) in Area B.

813. A harp peg, slightly smaller than no. 812 but similar in every other way (Fig. 6.7). L 92mm; D at perforated end 5mm; D at square-sectioned end 6.5mm. From a layer (F97) beneath the destruction rubble in Area C.

Tuning pegs have been found in late medieval and early modern contexts in Ireland and elsewhere and can be made of bone or copper alloy. Smaller examples from Clontuskert Priory made of copper alloy (L 64.5mm)

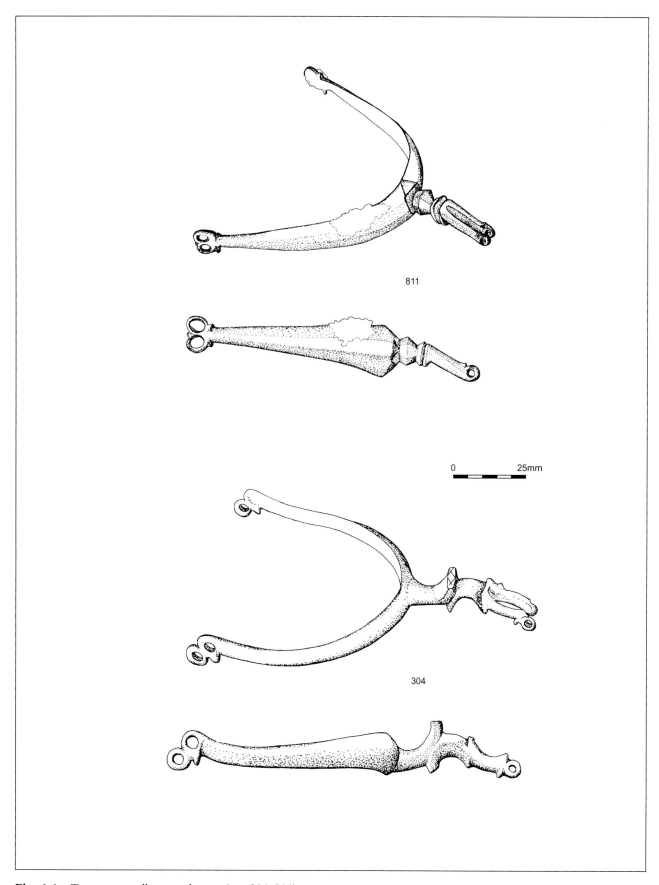

811

0   25mm

304

Fig. 6.6—Two copper–alloy rowel spurs (nos 304, 811).

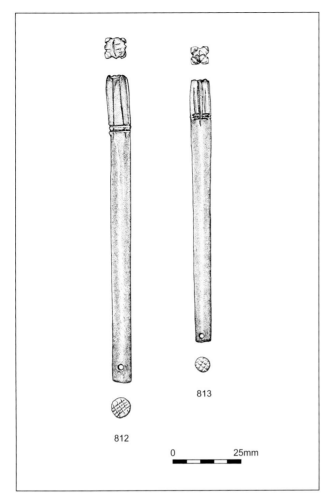

Fig. 6.7—Two harp tuning pegs (nos 812, 813).

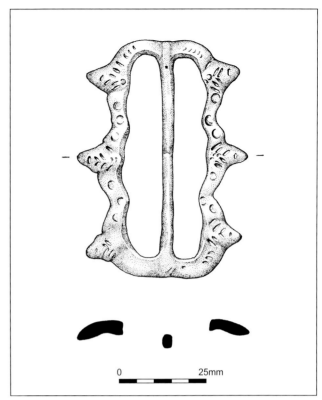

Fig. 6.8—A decorated buckle (no. 655).

and bone (L 56mm) and a single complete example in bone from Kells Priory (55.6mm) may have been for smaller stringed instruments (Fanning 1976, 147–9; Clyne 2007, 417–18). Larger copper-alloy examples, such as the three found at Parke's Castle, Co. Leitrim, which are between 78mm and 82mm in length (Foley and Donnelly 2012, 88), and the two from Clogh Oughter, which are longer still, are certainly for Gaelic-type harps and can be compared with surviving harps from Ireland and Scotland dating from between the fifteenth and eighteenth centuries, even down to the qua-trefoil decoration on the heads (*ibid.*). A cache of 24 copper-alloy harp pegs was found at Montgomery Castle in Wales in post-1649 destruction rubble. They ranged from 102mm to 105mm in length and had filed decoration on the square-sectioned heads, somewhat like that on the Clogh Oughter examples (Knight 1993, 202–4; Lawson 1994, 197).

While one would naturally expect Irish harps to be associated with the Gaelic population, it is worth noting that Robert Parke had his own Irish harper at Parke's Castle in the 1640s (Foley and Donnelly 2012, 13) and that a New English resident in County Cavan,

Lieutenant Arnold Cosby, listed an Irish harp among the many items he claimed were lost to him from his house at Sweden (Swellan, beside Cavan town) as a result of the 1641 rebellion (TCD MS 833, 124–5).

Buckle

655. Oblong buckle with a double-loop frame and no pin surviving (Fig. 6.8). The frame has similar decoration on each side, consisting of three evenly spaced pointed projections with stab and curving decoration. L 66mm; W 50mm. From destruction rubble (F30) in Area C.

This example, being broader along the strap bar than across the frame, is of a type designed for waist- or sword-belts, as opposed to other uses such as for shoes or hats (Whitehead 1996, 74–8). According to Webb (1981, 25–6, no. 93), very elaborate examples of this type of buckle were made during the seventeenth century.

Candlesticks

188. Candlestick, lacking its base (Fig. 6.9). It is circular in section throughout, with a flat projecting flange at the rim of the socket and two further flat flanges further down the exterior of the socket. Beneath these is a bulbous expansion that narrows downwards to the stem, which has a further small flange and a widening towards the base. Beneath this is a narrow tenon (D 12mm) for

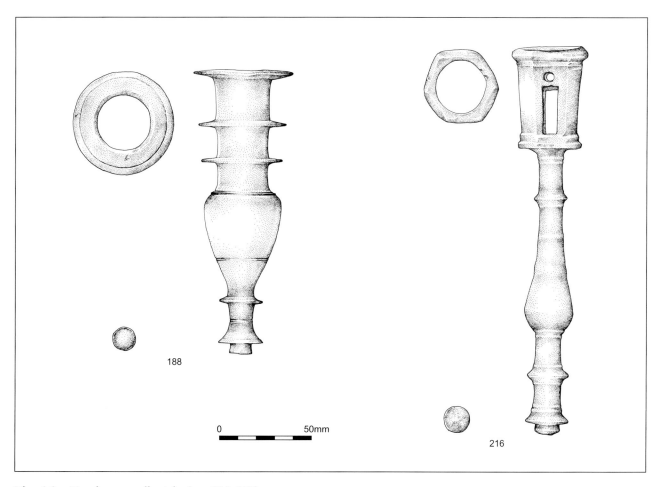

Fig. 6.9—Two brass candlesticks (nos 216, 188).

attachment to the base. The three large flanges have an incised line forming a circle on their upper edge, while there are double lines encircling the upper and lower parts of the bulbous projection and at the narrowest part of the stem. This object appears to have been finished on a lathe after casting. The socket, which still has en-crusted material in its base, is 30mm in D at the mouth and narrows to its present measurable depth of 55mm. L 149mm; max. W 55mm; min. W of stem 12.5mm. From destruction rubble (F30) in Area C.

216. Candlestick, lacking its base (Fig. 6.9). The long stem of this candlestick is circular in section, but the socket is six-sided with a large, upright, rectangular opening beneath a small circular hole in two opposing sides. The large openings were to facilitate the removal of the candle stub, while the circular ones may have been intended to hold the candle-snuffer. The stem has a bulbous expansion towards the centre flanked by small flanges near the top and bottom. There is an expansion at the base, beneath which is a narrower tenon (D 14mm) for attachment to the missing base. At the top of the stem there is a flat circular flange (D 35mm), on top of which sits the hexagonal socket, which has an expanded moulded rim at the top. The socket is 49mm deep and narrows from a D of 28mm at the rim to 21mm at the bottom. L 206mm, max. W (at rim) 43mm; min. D of stem (near top) 12mm. From destruction rubble (F30) in Area C.

Book mounts and clasp

119. Book mount (Fig. 6.10). A decorated corner mount for the cover of a book, with a central boss surrounded by brambling decoration. There are three rivet holes and a zigzag decoration around the edges. The two edges that coincided with the edge of the cover are bent around to protect the edge of the book cover. A small remnant of the leather binding survived in the folded portion. L 39mm; W 33mm. From topsoil (F25) in Area C.

158. Book mount, very similar to no. 119 in form and decoration (Fig. 6.10). L 36mm; W 35mm. Also from topsoil.

These two book mounts are very similar in form and decoration to fifteenth-century book mounts on the single board of the oldest surviving binding of the Great

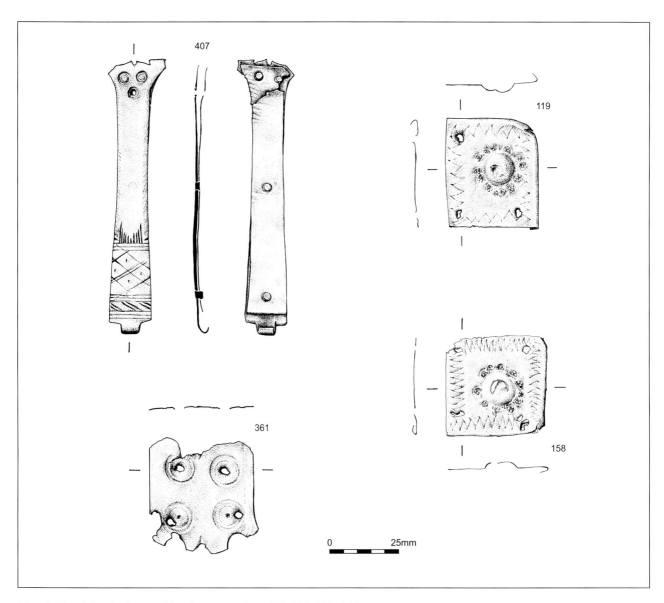

Fig. 6.10—A book clasp and book mounts (nos 407, 119, 158, 361).

Pl. 6.2—The surviving fifteenth-century cover of the Great Book of Lecan (National Museum of Ireland).

Book of Lecan in the National Museum of Ireland (Ó Floinn 2002, 268, 280) (Pl. 6.2). The only difference is that the ones on the latter book cover have a dot and concentric circles close to each corner and have four rivets in each case, as against three rivet holes on the Clogh Oughter mounts. These book mounts and the clasp below suggest that a large printed book or, more likely, an important bound manuscript may have been kept at Clogh Oughter during or just before the siege of 1653.

361. Possible book mount (Fig. 6.10). An almost square plaque with damaged edges and four concentric circles formed with a drill. Two of these have rough rivet holes punched through their centres, while the rivet holes in the two other cases missed the target. None of the edges is bent over as in nos 119 and 158 and the mount is thicker. It may be from another book or may be a rough replacement for a lost mount on the same book as the

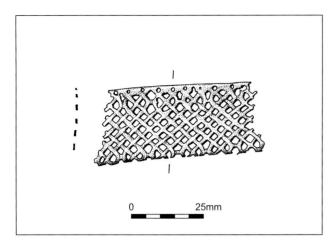

Fig. 6.11—An openwork mount with interlace design (no. 479).

latter two, possibly being placed on the corner nearer the binding. L 40mm; W 39mm. Found in a disturbed layer (F55) in Area A.

1034. Book or casket/box mount. Almost square mount, bent round on one side and with three rivet holes, one still containing a copper-alloy tack, along the opposite side. One of the other sides is damaged, while the last side has two incised lines running parallel with the edge. Some organic material, possibly wood, was preserved with the mount. L and W 35mm. From layer (F49) beneath destruction rubble in Area C.

407. Book clasp (Fig. 6.10). A long, flat piece with a thinner plate riveted to its underside. It ends in a flat, shallow hook at one end. The other end is expanded with a jagged edge and three rivet holes, two of which still contain rivets, which held something like a leather strap between the two metal plates. Each of these rivet holes had a circle round it and the other end of the piece has an incised design. L 97mm; W at clasp end 15mm; present max. W at other end 22mm. Found in destruction rubble layer (F27) in Area A.

This is similar to a book mount, dating from 1630–40, from Southampton (Platt and Coleman-Smith 1975, vol. 2, 267–8) and others found at Montgomery Castle, Wales (Knight 1993, 202–3), and Basing House, Hampshire (Moorhouse 1971, 58–9).

Shrine mount

479. Part of an openwork mount, possibly from a shrine (Fig. 6.11). Only one original straight edge survives, with small circular holes along it, some of which could have been used for rivets. The pattern is a plain interlace finishing along the surviving edge and cut along a

straight line very close to what must have been the edge on the opposing edge. The top and bottom edges are more roughly cut. Max. L 59mm; W 25mm; T 1mm. Found in clay layer (F48) beneath destruction rubble near entrance in Area C.

Sheeting

427. A broken piece of sheeting with the remains of three large (D 4mm) cut rivet holes. The original edge, along which the rivet holes were cut, curves somewhat. Max. L 71mm; W 52mm; T 0.5mm. From F30, Area C.

1083. A broken piece of sheeting with rough edges all around. Max. L 51mm; W 45mm; T 1mm. From F47, Area C.

364. A large, five-sided, flat piece of sheeting with heavy rivets along the edges. One piece is broken away, with up to three rivets/rivet holes. Up to nine of the rivets survive, with large round heads up to 10mm in D. Three empty rivet holes are perfectly circular and almost 6mm in D. Other rivet holes are smaller in D (c. 4mm). The outer side with the rivet heads has the remains of what looks like limewash. This piece looks like a patch for a rectangular water tank. Max. L 211mm; max. W 140mm; T 1mm. From destruction rubble (F27) in Area A.

Pestle

1105. A well-made pestle with moulding along the shaft (Fig. 6.12). There is a short tenon or tang at the handle end, which is only slightly narrower than the shaft. The working end shows evidence of wear. It is possible that, rather than having a handle, this was a double-ended pestle, with the missing end attached like a sleeve over the tenon. It could then have been similar to a double-ended pestle found on the Dominican Priory site in Cork City (Hurley and Sheehan 1995, 118–19). L 128mm; D of shaft 12mm; D of business end 30mm. Found in F107 in Area C.

Piping

277. A piece of piping with an added junction collar at one end and a worked narrowing at the other (Fig. 6.12). The seam is well finished and soldered. L 131mm; L of collar 18mm; external D of collar 15mm; external D of pipe 13mm; D at narrow end 9mm. From F22 in Area A.

382. Two broken short pieces of piping with obvious seams, which fit together (Fig. 6.12). The longer piece

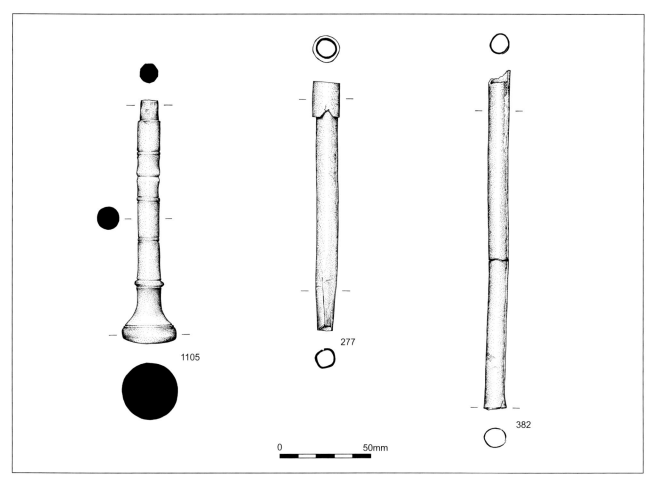

Fig. 6.12—A pestle (no. 1105) and pieces of piping (nos 277, 382).

(broken at both ends) is 100mm L. External D 10mm, internal 8mm. The shorter piece (L 79mm) has one original end, which flares slightly to an external D of 12mm. Found in floor layer (F31) in Area A.

These pipes could have been used as part of an apparatus for distilling spirits, such as that illustrated by Wilde (1861, 537).

Miscellaneous

1118. A flat broken piece with two original straight sides externally and part of a large circular hole internally (Fig. 6.13). The sides of the circular hole curve in one direction. It could be part of the base of some object such as a candlestick. Max. surviving L 87mm; present W 52mm; estimated original D of hole 32mm; T 1mm From F1.

320. Flattened and broken piece of a cylindrical vessel with a single vertical seam. It had a simple plain rim, most of which survives, but the lower part is roughly cut away at a point 47mm below the rim. Estimated original D at rim *c.* 40mm. T 0.8mm. Found in floor build-up layer (F32) in Area A.

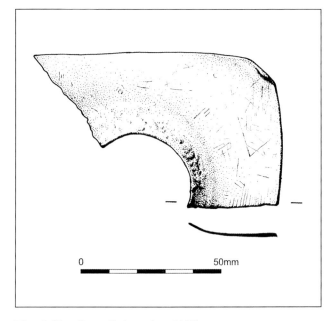

Fig. 6.13—Part of a base (no. 1118).

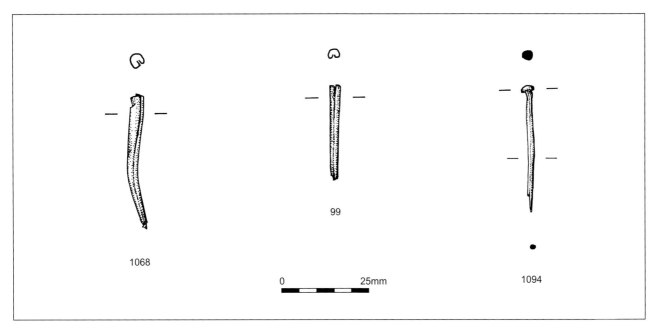

Fig. 6.14—Two lace-chapes (nos 99, 1068) and a pin (no. 1094).

584. Curtain ring? External D 25mm; internal D 21mm; T 2mm. F1, Area C.

1094. Nail or pin (Fig. 6.14). L 36mm; D of shaft 2mm, of head 4mm. From F97 in Area C.

99. Lace end or chape (Fig. 6.14). L 24mm; tapering from D of 3mm to 1.3mm. From F1.

1068. Lace end (Fig. 6.14). L 33mm; tapering from D of 3mm to 1.2mm. From F107 in Area C.

Cooking pot

183. A fragmentary cooking pot with one surviving leg (Fig. 6.15). About half the circumference survives, with only about 110mm of the rim. The rim is only marked by a narrowing to the almost blade-like edge. There are two large holes in the surviving side, which were patched; the patches, made of bronze and rectilinear in one case and rounded and made of bronze and iron in the other, survive detached. There are also four other broken fragments of the side and base. The leg has three

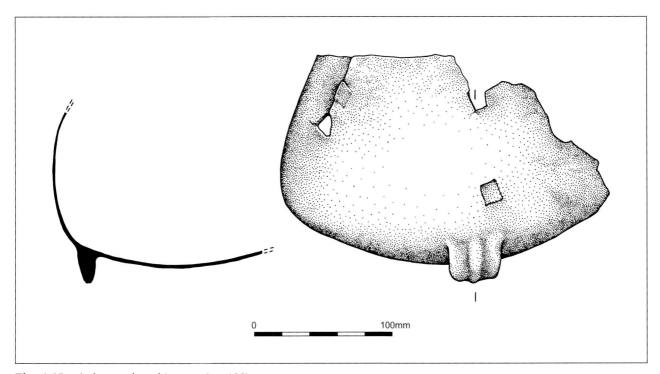

Fig. 6.15—A damaged cooking pot (no. 183).

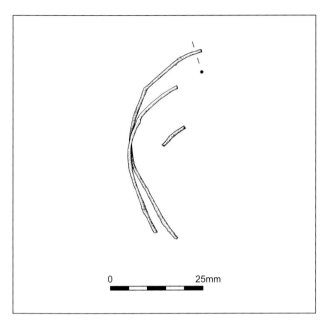

Fig. 6.16—A fragmentary wire bracelet (no. 1123) found on Skeleton D.

vertical ridges on the outside. It displays considerable evidence of use and is heavily blackened internally and externally. Estimated original D 230mm; H 150mm. Found in the destruction rubble (F30) in Area C.

Comparison with cast-bronze cooking pots of medieval type in the Ulster Museum (Marshall 1950) indicates that the present rim is not original and that, when new, the pot would have been taller with an everted rim, which is now missing, and two handles connecting the body and rim. A number of pots of uncertain date in the Ulster Museum, including ones from the River Erne near Belturbet and one from Lough Oughter (*ibid.*, 67, 69), have a curved angle between the base and side, as in the case of this one from Clogh Oughter. The pot from Lough Oughter (exact find-spot not recorded) also shows evidence of repairs (*ibid.*, 69, 74). A number of the pots in the Ulster Museum have stubby, possibly damaged, ribbed legs, as in this case. It is of somewhat similar shape to a larger pot bearing the date 1640 from Macroom, Co. Cork (Wilde 1861, 535, fig. 414).

Wire bracelet

1123. Fragmentary bracelet of thin bronze wire (Fig. 6.16), found on wrist of Skeleton D. It consisted of two strands of wire whose ends were joined by being twisted around each other. D of wire 1mm; estimated D of bracelet 60mm. Found in Area C subsequent to the excavation in 1989.

Modern finds

100. Thimble. This appears to be machine-made, with tiny hollows laid out in perfect lines and with the remains of numbers or letters at the base. H 21mm; D at base 16mm. From F1. Presumably lost on the site in modern times by visitors.

193. A plain circular button with an attachment loop at the back. D 24mm. Surface appears to have been tinned and shows evidence of much polishing. From topsoil.

Two bullet shells from a .22 rifle (nos 17 and 690) and a thin brooch or tie-pin with floral decoration (no. 886) were found in the topsoil.

IRON OBJECTS

Cooking pot fragments

817. A large sherd with rim, handle and part of curving body of a cast-iron cooking pot (Fig. 6.17). The rim section is vertical and 90mm high. The body curves out below this. The handle is L-shaped and connects the top of the rim and the rounded body. It is circular in section, with a diameter of 16mm. L of upper horizontal arm of handle 40mm, of vertical part 100mm. There is a moulding just below the rim. Estimated D of rim *c.* 330mm. From a layer (F97) beneath the destruction rubble in Area C. This piece fits body sherd 1084.

1084. Part of the body of a cooking pot, which joins no. 817 above. From F104, Area C.

29a. Part of the rim and body of a cooking pot similar to no. 817. There is a white limey encrustation on the inside of the rim, with impressions of seeds like grain. From destruction rubble in Area A (F22).

367. A badly rusted piece of the rim and body of a cooking pot. The vertical portion at rim is 90mm high but it is hard to tell whether there is a moulding at the rim. From destruction rubble (F27) in Area A.

475. L-shaped handle of a cooking pot, with a small portion of the vessel attached to the upper part. D of handle 15–17mm; L of upper horizontal arm 40mm, of vertical portion 88mm. From a layer (F48) beneath the destruction rubble in Area C.

454. The badly rusted L-shaped handle of a cooking pot. D 16–19mm; L of upper horizontal arm 45mm, of ver-

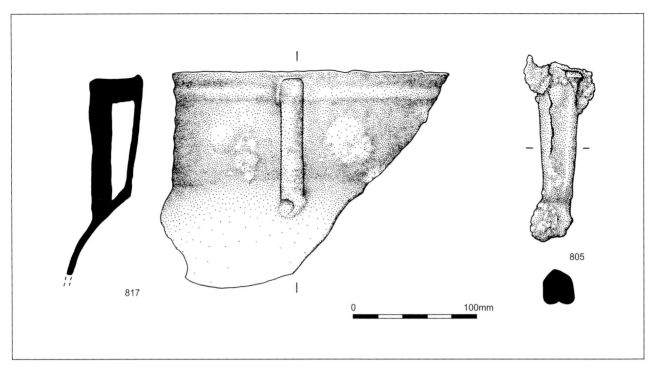

Fig. 6.17—Part of a cast-iron cooking pot with handle (no. 817) and a pot leg (no. 805).

tical portion 112mm. From a floor layer (F32) beneath the destruction rubble in Area A.

This handle may fit rim and body sherd 367.

426. The leg of a cooking pot. It is roughly five-sided in section and the wide inner side has a slight hollow angle down its centre. It widens slightly at the foot. L 106mm; W 22–34mm; T 17–25mm. From the destruction rubble (F30) in Area C.

805. The leg of a cooking pot (Fig. 6.17). It is five-sided with a pronounced foot at the base. The inner side has a slight hollow angle down its centre. L 122mm; W 21–31mm; T 21–32mm. From the old surface layer (F40) beneath the destruction rubble in Area C.

Up to 40 featureless body sherds, all apparently from a cast-iron cooking pot or pots, were also recovered, mainly from the destruction rubble (F30, F27 and F22).

The existence of three handles of different heights would suggest that at least three cast-iron pots are represented here. Virtually all of the fragments were found in layers sealed by the 1653 destruction of the castle. The technology of casting iron was introduced into England in the sixteenth century and was at first used mostly for making cannon and shot. By 1573 there were ten founders of iron guns, mostly in the Weald, south of London (Straker 1931, 142–540). Firebacks were also cast at these foundries, as well as pots, pans, skillets and gressets (*ibid.*, 176–7). Copper-alloy cooking pots were

Pl. 6.3—A cast-iron cooking pot in the collection of the Royal Society of Antiquaries of Ireland.

common in later medieval times, and indeed the excavation produced a large portion of one (no. 183), with a different shape from the cast-iron examples. A fine complete example of a cast-iron pot very similar to those represented here is in the collection of the Royal Society of Antiquaries of Ireland at its house on Merrion Square, Dublin (Pl. 6.3). Like the examples represented at Clogh Oughter, it has a belly and a high collar with a slight moulding 30mm below the rim. It has two L-shaped handles like those from Clogh Oughter and three legs. Its overall height is 320mm, and its greatest width, at the belly, is 340mm. The diameter at the rim is 280mm, the collar being 105mm high and 250mm in internal diameter at the junction between the belly and collar. A casting seam is visible, running vertically down one side, around the base and up the other side. An inventory of 1639, probably relating to Kilkenny Castle, includes two iron pots in the kitchen (Fenlon 2003). These were undoubtedly cast-iron pots. In his deposition of May 1642, Arnold Cosby of Swellan, Co. Cavan, listed iron and brass pots among the items of which he was despoiled or deprived as a result of the rebellion (TCD MS 833, 124–5). Without further research it is not clear whether the cast-iron cooking pots from Clogh Oughter were imported from England or made in Ireland, though, given the number of iron-works that were operating in Ireland in the early seventeenth century (see below, under the fireback), it is quite possible that they were locally made.

Chain links

231. An oval link with ends slightly detached. L 64mm; W 40mm; T 6mm by 5mm. F38.

261. A flattened oval link with ends detached. L 70mm; T of bar 4–8mm. F38.

560. A hook for a light chain with broken links attached. The complete link is looped at each end, with a straight bit between. L 50mm; T of bar 4–5mm. F57.

422. An iron fitting with expanded perforated terminals at each end. It is bent almost at right angles at the centre. L (straightened out) 145mm; W 20–27mm; T 5–6mm; D of perforations 11–15mm. F30.

27. A swivel connection for a chain with a possible spring-loaded opening connection. L (overall) 105mm; dimensions of transverse link 65mm x 30mm, and of spring-loaded link 75mm x 35mm. F1 (may be modern).

Hooks

259. Hook. L 45mm; it narrows towards end of hook to 2mm x 1.5mm. Other end 4mm x 6mm, set at right angles. From destruction rubble (F38) in Area A.

614. Suspension hook with a slight knob at the hook end and screw thread for 25mm at the pointed end. L 102mm; W 5–7mm; T 4–7mm. From a floor layer (F64) in Area B.

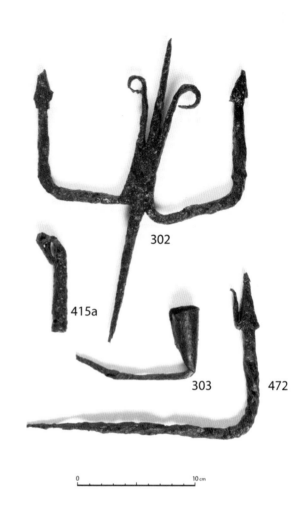

Pl. 6.4—Iron candle-holders (Photographic Unit, NMS).

Candle-holders

302. A large, three-branched, pricket candle-holder (Pl. 6.4). The central spike is flanked by spiral volutes. The side arms are made of twisted square-sectioned bars with expanded arrow-like spikes. The base is a sharp tang for insertion into a block of wood. L 254mm; W across arms 172mm; W of arms 10mm. From the destruction rubble (F30) in Area C.

There are parallels from the excavations in Cork and Waterford cities, and similar candle-holders, sometimes associated with rushlight-holders, were in use until the late nineteenth century (Drury 1925).

303. A cupped candle-holder (Pl. 6.4). The cup is made of a curved piece of sheet iron, while the stem is set at right angles for driving into a wall or timber upright. L 100mm; L of cup 55mm; W of cup at mouth 20mm; W and T of stem 10mm by 6mm. From the destruction rubble (F30) in Area C.

This type of candle-holder, with both straight and right-angled stems, is known from the late thirteenth

Pl. 6.5—An iron fireback (no. 199) (Photographic Unit, NMS).

century onward (Egan 2010, 142–3). Examples dating from the seventeenth century were found at Glanworth Castle (Manning 2009a, 79).

472. Large L-shaped piece of square section, partly twisted (Pl. 6.4). It is pointed at the long end and has an arrow-like terminal at the other end, with remains of fused flanking pieces at each side. It is probably a pricket candle-holder for insertion into a wall or wooden partition. L of long arm 190mm; L of pricket section 130mm; bar mostly 9mm x 10mm. From a layer (F48) beneath the destruction rubble in Area C.

415a. A socketed object with a flat, perforated, curved-out terminal, through which a small link, pointed at one end, is looped (Pl. 6.4). It has a slit in one side close to the socket. It could possibly be part of a pricket candle-holder. L 80mm; W at socket (external) 13mm, (internal) 9mm. From layer beneath destruction rubble (F32) in Area A.

Fireback

199. A large, complete fireback of cast iron, decorated in relief with a central motif that could be either ostrich plumes or a firing gun/mortar and three rosettes (Pl. 6.5). The sides and lower edge are straight, but the top is semicircular with short straight shoulders, of unequal lengths, at each side. H 600mm; W 500mm; T 30mm. From the destruction rubble (F30) in Area C.

This is at present on display in a furnished room above the gate passage in Parke's Castle, Co. Leitrim. Firebacks served to protect masonry at the back of a fireplace and to reflect heat back into the room. They became common especially in the seventeenth century, and many cast-iron examples are decorated with foliate ornament, dates, coats of arms, figurative scenes etc. (Hodgkinson 2010). The emblems on the Clogh Oughter example do not appear to be heraldic and may be purely decorative, though the form of the central motif resembles a crest. More ornate firebacks, one of which bears the date 1608 while the other has the royal arms and the initials 'CR', indicating the reign of Charles I, were found in Basing House, Hampshire (Moorhouse 1971, 56–7, pl. IVA, B). Firebacks are mentioned in seventeenth-century inventories of household furnishings from Ireland (Fenlon 2003, 50–62).

As the size and form of this fireback are not easily paralleled in England, it is worth considering the possibility that it might have been made in Ireland. There were a number of large ironworks in Ireland in the early seventeenth century, made viable more by the availability of woods for producing the necessary charcoal than by the availability of local iron ore (McCracken 1957). In the south of Ireland the main entrepreneur in this business was Richard Boyle, the earl of Cork (Kearney 1953), who set up a number of ironworks in counties Waterford and Cork and did on at least one occasion manufacture some firebacks. One of the other great entrepreneurs in the iron business was Sir Charles Coote, who is reported to have employed 2,500 English and Dutch workers in a number of ironworks around the borders of counties Cavan, Leitrim and Roscommon, where there was iron ore as well as extensive woods (McCracken 1957, 123). These works were attacked at the start of the 1641 rebellion; the losses he claimed to have suffered are detailed in a number of depositions and included iron bar and cast iron (Canny 2001, 359). Some of these works were re-established in the later seventeenth century, and a fireback thought to have been made in one of them bears a version of the O'Rourke arms, the initials OO'R (Owen O'Rourke) and the date 1688 (Meehan 1906, 123). Another fireback from the area bore the date 1692 (*ibid.*, 136). A fireback with a 'diamond pattern', which was thought to have been made in one of the local ironworks, was supposed to have been retrieved from Manorhamilton Castle after it was burnt in 1641 (*ibid.*, 132–3). This all strongly suggests that the Clogh Oughter fireback could have been produced relatively locally.

Pl. 6.6—A spur with decorative silver inlay (no. 104) (Photographic Unit, NMS).

Pl. 6.7—A spur with decorative silver inlay (no. 1121) (Photographic Unit, NMS).

Pl. 6.8—A spur with rowel still in place and traces of copper-alloy plating (no. 64) (Photographic Unit, NMS).

Window bar

833. A short piece of a square-sectioned bar, probably from a window, part of either a stanchion or a saddlebar. It is broken at one end but sharply tapered at the complete end for insertion into the bar hole of the stone surround of the window. L 83mm; W and T 12–13mm. From destruction rubble (F30) in Area C.

Spurs

The terminology used to describe the spurs is adopted from Ellis 1995, 126–7.

104. A highly decorated fragmentary spur with most of one side and the end of the neck missing (Pl. 6.6). The complete terminal is of figure-of-eight type. There is no drop in the sides but the neck has a downward turn. Conservation revealed remains of decorative silver encrustation, consisting of strips along the edges and twining floral and leaf decoration in the centre. See Appendix 3 for report on metal composition. L (at present) 90mm; W of sides 14mm, T 3-4mm; L of neck (at

present) 33mm, W and T 14mm. From destruction rubble (F27) in Area A.

1121. A highly decorated fragmentary spur with the ends of the sides detached but with the full neck, split at the end to hold the missing rowel (Pl. 6.7). The detached terminals are of figure-of-eight type and there is an iron attachment still in one of them. There is no drop in the sides. Conservation revealed remains of decorative silver encrustation, consisting of strips along the edges and floral decoration like a vine scroll on the external surface. See Appendix 3 for report on metal composition. L (at present) 80mm; W of sides 13mm; L of neck 31mm. From destruction rubble (F30) in Area C.

64. An almost complete spur with one side complete to its figure-of-eight terminal and with the rowel still in place at the end of the neck (Pl. 6.8). There is a slight drop in the sides. Conservation revealed slight remains of brass and silver plating (see Appendix 3). L 130mm. Max. W of sides 20mm, T 6mm. L of neck with rowel 54mm. The rowel is five-pointed with fleur-de-lis-

Pl. 6.9—A fragment of an iron rowel spur (no. 354) (Photographic Unit, NMS).

Pl. 6.10—A curry-comb with semi-cylindrical blade (no. 301) (Photographic Unit, NMS).

shaped points (D 28mm). From destruction rubble (F27) in Area A.

354. A fragmentary spur with much of the sides and most of the neck missing (Pl. 6.9). The sides do not drop at the centre. L (at present) 74mm; W of sides 13mm, T 3–4mm; L of stub of neck 13mm, W and T 7–8mm. From destruction rubble (F30) in Area C.

There was a fashion for encrusting iron sword hilts, spurs and buckles with silver decoration, starting from the late sixteenth century and continuing into the seventeenth century (Norman 1980). A spur of this period with somewhat similar decoration to nos 104 and 1121 was found at Kettleby Thorpe in Lincolnshire (Russell 1974, 34), and in the Ashmolean Museum, Oxford, there is a particularly fine pair of spurs with silver encrusted decoration that belonged to Charles I (Hibbert 1968, 214). Many iron spurs from medieval times onward were coated with tin, as no. 64 appears to have been (Ellis 1995, 127).

Horseshoes

The terminology used to describe the horseshoes is adopted from Clark 1995, 81–4.

474. The heel and quarter of a wide horseshoe, broken across one nail hole and with two other nail holes. L 125mm; W 24–33mm; T 4–5mm. F48.

29d. The heel of a narrow horseshoe, broken across one nail hole and with one other nail hole. L 70mm; W 24mm; T 4mm. F22.

222. The feathered heel of a horseshoe with one nail hole. L 70mm; W 20–30mm; T 7mm. F30.

329. A badly worn and badly corroded quarter fragment of a horseshoe with remains of two or three nail holes. The surfaces have split off. L 75mm; W 20mm; T 3mm. F31.

470a. The branch and part of the well-worn toe of a small horseshoe with a folded calkin, two complete holes and the possible remains of one other. L 110mm; W 16–24mm; T 3–4mm, at calkin 7mm. F48.

470b. Possibly the toe of a horseshoe with four corroded-over nail holes. L 1–4mm; W 25mm; T 2–3mm. F48.

Horseshoe nails

1067d. A horseshoe nail with a flat fragmentary shaft. L (at present) 32mm; W and T of rectangular head 10mm x 7mm; W and T of shaft 5mm x 1.5mm. F107.

378a. A horseshoe nail, bent at the pointed end. L (straightened out) 55mm; W and T of rectangular head 9mm x 6mm; W and T of shaft 4mm x 4mm. F31.

Curry-combs

301. A curry-comb of post-medieval type (Pl. 6.10) with semi-cylindrical blade (Clark 1995). One of the three attachment arms of the handle is still attached, while the rest of the tanged handle is detached. L of

Pl. 6.11—The blade of a flat-backed curry-comb (no. 302a) (Photographic Unit, NMS).

Pl. 6.15—Part of what may be the domed case of a watch with applied copper-alloy bands (no. 316) (Photographic Unit, NMS).

blade 195mm; W 45mm; T 3–4mm; L of handle 170mm, W and T of tang 7mm x 5mm and narrowing towards end. From the destruction rubble (F30) in Area C.

56a. A short broken rod, expanded for attachment at one end. Could be part of the handle of a curry-comb and might even fit no. 301 above. L 60mm; W and T of arm 3–4mm. F32.

464. The junction of a forked object with a broken tang-like projection rather than a socket. Could be part of the handle of a curry-comb. L of tang 30mm; W and T 10mm and 4mm; W of arms 11–15mm; T of arms 3–4mm. F44.

254. A short broken rod, expanded for attachment at one end. It could be part of the handle of a curry-comb. L 50mm; W and T of head 16mm and 2mm; W and T of shaft 5–6mm and 3.5–4.5mm. F25.

302a. Part of a curry-comb (Pl. 6.11). It has perforated lugs for attachment at each end, the flat planes of which are set at right angles to the blade. L 167mm; H of blade 16mm, T 1.5mm; number of teeth per 10mm = 4.5; W of attachment lugs 12mm, L 12mm, D of perforation 2mm. From the destruction rubble (F30) in Area C.

This comes from a flat-backed 'modern' form of curry-comb, which was introduced in the post-medieval period and continued in use until recently (Clark 1995, 161, 165; Egan 2005, 186, fig. 174:a).

Watch

316. Appears to be part of the domed case of a watch (Pl. 6.15), with the remains of eight attached 4mm-wide copper-alloy strips radiating from the centre point of the dome. D 56mm; H 20mm; T 3–4mm. From a layer (F32) beneath the destruction rubble in Area A.

A silver watch owned by Oliver Cromwell and pre-served in the Ashmolean Museum, Oxford (Hibbert 1968, 214), has an opening side very similar to this and has six similar raised strips. Coincidentally, we know that Viscount Montgomery of Ards had a watch with him when he was a prisoner at Clogh Oughter in 1646, as recorded by Massari, who visited him at the castle (see pp 28–9).

Keys (Pls 6.12 and 6.13)

15. The shaft and bow of a key bearing considerable re-mains of copper alloy. The bow has two openwork loops within it. L 60mm; W of shaft 10–12mm; W of bow 32mm; T of bow 9–10mm. F1.

47. Possibly the bow of a key, now in three pieces (not illustrated). D-shaped. W of bow 40mm; T 6mm. F81.

1095. A very large key, very corroded, with part of the bit and a complete bow. Conservation revealed copper-alloy surface remains at the junction of the bow and the shaft. L 165mm; bow 60mm x 46mm; D of shaft 10–12mm; projection of bit 25mm. F25.

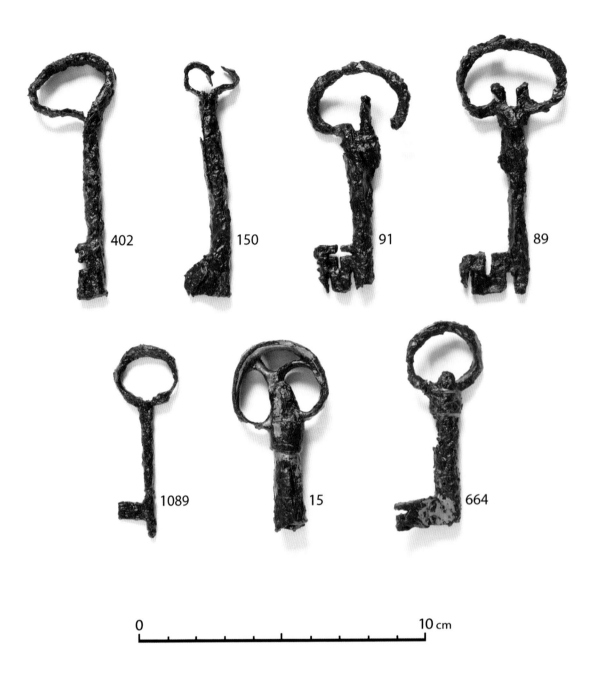

Pl. 6.12—Keys.

1089. A small key with oval bow and plain rectangular projection for bit. L 62mm; bow 23mm x 21mm; bit 9mm x 6mm; T of shaft 5mm. F97.

712. The bow and shaft of a key in two pieces. The bow is in the form of a pelta with loops at each side. Conservation revealed strips of copper-alloy inlay on the shaft. The bit is missing. A fragment of wood is fused accidentally to it. L 83mm; W of bow 41mm, T 8mm; D of shaft 13mm. F49.

263. A large key with two thirds of bow and plain flat rectangular bit. Conservation revealed some copper-

alloy surface remains. L 120mm; original bow 36mm x 22mm, T 7mm; D of shaft 9mm; W of bit 22mm, projection 17mm. F27.

664. A short stubby key with bit and oval bow. Conservation revealed considerable copper-alloy surface remains. L 75mm; D of shaft 10mm; W of bow 28mm; W of bit 12mm, projection 15mm. F57.

73. A large key with damaged bit and D-shaped bow. L 152mm; D of shaft 11–14mm; W of bow 43mm; W of bit 30mm, max. projection 25mm. F1.

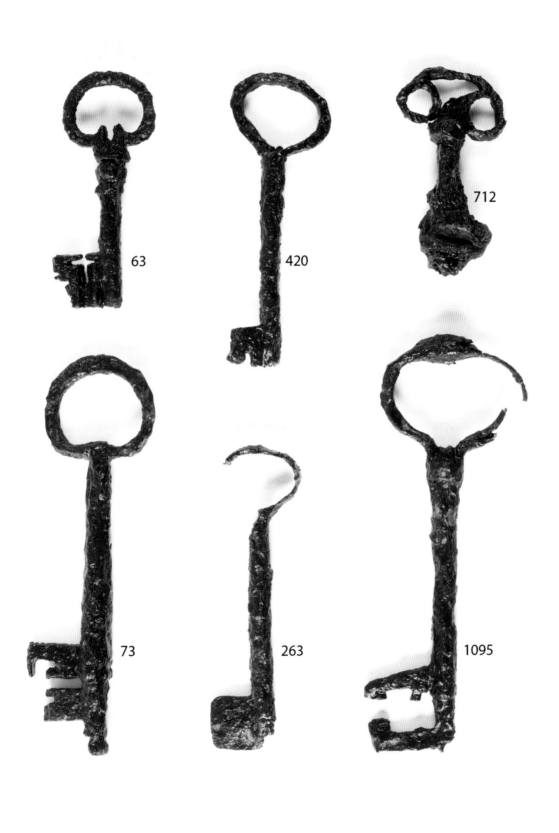

Pl. 6.13—Keys.

402. A key very encrusted with mortar, especially the bit, whose shape is unclear. Conservation revealed copper-alloy surface remains. L 80mm; W of bow 30mm. F27.

150. A very badly corroded key with part of bow and bit. L 75mm; D of shaft 8–9mm. F30.

63. A key with D-shaped bow, slightly damaged bit and collar around top of shaft. Conservation revealed copper-alloy surface remains. L 95mm; D of shaft 8–9mm; bow 30mm x 34mm; W of bit 24mm, projection 22mm. F27.

89. A badly corroded key with damaged kidney-shaped bow and bit. L 90mm; bow originally 37mm x 30mm; D of shaft 6mm but widens to 10mm at top; W of bit 14mm, projection 16mm. F22.

91. A badly corroded key with bit and D-shaped bow. L 75mm; bow 36mm x 24mm; D of shaft 7mm; W of bit 16mm, projection 13mm. F27.

420. A badly corroded key with only the bow, shaft and part of the bit surviving. Bow not in line with bit, as if twisted out of line by force. Conservation revealed copper-alloy surface remains. L 87mm; D of shaft 10mm, bow 43mm x 35mm. F30.

Padlocks and fetters

167. A spherical padlock, complete with its loop (Pl. 6.14). It has decorative copper-alloy inlay consisting of thin lines continuing from the sides of the loop around the body. The area of the keyhole appears to have been smashed in. D of sphere 33mm; W and T of loop 6mm and 4mm. F1.

Similar padlocks have been found at Montgomery Castle in Wales and at Nonsuch Palace in Surrey (Knight 1993, 203–4; Biddle 2005, 386–7).

155b. Possibly a spring from a barrel padlock with part of one side spring intact (Pl. 6.16). L 75mm; W 10mm; T of centre bar 3–4mm. From destruction rubble (F30) in Area C.

415b. A broken socketed object with a curved-down piece at the broken business end. It could be the barrel of a padlock, possibly for a fetter (Pl. 6.17). Compare one from Trim Castle (Hayden 2011, 359) and a fetter in the National Museum of Ireland (Anon. 1960, 33). L 85mm; D of stem 14mm. From a layer (F32) beneath the destruction rubble in Area A.

Pl. 6.14—A spherical padlock with copper-alloy inlay (no. 167) (Photographic Unit, NMS).

Pl. 6.16—The spring of a barrel padlock (no. 155b) (Photographic Unit, NMS).

Pl. 6.17—Part of a barrel padlock (no. 415b) (Photographic Unit, NMS).

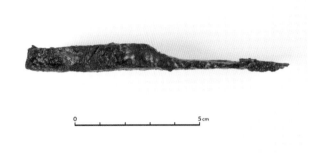

Pl. 6.20—Side view of the lock bolt (no. 321) (Photographic Unit, NMS).

Pl. 6.18—Part of a leg iron with traces of copper alloy (no. 240) (Photographic Unit, NMS).

240. A semicircular strap, roughly broken at one end and with the remains of a box-like feature at the other, which has the remains of copper-alloy coating and may be part of a lock (Pl. 6.18). It could be part of a prisoner's leg iron. The strap has three grooves lengthwise along its outer face. Present overall L 115mm; W of strap 17–19mm; T 4–5mm. Surviving side of box (lock) measures *c.* 27mm x 27mm. From destruction rubble (F30) in Area C.

The holding of prisoners in irons at the castle is mentioned in accounts relating to late 1641 and 1642 (see pp 26–7 above).

Mounted locks

321. Fragments of a door lock with a fragmentary bolt and pieces of sheet iron from the casing of the lock (Pl. 6.19). The end of the bolt that held the door when locked is thicker than the rest (Pl. 6.20). Parts of the rest of the bolt with the projections that engaged with the key also survive in fragments. A complete example dating from the eighteenth century was found at Cowlam deserted village in Yorkshire (Hayfield 1988, 54–5). L of bolt piece 93mm; W 29mm; T 7–8mm for 45mm at complete end, narrowing to 2–3mm for remainder to its broken end. Found in a layer (F45) outside the entrance in Area C.

Pl. 6.19—The bolt of a mounted door lock (no. 321) (Photographic Unit, NMS).

Pl. 6.21—Mounted lock bolts (Photographic Unit, NMS).

1106b. Part of the bolt of a door lock, with the thicker portion that secured the door surviving but only the start of one of the projections that engaged with the key (Pl. 6.21). L 117mm; W 25mm; T 7mm for 33mm at complete end, narrowing to 2mm for remainder. Found in a layer (F107) beneath the old surface and destruction rubble in Area C.

94. A bolt for a mounted lock on a chest, which would have engaged with a staple hasp to lock the chest. It has two subtriangular projections from the middle of one side for engaging with the key (Pl. 6.21). L 130mm; W of bolt (excluding projections) 10–13mm; T 6mm. Found in a disturbed layer (F39) in Area D.

Locks of this type have been found from as early as the late thirteenth century in London (Egan 2010, 103–10).

153. Part of a mounted-lock bolt, probably for a chest (Pl. 6.21). The upper part of one of the projections to engage with the key is missing. Both ends are broken. L 103mm; W at complete projection 25mm, otherwise 12–16mm; T 2mm. From destruction rubble (F30) in Area C.

Pl. 6.22—Ward-plates (nos 156, 296a) from mounted door locks and part of lock casing (no. 296b) (Photographic Unit, NMS).

0   10 cm

Pl. 6.23—Part of a mounted lock with a keyhole and with a key guard to the rear (no. 867) (Photographic Unit, NMS).

30c. Part of a mounted-lock bolt with two projections for engaging with the key (Pl. 6.21). L 88mm; W 20mm; T 5–6mm. From destruction rubble (F22) in Area A.

156. The ward-plate of a door lock and fragments of sheet iron, possibly part of lock casing. The ward-plate has a hole for the key, which is open at the base and has four pieces set vertically in the plate and projecting from each side to fit a key with a symmetrical bit (Pl. 6.22). This type of lock is for a door and could be locked or opened from either side. There are parallels from sixteenth-century London (Egan 2005, 75–6), while examples from the late seventeenth century were found at Aldgate, London, and at Nonsuch Palace in Surrey (Thompson *et al.* 1984, 97, fig. 48: 25; Biddle 2005, 386–7). Present L 77mm; max. W 29mm; T 1–1.5mm; D of circular hole for key 7mm. From destruction rubble (F30) in Area C.

296a. Ward-plate of a door lock with a hole for a key, open at the base (Pl. 6.22). There are no pieces set vertically to the plate in this case and no clear traces that there were any. L 90mm; W 30mm; D of circular hole for key 9mm. From destruction rubble (F30) in Area C.

296b. Part of the casing of a door lock with one right-angled corner and possibly the lower part of a keyhole (Pl. 6.22). There is a large, decorative copper-alloy rivet head adjacent to one edge. Present L and W: 61mm and 52mm. T 2–3mm. D of rivet head 15mm; D of rivet shaft 4.5mm. From destruction rubble (F30) in Area C.

867. Large fragment of the casing of a mounted lock with a complete keyhole and some other fragments (Pl. 6.23). The main piece has two complete corners with small nail holes and remains of other parts of the lock compressed and corroded with wood remains against the back of the keyhole. A key-guard plate (Egan 2010, 104, fig. 77) survives in place at the back of the keyhole. From its size this would appear to have been a lock for a cupboard or chest. Original H of lock 86mm; surviving W 90mm; T 1.5–3mm. H of keyhole 23mm; max. W 8mm. From a layer (F97) close to the entrance and beneath the destruction rubble.

300. Fragments of what appears to be a mounted door lock. Some bits fit together and at least one forms a right angle. Possibly timber in corrosion product. F30.

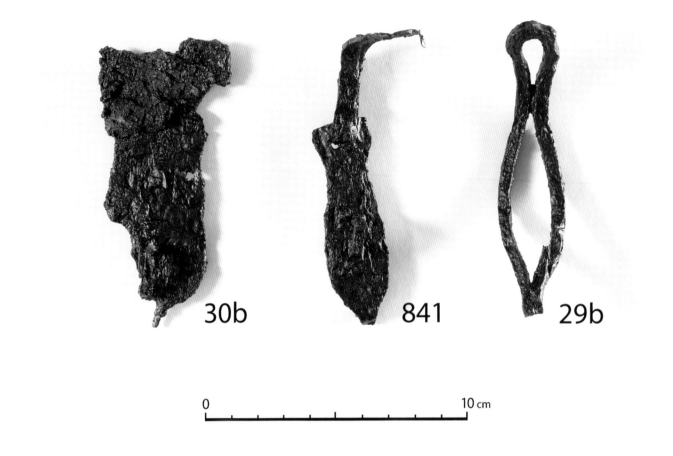

Pl. 6.24—Two staple hasps and a loop hasp (Photographic Unit, NMS).

832. Possibly small pieces of a door lock with square corner. F97.

477. Four pieces of sheet iron, one with a straight edge, possibly part of a door lock. L of piece with straight edge 70mm; W 31mm; T 1–1.5mm. F48.

453c. Pieces of sheet iron with wood in accretion matter attached. L of largest pieces 80mm. One piece has a nail or rivet hole, D 2.5mm. Possibly pieces of door lock. F31.

There are four pieces (nos 649, 49, 151, 800) that might be fragmentary springs for mounted locks. These are described and illustrated below under the miscellaneous heading.

Lock or staple hasps

30b. Large staple hasp (Pl. 6.24). L 115mm; W 35–55mm; T 3mm; staple L 20mm; projects 10mm. From destruction rubble (F22) in Area A.

268. Small fragment of a staple hasp. Staple L 20mm; projection 14mm; T of hasp 2–4mm. From destruction rubble (F27) in Area A.

841. Staple hasp for a chest or large box (Pl. 6.24). It is fish-shaped with a curled-out terminal. Two nail-like spikes at other end set at right angles. L 100mm; W 10–24mm; T 4mm. From modern surface layer (F25) in Area C.

19. Fragmentary band of iron with a possible nail hole and a nail, bent at end, protruding from it though appearing to be part of it. Could be part of a staple hasp. L 57mm; W 30mm; T 1–3mm; nail 2mm x 4mm, L 20mm. F1.

762. A badly corroded hasp, possibly from a chest. L 70mm; max. W 20mm; T 2–5mm. F98.

These hasps were used to lock chests. With the staple of the hasp inserted through a slot in the mounted lock, the key would have moved a bolt, like nos 94, 153 and

30c above, to lock it in place (Egan 2010, 81–4; 2005, 76–8). Examples have also been found at sites such as Kells Priory, Co. Kilkenny (Clyne 2007, 364–5, 372–3), and Nonsuch Palace in Surrey (Biddle 2005, 386–7).

Pl. 6.25—Two loop hasps (Photographic Unit, NMS).

Loop hasps

29b. Loop hasp with one small loop and one long lentoid loop with a looped tab at its end (Pl. 6.24). L (straightened) 115mm; W 18–25mm; T 5mm; bar 5–7mm. From destruction rubble (F22) in Area A.

220. A simple loop hasp (Pl. 6.25). L (straightened out) 145mm; 8mm by 4mm. From destruction rubble (F30) in Area C.

1005. A simple loop hasp (Pl. 6.25). L 100mm; W 35mm; T of bar 6–7mm. From the modern surface layer (F25) in Area C.

Five other complete or fragmentary loop hasps were found. These were used in conjunction with padlocks to secure doors, gates, chests etc. Parallels have been found in medieval contexts in London (Egan 2010, 57–8).

Hinges and straps (Pl. 6.26)

467. Large, long strap hinge for a door, with longer end broken. L 300mm; W 27–38mm; T 3–4mm. Found in a layer (F48) close to the entrance and beneath the destruction rubble in Area C.

Pl. 6.26—Iron hinges (Photographic Unit, NMS).

781. Long, narrow strap hinge with expanded pointed terminal with nail hole at centre. L 150mm; W 13–20mm; T 2.5mm. From the destruction rubble (F30) in Area C.

786. Strap hinge fragment with nail holes and some wood attached. L 72mm; W 22–32mm; T 2mm. From the modern surface layer (F25) in Area C.

1077. Hinge with nail holes for a cupboard door or the like. L 65mm; W 26–34mm; T 1.5–2mm; pivot bar D 5mm. F104.

52b. Part of a strap hinge for a door, in two pieces. L 140mm; W 26–37mm; T 1.5–2mm. Another narrower piece (L 63mm; W 23–29mm) with it. From floor layer (F31) beneath the destruction rubble in Area A.

30d. A strap, bent upward at one end. L 96mm; W 25mm; T 2–3mm. From destruction rubble (F22) in Area A.

113. Part of a hinge. L 45mm; W 27–34mm; T 1.5mm. F22.

1106a. Strap fragments with wood. One piece is looped over for a hinge at one end. Other fragments have nail holes. W 20–25mm; T 2–4mm. F107.

265. A bent pointed spike with a loop at its wide end forming an eye, possibly a hanging eye for a cupboard door. L (straightened out) 115mm; max. W and T 7mm x 7mm; D of eye, internal 6–7mm, external 17mm. From destruction rubble (F27) in Area A.

Binding strips

29e. A flat band with two nail holes. L 70mm; W 23–27mm; T 1.5mm. F22.

289. A trapezoidal mount for a chest with two nail holes. Shaped at wide end with three indentations. L 62mm; W 23–34mm; T 1.5mm. F30.

375. The shaped terminal of a binding strip with a nail hole. L 54mm; W 11–17mm; T 1.5mm. F31.

450. A heavy iron strap with three punched-through nail holes. L 77mm; W 21–24mm; T 3mm; D of nail holes 4mm. F25.

Pl. 6.27—Iron handles (Photographic Unit, NMS).

785. Fragment of a binding strip with two nail holes, one with a nail in place. L 40mm; W 15–20mm; T 1.5mm; L of nail 13mm, W and T 2mm and 4mm. F25.

Handles (Pl. 6.27)

403. A drop handle for a chest, with an upward projection to hold it horizontal when being lifted. The straight part of the handle is 93mm long, while it projects 34mm. W and T 5–8mm. L (overall) 125mm. W of perforated expansion 15mm. From destruction rubble (F27) in Area A.

834b. A long, thin piece, bent at one end and with a perforated expansion at the other (cf. Knight 1993, no. 125, pp 236 and 239; Moorhouse 1971, no. 143). L 140mm; W and T 4mm x 3mm; W of terminal 16mm. From a layer (F97) beneath the destruction rubble in Area C.

1102. A flat handle or staple with a tapering projection at each end extending in the same direction. There are traces of copper-alloy inlay. L 120mm; max. W of strip 14mm; T 4–6mm. L of projections 25mm. From a partly disturbed floor layer (F53) in Area A.

Buckles (Pl. 6.28)

164. Possibly part of a figure-of-eight buckle. W 45mm. From destruction rubble (F30) in Area C.

405. Part of a buckle with a double frame—one side D-shaped, the other rectangular. L 37mm; W 27mm; T 5–7mm. From destruction rubble (F27) in Area A.

105. A plain rectangular buckle with a pin, W 40mm; present L of pin 31mm. F27.

652. A plain D-shaped buckle with a pin. L and W 35mm and 31mm; L of pin 27mm. F30.

957. A trapezoidal buckle with part of loop of pin (not illustrated). L and W 35mm and 32mm. F30.

574. Most of a D-shaped buckle (not illustrated). L and W 38mm and 33mm. F69.

253. Most of a rectangular buckle with pin. L and W 45mm and 42mm; L of pin 50mm. F25.

229. Part of a buckle with a tongue looped over it and now fused in place (not illustrated). L 50mm; W 24mm; T 2–5mm. F38.

30a(1). A small, plain rectangular buckle attached to a thin iron strap end. The pin is missing. There are two rivet holes in the strap end. L and W of buckle 31mm and 23mm; L and W of strap end 51mm and 25mm. The back portion of the strap end is only 21mm L; the remainder is missing. From destruction rubble (F22) in Area A.

Eye and hook attachments

397a. Part of an eye and hook for securing clothing (Egan 2005, 51; Manning 2009a, 81). This thin bar is twisted tightly in different directions at the terminal. L 37mm; D of rod 2mm. F27.

675a. Possibly the hook of an eye and hook for securing clothing. L (at present) 19mm; W and T 3.5mm x 2.5mm. Further piece of shaft? with it. F84.

Dress-pin

968. A dress-pin with a damaged expanded head. L 92mm; D 3mm, narrowing to the point; max. W of head 6mm. F25.

Pl. 6.28—Iron buckles (Photographic Unit, NMS).

Pl. 6.29—Bent knife with part of wooden handle (no. 152).

Jew's harps

1122. A jew's harp, complete apart from tang. L 61mm; W at bow 31mm; W across arms 16mm; T 7mm. F30.

232. Part of one arm and part of the bow of a jew's harp, with the stub of the tang. Estimated W of bow 32mm; T 6mm; L of stub of tang 5mm. F38.

Knives

See Cowgill *et al.* 1987 for terminology.

152. A knife with a broken scale-tang handle, with parts of the iron-oxide-impregnated wooden handle surviving (Pl. 6.29). The blade has been deliberately and carefully bent at right angles at three points, so that the narrow end of the blade is now touching the handle. L (at present) 82mm, L of blade straightened out 145mm; L of surviving stub of handle 20mm; W of blade 15–17mm; T at back 2mm. From destruction rubble (F30) in Area C.

370a. A fragmentary iron knife with a whittle tang and bolster (Pl. 6.30). The blade is broken in two and missing its end. L (at present) 115mm; W of blade 18mm; T at back 2–3mm; L of bolster 30mm. From destruction rubble (F27) in Area A.

370b. A flat oblong piece of iron that may be part of a small knife blade. L 48mm; W 15mm; T 2mm. F27.

454. A relatively well-preserved whittle-tanged knife with its point missing (Pl. 6.30). The blade is triangular in shape and there is a shoulder between the back of the blade and the tang. L 195mm; L of blade 117mm; max. W of blade 22mm; max. T of back 5mm; tang narrows from 11mm by 5mm at junction with blade. From destruction rubble (F30) in Area C.

837. The end of a knife blade. L (at present) 58mm; max. W 17mm; T at back 2mm. F30.

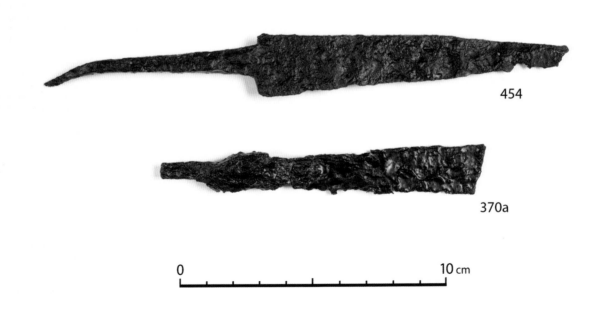

454

370a

Pl. 6.30—Two iron knives (Photographic Unit, NMS).

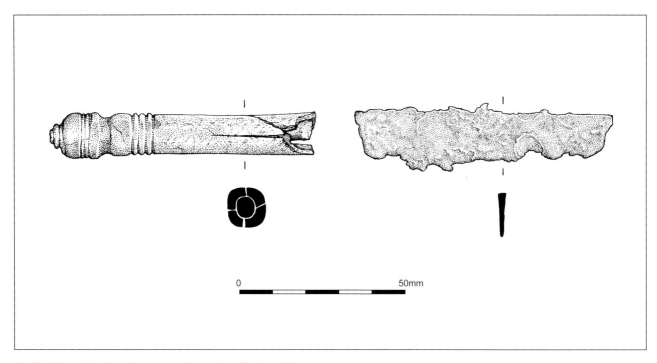

Fig. 6.18—A knife with a turned bone handle (no. 70).

453b. The parallel-sided blade of a knife (in two pieces), widening at the handle end to what was probably a bolster. L 100mm; W 16mm; T at back 3mm. F31.

838. The blade of a very small knife in two pieces, with the butt of a whittle tang. L 55mm; W 13mm; T of back of blade 2.5mm. F30.

70. A whittle-tanged knife in two pieces (tip missing) with a finely turned bone handle (Fig. 6.18; Pl. 6.31). L (overall) 154mm; L of surviving blade 72mm; W of blade 16mm; L of handle 81mm, D 12mm. Handle cracked by corroding iron—one piece detached. Turned bone plug at end. From destruction rubble (F27) in Area A.

Pl. 6.31—Knife with bone handle (no. 70) after conservation (Photographic Unit, NMS).

Chape

359a. A very corroded narrow chape, oval in section (Pl. 6.32). It tapers from the open end, now clogged with corrosion product, towards the narrow end, which comes to a point. Conservation revealed copper-alloy inlay, partly consisting of diagonal strips and a wide horizontal band close to the point. It is presumably from the scabbard of a narrow-bladed dagger or a rapier. L 53mm; W and T at wide end 16mm x 11mm; T of iron at top 2mm. From destruction rubble (F30) in Area C.

A number of copper-alloy chapes and one made of iron were found at Trim Castle (Hayden 2011, 333–5, 345, 347), but these were mainly of medieval date.

Tools

106. A plumb bob—a heavy, rounded, cone-shaped piece with a narrow central perforation (Pl. 6.33). H 50mm; W at base 31mm. From destruction rubble (F27) in Area A.

469. The broken-off blade of an axehead, widely splayed on one side (Pl. 6.34). L 80mm; W of blade 90mm; W at broken end near shaft 32mm; max. T 9mm. From layer (F48) beneath destruction rubble in Area C.

0   2 cm

Pl. 6.32—Scabbard chape (no. 359a) (Photographic Unit, NMS).

0   3 cm

Pl. 6.33—Iron plumb bob (no. 106) (Photographic Unit, NMS).

469

952

0   10 cm

Pl. 6.34—Axe (no. 469) and saw (no. 952) fragments (Photographic Unit, NMS).

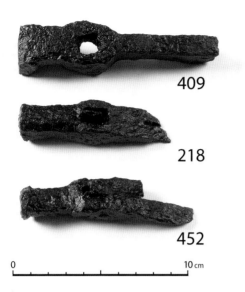

Pl. 6.35—Two hammer heads and an unidentified object (Photographic Unit, NMS).

Pl. 6.36—A pair of dividers and a pair of scissors (Photographic Unit, NMS).

952. Fragment of a saw blade with part of the section to which the handle was attached, including a rivet hole (D 3.5mm) (Pl. 6.34). L 132mm; W 45–47mm; T 2mm. Section with teeth 75mm L. Two teeth to every 22mm. From destruction rubble (F30) in Area C.

452. The head of a claw-hammer, with one arm of claw missing (Pl. 6.35). L 103mm; D of socket *c.* 12mm. D of head, burred from use, 18–23mm. From floor layer (F31) below destruction rubble in Area A.

218. A hammer head, slightly burred at business end (Pl. 6.35). It is broken at the other end but there is no sign of the division for claws. L 100mm; socket appears rectangular (*c.* 17mm x 9mm); D of business end 20mm; dimensions of broken end 22mm by 8mm. From destruction rubble (F30) in Area C.

409. A heavy, bar-like iron object with a circular perforation near one end (Pl. 6.35). This end also expands and is turned down for a length of 5mm. The longer end is square in section (16mm x 16mm). L 133mm; D of perforation 10mm; W of expanded end 33mm. Found in Area B in a layer disturbed by nineteenth-century digging (F44).

69. A pair of dividers with one arm missing (Pl. 6.36). The head is globular, with a D of 14–15mm. L 130mm; arm decreases from 8mm x 5mm to a point. From destruction rubble (F27) in Area A.

Two pairs of iron dividers, dating from the early seventeenth century, were found at Glanworth Castle, Co. Cork (Manning 2009a, 71–3).

286. A damaged pair of scissors, badly corroded (Pl. 6.36). The finger loops are both partially present, while the tip of one blade and most of the other are missing. L 142mm; W across finger loops 46mm; W at pivot 17mm. From destruction rubble (F30) in Area C.

299. A heavy, spear-like object, possibly the head of a poker. The broken shaft (9mm x 10mm) widens to 16mm x 20mm for the head, which tapers from that to 5mm x 5mm at the point over a length of 90mm. F30.

297. A small, fragmentary, trapezoidal flat piece with a broken handle (?) projecting from one corner. Part of a trowel? L 57mm; present W and T of flat piece 21mm and 1–3mm; handle widens to 10mm x 11mm where broken. F30.

453a. A pointed object tapering towards both ends, though one appears broken. L 165mm; W and T 15mm and 12mm at centre, broken end 6mm x 6mm. F31.

789a. A tanged chisel. L 90mm; W of blade 11mm; max. W and T of shaft 7mm x 5mm. F25.

687. A short, heavy punch, possibly broken. L 68mm; narrows from 16mm x 10mm to 13mm x 5mm. F40.

778. A short, tapered bar, possibly a broken punch. L 60mm; W 15–20mm; T 9–11mm. F30.

348. A flat, triangular, blade-like object, with a narrow piece projecting from one of the corners at the wide end and set laterally to the blade. Possibly a blade from a pair of shears. It is at present bent in a slight curve. L 170mm; L of blade 145mm; W at wide end 40mm; T 2–3mm. F27.

Staples and U-shaped pieces

52a. A fine staple. L 55mm; W 24mm; T 2–5mm. F31.

315. A hook or broken staple. L of long arm 53mm, of short arm 30mm; T of bar 4–6mm. F32.

353. A staple or broken chain link. L 44mm; W 37mm; T 6mm. F30.

421. A staple with points bent in opposite directions. L (original) 59mm; bar 5mm x 4mm, tapering to ends. F30.

476. A hook or broken staple. L of arms 36mm. One arm has another bar fused onto it. It could be the curved-down piece of a pricket candle-holder. F48.

573. A hook or broken staple. L of long arm 55mm, of short arm 26mm; T 3–7mm. F69.

780. A staple. L 43mm; W 32mm; T 3–7mm. F30.

Rings

65. Ring. D external 43–45mm, internal 36–37mm; W 12–14mm; T 2–4mm. F27.

363. Flat ring, folded from one piece. D external 33–35mm; W 32mm; T 2mm. F60.

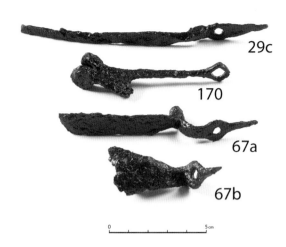

Pl. 6.37—Unidentified forked/hinged pieces of iron (Photographic Unit, NMS).

468. Heavy ring. D external 55–58mm, internal 40–44mm; T 5–6mm; W 25–28mm. F48.

568. D-shaped ring. D 73mm x 50mm; W 20mm; T 6–9mm. F57.

956. Heavy ring. D 40mm; W 21–24mm; T 4–5mm. F30.

Forked/hinged pieces with perforated terminals

29c. Two strips, possibly binding strips for a small wooden chest or box. One has a terminal with a nail hole and possibly a hinge connecting it to the remainder of the strip (Pl. 6.37). L 155mm; W 6–13mm; T 2–3mm. The second piece is twisted and broken at both ends. L (straightened out) 130mm; W 5–9mm; T 2mm. From destruction rubble (F22) in Area A.

67a. A complicated heavy binding strip with a nail near one end and an expanded perforated terminal at the other, which continues to a point (Pl. 6.37). L 110mm; W of main strap 14mm; T 5mm. Smaller strap W 7–14mm; T 3mm; D of nail hole 4mm. From destruction rubble (F27) in Area A.

67b. A broken binding strip or strap hinge terminal, which was getting wider at the point where broken (Pl. 6.37). L 65mm; W 12–27mm; T 2–3mm. There is a curved expansion at the terminal with a central nail hole and a continuation ending in a point. D of nail hole 3mm. F27.

Pl. 6.39—Unidentified looped objects (Photographic Unit, NMS).

Pl. 6.40—A pin with a ring (no. 580) and an unidentified object (no. 800) (Photographic Unit, NMS).

800. A flat piece of iron, shaped like a large spatula or parallel-sided spoon (Pl. 6.40). It has a number of small rivet holes in it. L 125mm; W 40mm; W of neck, where broken, 17mm. From a small deposit (F105) in the floor of the entrance doorway.

296. A tapering, curving narrow piece, complete at the narrow end. L 72mm; W 9–21mm; T 2–4mm. F30.

358. A flat bar, wide in the middle, narrowing almost to a point at one end and more slightly at the other broken end. L 140mm; max. W 16mm, W of broken end 13mm; T 4–8mm. F30.

787. A broken flat piece with a swelling at the middle and pointed at each end. L 134mm; W 16mm at centre, tapering to 6mm at ends; T 11mm at centre, tapering to 4–5mm at ends. F25.

580. A large pin with a ring, possibly a large dress-pin (Fig. 6.19; Pl. 6.40). The pin is looped over the ring, with a slight collar below the loop. The lower end of the pin is missing. L 85mm; D of shaft 7–8mm; external D of ring 42mm; internal D of ring 26mm. From a floor layer (F63) in the western part of Area A.

1091a. A heavy fragment of flattened oval section, like a strap handle with a curve in it. L (at present) 45mm; W 55mm; T 27mm. F97.

1091b. A heavy fragment of flattened oval section, like a strap handle. L (at present) 47mm; W 53mm; T 20mm. F97.

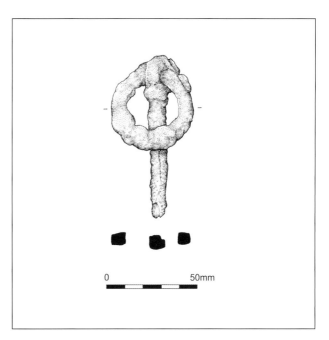

Fig. 6.19—An iron pin and ring prior to conservation (no. 580).

1091c. Heavily corroded pieces of sheet iron connected with corrosion product. These could be fragments of sheet armour. L 90mm; W 50mm; T of individual sheet 1.5mm. F97.

401. Heavy fragment of flattened oval section, broken at one end and expanding towards the other. L 75mm; W and T at narrow end 55mm x 22mm; the wide end is hollow, being 10mm deep at the centre; W and T 62mm x 47mm. F27.

66b. Fragments of sheet iron that could be bits of armour. Largest piece 60mm x 30mm; T 1mm. F27.

359b. Some pieces of sheet iron, especially one large piece consisting mainly of corrosion matter. T 2–4mm. F30.

423a. A looped-over flat band. L 75mm; W 10–12mm; T of band 3mm. Could be a rein end fitting. F30.

1087b. A contorted rod that could be part of a chain link. L 60mm; W 40mm; W and T of rod 5–6mm x 3mm. F104.

651. A broken, bent-over piece of sheet iron, possibly part of the open socket of a bladed implement or the iron blade of a wooden spade or shovel. L 57mm; W 30mm; max. T of socket 12mm; T of sheet iron 1.5–2mm. F30.

293b. A wedge-shaped piece, slightly too big to be a horseshoe nail. It is broken at the narrow end. L 48mm; W and T at wide end 10mm x 9mm, narrowing to 3.5mm x 4mm. F30.

357a. An almost square-sectioned bar with a right-angled turn at one end. The other end is broken. L of main bar 100mm, of right-angled piece 24mm; max. W and T 8mm x 6mm. F30.

357b. A thin band with an expanding terminal at an obtuse angle. The other end is missing. Part of a handle? L 90mm, L of angled end 30mm; W and T 8mm x 3mm. F30.

1011. A wedge-shaped piece. L 57mm; max. W and T 15mm x 10mm, at narrow end 5mm x 1.5mm. F30.

234a. Possibly pieces of plate armour, 40–50mm across. T 2mm. F38.

45. A curving L-shaped piece, widest at long straight end and blunt at short pointed end. L 95mm; W 4–11mm; T 4–9mm. F39.

1099. A complicated piece of curving sheet iron with solid bits attached and with smooth clay or mortar at-tached. Part of lock or gun? Measures 80mm by 60mm. F30.

BONE OBJECTS

487. A well-turned small, deep button with raised mouldings on the front and a central perforation. D 15mm; D of central perforation 2.5mm; T (max.) 5mm. From the old surface layer (F40) beneath the destruction rubble in Area C.

One of the iron knives has a finely turned bone handle. For a description and illustrations see under iron knives.

STONE OBJECTS

Quernstones

200. The complete base stone of a rotary quern made of sandstone (Fig. 6.20). There is a slight raised rim around the central perforation and evidence of random pocking on the grinding surface. D of central perforation 47.5mm; overall D 435mm; T at edge 127.5mm, at centre (including raised rim) 150mm. From the destruction rubble (F30) in Area C.

818. A complete base of a rotary quern of sandstone, which shows considerable evidence of use (Fig. 6.20). The grinding surface has been worn down, leaving a slight raised lip in parts around the edges. D of central perforation 50mm; overall D 470–480mm; T at edge 85–95mm, at centre 111.5mm. From the destruction rubble (F27) in Area A.

45. Segment of an upper stone with part of the central perforation. T 55–56mm; L from central perforation to edge 160mm, indicating an original overall D of *c.* 410mm. From disturbed layer (F39) in Area D.

514 and 515. Small segments of the upper stones of querns. They stop short of the central perforation and have no other features. T 60–64mm. From partly disturbed floor layers (F57 and F56) in Area B.

516. Part of the rim of an upper stone. T 57–65mm. F56.

517. Almost a quarter of an upper stone. T 57–60mm; L from edge to central perforation 170mm; estimated original overall D *c.* 430mm. F56.

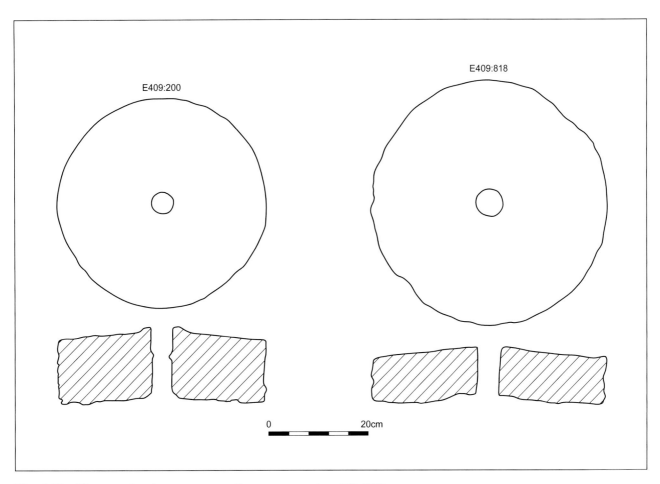

Fig. 6.20—The complete bottom stones of rotary querns (nos 200, 818).

859. A rough segment of an upper stone with part of the central perforation. Max. L from edge of central perforation 150mm; estimated overall original D *c*. 390mm. From a layer (F49) near the entrance and beneath the destruction rubble in Area C.

527. Part of the edge of a thick quern showing little or no wear. It could be from either an upper or a lower stone. T 90–100mm. F57.

964. A large fragment of an upper stone with part of the central perforation. While the underside is well dressed and smooth at the edge as a result of being lifted to remove the flour, the upper surface is uneven and natural in appearance. T 40–60mm; L from central perforation to edge 180mm; estimated original overall D 450mm. From a layer (F97) near the entrance and beneath the destruction rubble in Area C.

1008. About a quarter of an upper stone, with half of a handle perforation and a small bit of the central perforation. T 30–56mm; L from central perforation to edge 170mm; estimated original overall D 330mm; D of handle hole 30mm. F56.

891. Part of a thick upper stone of a quern, with part of central perforation. The grinding surface is pock-dressed and the upper surface is partly smooth from having been used for sharpening. There is also a sharpening groove on this surface that contains a brown ferrous stain. T 73–83mm; L from central perforation to edge 155mm; estimated original overall D *c*. 400mm. F49.

1009. About a quarter of an upper stone of a quern, with part of central perforation and part of handle hole. T 57–65mm; L from central perforation to edge 185mm; estimated original overall D 460mm; D of handle hole 30mm; depth 40mm. F57.

Unnumbered. Part of a very small upper stone with part of central perforation, part of a handle hole and part of the sloping edge. T 60mm; L from central hole to edge 125mm; estimated overall original D *c*. 330mm; D of handle hole 25mm; depth of handle hole 36mm. Chance find.

Querns continued to be important tools for the grinding of grain into the seventeenth century and later. They were very important in war conditions, when mills were

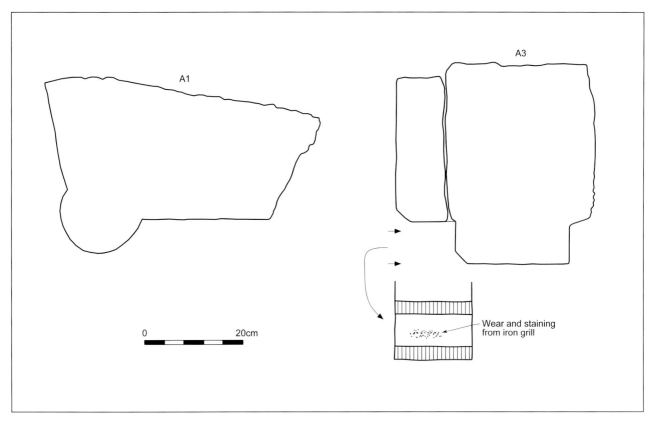

Fig. 6.21—A sandstone newel for a spiral stair (A1) and a limestone jamb from the seventeenth-century ground-floor doorway (A3).

often destroyed, as is clear from a letter written from Cashel, Co. Tipperary, by the earl of Inchiquin in 1647, in which he requested 'handmills (for which I have often and earnestly written), the water mills being either burnt or deserted' (McNeill 1943, 266). They were of course particularly important under siege conditions, as at Clogh Oughter in 1653, where they were essential for grinding the stores of grain for the making of bread, porridge etc. This is clear from the account of the siege of Ballyaly Castle, Co. Clare, in 1642, where querns are mentioned on two occasions (Croker 1841, 19, 21).

Rotary sharpening stones

271. A small segment of a rotary sharpening stone of sandstone. A length of the well-used sharpening edge survives but no part of the central perforation. Estimated original D at least 500mm. T 70–74mm. Context not recorded.

14. A small segment of a rotary sharpening stone with only half its thickness surviving. Probably from the same object as no. 271. T (at present) 37mm. Edge very smooth from use. F1.

Stone disc

480. A roughly shaped thick stone disc. D 64–70mm; T 26mm. F48.

Flint

55. A small waste flake of good-quality light brown flint. L 30mm; W 20mm; T 2–5mm. F32.

During conservation a piece of flint was found in corrosion product attached to the cock of a snaphaunce (flintlock) musket (no. 217) (see p. 150).

ARCHITECTURAL STONE AND OTHER BUILDING MATERIALS

Loose architectural stones

A1 (Fig. 6.21). A large cut piece of sandstone with two faces at a slightly obtuse angle and with a circular moulding at the angle. L 560mm; W 360mm; T 260mm. D of circular moulding 160mm. Surface find. A second similar newel stone (A4) (T 170mm) was found by the conservation team, and both were securely displayed in front of the fireplace in Area A. A site visit in May 2012

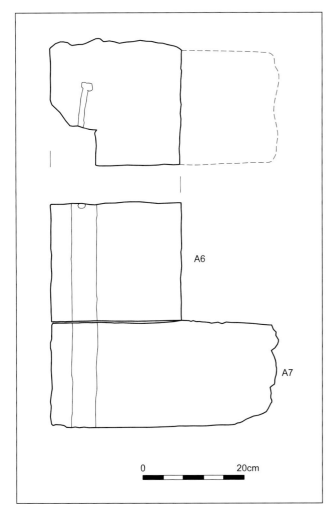

Fig. 6.22—Sandstone jambs from a thirteenth-century window (A6, A7).

revealed that both had been displaced by vandals but were still on site. These are newel stones from a spiral stair.

A2. The jamb stone of a door or window with a bolt hole in it. L 400mm; present W 230mm; T 245mm. Bolt hole 70mm x 55mm x 60mm deep. Found by the conservation team in rubble close to the doorway in the cross-wall.

A3 (Fig. 6.21). The displaced jamb stone of the late ground-floor doorway. Made of good-quality limestone, it has an external rebate for an iron grill or yett. L from front to back 400mm; W 400mm; T 155mm. The rebate was 120mm deep from the front and 72mm deep from the door opening, with chamfers on both corners. The face of the rebate facing the opening had evidence of wear and iron staining from the iron grill rubbing against it. The rebate for the wooden door survived on the inside as an obtuse angle 70mm in from the door opening. It was found directly in front of the ragged doorway and only 0.25m from it. A site visit in May

2012 revealed that a second, similar stone (A5) (T 180mm) had been found by the conservation team after the excavation. Both are displayed at the fireplace in Area A.

A6 and A7 (Fig. 6.22). Two pieces of cut sandstone, probably from a window jamb, which were found by the conservation team and are secured within the fireplace in Area A. A6, the uppermost of the two stones, is finely dressed on three sides, the other side being broken. It has an external rebate for a shutter and a groove on the upper surface for an iron hinge fitting for a shutter. There is also a chamfer between the rebate and the inner part of the jamb. L 260mm; W 230mm; T 250mm. A7 is a similar piece, which does not have a third dressed face but extends on roughly for another 180mm in length.

A8. Part of a sandstone window jamb with a wide chamfer. It has a groove for an iron hinge fitting for an internal shutter. L 350mm; W 220mm; T 250mm. This is from a window similar to the first-floor east window, two stones of which survive *in situ*.

A9. A sandstone jamb from a window or door. It has no chamfers. The dressed jamb itself is 220mm wide with a 70mm-deep rebate on the inside, beyond which the stone is broken. The outer face is well dressed for a length of 240mm, beyond which it shears off at an angle for another 130mm. There is a square hole as for a bar in the outer face (40mm x 40mm x 20mm deep). L 370mm; W 270mm; T 370mm.

A10. A badly damaged piece of sandstone with the remains of a rebate, as for an internal window shutter, and part of the outer face.

A11–15. Gutter stones from the roof level, like those still in place at the top of the tower (Pls 3.28 and 3.29). The gutter groove is 110mm wide and 20–30mm deep. These have been secured with mortar in a curving line on top of the remains of the south wall. Similar stones are still in place at the top of the tower.

Other building materials

Brick

A number of pieces of brick were found in the rubble. Two, one complete and one almost complete, were kept as samples.

Sample 2 is a coarse orange-coloured brick, which had one end neatly cut off. One side, which is relatively smooth, shows mortar staining. L (incomplete) 160mm, W 98mm, T 50–54mm (6+in. x 3.75in. x 2–2.25in.). Found in destruction rubble (F22) in Area A.

Sample 23 is a complete coarse orange-coloured brick. It has a 20–25mm-thick layer of mortar attached to one side and overlapping the one end and edge. L 210–215mm, W 105mm, T 51–55mm (8.25–8.5in. x 4.25in. x 2–2.25in.). Chance find by the conservation team.

Unlike in England and parts of the Continent, brick was not generally made or used in Ireland in medieval times. The earliest known use of brick in Ireland is in the gun-ports in Carrickfergus Castle, dating from the 1560s. There is good documentary evidence for the manufacture and use of brick in Ulster in the early seventeenth century by the London companies and by English undertakers who took part in the Plantation of Ulster (Meek and Jope 1958, 113–14; Robinson 1979, 15, 21–2; Reeves-Smyth 2007, 299–300). One of the English undertakers in County Cavan, John Fishe, arranged for the manufacture of bricks locally and built a house or castle of brick at Lisnamaine, some 4.5 miles north-north-west of Clogh Oughter, by 1613 (O'Reilly 1985, 265). Another of the English undertakers in the barony of Loughtee, Sir Nicholas Lusshe, had bricks and roof tiles made on site for his building works at Lisreagh (Robinson 1979, 22). The sizes of bricks vary a lot at this period in Britain and Ireland, but the two bricks from Clogh Oughter are within the range of dimensions for early seventeenth-century bricks in England (Campbell and Saint 2002, 181) and closely comparable with Ulster bricks of the period, which averaged 8.5–9in. x 4.25in. x 1.75–2in. (Meek and Jope 1958, 113). The bricks at Clogh Oughter may only have been used for the chimney-stack and/or for lining flues. While the very limited number of bricks required for the work on the castle would not have warranted a brick-making operation for this project, it is likely that the bricks were made relatively locally (see report on Sample 2 below).

Report on visual examination of brick (Sample 2)
SARA PAVIA

The sample is a red/orange fired-clay brick, which contains cinders and rock fragments. The brick was made with a mild or sandy clay including a significant amount of sand and rock fragments. This suggests that the brick was probably made locally with a glacial drift (boulder clay). Such deposits occur widely in Ireland and were often used historically for brick-making in the south-east, the east, and counties such as Mayo and Leitrim.

The rock fragments also indicate that the clay underwent little processing or preparation. The presence of abundant cinders suggests, however, that combustible matter was added to the raw material as a fuel to assist firing. Some of the limestone fragments in the raw clay have become lime as a result of firing.

Daub
Sample 24 consists of two pieces of daub with impressions of wattle in them. The larger piece is a fine biscuit-coloured daub with small pieces of stone. It has a very rough and uneven surface on one side and roughly parallel impressions of wattle (D 11–13mm) on the other. L 80mm, W 100mm, T 22–46mm. The smaller piece has a reasonably flat surface on one side and wattle impressions on the other. L 58mm, W 36mm, T 10–16mm. Found by the conservation team.

These could have been part of partitions within the castle as rebuilt in the early seventeenth century (Phase 3). Such partition walls were usually timber-framed, with either brick or wattle-and-daub being used to fill the open panels. At Clogh Oughter such partitions might have been used to divide the wooden stair from adjacent rooms, or for internal lining of the passage leading to the doorway that gave access to the parapets. A partition wall of this type survives at Tintern Abbey, Co. Wexford (Lynch 2010, 24–5).

MILITARY ARTEFACTS
DAMIAN SHIELS

Introduction

The excavation produced a large number of military-related artefacts. This report includes technical descriptions and discussion of object function, and attempts to place the material in its historical military context.

The siege of Clogh Oughter Castle

There are few surviving details regarding the particulars of the fall of Clogh Oughter in 1653. The castle was being held by a Confederate/Royalist Irish force under Colonel Philip O'Reilly when it was placed under siege by Parliamentarian forces commanded by Colonel Barrow in or around March of that year (see p. 30). Colonel Jones reported on 1 March that:

'We have intelligence from Colonell Barrow that Trinity Island, in the county of Cavan (as I take it), and some other islands therabouts, are delivered up unto him, and that he is now before Cloughwater Castle, and hath by a fiery floate burnt their boates or cottes (as he hopes), and with sluges hath burnt their corne, and hopes in a short tyme it will be rendered or quitted' (Gilbert 1879–80, vol. 3, 371).

Articles of surrender survive which indicate that the castle was offered up to the Parliamentarians on 27 April (see pp 31–2). Aside from these details, there are no historical accounts available to indicate how the siege was prosecuted. Local tradition names a hill in the townland of Inishconnell, on the mainland to the south of Clogh Oughter, as 'Camp Hill'. In addition, a road leading to this elevation is known as 'Cromwell's Road'. Both of these names were incorporated into the Ordnance Survey six-inch mapping for the area, which was carried out in 1835 (see p. 34). The use of the term 'Cromwell's Road' is common throughout Ireland in places where routeways were thought to have been developed for use by Parliamentarian forces, often in order to facilitate the transport of artillery.

It is clear that the siege of Clogh Oughter was of significant duration. Almost two months elapsed between the initial report that the castle was besieged and its eventual capitulation. This is a testament to the strong defensive position occupied by the fortification, located as it was on an island in a lake. Irish castles often succumbed very quickly to siege once artillery was employed; for example, Carrickmines in County Dublin, which was besieged in 1642, fell after only two days (Clinton *et al.* 2007, 196–9).

Given the paucity of detail regarding the particulars of the siege operations, we must turn to the archaeological evidence to furnish us with indicators as to its intensity and effect. The assemblage of 180 artillery projectile fragments recovered during the excavation represents the largest known from a site of this type in Ireland. This provides ample evidence to suggest that the Parliamentarians employed a variety of ordnance against the castle, and did so intensively.

The artillery projectiles

A total of 180 artillery projectiles were recovered from the excavations at Clogh Oughter Castle. Of these, 179 were fragmented, suggesting that they had been fired and had broken apart following detonation or impact. One example of an extant projectile was also recovered. Two broad forms of projectile were identified during analysis. The first are solid shot, consisting of solid iron balls of varying sizes, designed to weaken and destroy masonry. The second are mortars, which fired hollow spherical iron balls or 'bombs' filled with powder and designed to detonate above a target.

Owing to the highly fragmentary nature of much of the assemblage it was not possible to identify the majority of projectiles. Table 6.1 presents the material from Clogh Oughter by projectile type.

Table 6.1—Clogh Oughter assemblage by projectile type.

Projectile type	Number
Indeterminate	131
Mortar	9
Mortar?	27
Solid shot	7
Solid shot?	6

Almost 50% of the projectiles retained a portion of their original curved surface. In some instances this allowed an estimation of the original diameter of the balls. Drawings of the curvature produced during the physical examination of the assemblage were digitally scanned. These scans were then used in conjunction with Adobe Illustrator to provide an estimate of the potential original diameter of the projectiles prior to fragmentation. Although such data need to be treated with caution, the main aim was to establish whether any groupings were apparent which would allow for discussion of the potential projectile calibre employed by the Parliamentarians during the siege. Fifty-one of the fragments (plus the one intact ball) were used in this analysis. The results are provided in Table 6.2.

The results highlight four clusters around the 80–100mm, 110–130mm, 140–160mm and 230–250mm diameters. The most pronounced cluster is formed around the 110–130mm range, with twenty fragments producing potential diameters at this size. It is possible to use this information to speculate as to the types of artillery pieces being used by the Parliamentarians at Clogh Oughter, as set out below.

Artillery pieces: solid shot

Projected diameters were attempted for ten of the thirteen fragments that fell into the 'solid shot/solid shot?' category. The results are set out in Table 6.3.

Table 6.2—Number of projectile fragments that fell into projected diameter ranges (where a range of diameters was possible, a median of the two was selected for the analysis).

The projected diameters were converted to inches (the standard measurement of calibre) and matched with the known calibres of mid-seventeenth-century artillery pieces. Four types of gun were suggested: saker, demi-culverin/small culverin, culverin and demi-cannon. The characteristics of these weapons are set out in Table 6.4.

These findings suggest that the Parliamentarian besiegers may have employed at least four different types of artillery to fire solid shot against the defenders of Clogh Oughter.

As noted above, only a small proportion of the assemblage was firmly identifiable as solid shot. The principal reason for this is the extremely fragmentary nature of the surviving material (Pl. 6.41). Only a small number of the projectiles retained anything close to 50% of their original form, with examples such as no. 159 (Pl. 6.42) unusual in their completeness.

It was possible on some of the examples to identify remnants of the manufacturing process; no. 796 retained a portion of its mould seam, indicative of the join between the two halves of the ball mould (Pl. 6.43).

Although not firmly identifiable as solid shot or mortar, a number of other projectiles presented evidence that provides an insight into the manufacturing

Table 6.3—Potential guns that fired solid shot at Clogh Oughter.

Identification	Projected diameter (mm)	Projected diameter (inches)	Potential gun
Solid shot?	*c.* 90	*c.* 3.5	Saker
Solid shot	*c.* 110	*c.* 4.3	Demi-culverin/ small culverin
Solid shot	*c.* 120	*c.* 4.7	Demi-culverin/ small culverin
Solid shot?	*c.* 120	*c.* 4.7	Demi-culverin/ small culverin
Solid shot	*c.* 130	*c.* 5.1	Culverin
Solid shot?	*c.* 130	*c.* 5.1	Culverin
Solid shot	*c.* 160	*c.* 6.3	Demi-cannon
Solid shot	*c.* 170	*c.* 6.7	Demi-cannon
Solid shot?	*c.* 150	*c.* 5.9	Demi-cannon

process. Impurities such as air bubbles were apparent on a number of examples, such as no. 963a (Pl. 6.44). This could have been caused by the quality of metal used to

Table 6.4—Characteristics of potential solid-shot guns at Clogh Oughter (after Eldred, *The gunners glasse* (1646), and Nye, *The art of gunnery* (1647), in Blackmore 1976, 396–7).

Gun type	Calibre (in.)	Length (ft)	Weight (lb.)	Diameter of shot (in.)	Point-blank range (yds)
Saker	3.5–4	8–10	1400–1800	3.25–3.75	360
Demi-culverin/ small culverin	4.25–5	9–13	2000–4000	4–4.75	400
Culverin	5.25–5.5	10–13	4500–4800	5–5.25	460
Demi-cannon	6.25–6.75	1–12	5400–6000	6–6.5	–

Pl. 6.41—Fragments typical of the Clogh Oughter assemblage (nos 349a–k).

Pl. 6.43—Impacted solid shot with evidence for mould seam (no. 796).

Pl. 6.42—The most complete of the impacted solid shot assemblage (no. 159).

Pl. 6.44—Cavities caused by imperfections in the manufacturing process (no. 963a).

produce the ball, or the weather conditions under which the shot was produced.

It was noted that a number of the projectiles had fragmented in a linear or layered fashion. Although the reason for this cannot be determined with any certainty, it seems likely that the manufacturing process gave rise to linear weaknesses, along which fractures often occurred on impact (e.g. nos 645a, 866a, 955b).

Artillery pieces: mortar bombs

There were 36 fragments of mortar/mortar? identified in the assemblage. Projected diameters were attempted for 28 examples. Of these, nine were firmly identified as mortars and were used to assess potential mortar types, set out in Table 6.5 below.

Table 6.5—Potential mortars that were fired at Clogh Oughter.

Identification	Projected diameter (mm)	Projected diameter (inches)	Potential mortar size (in.)
Mortar bomb	120	4.7	5
Mortar bomb	120	4.7	5
Mortar bomb	140	5.5	6
Mortar bomb	160	6.3	7
Mortar bomb	170	6.7	7
Mortar bomb	230	9.1	10
Mortar bomb	230	9.1	10
Mortar bomb	240	9.4	10
Mortar bomb	240	9.4	10

Pl. 6.45—Complete mortar bomb filled with lead (no. 1126).

Pl. 6.46—Detail of fuse cavity with lead visible (no. 1126).

Significantly less is known about the range and calibre of mortars employed during the seventeenth century than about other artillery pieces. It is thought that only one example from the period survives in Britain (Bull 2008, 108)—the mortar known as Roaring Meg, which is on display at Goodrich Castle in Herefordshire. The evidence from Clogh Oughter suggests that at least two and probably three sizes were in use. Nye, in his 1647 *Art of gunnery*, felt that the optimum size of a mortar bomb (or 'granadoe') was 9in., as this was large enough to cause significant damage but not so large as to present major logistical problems (*ibid.*, 13). The projectiles could range in size, however, from small examples that could double as hand grenades through to bombs of 18.5in. diameter (*ibid.*). All of the Clogh Oughter examples fit within this range and were most probably a mix of small and medium mortars. The type of mortars used on the castle in 1653 were capable of firing significant explosive shells; at the siege of Basing House during the English Civil War, a 10in. mortar and a 6in. mortar were employed, with the bombs weighing 80lb. and 36lb. respectively (*ibid.*, 115).

The most notable mortar bomb from the assemblage is no. 1126, which also constitutes the only complete projectile among the 180 artefacts (Pl. 6.45). Although heavily corroded, it had a surviving diameter of 7in. (178mm). The heavily corroded fuse hole was some 2.2in. (56mm) in maximum diameter (Pl. 6.46). Unusually, this bomb appears to have been at least partially filled with lead rather than explosive powder. A parallel for this has yet to be identified, but a likely scenario is that the besiegers were seeking to increase the projectile's weight in order to convert it into a solid shot. Lead has more mass than cast iron, and therefore a lead-filled mortar bomb would be a heavier projectile than a cast-iron solid shot of equal size (no. 1126 weighs 14.42kg). Theoretically this would provide a lead-filled mortar with more destructive power than a complete cast-iron equivalent, although it would also bring with

Pl. 6.47—A mortar-bomb shell (no. 18), illustrating intact internal and external surfaces.

Pl. 6.49— Example of a surviving fuse cavity (no. 1127).

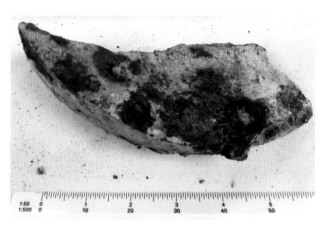

Pl. 6.48—A mortar fragment 'slice' (no. 866).

Pl. 6.50—An iron plug, possibly from a mortar bomb (no. 645d).

it increased risk to the gun (and gunners), as more powder would be required to propel it. It is possible that this object represents an attempt by the besiegers to inflict increased damage on the masonry of Clogh Oughter, or it may have been an emergency measure if they found themselves running short of solid shot. In either case it is an extremely interesting survival.

A number of the mortar fragments retained portions of both their outer and inner surfaces, allowing for measurements to be taken of the shell thickness (Pl. 6.47). Examples such as nos 18, 237a and 1066 had a shell thickness of 2in. (51mm). Other fragments, such as nos 168c and 198, had thinner surviving shells of 1.25in. (32mm), while no. 1127 had a shell of 1.75in. (44mm).

The extreme forces to which the mortar bombs were subjected upon detonation is reflected in the assemblage. Many of the fragments broke into 'slices' of the original spherical bomb, testament to the destructive force of the explosion (Pl. 6.48).

Some of the fragments retained a portion of their original surface which incorporated some of the original fuse cavity, such as no. 1127 (Pl. 6.49). On this example the remains of a portion of the hole for the fuse are visible towards the bottom right of the fragment.

One unusual fragment was noted amongst a group of fourteen fragments under the number 645a–n. No. 645d took the form of a metal plug measuring 1.2in. (30mm) in diameter and 1in. (25mm) thick (Pl. 6.50). The function of this object has not been determined during this analysis but it is possible that it represents part of a plug from a mortar bomb, potentially to hold the fuse in place.

Projectile distribution

The 180 projectile fragments were distributed across nineteen contexts, as set out in Table 6.6.

The vast majority of projectiles were located in Areas A and C. This is the expected distribution, given the probable location of the Parliamentarian siege artillery on the mainland to the south of Clogh Oughter. Area A represented the southern half of the interior of the castle, including the late external ground-floor doorway, while Area C consisted of the area immediately outside the doorway on the south side (see pp 79–93). Area B was located in the northern portion of the castle and as a result produced fewer projectiles.

Table 6.6—The distribution of the solid shot and mortar fragments by context and area.

Context no.	Description	Area	Fragment no.
F1	Topsoil and sod	Area C	7
F22	Rubble layer	Area A	6
F23	Same as F30	Area C	1
F25	Topsoil and sod	Area C	14
F27	Rubble destruction layer with soil content	Area A	27
F30	Rubble collapse	Area C	67
F31	Burnt clay with charcoal and bone	Area A	6
F32	Gravelly mortar layer with soil and small stones	Area A	6
F38	Mottled soil and sand mix with yellow clay and mortar	Area A	5
F40	Brown fine sandy soil	Area C	2
F44	Disturbed layers	Area B	1
F48	Clay amongst stones outside entrance	Area C	1
F56	Loose brown soil	Area B	2
F57	Purplish-brown loose soil with stones	Area B	1
F62	Disturbed layer	Area A	1
F97	Cobbling	Area C	2
F104	Brown soil under which burials were dug—under F30	Area C/Area E	3
F107	Black loamy soil	Area C	1
F108	Sandy grey-brown clay	Area C	3
Unknown	–	–	24

In addition to the evidence provided by the distribution of projectiles, impact scarring was also noted on one of the upstanding walls of the castle on the southeastern side. These scars are the result of solid-shot impacts during the course of the siege. While one of the strikes has destroyed portions of three pieces of masonry in a sporadic fashion, the other is a potentially valuable piece of evidence with regard to identification of the guns used to reduce Clogh Oughter. This larger impact scar has preserved the impression of the solid shot that created it, and is surrounded by a shatter zone of 0.35m. The probable diameter of the shot used was 80–100mm (3.1–3.9in.), which is commensurate with a saker, one of the potential weapons identified as a result of the projectile analysis. Although a systematic study of impact scarring as a result of artillery fire has yet to be conducted in Ireland, such an undertaking would provide significant information about the conduct of siege warfare on the island. The Clogh Oughter example is an important addition to the range of known sites that exhibit impact scars, such as Lisacarroll Castle, Co. Cork, and Birr Castle, Co. Offaly.

The lead shot and casting headers

Seven lead shot were recovered during the original excavations at Clogh Oughter, with a further seven recovered during the 2012 underwater survey. The details of these are outlined in Table 6.7.

The lead shot assemblage from the original excavation is representative of bullets for three different types of weapons. The majority (nos 441, 1091c (A), 25 (A), 25 (B)) fall into the weight-to-the-pound range expected for muskets. Two of the bullets (nos 972, 1091c (B)) are

Table 6.7—The lead shot.

Artefact no.	Weight (g)	Diameter (mm)	Weight to the pound	Mould seam	Sprue	Fired	Comments
972	23	16	19.7	None visible	Clipped	No	Grey patina
882	8.3	11	54.6	Visible	Clipped, raised	No	Grey patina
441	30.9	18	14.6	Visible	Clipped	No	Grey patina
1091c (A)	31.8	17	14.2	None visible	Over-clipped	No	Grey patina
1091c (B)	22.6	16	20	Visible	Clipped	No	Grey patina
25 (A)	33.8	19	13.4	Visible	Over-clipped	No	Grey patina, subspherical owing to mould
25 (B)	33.7	19	13.4	Visible	Over-clipped	No	Grey patina, subspherical owing to mould
12D0012:01	31	N/A	14.63	None visible	Not visible	Yes	Heavily impacted, impressions of other balls and textile, hail shot
12D0012:02	29	15	15.64	Visible	Not visible	Yes	Heavily impacted, compression to one half of ball
12D0012:03	19	N/A	23.87	Not visible	Not visible	Yes	Heavily impacted, pancaked from high-velocity strike
12D0012:04	31	13 (estimated)	14.63	Not visible	Clipped	Yes	Heavily impacted, compression to one half of ball
12D0012:09	31	13 (estimated)	14.63	Not visible	Clipped	Yes	Heavily impacted, compression to one half of ball
12D0012:10	26	N/A	17.45	Not visible	Not visible	Yes	Heavily impacted, pancaked from high-velocity strike, possible stone fragments survive
12D0012:11	7	8	64.80	Visible	Clipped	Yes	Clear banding around the ball, indicating compression against barrel when fired

more likely to have been intended for a lighter weapon such as a carbine. The smallest example (no. 882) is of a type that could be used as pistol or buckshot. None of the balls produced clear evidence for firing, although the mould sprues had been clipped, suggesting that they had been prepared for use. It seems likely that they were lost or discarded by the defenders prior to the fall of the castle, or by the besiegers following its capitulation.

In addition to the completed bullets, evidence was also revealed during excavation for the on-site production of lead shot in two-piece moulds. This took the form of two casting headers (nos 1100a and 1100b), with the space between the runners being *c.* 5mm (Pl. 6.51). The lead that connects each of the runners is ev-

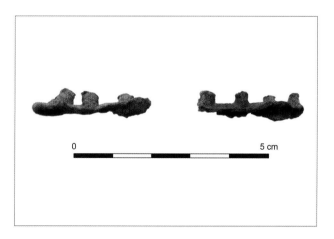

Pl. 6.51—Lead bullet-casting headers (nos 1100a and b).

idence for the run-off channel on the mould; the location of the sprue on a completed ball is indicative of where it connected with these runners prior to clipping. Similar examples of casting headers have been uncovered at a range of defended sites, such as Camber Castle in Rye, East Sussex, where a number of examples similar to the two discovered at Clogh Oughter were excavated (Scott 2001, 200–3).

In contrast to the lead shot from the excavation, the seven bullets recovered from the 2012 underwater investigation have all been fired. They may represent evidence for the lake expedition launched by the Parliamentarians against Clogh Oughter and referred to in the 1 March 1653 report of Colonel Jones. The recovery of two logboats, one of which has been dated to the sixteenth or early seventeenth century (see Appendix 2), presents at least the possibility that these vessels are the 'boates or cottes' referred to by Jones.

Determining the different weapons utilised becomes more difficult when projectiles have been fired, as there is often deformation and a loss of original weight. It can be stated with some confidence, however, that the majority of the examples recovered during the underwater survey were intended for a musket. Of those not clearly of musket bore, no. 12D0012:03 has been so severely deformed from impact that it may well have originally been for a musket; the same is also true of no. 12D0012:10. The exception is no. 12D0012:11, which was fired from a pistol.

The impaction patterns on the underwater assemblage reveal some important information about how these balls were utilised. The most important of the bullets in this regard is no. 12D0012:01. Although this ball was intended for use in a musket, it appears to have been employed as 'hail shot'. The ball carries nine hexagonal impressions, which suggest that it was fired while packed together with a number of other bullets. These were wrapped in a textile container, the impressions of which can clearly be seen on the bullet surface. This bag of bullets would then have been fired from an artillery piece. Identification of firing of this type at Clogh Oughter is extremely important and is, to the author's knowledge, the first instance of the use of hail shot identified archaeologically on the island. It is possible that some of the other bullets in the underwater group were also used as hail shot, such as no. 12D0012:3, although owing to their level of impaction it is not possible to confirm this with certainty.

Of the other bullets, some, such as no. 12D:0012:4, may have been fired as part of a double load, where two bullets were placed in the barrel at once. The majority carry impact scarring, although only nos 12D0012:3 and 12D0012:10 are likely to have hit a surface such as stone; the latter example retains some fragmented stone appended to its surface from the strike. A lead ball striking stone at relatively short range usually displays catastrophic impaction, whereas most of the bullets in the Clogh Oughter underwater assemblage are reminiscent of impact with softer materials, such as wood or earth.

The pistol ball 12D0012:11 displays an interesting feature that demonstrates that it has been used. It carries a distinctive 'band' across its surface, created when the bullet was fired. The ignition of the powder caused the lead bullet to expand and grip the interior of the barrel as it was propelled forward, creating a banding effect that is a tell-tale signature of firing. It is interesting to note that beyond this banding little other deformity is evident on the ball's surface.

The weapon furniture

A number of firearm parts were discovered during excavation. These are all seventeenth-century in date and are presumably the defenders' weapons, which were lost or destroyed during the siege.

Pl. 6.52—Sear from matchlock musket (no. 843a) (Photographic Unit, NMS).

Pl. 6.53—Probable matchlock mechanism (no. 30a) (Photographic Unit, NMS).

Pl. 6.54—Snaphaunce lockplate mechanism (no. 662) (Photographic Unit, NMS).

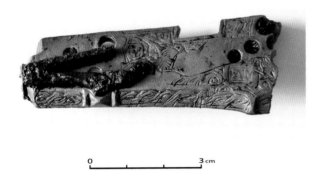

Pl. 6.55—Snaphaunce copper-alloy lockplate fragment with incised decoration (no. 26) (Photographic Unit, NMS).

Pl. 6.56—Detail of snaphaunce lockplate fragment with decoration and initials (no. 26) (Photographic Unit, NMS).

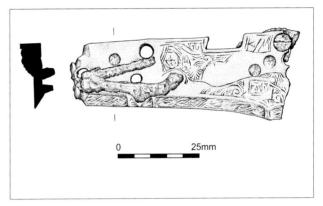

Fig. 6.24—Snaphaunce pistol lockplate with decoration and maker's initials (no. 26).

843a (Pl. 6.52). A piece from a matchlock musket, namely the sear (Cotter 1958, 177; Straube 2006, 55). It measured 160mm in length and 10mm in average diameter. The sear was the trigger portion of the weapon, which when depressed would bring the serpent (carrying the lit match) into contact with the pan and cause the weapon to be discharged. F25.

30a (Pl. 6.53). Three fragments of metal, two of which fitted together during conservation. This object most likely formed part of a matchlock mechanism. The main fragment was 85mm in surviving length and retains a portion of the serpent, which would originally have held the match. One fragment has been bent, suggesting that it was subjected to significant force prior to its deposition, possibly during the siege. F22.

662 (Pl. 6.54). A lockplate from a snaphaunce (Cotter 1958, 177; Straube 2006, 57)—an early form of flintlock mechanism, which would eventually supplant the older matchlock type and was becoming more popular by the

mid-seventeenth century (Peterson 1964, 304–5). It measured 220mm in length before conservation, and has a minimum height of 22mm and maximum height of 42mm, with a thickness of 4mm. F57.

26 (Pl. 6.55; Fig. 6.24). A portion of a snaphaunce lockplate mechanism. Unlike no. 662, it has been broken and only partially survives to a length of 70mm, a maximum height of 25mm and a maximum thickness of 2.5mm. Conservation revealed that the copper-alloy plate had been decorated, with what appear to be the initials 'AM' enclosed within an incised rectangle surrounded by scrollwork (Pl. 6.56). The orientation of the plate suggests that this may form part of a rare left-handed snaphaunce pistol, originally one of a pair (the partner of which would have been designed for the right hand). It is strikingly similar in form to a pair of Scottish brass-stocked snaphaunce pistols dated 1622 by the master 'AG', offered for sale by Peter Finer Antique Arms (Pl. 6.57).[1] Although the decoration on the Clogh Oughter

---

[1] See www.peterfiner.com/current-stock/item/1549/, accessed 28 March 2012. I am grateful to Boyd Rankin of Irish Arms for drawing my attention to this parallel.

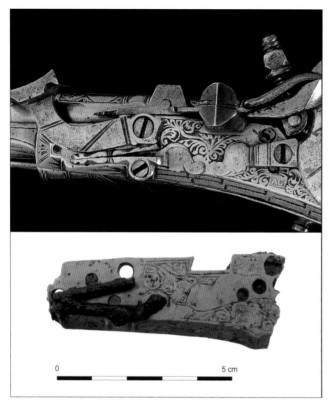

Pl. 6.59—A possible snaphaunce lockplate (no. 663a), badly corroded (Photographic Unit, NMS).

Pl. 6.57—Comparison of Clogh Oughter E409:26 with a Peter Finer 1622 Scottish left-handed snaphaunce pistol.

Pl. 6.60—Part of a sear (no. 663b) (Photographic Unit, NMS).

Pl. 6.58—Part of a cock from a snaphaunce musket with portion of flint intact (no. 217) (Photographic Unit, NMS).

Pl. 6.61—Possible portion of lock mechanism (no. 376) (Photographic Unit, NMS).

example seems somewhat cruder, it is undoubtedly of the same style, and the maker 'AM' may well have operated in Scotland during the same period. F1.

217 (Pl. 6.58). Part of the cock of a snaphaunce musket. It is now in two pieces, with the major portion measuring 57mm in maximum length. This is the part of the gun that held the flint, and following conservation it was discovered that a portion of the original flint survives, corroded in place by the metal surrounding it. When the trigger of the weapon was pulled, the flint hit the steel

of the weapon, creating a spark which ignited the powder in the pan and discharged the weapon. F30.

663a (Pl. 6.59). Found in association with no. 663b. Although heavily corroded, it most likely represents a snaphaunce lockplate, similar to no. 662. It measures 185mm in maximum length and 30mm in maximum height. F57.

663b (Pl. 6.60). Found in association with no. 663a. It is heavily corroded and part of the object appears to

0 ⌞_____⌟ 10 cm

Pl. 6.62—Musket barrel (no. 28) (Photographic Unit, NMS).

have broken off. It is most likely a sear and resembles no. 843a, albeit in much poorer condition. It measures 145mm in maximum surviving length and 15mm in maximum surviving height. F57.

376 (Pl. 6.61). A possible portion of a firearm, which may have formed part of a pivoting section of the mechanism, perhaps the lock. It measures 51mm in length and 10mm in thickness. F31.

28 (Pl. 6.62). A portion of a musket barrel, surviving to a length of 312mm. The barrel is hexagonal in form for 70mm of its length and cylindrical for the remainder. The barrel is some 30mm in maximum diameter, with a wall thickness of 6mm (Pl. 6.63). Although corrosion has reduced the bore of this weapon, it survives to a maximum diameter of 18mm (0.7in.). Allowing for corrosion, this bore is consistent with that of a musket. It is similar to examples that have been excavated in Jamestown, Virginia (Cotter 1958, 177). F1.

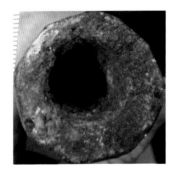

Pl. 6.63—Detail of barrel bore (no. 28), before conservation.

The National Museum of Ireland material

The National Museum of Ireland holds a number of military-related objects that are provenanced to Clogh Oughter. The NMI register entries for the material are as follows:

Register 1865-. Two swivel guns, iron. Presented to Royal Irish Academy by Lord Farnham: R2145/Wk134. 'Gun barrel. Iron.

Pl. 6.64—
Seventeenth-century snaphaunce mechanism from Clogh Oughter, found in the nineteenth century (NMIHA1995:1174).

Much rusted. Length six feet.' Found in 1851. R2146/Wk135. 'Gun barrel. Iron. Much rusted. Length five feet six inches.' Found in 1852.

Wakeman Catalogue (Wk169/HA:1995.1174). Flintlock of a musket, much rusted but fairly perfect. 10". Presented by Lord Farnham in 1887.

Unfortunately, the National Museum was unable to locate the two swivel guns, which prevented their analysis and inclusion in this report. They are reported to be 6ft and 5ft 6in. in length respectively, and were reportedly discovered at Clogh Oughter Castle. If this is the case, they may well represent part of the defenders' wall-mounted armaments, and may have been the largest calibre weapons available to the besieged garrison in 1653.

The musket mechanism, which is also purportedly from Clogh Oughter Castle, was analysed (Pl. 6.64). The object is 254mm in length and is part of a snaphaunce mechanism. It is in good condition, having survived virtually intact. This contrasts with the excavated examples from the site, which were heavily degraded. The mechanism is of seventeenth-century type (Blackmore 1961, 20–1) and may well therefore be associated with the siege of the castle in 1653.

Discussion

The analysis of the military material from Clogh Oughter has provided us with further details regarding the range of weaponry used during the 1653 siege of the castle. The Parliamentarian forces had brought a siege train that consisted of a variety of artillery pieces, most probably including a saker, demi-culverin/small culverin, culverin, demi-cannon and up to three types of small and medium mortars. To combat this, the de-

fenders were armed with small arms such as matchlocks and the more up-to-date snaphaunce, an early form of flintlock. Despite the disparity in firepower, the siege was a protracted one, taking up to two months to prosecute.

It has been shown that the principal concentration of projectiles was on the southern side of the castle, as would be expected from artillery bombarding the position from the mainland to the south. The high degree of fragmentation visible in the projectile assemblage suggests that the artillery was located in relatively close proximity to the castle. Projectiles lose velocity—and, as a result, energy—the further they travel from their source. Fragmentation at this level indicates that the shot was hitting the walls at close to full power. Table 6.4 highlights the 'point-blank' range of some of the artillery that may have been employed by the Parliamentarians at Clogh Oughter, which varies from 360yds to 460yds (329–420m). Figure 6.23 illustrates two potential locations for the Parliamentarian artillery at Clogh Oughter (A and B), both of which are plausible scenarios. Position A places the artillery at a range of 393.7yds (360m) from the castle, within range to inflict significant damage, with projectiles striking the castle at close to full velocity. Position B, however, is perhaps the more likely original location of the Parliamentarian artillery. Placed here, the pieces would have been on commanding ground on the hill at Inishconnell; they would also have been within the optimum range necessary to reduce the castle (at a distance of 388.2yds or 355m). In addition to these factors, 'Cromwell's Road' is ideally located to disgorge artillery atop this hill, while the surviving impact scarring on the castle discussed above suggests that the artillery may have been firing from the south-east, a factor which supports a position in this vicinity.

Given the type of ordnance that we suspect was being employed by the Parliamentarians at Clogh

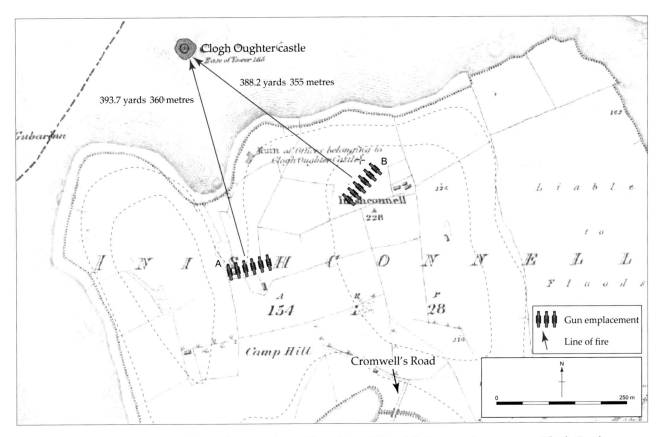

Fig. 6.23—Potential locations of the Parliamentarian artillery (A and B) and their respective ranges to Clogh Oughter Castle superimposed on first-edition OS six-inch map, which also shows Camp Hill and Cromwell's Road.

Oughter, it is also likely that the besieging force would have experienced considerable difficulty in transporting the pieces and manoeuvring them into position. Troops were commonly forced to construct roads through the landscape in order to secure passage for their artillery train. Table 6.8 demonstrates the number of animals required to move this artillery through the landscape.

Given the weight of the pieces and the number of animals needed to haul them, it is plausible that 'Cromwell's Road', although not constructed by Cromwell himself, was originally laid out by Parliamentarian forces seeking to bombard Clogh Oughter.

The two different types of artillery were brought to Clogh Oughter to play different roles. While the solid shot was intended to batter down the walls of the castle, the mortar was a terror weapon, designed to fire explosive bombs over the walls and set fire to wooden structures and supplies. It is likely that the contemporary account's statement that the attackers had 'burnt their corne' with 'sluges' (Gilbert 1879–80, vol. 3, 371) is a reference to the use of mortars to set fire to the defenders' supplies. At this time the majority of mortars were made from cast bronze, and were small, squat artillery weapons operated from a flat bed. They fired at a higher trajectory and a lower velocity than other ordnance.

Table 6.8—Crew and horses required for the range of guns at Clogh Oughter (after Barratt 2000, 58).

Gun	Crew	Horses
Saker	6	24
Demi-culverin	7	36
Culverin	8	50
Demi-cannon	16	60

They were usually employed at an elevation of 45 degrees or more in order to gain the height they needed to pass over defensive walls and onto exposed areas such as wooden roofs (Bull 2008, 12–14). The bomb itself was a hollow metal sphere packed with powder, which was detonated by means of a lit fuse, cut to different lengths depending on when the operator wanted the projectile to detonate. The fuse was a heavy rope or linen tow, which was soaked in alcohol or water mixed with saltpetre (Hutton and Reeves 1998, 205–6). In certain situations different types of incendiary bomb might also be used, particularly when attempting to set fire to a target. The complexity of the mortar usually required its handling by an engineer rather than a gunner (Bull 2008, 12–14).

Although the other artillery pieces present could fire forms of projectile such as grapeshot, it seems likely that they were used exclusively for solid shot at Clogh Oughter. Hutton and Reeves (1998, 205–6) have assessed the effectiveness of each of the four potential solid-shot guns that may have seen action at the castle in 1653. While the saker and demi-culverin could destroy battlements, gates and turrets, and the culverin could crack stonework, none of them could be expected to bring down a serious stone wall. For this the demi-cannon was required. As seen above (Tables 6.4 and 6.8), this weapon was both large and cumbersome. If horses were not available to haul the piece, it would require 30–40 oxen or around 100 men in their place. The demi-cannon and guns of a similar calibre would dominate siege warfare until well into the nineteenth century (*ibid.*, 205). In a siege situation it would be usual for these pieces to be entrenched or protected by earth-filled baskets known as gabions in order to protect them from the defenders' fire. Gunners also often used pre-existing fortifications in the landscape to their advantage, as occurred during the English siege of the Spanish garrison at Kinsale in 1601, when early medieval ringforts were adapted by the attackers (Shiels 2007, 178).

When firing a gun such as a saker or demi-cannon, the gunners would first set the piece in their chosen position. The barrel was then checked to see whether there were any obstructions in it, after which it was sponged out with a staff mounted with wet sheepskin, a process which put out any embers if the gun had just been fired and cleaned the barrel if it had not. Powder was then put down the barrel using a ladle, also attached to a long staff, and this was driven home with a rammer. A wad was added next, followed by the solid shot itself. Aim and elevation were checked, after which the gunner filled the vent in the barrel with powder, which was then ignited using a lit fuse attached to a linstock, thus discharging the weapon (Henry 2005, 24–33).

The seven impacted lead bullets recovered as part of the 2012 underwater investigations to the immediate north of Clogh Oughter Castle are also extremely important for furthering our understanding of events in 1653. The evidence suggests that at some point during the siege a sharp engagement took place between defenders located on the northern side of Clogh Oughter island and besiegers attempting to assault them from the lake. The firing of hail shot suggests an anti-personnel role, and it is possible that a Parliamentarian raiding party was sent across Lough Oughter to detach the defenders' vessels from the garrison, leaving them isolated

and with no means of resupply. The northern end of Clogh Oughter island would have been the logical position for the defenders' boats, as it was the most sheltered from the lough's southern shore, where the enemy artillery had been established. The variety of bullets in this small assemblage also suggests that the defenders vigorously defended themselves against the Parliamentarian attack. It is possible that a number of attempts on the Confederate boats were made before the successful use of the 'firey floate', and we cannot say with absolute certainty that these projectiles directly relate to that specific historically recorded attack. If the material is not from that incident, however, it is certainly from a closely related one during the 1653 siege and adds an important new layer of archaeological information to our knowledge of the castle's final days.

What type of weapons were in the possession of the defenders? Articles of agreement for the surrender of Sir Francis Hamilton's castles in Cavan in June 1642 provide an insight into what might have been available. The defenders on that occasion were allowed to leave with 'the Kings Majesties armes, together with all carrabins, petronels, pistols, horsemens-peeces, bandeliers, swords, rapiers, daggers, horses, with all the horse furniture belonging to them, partisans, holberts, and that the souldiers belonging to Sir Francis Hamilton shall march away with drums beating, colours flying, and bullets in their mouthes' (Gilbert 1879–80, vol. 1, 494). The reference to carrying bullets in their mouths is a notable one, suggesting that the men were ready for combat. In action, soldiers of this period often carried the lead balls in their mouths so that they could spit them into the barrel, saving precious seconds as they sought to reload.

Details of a muster roll of 'undertakers' in Ulster from *c.* 1630 offer further insight into the type of weapons that were generally available at the time. At this date the chief tenants of the county were capable of raising 795 men, with 166 swords, 100 pikes, seventeen muskets, eight calivers, 46 snaphaunces and three halberds available (Gilbert 1879–80, vol. 1, 332). A more detailed breakdown of the arms and material available to Sir James Craig and Sir Francis Hamilton is worthy of closer examination. As discussed above (pp 23–7), both of these men's castles initially held out against the Confederates before being forced to surrender in June 1642. Much of this equipment would then have been used in their cause, and it is not beyond the realms of possibility that some of it was retained in the area for use by the Clogh Oughter garrison.

In total, Sir James Craig could muster from his 2,000 acres 54 men armed with sixteen swords, fifteen pikes, six muskets and one halberd. Sir Francis Hamilton

Table 6.9—Sir James Craig's muster: distribution of arms (after Hunter and Perceval-Maxwell 1977, 212–13).

Weapons	No. of men
Pike only	6
Sword only	0
Musket only	1
Halberd only	1
Sword & pike	10
Sword & musket	6
No arms	30

Table 6.10—Sir Francis Hamilton's muster: distribution of arms (after Hunter and Perceval-Maxwell 1977, 210–12).

Weapons	No. of men
Pike only	3
Sword only	6
Snaphaunce only	2
Halberd only	0
Sword & pike	26
Sword & musket	6
Sword & snaphaunce	7
Sword & caliver	1
No arms	85

from his 3,000 acres had 136 men carrying a total of 46 swords, 29 pikes, nine snaphaunces, six muskets and one caliver (Hunter and Perceval-Maxwell 1977, 206–22). Swords and pikes dominated the weapons available to both Craig and Hamilton. Three types of firearm are recorded, the snaphaunce, musket and caliver.

Pike and sword

The pike was the principal infantry weapon of the mid-seventeenth century. Its optimum use was in a mass formation, which would engage their adversaries in a 'push of pike'. Pikes were generally made of ash with a steel head, and were between 15ft and 18ft in total length. The *Directions for musters* of 1638 recommended that the 'Pikeman must be armed with a Pike seventeen foot long, head and all; (the diameter of the staff to be one inch 3/4, the head to be well steeled, 8 inches long, broad, strong and sword-pointed; the cheeks 2 foot long, well riveted; the butt-end bound with a ring of iron) a Gorget, Back, Breast, Tassets and Head-piece, a good sword of 3 foot long, cutting and stiff-pointed, with Girdle and Hangers' (Roberts 2002b, 22). In reality, few pikemen wore the prescribed armour in the wars of the 1640s, as it restricted manoeuvrability and was an added expense. The length of a pike could be of crucial advantage in a battle, and it has been claimed that one of the reasons for the defeat of Monro's army at the Battle of Benburb in 1646 may be that the Scot's army shortened their pikestaves to reduce weight, thereby placing them at a disadvantage when facing the Irish 'push of pike' (Lenihan 2001, 206). As can be seen from the *Directions for musters*, carrying a pike in combination with a sword was seen as the ideal; the smaller weapon was to be used in close-quarters fighting during the

'push of pike' or when an enemy had managed to get around the pike's reach.

Musket

The musket of the seventeenth century was the matchlock. The matchlock was the first mechanical device developed to fire a weapon (Peterson 1964, 199–200). An arm, called the serpentine, gripped a lit match that was lowered to the pan by pulling the trigger, firing the gun. A matchlock musketeer would carry with him his gun, a pouch with musket-balls, a cleaning kit, matchcord (made of flax or hemp), a flask of fine priming powder for use in the pan and a bandolier of cartridges containing powder for the barrel (Roberts 2002a, 9). This weapon had a number of drawbacks owing to its need for a lit match: it was difficult to operate in wet conditions and gave away the position of its owner in darkness.

Snaphaunce

This was an early form of flintlock, which, instead of relying on a lit match to discharge the weapon, now carried a flint, held in place by a cock. When the trigger was depressed, the cock, carrying the flint, moved forward to strike a piece of steel, creating a spark that ignited the powder in the priming pan. The name derives from the Dutch *schnapp-hahn*, meaning 'pecking cock', a reference to the action of the cock in striking the steel (Peterson 1964, 304–5). Although in modern usage a snaphaunce refers to the form of flintlock in which the steel and pan cover were separate components, in the seventeenth century the term was often used for any form of firearm that discharged using a striking cock (*ibid.*). Many of the troops who carried flintlock types during the Confederate Wars were referred to as 'firelocks'.

Caliver

This was a lighter weapon than the matchlock musket and had become popular among English armies in Ireland during the Nine Years War (1594–1603). What it sacrificed to the matchlock musket in terms of bullet size and range it made up for with its superior manoeuvrability, a result of its lighter weight. It was better suited for warfare in difficult terrain than its heavier counterpart (Peterson 1964, 72–3).

Conclusion

The military assemblage from Clogh Oughter Castle is among the most impressive from any seventeenth-century Irish site. It is all the more important in view of the paucity of available information regarding the conduct of the siege. The evidence suggests that the Parliamentarians employed a wide range of ordnance in their siege train and went to considerable effort to position their pieces and reduce the island fortress. The quantity of surviving projectile fragments is testament to the withering fire to which the defenders were subjected, which would eventually force them to seek terms. Differing calibres of solid shot and mortar bombs descended on the castle and undoubtedly caused considerable damage and destruction. It is unlikely that the defenders had any significant means of responding to this bombardment, although evidence from the 2012 underwater survey suggests that they did use ammunition such as 'hail shot' in anti-personnel roles when the need arose. This small assemblage of fired bullets also indicates that on at least one occasion there was some relatively close-order fighting taking place. For much of the siege, however, they were most probably forced to satisfy themselves with small-arms fire aimed at any of the besiegers who exposed themselves on the lake shore, and it is clear that some of these weapons were damaged or lost during the bombardment.

Skeletal analysis undertaken by Laureen Buckley on the human remains recovered during the excavation at Clogh Oughter suggests that, in addition to the male garrison, women and children may also have been present in 1653. Skeleton C, a male adult, exhibited a perimortem fracture of the right leg and was buried in a formal manner (Buckley, this volume). It is tempting to

consider that this injury may have been caused by collapsing masonry during the course of the siege, and that he represents one of the fallen garrison buried by his comrades while the investment was ongoing.

Taken as a whole, the 1653 Clogh Oughter assemblage provides us with information denied to us in the historical record, enabling us to understand better the conditions and events of the siege. It is undoubtedly one of the most important and complete archaeological records of a siege site ever excavated in Ireland.

TEXTILES
ELIZABETH WINCOTT HECKETT

Four pieces of textile were found at Clogh Oughter, consisting of two similar pieces of gold lace (1120) found together and two similar pieces of silver lace (1119) found together. No other pieces appear to have survived and these pieces may have done so because they were woven from metal thread. They would be described as 'gold lace' and are narrow bands woven from threads consisting of silk cores around which finely beaten metal strips have been twisted. The protection provided by the metal stripping may have contributed to their survival on this dry site, where conditions do not appear to be particularly favourable to the survival of textiles. This report first discusses the pieces and presents some comparanda. Then technical details are catalogued and a glossary of terms is included.

The two pieces of gold lace (1120) consist of a narrow-weave band in a chevron pattern with a wide rib at each side and in the centre (Pl. 6.65; Fig. 6.25). The pieces vary from 26mm to 32mm wide and are 275mm and 190mm long respectively. Both warp and weft systems are metal thread; a further two strands of finer metal thread have been inserted on either side of the wide rib at each edge and of the central rib. The thread used in the main systems, and the finer threads, consist of a twisted silk core covered with metal stripping. The metal covering has deteriorated over some of the band but enough remains to demonstrate the clear gold colour that originally would have made this band an imposing and luxurious decoration.

These pieces were found in a layer (F97) associated with cobbling in front of the Phase 3 entrance and beneath the destruction rubble in Area C.

This Clogh Oughter gold lace is unusual in that both the warp and weft systems are made from the same gold metal thread. Barker (1980, 14) states that in later times the typical way for narrow bands to be woven was

Pl. 6.65—The pieces of gold (no. 1120) and silver (no. 1119) lace (Photographic Unit, NMS).

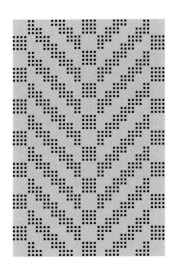

Fig. 6.25—A diagram of the weave of the bands of gold lace (no. 1120).

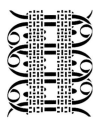

Fig. 6.26—A diagram of the weave of the bands of silver lace (no. 1119).

for the warp system to be of dyed silk or cotton yarn, while the weft (the more noticeable system) would be of metal thread. This type of band is known as orris lace. It would, of course, be more expensive to use metal thread for both systems. This also means that the weave is balanced and regular, since both warp and weft threads are of equal weight and diameter. The weave, however, has been varied in such a way that the eye would have been drawn to the central rib and the two outer edges of the lace. This has been achieved by using four threads for these ribs while the chevron pattern is worked in a 2/2 twill weave. The effect of the ribs is further enhanced by four metal threads that have been interlaced in pairs on either side (Fig. 6.25) so that a

continuous stripe is produced. Best-quality gold filament would have been made from 2% gilt (gold leaf) on 90% silver alloyed with some copper (*ibid.*, 7).

The two pieces of silver lace (1119) consist of a delicate and decorative metal narrow-weave band. Two adjacent narrow-woven bands, 2mm wide, each made of four metal threads, hold in place thicker metal threads which extend outside the bands in convoluted arcs (Pl. 6.65; Fig. 6.26). The lace is quite distorted, so that it is difficult to see the original form. The pieces are 5–8mm wide and 80mm and 48mm long respectively. A useful visual analogy for a modern reader (although the structure is different) might be that of the narrow edgings that nowadays commonly trim lampshades. The width

Pl. 6.67—Portrait of Donagh MacCarthy, Viscount Muskerry (died 1665) (courtesy of the Hunt Museum).

Pl. 6.66—Portrait of Domhnall O'Sullivan Beare (*c.* 1605) (courtesy of St Patrick's College, Maynooth).

of the band is now only 7mm, so the whole piece is on a miniature scale and of a delicate appearance. It may be that this was silver rather than gold lace, since there is none of the appropriate gold colour remaining. If so, the best-quality silver filament would have been 90% silver alloyed with 8% copper (Barker 1980, 7).

These fragments were found in a deposit of loose silty soil (F105) on the floor of the Phase 3 entrance in Area A.

Discussion

There were two major changes that affected the availability of gold and silver threads in Europe by the seventeenth century. In the first, the techniques by which the filaments for gold and silver threads were produced have been clearly described by Barker (1980, 5–7). In the late sixteenth and seventeenth centuries a process of casting and drawing the thread replaced the beating and cutting techniques by which such threads had been made in antiquity and in the early medieval period. The

increased volume made possible by casting and drawing enabled great quantities of thread to be produced, so that decorative laces became widely available and fashionable.

In the second, vast amounts of gold and silver from South America were brought to Spain by its monarchy from the late sixteenth century onwards (Ferguson 2012, 100–1). Spanish courtiers became rich and powerful, and were able to wear many luxurious garments and ornaments. Perhaps the unusually rich gold lace found in Clogh Oughter is linked with Spanish contacts and influence in Ireland. The portrait of the O'Sullivan Beare, apparently painted in 1605 when he was in the service of King Philip of Spain, shows a martial leader with immaculate armour, helmet and plumes, and rapier/sword and baton of office. He is presented as being as sophisticated as any European nobleman. His trunk-hose, seemingly completely decorated with silver lace in a most elegant way, are an important part of the presentation (Pl. 6.66). By the mid-seventeenth century scarves and sashes were popular wear for men, and aristocrats and dignitaries showed their status by having expensive gold and/or silver threads woven into their own, as seen in the portrait of Viscount Muskerry (Pl. 6.67).[2]

[2] For further information on gold and silver lace in Ireland and for an account of these two paintings see Murray 2010, 18–21, 28–31, 60–3.

At the beginning of the seventeenth century there were some examples of gold and silver metal lace decorating high-quality clothes on these islands off the coast of continental Europe. In 1605/1615 in England, Sir Ralph Verney was wearing a gown with gold braid on the sleeves, armholes, front edges, hems and pockets, and in 1618 a gentleman of the Cotton family in Derbyshire owned a doublet also generously decorated with a similar lace (Arnold 1987, 98, 100, 88–9). As noted above, large quantities of gold and silver from their empire in South America were being imported into Europe by Spanish kings, so that these expensive embellishments became more widely available and were much sought after. It seems that individual craftsmen and women in Europe were making such laces and braids for wealthy patrons. Indeed, discarded pieces of metal thread were returned to the gold- and silversmiths and thread-makers to be melted down to be used again. It is likely that some laces would have been imported from Italy, since cities like Florence were centres of luxury cloth-making and decorative trimmings. By the early eighteenth century many of the noble Florentine families decided to have all their craftspeople, who had attended to each household individually, amalgamate into specific streets, such as the Via de' Tessitori, which still exists (Pretsch 1999, 63–4). It may be that in Ireland merchants and possibly even smugglers were successfully bringing these fashionable items ashore to sell to the gentry and aristocracy.

Although the middle years of the century did not reflect a particularly extravagant period in fashion (Dunlevy 1989, 68–9; Boucher 1965, 256), the use of gold and silver lace is evident from portraits of the time. Church vestments, too, were lavishly decorated with luxurious metal laces. Alternatively, the gold and silver laces represented here may have enhanced the sleeves or skirts of a lady or a pampered child of one of the local estates, trimmed a gentleman's doublet or breeches, or decorated a pair of fine leather gloves. Several persons of quality either visited or were held captive in the castle in the 1640/50s. These included Viscount Montgomery of Ards, a captive, Monsignor Dionisio Massari, companion to the papal nuncio, Hugh O'Reilly, archbishop of Armagh, Philip MacHugh O'Reilly and Owen Roe O'Neill (see pp 27–30). Any of these gentlemen might have sported gold lace of this quality.

Two other points should be taken into consideration here, however. The first arises from the SEM analysis, which showed very high concentrations of sodium chloride. This indicates body ether fluids or the decay of bodily tissues over a period of time. In this instance it may well indicate that the laces were worn by one of

the victims of the last attack on the castle. One male body was found quite near to the metal lace pieces, and a further three bodies, two male and one female, were hurriedly buried nearby (see above, pp 96–8). This interpretation is strengthened by the second factor, which is suggested by a comment of Mr A.D. Barker (pers. comm.). From his definitive knowledge of metal laces, he assesses the value of this piece as extraordinarily high; in different circumstances, as much as 97% of gold lace of much lesser value would have been returned to the makers to be melted down and reused when it had become useless. It is therefore very unlikely that a valuable cloth such as this would have been abandoned willingly. More than likely somebody would have retrieved it for his own personal use. The fact that this did not happen would strongly suggest that the gold lace ceased to be used in circumstances that were beyond the control of the wearer. Since the castle was subjected to a severe bombardment before being slighted, and since, moreover, the skeletons of those who died in the attack were found in the excavation, perhaps other defenders of the castle also lost their lives.

Comparanda

We know that some Irish people in the seventeenth century enjoyed wearing European fashionable dress. By the middle years of the century no person of any station in life who aspired to fashionable dress would have appeared without some such trimmings seemingly of 'gold' or 'silver' on their dress. For example, a description of Mrs Power of Credan, Co. Waterford, in the later seventeenth century records that 'her jacket was of the finest broadcloth, trimmed with narrow gold lace, the sleeves of crimson velvet striped with the same; her petticoat of the finest scarlet cloth bordered with two rows of broad gold lace, her coif trimmed with Brussels lace and her kerchief of clear muslin' (Dunlevy 1989, 85; Walker 1788, 73–4).

In connection with the use of gold lace on church vestments, Dr Dunlevy drew the author's attention to the possible seventeenth-century white satin stole, trimmed with gold lace, which is held in the Clonfert Cathedral Museum at Loughrea, Co. Galway. In addition, it would seem that both the back and front of the Clonfert chasuble, held in the same museum, may have high-quality gold lace sewn onto the orphreys (Dunlevy 2011, 24–7).

Another metal-thread band excavated from seventeenth-century levels in Dublin Castle (Wincott Heckett, forthcoming a) is of a much baser quality. This piece of belting has a linen warp and a weft of metal

Pl. 6.68—A highly magnified image of a metal thread in the gold lace (no. 1120).

Pl. 6.69—A highly magnified image of a metal thread in the silver lace (no. 1119).

thread around a linen core which is now bright green in colour, probably owing to the high copper content of the original thread. Copper with small amounts of silver could be made to look like gold. Presumably the Dublin Castle piece cost less and was worn by someone of lower social standing than the bands from Clogh Oughter.

Some pieces of decorative metal lace were found in excavations carried out between 2002 and 2008 on the first floor of the main chamber of Castledonovan, Co. Cork. A farthing coin of Charles I (*c.* 1625–44) provides a likely date. The seven lace pieces had been cut off a garment, since silk thread is still stitched along their edges and there are tiny remains of cloth on their undersides. Three have been carefully folded and stitched, so they would have outlined a panel of the skirt attached to a doublet. Two others, Y-shaped, were made up by one piece stitched at an angle to the other. Frequently such decorations were stitched into place in slanting stripes on a doublet or the bodice of a gown (Wincott Heckett 2012). Part of a garment made of fine-quality but well-worn ribbed twill silk cloth and perhaps part of a doublet was found in a seventeenth-century cesspit in South Main Street, Cork. On this cloth there are slanting lines of silk thread stitching, showing that the garment had been decorated with lace or braid ((Wincott Heckett, forthcoming b). Another find of decorative braids is linked with the journeys of a Spanish Armada ship. In 1588 *La Trinidad Valencera* was wrecked in Glenagivney Bay, Co. Donegal. Valuable silk braids and gold buttons, now on display in the Tower Museum, Derry, are part of officers' dress reclaimed from the wreck (Kelleher 2011, 125–7).

Conservation and analysis

Both pieces were washed in distilled water and a very weak solution of Synperonic NDB detergent, rinsed and straightened. They were then left to dry naturally and without tension, having been supported on frames throughout.

Scanning electron microscopy results for E409:1119 and E409:1120

The textiles were analysed using scanning electron microscopy. In the first instance, high-magnification images were obtained of the metal filaments spun around a silk fibre core (Pls 6.68 and 6.69). Secondly, EDX (energy dispersive X-ray) analysis was undertaken of the samples to determine the chemical elements present in the metal filaments (see also Appendix 3 (Table A3.1) for the results of another XRF analysis of these pieces presented in tabular form).

While the presence of copper in the sample analysis could indicate that it was present in the metal filament, it may also be related to the copper composition in the brass sample-holder.

E409:1119

Heavy element detection (no light, window closed): Very high detection of silver, high detection of chlorine, low detection of sulphur and silicon.

Light element detection (Be window open): Very high detection of silver but slightly less than in heavy-element detection, medium detection of chlorine, low detection of sulphur, very low detection of silicon.

Be window open: silk fibres: High detection of silicon, medium detection of silver, low detection of calcium, carbon and oxygen, very low detection of chlorine, sulphur and aluminium.

Be window closed: High and wide detection of silver and chlorine, high detection of sulphur.

E409:1120

Be window open, one grain 60,000 x: Very high detection of silver and chlorine, low detection of manganese.

Be window closed—area smooth: High detection of silver, low detection of chlorine, very low detection of sulphur and silicon.

Gold was identified in this examination.

Catalogue

Technical details listed in the catalogue are as follows: the warp system is listed before the weft system. The direction of twist and measurements of yarn diameter are given together with the densities of threads per cm and thickness of cloth. Colour gradings according to the Munsell Colour Charts are also listed with the verbal description first and then the gradings for hue, value and chroma.

1120. Narrow woven band of metal threads in two pieces, gilt metal strips wound around silk core, 2/2 twill in chevron pattern with rib at edges and centre of four weft picks; two pairs of finer metal threads outline either side of ribs; silk core yellow and brownish-yellow, 10YR 7/8 and 6/8, tarnished metal very dark gray, 10YR 3/1; (a) 280mm x 28mm, (b) 190mm x 28mm, two selvages; density of threads per cm: warp 12, weft 10; loose S-twist on both systems on silk core, very slight S-twist in metal stripping, width of metal strip *c.* 0.6–0.8mm; finer threads, very slight Z-twist, then two-ply S-twist width of metal strip 0.3mm; yarn diameter 0.86–0.75mm, finer threads 0.47–0.43mm; thickness of band 1.8mm. Known as 'Feather' design in the English eighteenth–ninteenth-century trade (A.D. Barker, pers. comm.).

1119. Two pieces of decorative woven band consisting of two bands of metal threads holding thicker metal-bound weft picks in place; light yellowish-brown 10YR 6/4, dark gray 10YR 4/1, yellowish-brown 10YR 5/4; 80mm x 7mm, 40mm x 7mm; two selvages; four warp threads in 2mm in two bands; warp/weft silk core loose S-twist, metal strips loose S-twist; width of metal strip round warp thread 0.33mm; warp silk core 0.45mm in diameter, with metal 0.55mm; weft metal strip width 0.6mm, weft core 0.5–0.8mm in diameter, with metal thread diameter *c.* 1mm; thickness of weave 2.42mm. Known as 'gimp' in the English trade. In England out of fashion after about 1650 (A.D. Barker, pers. comm.).

Acknowledgements

The late Dr Mairead Dunlevy, formerly of the National Museum of Ireland, was kind enough to supply the reference to the church vestment in Loughrea. My thanks are due to Mr Derek Barker for his generous help in sharing with me his great knowledge of gold lace and embroidery. The author wishes to acknowledge the support of Prof. G.T. Wrixon, then Director of the National Microelectronics Research Centre, now the Tyndall National Institute, University College Cork, for the use of the Centre's scanning electron microscopy facilities and technicians.

Glossary

BEATING AND CUTTING
: Produces a filament based on a flat section known now as BRIGHT PLATE.

BELTING
: A type of lace where the gold thread makes up the warp as structure with a silk, linen or (in the eighteenth century) cotton weft.

BRAID
: An incorrect name often used for narrow woven trimmings instead of the name 'laces'.

CASTING AND DRAWING
: Produces a round-sectioned filament known now as DULL or ROUGH SECTION, then rolled into flat section—BRIGHT PLATE.

CHASUBLE
: Church vestment worn by celebrant priest at the Christian service of Mass. From *casula* (little house, Latin), indicating a protecting and covering purpose.

CHEVRON TWILL
: Forms of twill where the direction of the diagonal lines is reversed over groups of picks or ends.

DOUBLET
: Close-fitting jacket with or without sleeves. Worn widely in Europe from the fifteenth to the seventeenth century.

END
: An individual warp end.

LACE — Narrow woven trimmings, often incorrectly called 'braids'. Laces made from gold or silver thread forming the weft-faced design on a warp structure of silk yarns are called orris lace.

ORPHERY — Decorative band on chasubles and other clerical vestments.

PICK — A single pass of the tool (shuttle) carrying weft threads through the shed (an opening in the warp).

RIB — A ridge on a cloth formed by the interplay of picks and ends. The rib may be horizontal, longitudinal or oblique.

SEAM — The joined line made by the sewing together of two or more pieces of cloth, or the stitching line of a fold in a single fabric piece, as in a dart.

SELVAGE — The firm vertical edges of a length of woven cloth closed by the weft loops.

SPIN (verb) — To twist together (with a stick or rod known as a spindle) fibres, other than silk filaments, into a continuous thread.

S/S, Z/Z — Terminology to denote both warp and weft having been spun or twisted in the same direction. Cf. S-SPIN and Z-SPIN.

STOLE — Church vestment worn by priests and deacons after their ordination.

S-TWIST or S-SPIN — Definition of twist or spin using the convention of following the direction of the central bar of the letter S, thus denoting an anti-clockwise direction in the yarn.

SYSTEM — Either the warp ends or the weft picks in a weave.

TABBY — A basic plain weave: each pick passes under one warp end, then over one, in the weft system.

TRUNK-HOSE — A type of breeches with decorative panels (panes), 1550–1650.

TWILL — A weave created by the weft system crossing over two or more warp ends, and continuing under one, over one. In the next row the sequence begins one warp end over, thus creating a diagonal pattern in the cloth and under one as above. In 2/2 TWILL the weft picks pass over two warp and then under two.

WARP — The system of threads that runs from top to bottom or from front to back on the loom. The warp ends are the individual warp threads.

WEFT — The system of threads that runs from side to side on the loom. The weft picks are the individual weft threads.

Z-TWIST, Z-SPIN — Definition of twist or spin to denote both warp and weft using the convention of following the direction of the central bar of the letter, thus denoting a clockwise direction in the yarn.

THE POTTERY

ROSANNE MEENAN

The pottery assemblage comprises 461 sherds representing at least 58 vessels, dating mainly from the seventeenth century but with some later pottery from surface and disturbed layers. Some fifteen different wares have been identified and it was not possible to classify six sherds. Each ware is described in turn, followed by a general discussion. The sherds were not abraded, suggesting that they had not been greatly disturbed since they were deposited.

Blackware

Thirty-six sherds of black-glazed ware were recovered from the excavation. There were two base sherds that may have come from flask- or bottle-like vessels. One of them (no. 225/226/306) had a splayed base (Fig. 6.27). There were prominent throwing rings on the interior surface of the base, the centre of which came into a small peak, while the exterior of the base had been trimmed with a blade or knife. The interior was not

Table 6.11—A classification of the pottery recovered. (The MVN is based on the number of rims present unless otherwise stated.)

Ware	Number of sherds	MVN	Vessel form	Date
Blackware	36	3	2 flasks/bottles (identified by base); drinking vessel	17th C
Raeren	3	2	Jug (identified by handle terminals)	17th C
Frechen	35	1	Bottle	17th C
Westerwald	8			17th C
Fulham-type stoneware	3			17th C
North Devon wares	8	2	Milk pans	17th C
Tin-glazed ware	90	6	1 wall tile, 2 drug jars, 1 fluted bowl, 1 porringer, 1 plate	17th C
Glazed red earthenware	136	19	2 milk pans, 1 storage jar, 1 jug	17th C
Medieval Ulster Coarse Pottery	103	20	20 vessels	17th C
Unidentified	6			17th C?
White earthenware	1			
Slipped earthenware	2			17th C
Mineral water bottle	7			19th C?
19th-century stoneware	7	2	Blacking bottle, food jar	19th C
Porcelain	8	1	1 cup	18/19th C
Transfer-printed ware	8	2	2 plates	18/19th C
TOTAL	461	58		

glazed and the exterior glaze was matte brown/purple in colour. Another base (no. 202) derived from a slightly larger vessel with a slightly less splayed base. The interior was unglazed but there were lumps of excess glaze. The exterior featured a matte brown/purple glaze.

There was evidence for two other vessels that may also have been bottles or flasks. One sherd (no. 176/251) had a very highly fired fabric, resembling stoneware, with a mottled brown/black exterior glaze and unglazed interior. There were two scars of a vertical handle springing from the neck of the vessel (Fig. 6.27). Another sherd (no. 752) came from the neck of a globular vessel (Fig. 6.27). The interior of the vessel was unglazed. The exterior had a glossy brown glaze. There

were two scars of a vertical handle springing from just below the neck of the vessel to just above the widest part of the vessel. Two parallel lines were incised on the shoulder of the vessel. There was evidence of a small opening at the top of the vessel with a diameter of approx. 20mm. Another group of sherds (nos 121, 189, 275) came from the same vessel but did not join. While both of these vessels featured handles on their shoulders, there was no evidence to indicate whether they had one or two handles.

The original form of these vessels is not known. The body sherds suggest that they had very narrow openings at the top, with handles springing from below the rim to just above the widest part of the vessel. This

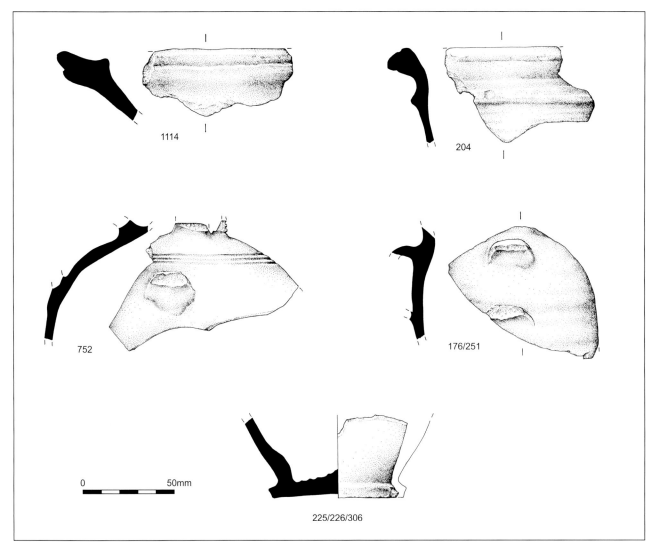

Fig. 6.27—Blackware and glazed red earthenware.

suggests a form such as a bottle or a flask. The *Guide to the classification of medieval ceramic forms* does not illustrate such vessels, pointing out that a bottle would not have handles and that flasks were not designed to stand upright. It is reasonably clear, however, that the Clogh Oughter vessels were designed to hold liquid, although they were not glazed on the interior, possibly as the openings at the neck were too narrow to ensure an even application of glaze. A similar vessel from the Sadler's Teapot Manufactory site, Burslem, Staffordshire, was illustrated by Barker (1986, 66, 75) and captioned as a 'bottle, two-handled'; it was recovered from a dump of pottery sherds, probably used communally by different potters between at least 1660 and 1720 (*ibid.*, 59). Small blackware vessels were, however, in production in England and Wales from the early decades of the seventeenth century (*ibid.*, 58–9).

A plain rim (no. 592) probably derived from a wide-mouthed drinking vessel. This had an all-over dark brown glaze. The remaining sherds, all body sherds, were similar in appearance to the possible bottle/flask sherds and were glazed on the exterior only. The stratified sherds were mostly found in the destruction rubble (F30, F22, F27, F38), while two (nos 445, 822) were found in layers beneath the rubble (F40, F97 respectively).

Raeren

Three sherds of stoneware were identified as Raeren stoneware. These were all body sherds but two (nos 505, 531) of them featured rat-tail handle terminals, indicating that two jugs were present. These sherds did not show evidence for any other decoration on the bodies of the jugs. A jug with similar handle terminals is illustrated by Hurst *et al.* (1986, 205) and dated to *c.* 1600. The third sherd (no. 503), from the shoulder of a panel jug, was decorated with two bands of impressed heart motifs. All three sherds were found in a partly disturbed floor deposit (F57) in Area B.

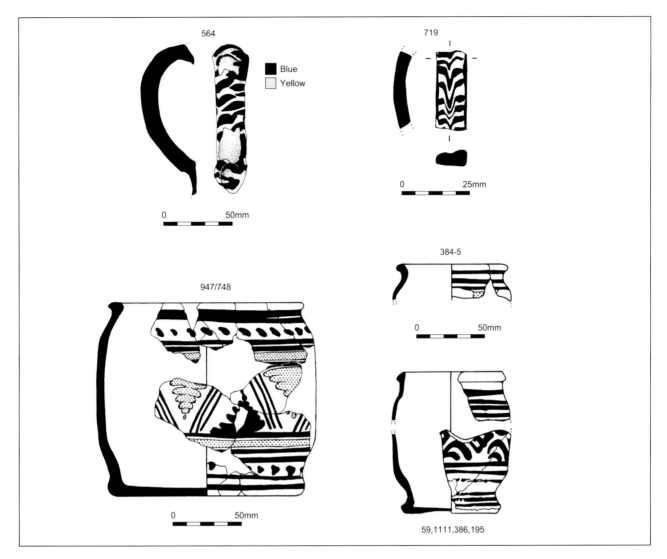

Fig. 6.28—Tin-glazed earthenware jars.

Frechen

Thirty-five sherds of Frechen stoneware were identified, all of them from bottles, with a minimum vessel number of one. Four body sherds were decorated. One medallion (no. 509) formed the lower portion of a *Bartmann* mask featuring a man's beard. The remaining three sherds (nos 444, 504, 510) were decorated with medallions containing rosettes, all of them contained within circular borders. Rosette motifs can be found on Frechen jugs throughout the seventeenth century (Hurst *et al.* 1986, 221). The remaining sherds were undecorated.

Of the stratified sherds, the majority were found in floor layers, some partly disturbed, in Area B (F56, F57, F64), while many were recovered from the destruction rubble (F30) in Area C. Three sherds were found in layers likely to be connected with the building works between 1610 and 1620: no. 711 in a rubble layer (F93) in Area F and nos 1057 and 1059 in a layer (F107) beneath the old surface in Area C.

Westerwald

It was not possible to identify vessel forms positively in this assemblage of eight sherds, although it is possible that they came from chamber-pots. Two of the base sherds showed evidence for wire marks on the exterior. Two of the body sherds were decorated with applied figures of lions, which were then painted over with cobalt. The use of the lion motif was developed in the first half of the seventeenth century and continued through into the middle of the eighteenth century; at first the lion motif was used as a support for a central medallion but then its use became debased (Hurst *et al.* 1986, 183).

Of the three stratified sherds, no. 511 was found in a floor layer (F57) in Area B, while nos 21 and 182 were found in destruction rubble, F27 and F30 respectively.

Fulham-type ware

Three sherds of stoneware with a white fabric and a mottled tiger glaze may have been from vessels made in John Dwight's factory in Fulham in London (Green 1999); these were made in imitation of the Rhenish stoneware vessels and have usually been dated to approximately the 1670s (Jennings 1981, 127).

One sherd, no. 548, was found in a floor layer (F57) in Area B and one, no. 624, in the old surface layer (F40) in Area C.

North Devon wares

The rims of two different milk pans in gravel-tempered fabric were present in the assemblage of eight sherds. They were very similar to each other in that they both had rolled-over rims with two grooves below the rim on the interior. Glaze was brought up to the lower of the two grooves. The body sherds probably came from one or other of those two vessels. One stray find in gravel-tempered fabric may have been part of a roof tile.

The presence of these sherds is a useful confirmation that North Devon wares were imported into Ireland in the first half of the seventeenth century.

The three securely stratified sherds (nos 621, 623 and 626) were found in the old surface (F40) in Area C.

Tin-glazed earthenware

The assemblage comprised 90 sherds, fifteen of which (nos 947, 748 etc.) (Fig. 6.28) formed part of the same drug jar—two sections of the rim, body sherds and a major section of the base. It was decorated with horizontal blue and orange lines, blue dashes and stepped triangular motifs. A second similar vessel comprised six sherds (nos 59, 195, 386, 387, 569, 1111), including a section of the base (Fig. 6.28). There is a pronounced constriction above the base, resulting in a splayed foot. It has a thin white glaze and was decorated with horizontal blue lines above the base, then a zone of blue concentric arcs. A third jar was represented by rim sherds (nos 384, 385) (Fig. 6.28); this was again decorated with blue lines under the rim. Another jar was distinguished by zones of decoration in blue with stepped triangles in orange.

There were eight other decorated sherds that might have originally formed part of one or more drug jars. Jars such as these were made in the Netherlands and in England at this period and the two areas of production are extremely difficult to distinguish.

The table wares were plain white apart from two handles (nos 564, 719), decorated with blue dashes on

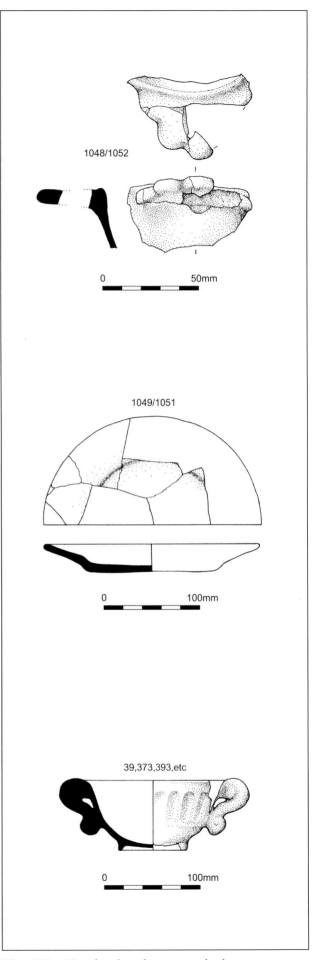

Fig. 6.29—Tin-glazed earthenware and other pottery.

Pl. 6.70—Tin-glazed earthenware wall tile fragments (Photographic Unit, NMS).

white, that were possibly from jugs. There was a group of thirteen sherds (no. 373 etc.) with a plain white glaze. These comprised a wide-mouthed, carinated bowl (Fig. 6.29) on a foot-ring, with a complete profile surviving on one side. The moulded decoration comprises fluting around the bowl above the carination. Both handle terminals are in a scroll shape. A handle/rim sherd (no. 1048/1052) (Fig. 6.29), with scalloping around the edge of the handle, probably came from a porringer.

There are the remains of another bowl or tazza (nos 499, 500, 501, 502); this again has a plain white glaze. The walls of the bowl were fluted, while the base pedestal is very pronounced; the rim of the pedestal shows evidence for wear and tear on its bottom surface. The vessel was made with pink/orange clay.

An undecorated plate was represented by rim and body sherds (nos 1049/1051) (Fig. 6.29).

Remaining small, undiagnostic sherds may have formed parts of other, now unrecognisable, vessels. Chamber-pots were not recognised in the assemblage. Plain white wares formed a very large proportion of total production and they would have been much cheaper to purchase than decorated wares (A. Dawson, pers. comm.).

The tin-glazed earthenwares present at Clogh Oughter were very probably made in England or in the Netherlands, as the earliest known production site in Ireland—Belfast—did not come into operation until the end of the seventeenth century (Francis 2000, 13). Tin-glazed earthenware was being made in Southwark, London, from as early as 1618 and in the Bristol area from the middle of the seventeenth century (Dawson 2010, 10–11); it was in production in Delft from *c.* 1620 (*ibid.*, 9). It is not possible to differentiate between the products of these two areas of production.

Two pieces of a wall tile (nos 588, 716) (Pl. 6.70) were present in the assemblage. The arc of the painted circle within the corner motifs represented a diameter of 120mm; it was 11mm thick. It was painted in blue and white with Wan Li-style motifs in the corners and a barbed border around a central panel, within which all that can be seen is the top of a tower. While one sherd (no. 588) was found in a modern surface layer (F25), the other (no. 716) was from the old surface (F40) beneath the rubble in Area C. Parallels, illustrated by Betts and Weinstein (2010, nos 188–90, 124–6), were Dutch in origin and probably found in London, and can be dated between 1620 and 1660/80.

These sherds were found widely across the site in the destruction rubble (F22, F27, F30), in floor layers in Areas A and B (F31, F57) and in layers beneath the destruction rubble in Area C. The porringer handle sherd (no. 1048/1052) and the plate (no. 1049/1051) were recovered from F107, a layer that may have pre-dated the 1641 occupation.

Glazed red earthenware

One hundred and thirty-six sherds of glazed red earthenware were found on the site. At least two vessels, made in the same fabric, were present; they were identified by the form of their rims. One (no. 204) (Fig. 6.27) was probably a storage jar, identified by a flat everted rim above a constriction. The other vessel (nos 519, 1114) (Fig. 6.27) was a milk pan or settling pan, represented by a flat everted rim with an internal diameter of 260mm.

The body sherds are very similar but it is not clear which of the two vessels they came from—some of them were unglazed on the interior while others were glazed on both surfaces. The glaze was orange-brown in colour; it was thinner in patches, becoming green in places with small black mottled spots. In places, where the glaze was very thin, the surface of the pot was purple. Throwing ridges were prominent. There were different stone inclusions in the fabric but mica was not visible. The fabric was brick red in colour and well fired. These two vessels were very similar in terms of fabric and glaze and may have been produced in the same kiln. Many of the body sherds recovered would have belonged to the vessels discussed above.

A third vessel (nos 703, 826, 84) was represented by a group of sherds sharing a fine orange fabric with an orange/brown glaze. No rim survived. The base was splayed, with a square profile. Throwing rings are visible. The interior was unglazed. The internal diameter of the vessel was 60mm. The vessel may have been a small jug or jar although that identification is not certain, as the interior was unglazed.

Another vessel was present in a different fabric, possibly a milk pan, recognised by a flat everted rim (no. 1113) with an interior diameter of 260mm. This has a finer red fabric, highly fired although partially reduced so that the glaze is green or orange depending on how the underlying fabric was fired. A base sherd (no. 687) in the same fabric may have been part of the same vessel; it had an interior base diameter of 120mm. The presence of milk pans in a situation where dairying was unlikely to have been carried out suggests that the pans may have been used for other purposes, such as food-mixing, washing etc. Milk pans produced in North Devon (see above) were also present in the assemblage.

There were seven sherds of a vessel (nos 16, 21, 190, 389, 571, 803, 1107) in a different glazed earthenware. This was a highly fired reduced ware with no visible inclusions, similar in appearance to North Devon gravel-free wares. The interior was unglazed, apart from splotches of what may have been accidentally applied glaze. The glaze on the exterior was dark brown/black with a greenish tinge in places. There were no sherds to suggest the shape of the rim, but the proportions of the vessel and the shape of the handle suggest that it was a jug. There is glaze on the outer surface of the base along with a stacking mark, indicating that the vessel was stacked on its rim during firing. While the place of the production of any of the glazed red earthenware found at Clogh Oughter is not known, it seems likely that the latter vessel was made in Britain owing to the nature of the fabric, which approaches the hardness of stoneware.

The bulk of the stratified sherds (over 90) came from the destruction rubble (F30, F27, F22), while the remainder came from layers beneath the rubble in Areas A and C. None was found in the floor layers in Area B.

Slipped earthenware

There were two body sherds from the same vessel; they were of red earthenware with the inner surface covered with a white slip, resulting in a pale yellow glaze. They probably represent the remains of a bowl or dish. One sherd, no. 323, was found in a disturbed layer and the other, no. 513, was found in a layer that appears to have been partly contaminated (F57) in Area B.

Medieval Ulster Coarse Pottery

In total, 103 sherds of this ware were recovered from the excavation. Coarse, hand-made cooking pottery from the western part of Ulster was described in the

nineteenth century as 'Crannog Ware', as much of it was found on crannogs there. A similar ware was also being found on excavations in eastern Ulster, where it became known as 'Everted Rim Ware', as it was classified according to its rim form. A new classification, Medieval Ulster Coarse Pottery, has been suggested by McSparron (2011, 101), as it is his opinion that the two types of pottery are too similar to justify two different categories.

McSparron (2011, 114–17) has broken down the group into two types: Type A, which is in general smaller, finer and thinner and dates from the mid-thirteenth century to the late fourteenth century, and Type B, which emerges in the late fourteenth/early fifteenth century. Type B vessels are bigger and thicker and there is a wider range of vessel forms. In addition, there is a wider range of rim styles. The colour of the fabric tends towards a dark grey/black colour, which he interprets as a slightly more sophisticated method of firing in which a conscious effort was made to regulate the supply of oxygen. Type B pottery is found on sites dating from the late fifteenth to the seventeenth century.

No complete vessels or profiles were recovered from the Clogh Oughter excavations but rims of twenty different vessels were present.

Rims

Four of the eight basic rim forms illustrated by McSparron (2011, 107) were present at Clogh Oughter. These were the less elaborate forms—pointed, rolled-over, flattened and rounded. The more elaborate forms, such as hammer-headed and splayed, were not present. Two of the three (nos 853, 1109) with flattened rims featured 'notched' decoration along the top of the rim (Fig. 6.30); the third flattened rim (no. 875) was very regular and squared in profile, suggesting that this vessel may have been finished off on a pottery wheel (McSparron 2011, 111). The remaining rim forms were simple.

Bases

No. 1030 was a base sherd whose upper surface showed a scar where the coil-built vessel wall had come away from the base. There were prominent grass marks on the exterior of this base. The pot wall separating from the base is a common feature of this pottery; Wakeman, when discussing similar pottery from crannogs in County Fermanagh, identified discs of baked clay as lids, but Raghnall Ó Floinn (pers. comm.) has identified them as detached bases. Two other base sherds (nos 898, 1019) showed evidence for having been laid down on grass prior to firing.

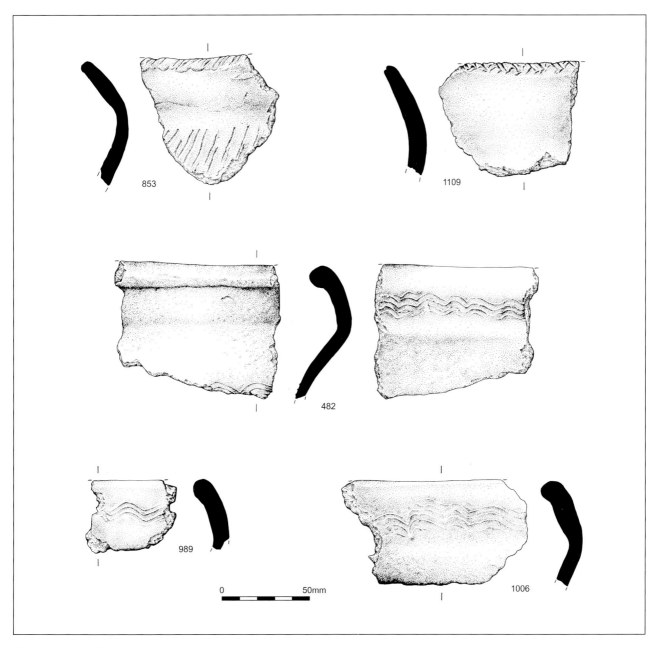

Fig. 6.30—Medieval Ulster Coarse Pottery rims.

Handle

There is no evidence on any of the sherds to suggest that the vessels were handled.

Decoration

Two sherds (nos 1109 and 853) were decorated with notching along the edge of the rim (Fig. 6.30), the latter also featuring diagonal slashing on the exterior shoulder. Three examples (nos 989, 1006, 482) featured combed wavy line decoration below the rim on the interior (Fig. 6.30); a three-toothed tool was used on each example but different pressure was used each time, so that the motif varied from sherd to sherd. No. 482 also featured wavy line decoration on the exterior (Fig. 6.30). Other rim sherds that were decorated on the interior may also

have been decorated on the exterior, but not enough survives of the sherds to exhibit the exterior decoration. Rims 606 and 607 were decorated with diagonal slashes, *c.* 5mm apart, on the interior just below the top.

Vessel type

It was not always possible to reconstruct the original diameters of the Clogh Oughter vessels from the rim sherds, but where it was possible the rim diameters varied from 150mm to 280mm, the measurements being taken at the exterior edge of the rim. McSparron (2011, 119) suggests that the largest vessels that he has examined, with rim diameters of up to 380mm, were not cooking vessels but rather may have been milk pans or used as large bowls. The Clogh Oughter rims, while everted, are not at right angles to the vessel walls, and in this respect they do not resemble milk pans that were in contemporary production in the North Devon wares or the black-glazed wares. In all cases the angles of the Clogh Oughter rims suggest that the vessels were globular rather than having straight, splayed walls, as would have been the case with milk pans.

The Clogh Oughter examples would tend to slot into the larger range of vessels and therefore can be identified as Type B, i.e. the type that McSparron considers can be dated to as late as the seventeenth century.

The vast bulk of the stratified sherds (47 out of 54) were found in F49, a charcoal layer directly in front of the seventeenth-century doorway and likely to have been deposited before 1641, possibly during the building works between 1610 and 1620. Two sherds were found in a post-hole in Area A (F74) connected with the seventeenth-century doorway, three on the old surface in Area C (F40) and only one in the rubble (F30). None was found in floor layers within the tower. This would strongly suggest that this pottery had gone out of use to a large degree on this site by the 1640s.

Unidentified

There was a very small quantity of very crude unglazed earthenware, which appears to have been used for cooking. Though this unidentified pottery looks as if it could be prehistoric, all of the pieces were found in rubble layers in Area A (F22, F27, F38), suggesting that it was in use within the castle before its destruction.

Stoneware (mineral water bottles)

Seven sherds were recovered, all of them possibly from the same mineral water bottle.

Production of mineral water bottles commenced in the Westerwald area of the German Rhineland from the middle or end of the seventeenth century; the volume of production increased substantially in the eighteenth century. The bottles bear the stamp of the source where they were filled with water (Gaimster 1997, 252). The letters 'INGE' remain from an inscription that was impressed around a roundel on one of the sherds (no. 941). The brown glaze of the Clogh Oughter examples suggests a nineteenth-century date of production (Hurst 1981, 264–5), as does the well-executed inscription.

Two sherds were found in floor layers in Area B (F56, F58) and two in the destruction rubble (F30) in Area C.

Nineteenth-century stoneware

Three vessels were represented in this group of seven sherds: a blacking bottle, a marmalade jar and a food jar. Six sherds were from surface or disturbed layers. One (no. 585), part of a blacking bottle, was found in floor layer F57 in Area B. This layer appears to have been partly contaminated by OPW works or nineteenth-century treasure-hunting or both.

Porcelain

Eight sherds of porcelain were recovered, six of them from the same cup with a floral pattern in dark red, blue and green along the rim. Although there was no evidence for a maker's mark, the vessel can almost certainly be identified as English porcelain and therefore not earlier than the eighteenth century.

These sherds were mainly found in disturbed layers, apart from one sherd, no. 596, from a floor layer (F57) in Area B that appears to have been partly contaminated.

Transfer-printed ware

Eight sherds were present in this assemblage, with a minimum vessel number of two plates. Both plates were decorated in blue, one with a 'cracked ice' pattern and the other with a floral pattern around the rim.

This ware was found in surface and disturbed layers.

Old finds of pottery from Clogh Oughter in the National Museum of Ireland

There are two Frechen bottles in the National Museum that were found on or in the vicinity of Clogh Oughter. One of these (1943:303) was found on the shore of the island and was presented to the National Museum in 1943 by George Poyntz. It stands 275mm high, with a basal diameter of 90mm and a mid-girth diameter of 190mm; a large portion of the body is missing. There is a bearded face-mask on the neck; the mouth and moustache area of the mask is very stylised and has been painted over with cobalt. There are two medallions, one under the mask and the other on the surviving side; there may have been a third medallion on the side that is now missing. The medallion is a ten-petalled double rosette enclosed by a ladder pattern.

The other bottle (1968:406) was found at Lough Oughter near Clogh Oughter Castle. It survives to a height of 155mm; its neck and rim are missing. The basal diameter is 60mm and the mid-girth diameter is

125mm (approx.). The beard is the only part of the face-mask that survives. The medallion is placed below the beard. The central oval panel of the medallion contains what looks like an upright trident; there is a saltire on the stem of the trident formed by what look like four nails. There are another two nails at the base of the stem. There are petals outside forming another panel, which in turn is enclosed by a ladder-type pattern.

Both of these vessels show wire marks on the exterior base, confirming their identification as being of Frechen manufacture. Parallels in shape and profile, as illustrated by Hurst *et al.* (1986, 214–21) and by Gaimster (1997, 212–23), suggest a date in the first half of the seventeenth century for both of these bottles.

Discussion

McSparron (2011, 102) indicates the presence of Medieval Ulster Coarse Pottery in south Ulster, showing examples in counties Monaghan, Cavan and Louth, along with a single example in north Meath; these are the most southerly occurrences of the ware. There is a concentration of find-spots of the ware in County Fermanagh along the Erne waterway. The presence of the Clogh Oughter sherds adds to the general distribution of the ware in south Ulster.

Dating

The occurrence of Type B Medieval Ulster Coarse Pottery at Clogh Oughter in the early seventeenth century confirms McSparron's conclusion that larger vessel forms belong to the later end of the spectrum (2011, 118). His figures 2 (103) and 12 (119) both indicate that the later, Type B pottery has been found in the south and west of Ulster, while the Type A is concentrated further to the north and east, although this dichotomy may be a result of the difficulty of dating later medieval sites in the north and east.

Much of the literature on Medieval Ulster Coarse Pottery deals with the date of its emergence. There is a smaller amount of discussion concerning the latest phases of its use and its disappearance. O'Sullivan (2001, 410–11) has studied the late medieval habitation of crannogs and describes the evidence for seventeenth-century occupation in which Medieval Ulster Coarse Pottery was present. Oliver Davies (1942) examined a series of crannogs in south Ulster. Pottery which he termed 'crannog ware' was found on several of them and in some cases it was found with glazed wares, for example at Farnham Lough, Corraneary and Aghavoher, all in County Cavan. The exact identification of the glazed wares was not offered, however, so a more exact

date range cannot be suggested, although Davies did state that some of these finds were seventeenth-century in date.

Medieval Ulster Coarse Pottery, associated with North Devon wares, was found on an early seventeenth-century Plantation site at Movanagher, Co. Derry. The excavator was of the opinion that although the settlers were English they were prepared to adopt Irish ceramic types (Horning 2001, 388). It is clear, therefore, that this coarse pottery was in use in seventeenth-century Ulster alongside fine imported wares. As the assemblages from County Cavan are still too small, there is not yet enough information to enable us to distinguish particular attributes and trends there.

Medieval Ulster Coarse Pottery and other wares on Clogh Oughter

Medieval Ulster Coarse Pottery has been shown to be present on Clogh Oughter island in the first decades of the seventeenth century, and was probably used by those engaged in carrying out the building works. This pottery was usually made locally, using locally available clays, possibly by itinerant potters (McSparron 2011, 112–13). It had become much less prevalent by the period of occupation between 1641 and 1653, but it is not clear why. It is possible that it was no longer in production in this area. It is possible that the occupiers of the castle chose not to use it, as other wares and/or other vessel types were available with which, culturally, they were more familiar or which they found more practical in garrison/prison circumstances.

The castle was occupied between 1641 and 1653. It was used as a gaol during some of those years to detain prominent persons who opposed the rebellion. When Bishop Bedell was imprisoned there between December 1641 and January 1642, he and his sons had to cook for themselves. They were provided with bread and flesh and got a pot for boiling and roasted or 'broiled' on coals. This suggests that the prison guards had access to cooking vessels such as the metal cooking pots that were found during the excavation.

The tin-glazed earthenwares and stoneware that were found were in common circulation at the time of the island's occupation. At this stage we cannot determine who owned the tin-glazed earthenwares and the stonewares. Unlike the cooking vessels, they had been imported into Ireland. We cannot know whether they were brought onto the island by captor or by captive. They may have been bought in nearby Belturbet or Cavan town. The ointment jars and their contents may have been brought onto the island for use by either captives or captors.

Conclusion

There are two groups of pottery that are dated stratigraphically to the works on the island in 1610–20. The first group comprises three sherds of Rhenish stoneware, identified as coming from Frechen, where pottery started to be produced in the mid-sixteenth century (Hurst *et al.* 1986, 214). The second group is the assemblage of Medieval Ulster Coarse Pottery, the bulk of which was recovered from the layers associated with the 1610–20 works.

A small group of plain white tin-glazed earthenware was found in a layer possibly pre-dating the main 1641 occupation (F107), but the pottery has hitherto usually been dated to the mid-seventeenth century.

The remainder of the assemblage that was recovered from the excavation can be broken down roughly into two chronological groups, based on stylistic considerations.

Seventeenth-century pottery

This group can be dated to the seventeenth century, mainly to the first half of that century. It can be safely associated with the occupation of the castle in the middle of the seventeenth century.

The assemblage contained two pottery types that are more commonly dated to the second half of the seventeenth century, i.e. North Devon ware and Fulham-type stoneware. North Devon ware was certainly imported into Ireland from the beginning of the seventeenth century (Grant 2005, 139) and therefore it is probable that the examples at Clogh Oughter do actually date from the mid-seventeenth century. The presence of the Fulham-type stoneware is more problematic, as it has heretofore been dated no earlier than the 1670s or 1680s.

Eighteenth- and nineteenth-century pottery

The second group comprises later wares, some of which date from as late as the nineteenth century. It is likely that this pottery was brought onto the island by visitors and tourists who would probably have brought picnics with them, as in William Ashford's painting (Frontispiece).

ROOF TILES
JOANNA WREN

Introduction

This assemblage comprised 413 sherds, all from peg tiles. A minimum number of 36 tiles is represented, judging from the number of sherds showing evidence for one or two holes. These tiles were similar in shape and fabric and they probably represent the remains of a single collapsed roof.

Methodology

The tile fabric was numbered Clogh Oughter Tile One (CLT1) and on visual examination it was identified as rough hard earthenware, which fired to brick red with an occasional dark grey core and voids where organic matter had burnt out during firing. Thin-section analysis of one of the sherds (see below) identified significant quantities of quartz, with smaller amounts of chert, sandstone, siltstone and feldspar, and indicated that the clay was probably sourced locally.

The tiles were grouped according to context and their deposition pattern was analysed, based on the percentages found in each phase. Dating was based on a combination of typology, contextual information and comparative material from other sites.

The tiles

Peg tiles were a clay imitation of the flatter forms of roofing, like slate or wooden shingles, which replaced curved tiles during the thirteenth century. They functioned better on the steep roofs required by our wet climate. The tiles consisted of flat, rectangular slabs of clay with peg/nail holes and/or clay nibs along their upper edges. The tiles were attached to the laths on the roof in horizontal rows, using pegs or clay nibs, and each row overlapped the one below it. The exposed lower sections were often protected with a glaze; however, there was no evidence that any of the Clogh Oughter tiles were glazed.

There were also no nibs on the Clogh Oughter tiles and they were probably attached to the roof using nails, as indicated by the size of the holes along their upper edges. The remains of nail holes survived on 36 sherds (Fig. 6.31). On one of the sherds (no. 194), however, the hole was incomplete and did not penetrate the tile. This apparent inconsistency may be explained by the fact that peg tiles were often further secured to the roof by *back*

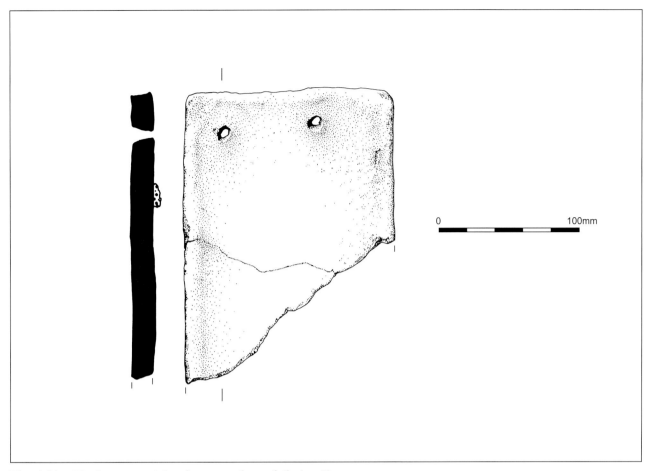

Fig. 6.31—The largest surviving fragment of a roof tile (no. 2).

pointing with mortar or plaster, from inside the building (Moorhouse 1988, 36).

The tiles came from contexts dating from the early seventeenth century onwards. The earliest deposits were two sherds (1%) from layers that may be associated with the adaptations to the castle carried out between 1610 and 1620 (Phase 3). The first of these (no. 212) came from a basal sand (F43) deposited against the ruins (F33) of structures on the northern side of the tower, and the second (no. 1060) was found in a black loam (F107) outside the tower to the south. The latter layer (F107) also contained a silver penny of James I (1603–25).

A further 17% of the sherds were deposited in contexts that ranged in date from 1620 to 1653. These included fifteen sherds (4%) from layers deposited between 1641 and 1653, when the island was used as a prison by the rebel forces. After the siege in 1653, the castle was slighted by the Cromwellian forces, resulting in the collapse of considerable amounts of tile, and 28% of the sherds came from contexts of this date (see pp 83–4 and 89). The other 54% of the sherds were found in later post-medieval deposits or amongst unstratified material.

The most complete tile, E409:2 (Fig. 6.31), has its two nail holes and its full original width of 145–8mm.

With its lower end missing, its present length is 195mm. The nail holes are 10mm in diameter on one side but only 5–7mm in diameter on the other, indicating that they were probably intended for nails rather than wooden pegs, while the remains of plaster on many of the fragments suggest that this may have been the main method of securing them on the roof.

Discussion

The most interesting feature of this assemblage is the fact that it consists entirely of peg tiles of one fabric, which appear to represent the remains of a single collapsed roof. The deposition pattern of the tile sherds allows us to infer certain facts about the history of this roof. Some 32% of the tiles were deposited in contexts dating from the first half of the seventeenth century and they were probably used to roof the castle sometime during this period.

In 1607 Lord Deputy Chichester described Clogh Oughter as 'an old castle without a roof', and in 1608 there were records of money spent on repairs, totalling £10 Irish. More extensive refurbishments, costing £200, were carried out between 1610 and 1620, when the castle was adapted as a prison for priests (see p. 18). Work on the castle in this period probably included the erection of a new roof, possibly with the peg tiles found in this assemblage.

While the tiles cannot be definitively linked to these renovation works, a number of factors could imply that they date from this phase of activity at the castle. Precise dating for roof tiles, on a purely contextual basis, can be problematic, as they can stay on a roof for over 150 years and they are often reused on later buildings (Harvey 1972, 23). At a number of sites, however, the writer has observed a pattern (Wren 1987, 44) whereby a few initial waste sherds are deposited when a roof is first tiled. The majority of sherds are then found in bulk deposits sometime later, when the buildings are re-roofed or demolished.

The two sherds (nos 212, 1060) from Phase 3 (1610–20) may represent the remains of accidental waste, deposited during the roofing process. The theory that the roof was erected in this phase is reinforced by the fact that broken tile sherds were also found reused during later refurbishments in Phase 4 (1641–53), when the tower was under the control of the insurgent Gaelic forces. The reused sherds probably represent accidental damage to the roof, at a time when it was beginning to decay.

The castle was empty during the period leading up to the rebellion; it is described at this time as 'worn all away to the bare stone walls' and 'having neither door nor window of glass' and floorboards 'rotten and broken with rain' (see p. 24). If the peg-tiled roof was equally dilapidated by this stage, it had probably been in place for some time, perhaps since the renovations of 1610–20.

The roof appears to have finally collapsed in 1653, when the castle was slighted by the Cromwellian forces. This attack focused on the southern side of the tower, in Areas A and C, and 33% of the sherds were recovered from rubble deposits and topsoil in this part of the site. The slighting ensured that the castle could not be reused, and in the late eighteenth century it was depicted as ruinous and overgrown (see pp 33–4). The roof tile sherds recovered from surface and disturbed levels were clearly residual debris from the Cromwellian attack.

In Ireland peg tiles were first produced in the thirteenth century, and in Dublin examples are known from an early thirteenth-century kiln, outside the city wall in Cornmarket (Wren, forthcoming a). As was the case at Clogh Oughter, the Cornmarket tiles had two round peg holes and were probably attached using wooden pegs. Similar tiles from Galway City may have been used

in roofing the thirteenth-century de Burgo castle (Wren 2004, 453).

Also in Galway, the town of Athenry produced a different form of peg tile, without peg holes but with a nib, which was moulded over the top edge of the tile. The Athenry tiles were probably imported from France (Wren, forthcoming b). During the later fourteenth and fifteenth centuries peg tiles combining peg holes and nibs became common; examples are known from a kiln at the abbey of St Thomas the Martyr in Dublin and from Trim Castle in Meath (Wren, forthcoming d; 2011, 382). Peg tiles in a variety of forms continued in use into the post-medieval period.

Peg tiles similar to those from Clogh Oughter, with two holes but in a yellow earthenware fabric, were found in 1980 forming part of an early floor surface at Portumna Castle, Co. Galway (C. Manning, pers. comm.). The castle was built sometime before 1617 (Fenlon 2012, 49). There are records of flat roofing tiles being produced locally for other buildings of the early seventeenth century in counties Cavan, Derry and Fermanagh (Reeves-Smyth 2007, 299).

Some post-medieval peg tiles that were closely comparable to the Clogh Oughter examples were recovered during excavations at Boyle Abbey in nearby County Roscommon (Wren, forthcoming c). The Boyle tiles dated from slightly later, as they appear to have been in use sometime in the later seventeenth or eighteenth century. The tiles from both sites were broadly similar in form nonetheless, and also in the fact that they did not appear to be glazed. This may be due to the fact that firing techniques had improved by this period, resulting in stronger tile fabrics which did not need a protective glaze.

The tiles at Boyle were made in a kiln on the site. Manufacturing on site was a practice often employed by itinerant tile-makers (Eames and Fanning 1988, 12), particularly when they were involved in elaborate building programmes such as that at Boyle. Itinerant craftsmen travelled long distances from one job to another. Jope (1961, 194) records medieval craftsmen in Cornwall travelling up to 40 miles to work on a building project—roughly the distance between Boyle and Clogh Oughter. Although this does not indicate any direct connection between the craftsmen working at these sites, it does imply that the form of peg tile found in each location could derive from a regional industry functioning in the north-west of Ireland in the seventeenth and eighteenth centuries.

Petrology of the roof tiles

RICHARD UNITT

Macroscopic description

The sample roof tile (E409:1a) was a surface find but is similar to all the other roof tiles. In hand specimen the tile contains sporadic large temper fragments up to 4mm (quartz and limestone) and a distinctive area of air cavities towards the centre of the section, suggesting that the clay was folded to form the correct thickness before firing. The remaining temper, seen with the naked eye, comprises mostly quartz up to 1mm in diameter.

Microscopic analysis

A small part of the roof tile was removed and prepared for petrographic analysis. The preparation involved resin impregnation of the tile in a vacuum to create a more stable medium for grinding and polishing. The resin block is attached to a glass slide and then ground down to a thickness of approximately 30μm for viewing under a petrological microscope.

The thin section showed that the temper consists of mainly quartz with lesser amounts of chert, sandstone, siltstone, opaques and heavily altered feldspar. The quartz has numerous fluid inclusion trails and may have been derived from quartz veins. There are also some relatively large fragments of organic matter and rare fragments of calcareous mudstone. The matrix consists of quartz, opaques, organic matter and clay minerals.

The sand and silt-sized particles form a typical assemblage for clays from this region, and the temper could also have been derived from local glacial deposits. Lough Oughter is underlain by Lower Carboniferous limestone, although a small granite body occurs a short distance to the south.

CLAY TOBACCO PIPES

JOSEPH NORTON

The assemblage comprises 59 stems and five bowls and, with one exception (no. 1117), all are early to mid-seventeenth-century in date. Three of the bowls are complete, one is incomplete and one is fragmentary. Two are flat-heeled, two are spurred, and the fragmentary bowl was also possibly spurred.

739. A flat-heeled bowl (Pl. 6.71). It has a barely legible stamp, which appears to be 'AL' in a circular serrated frame (Pl. 6.72), and seems to be a Chester pipe, based on bowl form and stamp. The closest parallel is Bowl form 67:iv (Rutter and Davey 1980, 117, fig. 40), which

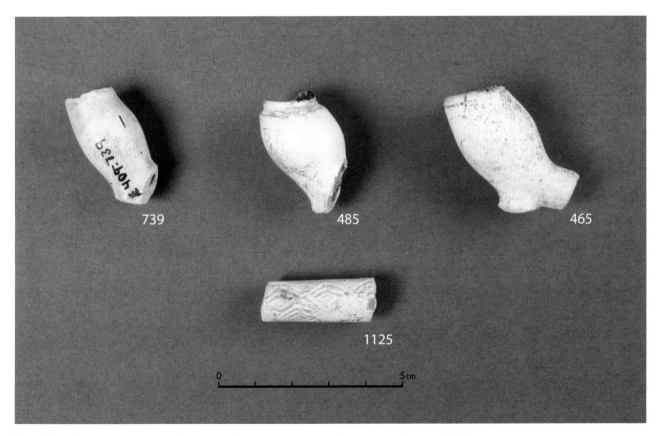

Pl. 6.71—Three clay pipe bowls and part of a decorated stem (Photographic Unit, NMS).

Pl. 6.72—Detail of the stamp ('AL') on the flat heel of pipe bowl no. 739 (Photographic Unit, NMS).

dates from *c.* 1630–60. If this 'AL', attributed to Alexander Lanckton, is correct, then this maker was operating earlier than previously thought, as the Chester maker of that name is first recorded in 1657. Pipes by this maker turn up in Civil War contexts in the northwest of England and the Isle of Man, making a pre-1653 date perfectly acceptable (Peter Davey, pers. comm.). This was found in the destruction rubble (F30) in Area C and therefore has a *terminus ante quem* of 1653.

485. A spurred bowl (Pl. 6.71), very bulbous, with rim milling and a polished glossy finish. The spur is tiny. It dates from *c.* 1630–50. This was probably made in London (Peter Davey, pers. comm.). Found in the old surface layer (F40) beneath the destruction rubble in Area C.

465. A flat-heeled pipe (Pl. 6.71) with a plain bowl and with milling at the rim. It is slightly bulbous in shape with a heart-shaped base. It dates from *c.* 1640–70, but must belong to the early part of this time-span (see below). This is somewhat similar to pipes found in Carrickfergus, which may have been locally made (Peter Davey, pers. comm.). Found in Area C in a clay layer (F48) that underlay the destruction rubble.

1064. A fragmentary bowl, probably dating from *c.* 1630–50. Found in a layer (F107) below the old surface in Area C.

1125. A decorated stem piece, having singly applied repeating patterns of fleurs-de-lys in lozenge-shaped frames (Pl. 6.71). The style is Dutch and the pipe from which it came would date from *c.* 1630–50, fitting into the overall date range of the pipe assemblage. Chance find.

1117. An extremely large, plain, spurred bowl, incomplete, of *c.* 1880–1910. It was obviously lost during this period, probably by a visitor to the island. Surface find.

Conclusion

All the seventeenth-century bowls must pre-date the slighting of the castle in 1653. This small collection of clay tobacco pipes is therefore rare in having so definite a terminal date.

Acknowledgement

I am very grateful to Dr Peter Davey, University of Liverpool, for advice on these pipes.

GLASS

SIOBHÁN SCULLY

Introduction

The assemblage comprises 22 glass fragments and includes bottle glass, fragments of drinking glasses, small sherds of flat glass which probably represent window glass, a possible eyeglass and a lump of glass slag. Most of the fragments date from the use of the castle in the decades up to 1653, while some later pieces were also found in surface or disturbed layers.

Bottle glass

There are six sherds of bottle glass, all probably from wine bottles. One neck sherd (no. 616) is probably from a shaft-and-globe bottle dating from *c.* 1650. A complete base (no. 618) from an 'onion' bottle dates from around the 1680s. There are three body sherds (nos 586, 590, 855) from free blown bottles but they are too fragmentary to be closely dated and can only be given a general date of between the seventeenth and nineteenth centuries. One body sherd (no. 871) is

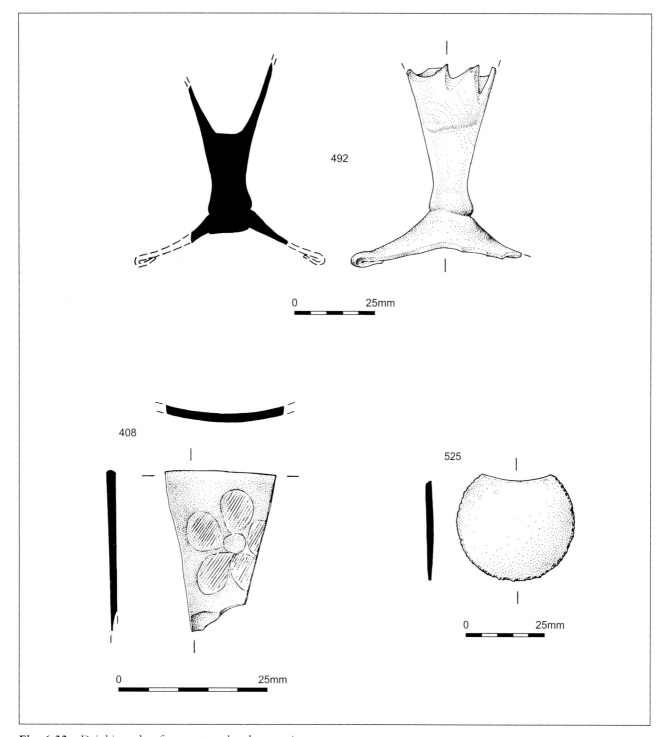

Fig. 6.32—Drinking-glass fragments and a glass eyepiece.

probably from a cylindrical bottle dating from the eighteenth or nineteenth century.

Drinking glasses

Of the five fragments of drinking glasses, two sherds (nos 308, 565) are from the feet of drinking glasses which probably date from the late sixteenth or early seventeenth century. Only small sections of the feet remain, but both have folded edges similar to those found on pedestal beakers of this period (see Willmott 2002, 45–9). One drinking glass (no. 492) has the remains of a folded foot, a short plain stem and the narrow base of a conical bowl (Fig. 6.32). It is similar to eighteenth-century drinking glasses in the collection of the Museum of London (accession numbers A12586, 34.139/328, NN23921). A very small fragment of a rim of a drinking glass (no. 408) has a flower engraved on it (Fig. 6.32). Engraving was done after the vessel had been formed and was cold. The surface was scored with a diamond-tipped instrument. The outline of the motif was executed first and then filled in with hatching (Willmott 2002, 18). This type of scratch engraving was used on Venetian and German drinking glasses during the sixteenth and seventeenth centuries and on seventeenth- and eighteenth-century English glass (Bickerton 2000, 23). There is one very small body sherd (no. 673) of clear glass which may also be from a drinking glass.

Eyepiece

An unusual find from Clogh Oughter is a possible glass eyepiece (no. 525). This disc of clear glass has a crescent-shaped notch, a diameter of 37mm and a thickness of 1.5mm at the outer edges, increasing to 2.2mm at the centre of the lens (Fig. 6.32). While a small number of bone spectacle frames are known from excavations in London and across Britain (Stevenson 1995, 321), no finds of glass from spectacles before the mid-seventeenth century have as yet been identified in Britain (Egan 1998, 277; Stevenson 1995, 324). Glass lenses for spectacles were developed in Italy at the end of the thirteenth century, and spectacles are known in Britain from the early fourteenth century. From the late fourteenth century they were being manufactured in large quantities in Flanders and the Netherlands, and the earliest recorded manufacture of spectacles in London dates from the mid-fifteenth century (Stevenson 1995, 324). Bone spectacles found from excavations in Britain range in date from the fifteenth century to the mid-sixteenth/mid-seventeenth century (*ibid.*, 322). The bone spectacle frames from Swan Stairs, City of London, would have held a lens that had a diameter of 31mm and a thickness of 2mm (*ibid.*), which compares well with the lens from Clogh Oughter.

Flat glass

There are nine sherds of clear flat glass that may possibly be the remains of window glass. The fragments range in thickness from 1.3mm to 2.3mm. Three fragments (nos 512, 539, 1074) have marks that may have been made by window leading and may be seventeenth-century in date (Hume 1969, 233).

Glass slag

A lump of vitrified material (no. 307) may possibly represent glass slag or gall, which may have been produced when the raw ingredients from the manufacture of glass were first heated in the crucible (Tyler and Willmott 2005, 42).

Catalogue

307. Lump of glass slag or gall. Blue in colour, banded with white. Some patina. L 42mm, W 30mm, T 26mm. From rubble in Area A (F27).

308. Fragment of folded foot from drinking glass. Clear glass. Late sixteenth to early seventeenth century. From floor deposit under rubble in Area A (F31).

408. Drinking glass. Small rim fragment from bowl. Engraved flower design. Sixteenth to eighteenth century. From floor deposit under rubble in Area A (F53).

448. Very small fragment of flat glass. Clear glass. Heavy patina. T 2.3mm. From old surface under rubble in Area C (F40).

492. Drinking glass. Foot, stem and base of bowl. Circular foot folded at the edge with an unpolished pontil mark. Short, plain, circular stem with only a slight merese at the junction of foot and stem. Only the narrow base of a conical bowl remains. Eighteenth century. From floor deposit in Area B (F56).

512. Two fragments of flat glass that do not refit. Clear glass. Heavy patina. (a) T 1.6mm. (b) T 1.6mm. From floor deposit in Area B (F57).

525. Eyeglass piece. Clear glass. Notch in edge. Patina. D 37mm, T 1.5–2.2mm. From F62, Area A, disturbed layer with seventeenth-century artefacts and later artefacts.

539. Three fragments of flat glass. Clear glass. (1) T 1.6mm. (2) T 1.3mm. (3) T 1.5mm. From floor deposit in Area B (F57).

565. Fragment of folded foot from drinking glass. Clear glass. Patina. Early sixteenth to late seventeenth century. From floor deposit in Area B (F57).

586. Body sherd of bottle glass. Olive green glass. Heavy patina. Seventeenth to nineteenth century. From old surface below rubble in Area C (F40).

590. Body sherd of bottle glass. Olive green glass. Heavy

patina. Seventeenth to nineteenth century. From topsoil in Area C (F25).

616. Possible neck sherd from shaft-and-globe bottle. Olive green glass. Heavy patina. From *c.* 1650. From topsoil in Area C (F25).

618. Wine bottle. Base. Wide base with glass-tipped pontil. Olive green glass. Heavy patina. 'Onion' bottle, *c.* 1680s. From F62, Area A, disturbed layer with seventeenth-century artefacts and later artefacts.

673. Very small fragment, possibly from a drinking glass. Very thin glass. Clear glass. Heavy patina. From floor deposit in Area B (F57).

849. Fragment of flat glass. Clear glass. Patina. T 3mm. From topsoil in Area C (F25).

855. Body sherd of bottle glass. Clear glass. Heavy patina. Seventeenth to nineteenth century. From rubble in Area C (F30).

871. Body sherd of bottle glass. Light olive green glass. Heavy patina. Eighteenth to nineteenth century. From topsoil in Area C (F25).

1074. Fragment of flat glass. Clear glass. Patina. T 1.7mm. From below rubble in Area C (F104).

1085. Fragment of flat glass. Clear glass. Patina. T 2mm. From below rubble in Area C (F104).

Internet references

Museum of London, The Ceramics and Glass Collection (on-line). Available at http://www.museumoflondon.org.uk/ceramics/ (accessed 13/06/2011).

Drinking glasses
Accession No. A12586:
http://www.museumoflondon.org.uk/ceramics/pages/object.asp?obj_id=465913

Accession No. 34.139/328:
http://www.museumoflondon.org.uk/ceramics/pages/object.asp?obj_id=528962

Accession No. NN23921:
http://www.museumoflondon.org.uk/ceramics/pages/object.asp?obj_id=513409

HUMAN SKELETAL REPORT[3]

LAUREEN BUCKLEY

Introduction

Four burials, three adult males (A, B and C) and an adult female (D), were excavated, and fragmentary remains of at least two other individuals (an adult and a juvenile) were recovered. The four skeletons had been sent for examination to the Department of Anatomy, UCC, many years ago; unfortunately, two of them (A and C) and the skull of B were mislaid there and cannot now be located (C. Manning, pers. comm.). This report is therefore based on photographs of the burials *in situ* and an examination of all the bones of D, as recovered in the excavation, and all the bones of B, apart from the skull, as well as the other fragmentary remains.

Burial types and position

The remains all appeared to be in simple graves. Skeletons B, C and D were lying in a supine extended position, and Skeleton A had been buried in the prone position (Pls 5.21 and 5.27). Apart from Burial A, which had been disturbed prior to excavation, and the lower legs of Skeleton D, which were disturbed by the conservation works team, the graves had been relatively undisturbed.

The arm position varied in each skeleton. Skeleton A was face down with the arms under the body. The upper right arm was drawn across the chest, with the lower arm flexed at 90° and tucked between the upper and lower left arm. The upper left arm was adducted, i.e. drawn away from the body, with the elbow tightly flexed so that the lower arm went under the body. This body did not appear to have been buried with care and may have been flung into the grave.

In Burial B the body was formally laid out, with the arms slightly flexed at the elbow and the hands crossed in the pelvic area (Fig. 5.12; Pls 5.28 and 5.29). It appeared to have been squeezed into a narrow grave-cut, however, forcing the rotation of the right shoulder and upper arm.

---

[3] This report is a summary. The full report, including the skeletal inventory and methods used, is on file in the National Monuments Service, Department of Arts, Heritage and the Gaeltacht.

Burial C was a formal burial, with the arms extended by the sides (Fig. 5.12; Pl. 5.30). Burial D was also a formal burial: the left arm was flexed at the elbow, with the lower arm over the waist, and the right arm was slightly flexed, with the lower arm and hand over the pelvic area (Fig. 5.13; Pl. 5.31).

Preservation and completeness

It is important to comment on the completeness and preservation of the skeletal material recovered, as this could have an impact on the amount of information derived from the analysis.

The two skeletons examined were in an excellent state of preservation and fragmentation of the bone appeared to be low, although some reconstruction had been carried out at some time in the past before they were received for analysis. From the photographic evidence it seems that Skeleton A and Skeleton C were also well preserved.

Skeleton A was less than 50% complete, whilst Skeletons B, C and D appeared to have been nearly 100% complete at the time of excavation. Unfortunately, the skull from Skeleton B was not returned for analysis, and only the back of the skull remained from Skeleton D. The lower legs of Skeleton D had been disturbed prior to archaeological excavation but were recovered.

Population characteristics

Age and sex
Of the four skeletons, three appear to be male and one was female; Skeletons A and C were only examined from photographs, however, so they are only probably male. The female was Skeleton D.

Both Skeletons B and D appeared to be relatively young. Skeleton B was an early middle adult male, 26–35 years old at the time of death, and Skeleton D was a female of similar age, 25–29 years. It was only possible to describe Skeletons A and C as adults since all long-bone epiphyses appeared to be fused.

The mandible of a juvenile aged 6–8 years and a partial maxilla from a young adult were found near the graves as stray finds. Two partial adult long bones were also found.

A group of fourteen skeletons examined from King John's Castle, Limerick, which were dated to the siege of Limerick and hence to a similar period to the group from Clogh Oughter, consisted of the remains of one older male, females and juveniles. In fact, these remains consisted mainly of juveniles and so were probably

natural deaths or deaths due to starvation that occurred during the siege rather than those of soldiers (Buckley 1994).

Four burials recovered from outside the modern walls of the graveyard of Holy Trinity Church, Carlingford, were also thought to date from the seventeenth century. All four burials were male and were young adults or early middle adults, so were similar in age at death to the burials from Clogh Oughter (Buckley and McConway 2004).

Stature
The estimated living stature of the female was 160cm. The estimated statures of the males varied from 163cm to 168cm. It was possible to estimate the stature from bone measurements for Skeleton B only and it was 165cm. The statures for Skeletons A and C were determined from estimations of bone measurements from the plans. This means that they are more inaccurate and in fact, since the sex of these individuals has not been confirmed, may not be correct.

Assuming that the estimated statures are correct, it can be seen from Table 6.12 that the male stature from Clogh Oughter is slightly smaller than is found at other seventeenth-century sites apart from Smithfield in Dublin, where the remains were thought to be those of impoverished criminals who had been executed by hanging. The stature of the female from Clogh Oughter was slightly taller than that of females from most other sites from various periods but was similar to the average stature found at Church Street in Dublin. It must be remembered that the sample size at Clogh Oughter is too small to get a reliable average stature for the population.

Non-metric traits

Non-metric traits or discontinuous morphological traits are normal anatomical features which may be present or absent. There is thought to be a genetic control over their presence, but the extent of this or whether their frequency is affected by environmental factors is not fully understood. They are useful in establishing the 'distance' of one group from another (Brothwell 1981, 90). Skeletal non-metric traits were recorded for the skeletons and these follow the descriptions given by Berry and Berry (1967) and Finnegan (1978).

In the two skeletons examined, Skeleton B had a squatting facet on the right tibia and Skeleton D had bilateral squatting facets on the tibiae as well as a third trochanter on the right femur. The population size is too small to derive any conclusions from the frequency of the traits.

Table 6.12—Comparison of average statures (cm) from various Irish sites.

Site	Period	Males	Females (CM)
Bettystown[1]	1st millennium	170	157
Solar, Co. Antrim[2]	Early medieval	171	157
Dominican priory, Drogheda[3]	13th/14th century	171	155
Francis St., Dublin[4]	13th/15th century	171	158
Smithfield, Dublin[5]	17th century	168	-
Church St., Dublin[6]	17th century	171	162
Carlingford, Co. Louth	17th century	175	-
King John's Castle, Limerick[7]	17th century	-	154
Clogh Oughter Castle	17th century	-	160
St Peter's, Dublin[8]	17th–20th century	171	157
Modern population		174	161

1. Buckley 2001.
2. Buckley 2002.
3. Halpin and Buckley 1995.
4. Buckley 1996.
5. Buckley 2004.
6. Buckley *et al.* 2008.
7. Buckley 1994.
8. Buckley 2008.

Congenital developmental anomalies

A congenital abnormality is any defect that is present at birth or develops shortly afterwards. These abnormalities can be either harmful or benign. In the skeleton they usually take the form of missing or extra bones, unusual fusion or a failure of the ossification process. They occur most frequently in the spine and axial skeleton. In the two skeletons examined there were various anomalies in the spine.

Cranial shift

In Skeleton B the fifth lumbar vertebra was partially sacralised to the sacrum on the left side of the ala only. The posterior articular surfaces were not fused to the sacrum. Since this anomaly has the effect of shifting the lumbro-sacral border upwards it is known as a cranial shift. Since this is a unilateral cranial shift, i.e. it occurred on the left side only, it has more serious implications than a bilateral shift. It causes curvature and rotation of the lumbar spine, leading to a progressive scoliosis and giving rise to symptoms such as low back pain and sciatica (Barnes 1994, 110). It was evident from the photograph and could be deduced from the shape of the sacrum that this individual had developed a scoliosis. Apart from the back pain, scoliosis can also have implications for other organs, such as the lungs, where pressure can form.

Caudal shift

In Skeleton D the first lumbar vertebra had some aspects of a thoracic vertebra. Where variations occur at the borders between adjacent groups of vertebrae such as thoracic and lumbar there is said to be border shifting. In this case the first lumbar vertebra is the transitional vertebra, since it has thoracic characteristics in that there was a facet on the right side for a lumbar rib. Since the border between the thoracic and lumbar areas has now shifted downwards it is known as a caudal shift. Although caudal shifts are common, at the thoraco-lumbar border they are usually bilateral (Barnes 1994, 105), but in this case it was a unilateral shift since there were no changes on the left side. Lumbar ribs are less common than cervical ribs and they occur more often in females than in males (*ibid.*). The presence of lumbar ribs can cause pain and tenderness in the affected area of the back.

This skeleton also had a cleft in the first sacral vertebra. When there is a major delay in the development of the neural arches, the two halves of the arch do not meet together as normal and a cleft remains in the arch. This is sometimes referred to as spina bifida, although it does not arise from the same mechanism as spina bifida occulta. Cleft defects in the first sacral vertebrae are common and are asymptomatic, as the gap is closed with fibrous tissue.

Other anomalies

Another possible congenital anomaly was present in Skeleton D. The left second metatarsal had a deformed appearance in that the distal end was flat instead of rounded. This could be because the distal epiphysis had not developed. A differential diagnosis might be trauma but there was no indication of trauma to the rest of the bone or the phalanges. There was no sign of degenerative disease in the abnormal joint end.

Skeletal pathology

Pathology found on skeletal remains is limited to disease processes that were chronic, i.e. the individual had survived with them for a long time before death. Acute disease can cause rapid death but leave no trace on the skeleton, so the cause of death can rarely be determined unless death was caused by a trauma. Not all diseases leave traces on the skeleton. Therefore study of the pathological conditions found on human remains gives an indication of what was present in the living population but does not give an accurate account of disease prevalence. Further limitations are imposed when the fact that the response of bone is limited is considered. This means that different diseases can leave similar traces on the bone and therefore pathological conditions cannot always be related to a particular disease process.

Since there were only two skeletons available for detailed analysis, the results apply to the individuals and will tell us little about the overall health of the general population at this time.

Infections

Infections can be specific, i.e. the exact cause of the infection can be identified owing to the nature and pattern of bone involvement, or they can be non-specific, meaning that they could have been caused by a number of different organisms. The most common form of non-specific infection seen in archaeological material is periostitis. Periostitis may be caused by an infection in the overlying tissues of the bone or by spread of bacteria from an infection elsewhere in the body. In fact, toxins from the bacteria may spread to neighbouring bone and cause periostitis. Since it takes time for a bone reaction to form, the disease must have been present in the body for at least several weeks before death. Inflammation of the periosteum from infection or trauma causes new bone formation, which is easily identified in dry bone as a layer of grey, porous new bone, referred to as fibre bone on the original bone surface. As the disease becomes more long-standing, the new bone becomes thicker and more sclerotic and may distort the shape of the bone.

This was the case in Skeleton B, where long-standing, probably healed periostitis was present in the left tibia and fibula. The new bone that had formed over the surface of the original bone was thick and mostly striated or sclerotic bone. The effect of the new bone on the mid-shaft of the tibia distorted the shape of the bone so much that it had originally been mistaken for a healed fracture. There was no shortening of the bone, however, as occurs in untreated fractures.

The right tibia and fibula were slightly affected, with some slight new bone formation, but not nearly to the same extent as the left tibia and fibula.

Severe infections of the tibiae and fibulae can be indicative of syphilis infections, but both sides are usually affected equally and there are lesions elsewhere on the skeleton, including the skull. Although the skull was not analysed, the initial UCC report only mentions a few minor osteomas on the skull and does not indicate the presence of cavitations that could be diagnostic of syphilis. It is therefore unlikely that this infection was caused by syphilis.

A common source of infection is a dental abscess, and while there was an apical cist present in the mandible of this skeleton (see below), it does not appear to have been infected or to have developed into an abscess.

Nutritional deficiencies

There was no direct evidence, such as rickets or scurvy, of nutritional deficiency in the skeletons, but there was some indirect evidence in the form of enamel hypoplasia and osteopenia.

Enamel hypoplasia

Enamel hypoplastic defects take the form of lines, grooves or pits in the enamel of teeth crowns. They are thought to occur during development of the tooth, when the enamel production is temporarily halted owing to an acute infection or a period of dietary stress. Therefore they usually occur during early childhood, when most permanent teeth are formed, or during adolescence, when the third molars are formed.

Linear enamel hypoplasia was found in Skeleton B on the incisors, canines and first premolars. The episodes appear to have occurred at 3–6 years of age. Linear enamel hypoplasia was also found in the stray maxilla on the premolar tooth and occurred at 4–5 years of age.

Osteopenia

Osteopenia refers to a general loss of bone quantity without evidence for a specific cause. In archaeological material it is evident as the bone appears lighter than normal. There may be several causes for it, including osteoporosis, cancer and severe malnutrition (Ortner 2003, 410).

Osteopenia appeared to be present in Skeleton B. Since this is a relatively young male, osteoporosis is an unlikely cause. In the absence of other evidence for disease, it is probable that the osteopenia was caused by severe malnutrition, such as might occur during a siege.

Trauma

While there was no definite evidence for trauma in the two skeletons studied, there may have been trauma in Skeleton D and in the other two skeletons (A and C). Skeleton A, probably a male, had been buried hurriedly or disrespectfully in a face-down position. There was very little of the skeleton remaining so there may not have been evidence of trauma. As the skeleton could not be studied, it only remains a hypothesis that he may have been buried quickly after a violent death.

Skeleton C appeared to have a peri-mortem (around the time of death) fracture of the right femur. When a large bone such as a femur breaks, the powerful thigh muscles contract and pull the broken bone, so that it overlaps. Unless medical intervention occurs, the ends of the bone stay overlapped while the callus forms around it. An untreated fracture will result in shortening of the bone, provided that the patient survives. In this case the bone is overlapped but there is no evidence of healing, suggesting that this is a peri-mortem fracture. Fractures of the mid-shaft of the femur are usually caused by a direct blow. In this case the blow could have been from a weapon heavy enough to break the bone. A sharp weapon would also have severed the femoral artery, causing death by haemorrhage within four minutes. Again it is important to study the skeleton itself to find as much information as possible about this injury.

In Skeleton D, only the back of the skull was found in the grave, which had not been previously disturbed (Con Manning, pers. comm.). There were some old fractures in the occipital bone, which may have been peri-mortem. If only the back of the skull was present at the time of burial, these may be secondary fractures associated with the rest of the head being removed by a cannon-ball. While there is no way of proving this hypothesis, the skeletal evidence is not inconsistent with it.

Enthesophytes

Minor trauma to muscles can be evident in skeletal remains. Repeated and forceful use of muscles can leave lesions at the site of the muscle origins or insertions. These take the form either of ossification of the ligament or tendon, known as enthesophytes, or of lytic cortical defects in the bone. Collectively they are known as musculo-skeletal markers of stress and are frequently age-related (Knusel 2000, 387). By identifying the muscles affected, the range of movements or actions associated with this muscle can be determined and possible suggestions for the activities associated with these movements can be postulated. It must be appreciated, however, that many different activities can involve a similar use of muscles.

In Skeleton B, an early middle adult male, the muscles in the upper arms seem to have been well developed, as there were cortical defects in both humeri for the insertions of pectoralis major and latissimus dorsi muscles, with the right arm more developed than the left. These muscles are involved in adduction and medial rotation of the humerus, as well as extension of the humerus from the flexed position. There were also costal defects in the clavicles in the area of the costo-clavicular ligament. These muscles and ligaments could be involved in rotation movements of the arm and in swinging the arms above the head with extension of the elbow, such as the throwing of objects or the repetitive lifting of objects above shoulder height.

Skeleton D, the female, also had cortical defects for the costo-clavicular ligaments on both clavicles, with the right more affected than the left. This suggests that she was also involved in repetitive swinging motions of the arms. In this skeleton the right arm bones were of larger diameter than the left, suggesting that she was right-handed.

In addition, the ligamentum flavum was ossified in the lower thoracic vertebrae of Skeleton D. The ligamentum flavum is a deep ligament of the spine that is attached to laminae of adjacent vertebrae from the axis to the sacrum. It helps to maintain the upright posture and in straightening the vertebral column from the flexed position. Ossification of this ligament is often seen in skeletal remains and seems to be associated with stress on the spine. Skeleton D had slight compression of the sixth and seventh thoracic vertebrae as well as Schmorl's nodes (see below), suggesting that the spine had been subject to severe stress.

Schmorl's nodes

Schmorl's nodes are depressions in the middle of the end-plates of the vertebral column caused by herniations of the disc material. They are often caused by sudden traumatic incidents and chronic heavy stress, and therefore they occur more often in individuals engaged in heavy labour and they accumulate with age. Schmorl's nodes were observed in the vertebrae of Skeleton B in the mid–lower thoracic region. The nodes were very deep in most cases, and in the upper vertebrae the posterior edge of the vertebral bodies had split. This may have impinged on the spinal column, causing severe pain and neurological symptoms such as tingling of the limbs.

Skeleton D, the female, also had Schmorl's nodes but only the two lower thoracic vertebrae were affected.

Dental pathology

With only one partial dentition available for analysis and some teeth found in the disarticulated remains, it was not possible to give a definitive account of the dental pathology from this population.

Skeleton B had a complete mandible and some loose maxillary incisors that were found in the stray bone. Attrition was light, although this may be due to the individual's relatively young age rather than to the constituency of his diet. He also had light to moderate calculus deposits. Calculus deposits are a frequent finding on archaeological remains and they indicate a high level of plaque bacteria in the mouth and poor oral hygiene. There was no dental caries on the teeth of this individual.

The partial maxilla was found as a stray find and again attrition was light and calculus deposits were light. There was also no caries present. An unusual feature of this maxilla was that a deciduous molar tooth had been retained into adulthood.

A mandible from a juvenile aged 6–8 years was also recovered but there were no teeth remaining in the sockets.

Granuloma/cist

Skeleton B had a small cavity at the apices of the roots of the lower incisors. The cavity was approximately 6mm in diameter, suggesting that it may have been a cist.

Dental pulp has no ability to repair itself when damaged, whether by trauma or caries. Any inflammation in the virtually sealed pulp chamber increases the internal pressure, occluding the narrow blood supply in the roots and leading to death (necrosis) of the pulp. The necrotic material breaks down but will not be infected if there is no access for bacteria. The release of the breakdown products elicits an inflammatory response from the soft tissues around the apex of the tooth. This soft tissue lesion, a periapical granuloma, is a sphere of soft tissue surrounding the root apex and it creates a space in the surrounding bone.

Granulomata from different areas may eventually become confluent, forming larger areas. Slow enlargement over years produces a cystic space. A granuloma/cyst is highly likely to become infected, forming an abscess. Without a sinus tracking through the cortical bone indicating an abscess, all that can be said is that the teeth are non-vital (Ogden 2008).

In Skeleton B it appears that granulomata at the base of the central incisors had converged and formed a cist. Cavities more than 3mm in diameter are said to be cists rather than granulomata (*ibid.*). The cavity is smooth and porous but there is no indication of infection or surrounding periostitis, so it is unlikely to have developed into an abscess. The absence of caries in the other teeth of the mandible suggests that trauma may have been the cause of the pulp necrosis. Trauma to anterior teeth can be caused by direct violence.

Summary

The remains found at Clogh Oughter represent six individuals. Four were found in graves and two were represented by stray finds of dental remains. The four burials consisted of three males and one female. As two of the males were not examined, they were not aged beyond the fact that they were adults. The other male was an early middle adult, and the female was also an early middle adult. The male was 163cm in height and the female was 160cm in height. The living stature of the male is slightly lower than expected in comparison with average stature from larger populations of various periods.

There is indirect evidence for violence among the population. Skeleton A seems to have been buried face down, suggesting a hurried burial and raising the possibility that he may have died violently. Skeleton B had a cist in the mandible, indicating that the central incisors were not viable at the time of death, again raising the possibility that the damage to the teeth may have arisen as a result of interpersonal violence. This would not have had a bearing on the death of this individual, however. Skeleton C appears to have had a peri-mortem fracture to the right femur and this could have been responsible for his death. The fracture may have been the result of a blow from a weapon. Only the back of the skull remained from Skeleton D, and the presence of possible peri-mortem secondary fractures is consistent with the top of the head being blown off by a cannon-ball.

The two skeletons examined, the male Skeleton B and the female Skeleton D, had a link in that they both suffered from congenital malformations of the vertebral column. In Skeleton B this had given rise to a scoliosis of the spine, which may eventually have led to damage to internal organs. In Skeleton D the presence of a lumbar rib may have given rise to lower back pain. Variations of the spinal column are common, however, and the link between the two skeletons may not have been familial but rather a feature of the population from which they were derived.

The possibility of severe malnutrition before death was evident in only one skeleton, Skeleton B, who may have had osteopenia. Indirect evidence for either malnutrition or acute infection in early childhood was found in the form of linear enamel hypoplasia on the teeth of Skeleton B and in the stray adult maxilla. Malnutrition can exacerbate the effects of infection and Skeleton B bore evidence of a chronic infection. There was severe periostitis in the left lower leg, although the source of the infection was not located.

Both Skeleton B and Skeleton D appeared to have had strenuous lifestyles, with muscle strain evident in the shoulder and upper arm areas and the presence of Schmorl's nodes indicating that they had lifted heavy weights. Skeleton D also had stress to the spine and slight compression of two vertebrae.

Discussion

Although the remains from Clogh Oughter are few in number and only two of the four could be examined, they are an interesting parallel to the large sample found in Limerick Castle and dating from approximately the same period. The sample from Limerick consisted mainly of juveniles, although an old man and some females were also present. It seems likely that these people died natural deaths during the siege. At Clogh Oughter there were females and juveniles present but there were also three males, with at least one of these being relatively young. This, together with the evidence that one died from a broken femur, possibly as a result of a weapon blow, and that another may have suffered from interpersonal violence at some time during his life, suggests that the males may have been part of the defending garrison of the castle. The female may have been hit by a cannon-ball, which had removed most of the head. One male and one female bore evidence of a hard, strenuous lifestyle, with stress on the spine from

lifting heavy weights and stress on the muscle involved in stretching the arms over the head. It is not possible to say what activity might have caused this damage and it may have been caused by general heavy labour.

A similar small group of burials found at Carlingford and also dating from the seventeenth century were not directly associated with a castle but were definitely involved in defence, as they had all died from sword wounds. The six individuals from Clogh Oughter seem as a group to fall somewhere between the family members of the garrison found in Limerick and the fighting force found at Carlingford. There is evidence that the males were involved in fighting and the female may have been killed by a cannon-ball. Of course, some of the conclusions from Clogh Oughter are conjectural, and it would be of considerable assistance to the interpretation of the site if the remaining skeletons could be located and analysed.

THE FAUNAL REMAINS
MARGARET MCCARTHY

Introduction

The excavations at Clogh Oughter resulted in the recovery of a relatively small sample of animal, bird and fish bone. The majority of these came from general deposits and layers in an open area to the south of the tower (Area C). Lesser quantities of bone were found within the tower (Areas A and B), in an area outside the tower where two burials were found (Area E) and in a small cutting at the modern jetty (Area F). The remains mostly represent the food waste of an Irish garrison who occupied the castle between October 1641 and April 1653 and occasional prisoners held there during that time. Lesser quantities of bone originated from a phase of building works carried out between 1610 and 1620. Animal bones were found scattered in a relatively unspecialised manner on living surfaces within the tower and in external areas around the building. There appears to have been no organised approach to refuse disposal, although it is likely, given the extremely confined living conditions, that most of the food waste generated by the residents of the island was conveniently disposed of in the lake.

A total of 1,025 animal, bird and fish bones were recovered from various features associated with the use of the castle as a garrison and occasional prison in the seventeenth century. The largest and most varied samples came from various layers and deposits within

Table 6.13—Representation of species. ★ S/G = sheep/goat, LM = large mammal, MM = medium mammal.

	Horse	Cattle	S/G★	Pig	Dog	Rat	Red deer	Hare	Bird	Fish	LM★	MM★	TOTAL
Area A													
Floor leveller, F54	-	4	-	1	-	-	-	-	-	-	2	3	10
Post-pit, F78	-	-	-	-	-	-	-	-	10	-	-	-	10
Beam slot, F79	-	2	4	2	-	-	-	-	15	3	10	7	43
Area B													
Mortar surface, F58	-	2	3	-	-	-	-	-	-	-	5	4	14
Burnt clay, F64	-	1	2	-	-	-	-	1	2	-	5	8	19
Layers F56 and F57	1	66	17	15	-	1	-	-	60	3	58	40	261
Area C													
Building layers F107 and F108	-	16	7	3	-	-	-	-	-	-	10	7	43
Mid–17th-century occupation layers	-	100	60	20	1	-	1	-	10	1	129	96	418
Rubble collapse, F30	-	26	12	1	-	-	-	-	7	3	25	15	90
Area E													
Soil with burials, F104	-	42	11	4	-	-	-	-	-	-	37	18	112
Area F													
Dumped building rubble, F93	-	-	-	-	-	-	-	-	1	-	1	3	5
TOTAL	1	259	116	46	1	2	1	1	105	10	282	201	1025

the northern sector of the tower and from an external area to the south. These are dated to the middle of the seventeenth century, when the island was used as a garrison and prison, although, given the casual manner in which refuse was discarded, it was not possible to distinguish between the food waste of the garrison and that of the prisoners. The samples involved are too small to merit detailed analysis and emphasis is therefore placed on the bones themselves as indicators of the food items supplied to the island when it was occupied during the seventeenth century. Remains of the major livestock animals dominate the identified assemblage, although horse, hare, dog, rat, fish and various species of bird are also present. The faunal material is described chronologically below by individual excavated area.

Method of analysis

All material recovered from dated contexts was assessed in this report and the bones were identified using the reference collections housed in the Department of Archaeology, University College Cork. Data were recorded onto a database (MS Excel), which included categories for butchery, ageing and sexing as well as species and element identification. Bones not identified to species were categorised according to the relative size of the animal represented (i.e. large mammal, medium mammal and indeterminate). The material recorded as 'large mammal' in Table 6.13, for instance, is likely to belong to cattle but was too small to eliminate the possibility of horse and red deer, although the remains of these animals were not common in the assemblage. Similarly, specimens that in all probability were sheep but which may also have originated from goat, pig or large dog were recorded as 'medium mammal'. Owing to the anatomical similarities between sheep and goat, bones of this type were assigned to the category 'sheep/goat' unless a definite identification using guidelines from Boessneck 1969 and Prummel and Frisch 1986 was achieved. Ageing data were determined using procedures outlined by Silver (1971) for long bones and by Grant (1975b) for mandibles. The relative proportion of the different species was assessed using the fragments total (NISP) and the minimum number of individuals (MNI) represented.

Area A: southern half of interior of tower

Excavations in the southern half of the tower produced small samples of animal bones associated with the early to mid-seventeenth-century rebuilding and use of the tower. The bones originated from a sandy floor-levelling

deposit (F54) and from a large oval post-pit (F78). Faunal material was also found in a beam slot (F79) in the base of the cross-wall east of the doorway. The bones from F79 are less secure in their dating because material could only have accumulated in the slot, probably from other layers, after the beam had rotted.

Floor-levelling deposit (F54)

This floor deposit produced a total of ten animal bones. Identified remains include two adult cattle teeth and skull fragments, as well as a complete adult male pig maxilla. The remainder of the sample consists of two fragments of a rib from a large mammal, probably cattle, and three rib fragments from a smaller animal, similar in size to sheep/goat or pig. It is interesting that the diagnostic specimens are all from the cranial region of the body, as this suggests that whole animal carcasses were supplied to the individuals carrying out restoration work on the castle in the early seventeenth century.

Post-pit (F78)

This post-hole is associated with an early seventeenth-century phase of building works and the fill produced a total sample of ten bird bones, identified as the remains of two juvenile jackdaws (*Corvus monedula*). Jackdaws are gregarious birds often associated with man and may have nested in the roof of the castle during its occupation.

Beam slot (F79)

Preservation conditions in this feature do not seem to have been ideal, as the faunal sample is dominated by small, indeterminate fragments of large and medium-sized mammals. The identified sample contains the remains of cattle, sheep/goat and pig, along with a few bird and fish bones. The four sheep/goat bones are identified as the mid-shaft portion of a femur, a complete calcaneus and two unfused vertebrae showing traces of axial division. Ageing evidence indicates the presence of two individuals, an adult at least over three and a half years of age at slaughter and a younger individual around two years of age. Cattle and pig are each represented by two bones, vertebrae and upper and lower limb bones from individuals that were under two years of age at slaughter. The small sample of identified bird bones includes the remains of at least three jackdaws (*Corvus monedula*), a crow (*Corvus* sp.) and a lapwing (*Vanellus vanellus*), as well as various bones from domestic fowl and geese. The corvids are assumed to represent natural fatalities, while the lapwing may have been captured and eaten. Three pike bones (*Esox lucius*) were identified and these freshwater fish could easily have been taken from the lake as an additional food source.

Area B: northern half of interior of tower

Stratified faunal material from the northern half of the interior of the tower came from four deposits relating to the use of the island as a garrison and occasional prison between 1641 and 1653. The bones were recovered from a fragmentary mortar floor (F58), two layers (F56 and F57) and a burnt clay deposit (F64) exposed in the centre of the floor. These features together produced a total sample of 294 animal bones, of which 174 (59%) were identified to species level. The usual range of domestic mammals is represented, with cattle being dominant both numerically (69) and in terms of minimum numbers of individuals present (5). In general, the indications are of a high uptake of animals reared specifically for meat provisioning, including a calf less than four months of age. Most cattle were slaughtered at the prime meat-bearing stage (2–3 years), and the range of elements present suggests that complete carcasses were supplied to the island to be stored and dismembered for consumption when required. Butchery is quite common on the bones, with evidence for chop-marks on the upper limbs, division of the pelvis, separation of the shoulder from the main body of the carcass and numerous instances of axial butchery on vertebrae. A few metapodia were also chopped axially, presumably for the extraction of marrow.

Sheep/goat are second in importance numerically (22), and again the presence of almost the complete range of skeletal elements indicates that whole carcasses were supplied to the island. At least three individuals are present and, as with the cattle ageing evidence, indicate that the animals were slaughtered when they had reached their prime for meat production. Butchery evidence includes fine knife marks associated with meat filleting on two scapula fragments, and the proximal portion of a humerus was chopped horizontally during the separation of the scapula from the upper limb.

Pigs are the least frequently occurring of the main livestock animals, with just fifteen bones recovered from layers F56 and F57. At least two adult male individuals are represented. The sample is dominated by teeth, skull and mandible fragments, suggesting that pigs' heads were common food items.

All other mammalian species are very poorly represented. The fused distal portion of a horse metacarpus was recovered from layer F56. Heavy chop-marks indicate that the bone may have been broken for marrow extraction. Horseflesh was not consumed to any great extent, as this is the only equid bone represented in the assemblage. The mid-shaft portion of a hare radius was recovered from F64, and the finding of a rat mandible in F57 provides an insight into the living conditions that prevailed in the castle at this time.

Non-mammalian species include a relatively large number (62) of bird bones, of which just eight are from domestic fowl. The presence of medullary bone, a substance laid down in the internal cavities of the long bones of laying hens, indicates that fowl were kept on the island as suppliers of eggs. The avian assemblage is dominated by the remains of jackdaw (40%), representing at least eight individuals, including two adults. Two larger corvid bones are those of crow (*Corvus* sp.). The remains of two great black-backed gulls (*Larus marinus*) are also present in the assemblage. This species of gull is resident along Ireland's coastline but is usually only seen inland following storms. A few birds breed inland today on freshwater lakes in counties Mayo and Galway and it is likely that some pairs bred in Lough Oughter in the seventeenth century, when the castle was occupied.

Fishing for salmon (*Salmo salar*) and pike (*Esox lucius*) was also undertaken, evidenced by the recovery of two salmon vertebrae (representing a specimen *c.* 75cm in length) and a pike pharyngeal bone.

Area C: area immediately outside wall of tower to south

Excavations in this area immediately outside the southern circuit of the tower produced the largest quantities of animal bones from the site. These are associated with three different phases of activity: a small collection of bone from a layer (F108) possibly associated with an early seventeenth-century building phase, a larger sample from various deposits that accumulated during the occupation of the castle as a garrison and occasional prison in the mid-seventeenth century, and a collection of bones from a layer of rubble (F30) associated with demolition of the tower and the subsequent abandonment of the island. A disturbed upper layer of sand and topsoil (F25) contained 78 animal bones, and while these were given a cursory examination the results are not included in the following description.

Early seventeenth-century building works
A small collection of 43 animal bones was recovered from two deposits (F107 and F108) that accumulated in this area of the site possibly during restoration work on the tower in the early part of the seventeenth century. Cattle (16), sheep/goat (7) and pig (3) are all present, and the bones include a selection of the primary meat-bearing joints and peripheral elements, indicating that complete animal carcasses were transported onto the island for division and consumption. Ageing evidence from the state of fusion of the long bones shows that they represent single individuals that were slaugh-

tered when they had reached their maximum size for meat production, i.e. over two years of age. Butchery marks are quite scarce, but the upper limb bones of cattle have been chopped through the articulations and skull fragments are crudely broken and smashed, perhaps to gain access to the brains. Vertebrae of cattle are split medially, and knife marks are present on a pelvis and scapula where meat had been stripped from the bones. The proximal articular surface of a humerus is severely gnawed, indicating that the workmen may have brought their dogs onto the island during building works, either for companionship or for protection.

Mid-seventeenth-century occupation layers

A total of 418 bones were recovered from various deposits and layers that accumulated around the southern area of the tower during its use as a garrison and occasional prison in the mid-seventeenth century. Of these, 225 (54%) could not be identified to species level. The material is generally poorly preserved, with high values (21%) for loose teeth and eroded and abraded bone consistent with meat waste being left strewn on the surface for some time. Identification of the bones revealed that the main livestock animals form the greater part of the assemblage. The predominant species is cattle, which accounts for 100 specimens and represents at least six individuals. All parts of the skeleton are present, including the main meat-bearing upper elements of the body and the lower extremities such as phalanges and metapodial bones. The available epiphyseal fusion data indicate that most cattle (62%) were slaughtered between two and a half and four years of age, again suggesting that meat provisioning was significant. Two mandibles were sufficiently complete to be aged and the wear stages indicate that both individuals were mature at death, probably more than three years. Cut- and chop-marks occur on several cattle bones, including tibia, femur and transversely on several vertebrae. Many of the skull fragments were split open, presumably during the removal of the brains for consumption, and the majority of the vertebrae are split along the mid-line of the body. A few axially split metapodia indicate that marrow was also consumed.

After cattle, sheep/goat are the next most commonly represented animals, making up 31% of the identifiable material. A minimum of four individuals are present, including three adults and a lamb. Almost all parts of the skeleton were found, although the bones from the primary meat-producing areas of the carcass are more common than peripheral limb and cranial elements. As with cattle, a relatively large number of bones with unfused epiphyses are present and the emphasis

again appears to be on meat production. There is little evidence for butchery on the ovicaprid sample; a few scapula fragments have cut-marks associated with the separation of the shoulder from the limb, two vertebrae are chopped transversely and three upper limb bones have been chopped horizontally through the mid-shaft region of the bone.

Pig remains account for just 11% of the identified livestock assemblage and at least two individuals are represented, based on mandible fragments. All parts of the skeleton are present and the long-bone fusion evidence indicates that animals were mostly slaughtered in their first and second years, at a stage when pigs reach their optimum size for meat production.

The range of other taxa is extremely limited, confined to a red deer humerus from the main layer (F40) and a complete dog bone from a burnt clay layer (F49). The deer bone is chopped through and indicates that venison was occasionally consumed by the occupants of the castle. The dog bone is from an individual similar in size to a modern cocker spaniel. Bird bones are relatively frequent amongst the deposits, and the presence of bones of young chicks indicates that domestic fowl were kept on the island for the provision of meat and eggs. A single dentary of jackdaw is also present. Just one fish bone is present, identified as a pike skull fragment.

Layer of destruction rubble (F30)

A small quantity of 90 bones was recovered from this collapse layer associated with the destruction and abandonment of the castle in and after 1653. Of these, 55% could be identified to species level. The condition of the bone from this deposit is quite poor and many fragments have suffered severe surface abrasion. There is also a high proportion of weathered and gnawed bones, consistent with material lying scattered on floors or on the surface for some time. Identified mammalian remains include cattle, sheep/goat, pig and rat. Cattle are most frequent, in terms of both minimum number of individuals and identified fragments (26). Both prime meatbearing bones and peripheral elements are present, and ageing evidence indicates that the two individuals were between one and two years of age at death. Sheep/goat is represented by twelve elements, and epiphyseal fusion data indicate that the two individuals were slaughtered at over two and a half years of age. There is just one pig bone, the distal unfused portion of a metatarsus. Nonedible mammalian remains include a rat skull.

Seven bird bones were recovered and identified remains include jackdaw, domestic fowl and domestic goose. Three head bones of pike were also found.

Area E: outside wall of tower in soil where two burials were found

A loose brown soil (F104) outside the wall of the tower into which two burials had been inserted produced a relatively large sample of 112 animal bones, of which 51% were identified to taxon. Cattle dominate the identified assemblage, followed by considerably smaller amounts of sheep/goat and pig. At least three cattle are present in the sample, including a calf less than six months old at slaughter. Most parts of the carcasses were found, including the main meat-bearing elements of the body and the lower extremities. Ageing evidence indicates that the two adult individuals were over two and a half years old at slaughter. Butchery marks are frequent and include crude chop-marks on the limb bones as well as medially and transversely chopped vertebrae, all consistent with carcass division.

Sheep/goat and pig are present in almost equal amounts, with the former being marginally more frequent in terms of identified fragments. At least two adult sheep are identified and the sample contains a mixture of meat-bearing and peripheral elements, including upper limb bones, mandible fragments and loose teeth. The four pig bones are all from the peripheral region of the body and belong to a juvenile individual slightly less than a year old.

Area F: small cutting at the modern jetty at north-western edge of island

Excavations in this area of the site produced very few bones, with just five specimens being recovered from a layer of stone (F93) associated with the 1610–20 building works. The only identifiable specimen is a complete tarso-metatarsus of a wild gamebird, woodcock (*Scolopax rusticola*). The remaining specimens represent long-bone fragments from large and medium-sized animals, all probably domestic livestock.

Discussion

The small collection of bones from Clogh Oughter represents the food waste of an Irish garrison and their occasional prisoners who inhabited the castle between 1641 and 1653. The material was scattered in a somewhat unspecialised manner across the internal and external living surfaces of the tower, and it was not possible to distinguish between the food waste of the garrison and that of their prisoners. Some of the food waste is likely to be that of the garrison when under siege in March/April 1653. The prisoners kept in Clogh Oughter were mainly of high status and were apparently relatively well treated in terms of their diet. It is likely that there was little difference in the food that was supplied to these occasional prisoners, who were kept in various upper-floor rooms of the castle, and that of the garrison, who, when guarding the prisoners, were based on the ground floor.

The recovered bones suggest that the diet of the various seventeenth-century occupants of the castle was based mainly on the provision of beef, mutton and pork. The proportion of cattle remained stable throughout all phases of occupation, and beef would seem to have been the meat of choice for supply to the island. Skeletal element analysis interestingly indicated that all parts of the body are present, which suggests that whole carcasses were brought to the island for storage and eventual consumption. All ages of cattle are represented but the epiphyseal fusion data seem to indicate that there was a slight peak at three and a half years of age, corresponding to the optimum slaughter age for animals kept primarily for beef production. The recovery of a calf bone from a deposit outside the tower indicates that veal was also consumed on occasion. The cull patterns for sheep and pigs also indicate slaughter at a stage when the animals had reached their optimum size for meat production.

All other mammalian species are very poorly represented in the assemblage. A horse metacarpus was found in the interior of the tower and chop-marks on the bone suggest that horseflesh was occasionally eaten, possibly under siege conditions. The only wild animals to form part of the collection are red deer and hare, with single finds of each species being found in deposits associated with the mid-seventeenth-century use of the tower. The samples also include the remains of domestic poultry, wild birds and fish, but from the numbers involved it is clear that these food resources were not significant items in the diet. Domestic fowl dominate the domestic assemblage and there are indications that hens were kept on the island as suppliers of fresh eggs. Jackdaws are the most frequent species in the collection and probably nested in the roof of the castle during its occupation. Two species of locally available fish were exploited, i.e. pike and salmon. The introduction of pike into Ireland is generally attributed to monastic communities in the fourteenth century (Went 1957). This freshwater species of fish flourished in our inland lakes and rivers, and Longfield (1929, 49, 52) records that by the sixteenth century there was a vibrant trade in pike to Britain and Europe.

ENVIRONMENTAL REPORT

SUSAN LYONS

Introduction

This report discusses the results of the analysis of charcoal, wood and plant macrofossil remains from soil samples taken during the excavation.

Eight samples from four areas were submitted for analysis:

Area A: rubble layers F27 and F38;

Area B: floor layer F57 and layer of burnt clay F64;

Area C: rubble layer F30 and two samples of burnt layer F49;

Area F: rubble layer F93.

Pl. 6.73—Possible charred food debris.

Methodology

All samples were processed[4] prior to analysis. Three samples (F38, Sample 1; F49, Sample 10; and F57, Sample 8) contained material that was considered suitable for archaeobotanical analysis, while five samples (F27, Sample 14; F30, Sample 15; F49, Sample 12; F64, Sample 13; and F93, Sample 19) contained charcoal and wood.

The first part of this report will focus on the archaeobotanical or plant remains identified, while the second part will discuss the wood and charcoal identification results. They will later form part of an overall interpretation of environmental remains for the site in the concluding remarks.

Plant remains identification

Quantification and identification of plant remains

Sample 1, Sample 8 and Sample 10 were viewed under a low-powered binocular microscope (magnification x0.8 to x5) to determine whether there were any identifiable plant macrofossil remains present. Where preservation allowed, archaeobotanical remains were recovered and identified to species level, where applicable. All ecological remains were quantified numerically or recorded using an abundance key (DAFOR scale[5]) to highlight the concentrations of material identified from each sample: D = dominant, ++++ = abundant, +++ = frequent, ++ = occasional, and + = rare.

Results

The results of the archaeobotanical analysis are presented in Table 6.14.

Sample 1 contained a high volume of uncarbonised elderberry seeds (*Sambucus nigra*). Uncarbonised botanical material from archaeological sites is generally deemed to be associated with anaerobic conditions, where a lack of oxygen slows down the degradation process and allows organic material to survive in a stable environment. Based on the high number of elder seeds present, it is possible that Sample 1 represents the remains of an organic deposit that was sealed under destruction layers at the site.

Sample 8 is identified as the charred remains of possible food debris, in the form of processed foodstuffs. Despite the fragmentation of this material, it measures 8mm in thickness and is noted as having a slightly rounded edge (Pl. 6.73). The fragment is relatively flat and has an open porous structure on the underside. To confirm whether this material is a form of processed food, high-resolution morphological analysis and a series of chemical analyses would need to be undertaken.

Sample 10 appears to be the remains of partially burnt organic material, in the form of perhaps peat or animal dung. The material is of a crumbly nature, with a maximum thickness of 50mm. It has a densely packed composition, with fragments of plant fibres compressed into its structure (Pl. 6.74). These plant remains are similar to reeds, grasses or monocotyledon species.

---

[4] Soil samples were processed according to the standards and guidelines outlined by the Institute of Archaeologists of Ireland (2007) and Pearsall 2000.

[5] The DAFOR scale is a useful tool to visually assess the abundance of any species on a semi-quantitative level (Sutherland 1996).

Table 6.14—Composition of plant remains from Clogh Oughter Castle.

Area	Feature no.	Sample no.	Sample volume (g)	Feature description	Uncharred plant remains	Charred food debris	Comments
A	38	01	33.7	Destruction layer	++++		High volume of elder seeds (*Sambucus nigra*)
B	57	08	1980.7	Possible dried peat/dung	++++		Compressed remains of grass/reed-type plant remains and fibres
C	49	10	3.2	Burnt clay deposit		+	Possible remains of processed food

Table 6.15—Charcoal and wood identifications from Clogh Oughter Castle.

Area	Feature no.	Sample. no.	Wood identifications	Carbonised	Uncarbonised	No. of fragments	Weight (g)	No. of growth rings	Comments
A	27	14	*Quercus* sp. (oak)		⋆	1	3.2	4	
B	64	13	*Corylus avellana* (hazel)	⋆		17	4.3	5–6	Small roundwoods (x4)
			Salix sp. (willow)	⋆		1	1.2	6	
C	30	15	*Fraxinus excelsior* (ash)	⋆		19	2.3	3–11	Small roundwoods
	49	12	*Corylus avellana* (hazel)	⋆		19	3.1	4–6	Small roundwoods (x4)
F	93	19	*Corylus avellana* (hazel)	⋆		1	0.6	5	Small roundwood

Charcoal and wood identification

Wood and charcoal identifications were undertaken in accordance with Section 25 of the National Monuments Act, 1930, as amended by Section 20 of the National Monuments Amendment Act 1994.

Charcoal identification

Four samples (F30, Sample 15; F49, Sample 12; F64, Sample 13; and F93, Sample 19) contained charcoal fragments. Charcoal fragments were fractured to view the three planes (transverse, radial and tangential sections) necessary for microscopic wood identification. The wood species identifications were conducted under a binocular microscope using incident light and viewed at magnifications of x10 to x200. The charcoal fragments of each species identified were counted, weighed (grams) and bagged according to species.

The ring curvature of each charcoal fragment was also noted where applicable. Weakly curved annual rings suggest the use of trunks or larger branches, while strongly curved annual rings indicate the burning of smaller branches or twigs.

Wood identification

Sample 14 from F27 contained one fragment of waterlogged wood. Thin sections were cut from each of the three planes (transverse, radial and tangential sections) and mounted onto a glass slide in a temporary water medium. The wood was identified under a transmitted light binocular microscope at magnifications of x5 to x250.

All wood species identifications were made using wood reference slides and wood keys devised by Brazier and Franklin (1961), Schweingruber (1978), Hather (2000) and the International Association of Wood Anatomists (IAWA) wood identification manuals by Wheeler, Bass and Gasson (1989) (see also www.lib.ncsu/edu/insidewood).

Results

The results of the charcoal and wood identifications are presented in Table 6.15.

Three wood species, totalling 57 identifications, were recorded from the charcoal samples associated with F30, F49, F64 and F93. Hazel (*Corylus avellana*) dominated the assemblage, accounting for 37 identifications; nineteen fragments were identified as ash (*Fraxinus excelsior*), while just one fragment was identified as willow (*Salix* sp.).

The hazel and ash charcoal assemblages contained a number of small roundwoods, which had a diameter of 10–29mm. The hazel roundwoods contained 4–6

Pl. 6.74—Cross-section of organic peat/dung material.

growth rings, which were approximately 1.2mm in width. The ash roundwoods contained 5–11 growth rings, which were approximately 0.6–1mm in width.

The waterlogged wood sample from F27 was identified as oak (*Quercus* sp.). The fragment was a radial split, which measured 70mm in length by 87mm in width by 5mm in height. Since the growth rings were weakly curved, this material is from a larger piece of wood, such as a large branch or trunk wood.

Discussion

The samples analysed for this report were retrieved from features associated for the most part with destruction layers and collapse at the site. The charred and organic material identified was found alongside other domestic and occupational debris, such as pottery, tiles, bone, glass, iron objects and other metal and stone artefacts. This suggests that on-site waste material and refuse became incorporated into foundational layers and post-abandonment deposits at the site.

The only evidence for possible food debris at Clogh Oughter Castle was recorded from F49. The exact nature of this material would require further electronic scanning and chemical analysis to fully confirm the composition of the remains. A preliminary observation of the charred flattened material confirmed, however, that it was not wood; it could be the remains of processed food, such as bread, porridge or gruel. Medieval literary sources frequently mention the use of cereals for pot-based foods and breads (Sexton 1998). The only known evidence found in Ireland for a prepared foodstuff is a charred oaten biscuit from Lisleagh I, Co. Cork, dating from the seventh century AD (Monk *et al*. 2004, 20).

Material tentatively identified as partially charred peat or dung was recorded from F57. Peat has traditionally been collected and stored as a fuel source in Ireland. It has also been found associated with medieval occupation layers (floor deposits) at Ballinderry 2, Co. Offaly (Hencken 1942, 32), and at Antiville, Co. Antrim (Waterman 1971). During the medieval period, animal dung was commonly used as a component of daub (Johnston 2011, 370), as fertiliser to enrich soils (*ibid*.,

292; Kelly 1997, 364) and in making saltpetre, a key ingredient of gunpowder (Johnston 2011, 311).

The elderberry seeds recorded from F38 could represent the remains of once-waterlogged deposits that have dried out. The dense concentration of elder seeds suggests that it was a dumped deposit or that an elder tree grew here. Elder grows well on nitrogen-rich soils and is commonly found around farmsteads or areas of increased occupation. While the elderberries are insipid to the taste, they are used more in baking and in making jams and wine (Edlin 1951, 64).

The charcoal and wood assemblage recorded from the site contained wood species that are traditionally used in construction works and specialised activities. Hazel and willow are both pliable but strong woods and have been used in the making of hurdles, wattling, palisades and trackways from prehistoric times (Cutler and Gale 2000, 89, 236; Caseldine and Hatton 1996). Hazel and willow also have a history of being coppiced—the regular harvesting of brushwood and lighter round-woods from managed stands (Rackham 1980). Ash is also a very suitable building material, since its timber is easily felled and split to produce long posts. This species is considered the best firewood and its charcoal is highly regarded (Cutler and Gale 2000, 120). Oak is traditionally the main wood of choice in construction works from the prehistoric period and has a long history in the boat-building industry (*ibid.*, 204). This species also produces good, long-lasting fuel and is a major component in the curing and tanning of animal skins (Faber 1938).

Since the hazel and ash identified at the site were recorded as being small roundwoods, they are likely to represent the remains of structural wood associated with lighter structures, such as wattling, fences, or ancillary or internal walls. It is difficult to ascertain whether the charcoal recorded represents the remains of a structure that had burnt down or was a result of the construction methods used at the site. Posts and stakes might have been charred to prevent the timbers from rotting. Ash, for instance, rots quickly when exposed (Cutler and Gale 2000, 120), so perhaps ash posts would require charring to prevent such degradation occurring.

Conclusions

The samples associated with Clogh Oughter Castle contained both organic and charred ecofacts, which formed part of the occupational debris recorded at the site. The only possible evidence for food remains was charred organic material tentatively identified as a type of bread, gruel or porridge. The remains of what was interpreted as dried-out peat or dung was also recorded from the site. Both peat and animal dung would have had an economic value during the medieval period, being used in construction works, as fuel and as fertiliser. While charcoal from archaeological sites is commonly interpreted as fuel debris, the hazel and ash roundwoods recorded from Clogh Oughter are more likely to be the remains of structural wood. The preservation of oak wood and elderberry seeds suggests that some deposits at the site were once waterlogged, but the exact nature of this material is uncertain in the absence of more samples.

Acknowledgements

I would like to thank Mick Monk from the Archaeology Department in University College Cork for his comments on the bread/porridge/gruel sample.

7. DISCUSSION

THE CRANNOG OF O'REILLY

The earliest historical reference to the site appears to be under the name 'Crannog O'Reilly' in 1220, when Walter de Lacy captured it, as recorded in the *Annals of Loch Cé*. The next reference is in an Anglo-Norman document dating from 1224, where it is referred to as the castle of Crannog O'Reilly. The fact that there is no other certain crannog in this section of the lake (see Appendix 2) that the castle might have dominated makes it likely that the castle was built on the Crannog of O'Reilly. While the excavations uncovered no evidence for earlier occupation, their mostly limited nature and depth could at least partly account for this. The discovery of a wattle panel in the water close to the island with a radiocarbon date of 1210–80 (see Appendix 2) would lend support to the theory that the island itself is the crannog. Some crannogs in Ireland were made up of lake mud, sand, gravel, stones, timber and brushwood as well as soft organic occupation debris, which would not make a good foundation for a stone castle. The island at Clogh Oughter, however, is formed of stones thrown down on a base of bedrock and turned out to be an excellent foundation for a stone castle. If this is indeed the Crannog of O'Reilly, it may have been of relatively recent construction when the castle was built. Indeed, in its structure it may have been related to other island fortifications being built by the Irish in Connacht in the eleventh and early twelfth centuries (Naessens and O'Conor 2012). The Crannog of O'Reilly may have been an island cashel like Iniscremha in Lough Corrib or Caislen na Caillighe in Lough Mask (Naessens and O'Conor 2012, 262–5), and the kerb-like feature on the western side of Clogh Oughter could be a remnant of such a fortification.

Many crannogs were important royal and lordly centres and residences for the Gaelic Irish, from early historic times right up to the seventeenth century (Warner 1994; O'Conor 1998, 79–84; O'Sullivan 1998, 150–77; O'Conor *et al.* 2010). They were used as residences and secure bolt-holes by kings and lords and, along with ancient inauguration sites and dryland royal or lordly residences (often called a *dún*), came to symbolise the lordship of an area. This was particularly true of areas like County Cavan, where there are many suit-able lakes for the building of crannogs; but so important was this idea of a lordly lake-dwelling that, even in areas where there were very few lakes, small lakes, often since drained, were sought out as locations for crannogs. Lagore, Co. Meath, Lough Kent, Co. Tipperary, and Loughmerans, Co. Kilkenny, are good examples of the latter. The importance of such centres of power is often illustrated by the frequency with which manors and parishes—and even baronies—take their name from the crannog, usually in the form *inis*, or from the lake (*loch*) in which it was situated. It is in this context that the symbolism of the de Lacys building a castle most likely on O'Reilly's royal crannog needs to be seen. This was no longer the Anglo-Normans cooperating and living side by side with the O'Reillys but a direct attack on their lordship and an attempt at total subjection. Lough Oughter was the centre of O'Reilly power at the time, and Loughtee Upper and Lower, the present-day baronies in which Lough Oughter is situated, take their name from the mensal or household lands, *lucht tighe*, of the O'Reilly lords. William Gorm de Lacy, with his mixed Irish and Norman blood, would in particular have understood the importance and symbolism of building a castle at this location.

Both castle and crannog were also very strategically located, as they dominated a vital narrow point in the lake, Gubarinn, through which all boats going up or down the lake had to pass.

THE LOWER TWO STOREYS OF THE TOWER (PHASE 1)

The tower was clearly built in two distinct phases, though there may have been no real time-lapse between them. Both phases may have been built between 1220 and 1224. It is possible that Walter de Lacy built the first phase in 1220 to consolidate his position on the Crannog of O'Reilly and that phase 2 was built by William Gorm de Lacy as part of his strengthening of the grip of the de Lacys on Bréifne. The reference that he was to build specifically three stone castles in Bréifne for de Nangle is a rare documentary survival in an Irish context and in connection with Clogh Oughter may tie in with his work on Phase 2. The fact that de Nangle

Pl. 7.1—A reconstruction watercolour of Phase 1 of the castle (Phelim Manning).

is mentioned at all may be just a legal nicety resulting from the fact that he had already been given a grant of the area. While William Gorm's own half-brothers, the Blunds, figure prominently, de Nangle is not mentioned in Marshal's account of his campaign in Bréifne in 1224, and from this and Cathal Croibhdhearg's complaint to the king one gets the impression that William Gorm was operating on his own behalf and that his intention was to carve out a territory for himself.

While Phase 1 of Clogh Oughter was being built, the de Lacy motte-and-bailey castle of Kilmore, already established before 1211 and situated only 5km to the south, could have supplied military protection, resources and accommodation. It is also likely that the de Lacys had allied themselves with some faction of the O'Reillys, because in Gaelic medieval lordships there was never a shortage of dissatisfied minor branches, or even closer relatives of the lord, who would cooperate with an outsider to gain even limited power for themselves.

Phase 1 consists of the two lower storeys of the tower, which would have been a reasonably strong fortification, especially considering its location, surrounded by water. It may have had a stone parapet and probably a wooden hoarding from which it could be effectively defended, though no evidence was found for either. The

first-floor entrance would have added to the strength of the tower and would have been accessed by an external wooden stair. As it had no stone stair internally, some form of wooden stairs or ladders would have been necessary to access the ground floor and the parapets. No evidence survives regarding the form of the roof at this stage. While there may have been a fireplace in the missing southern part of the tower, the insertion of a cross-wall with fireplaces in the seventeenth century would suggest otherwise. A central brazier or even a hearth on a thick protective layer of clay or masonry above the timber first floor are possibilities. The two subsidiary doorways would suggest that there was an attached enclosure, perhaps curving round like crab's claws to protect the main entrance and a docking area for boats (Pl. 7.1). These doorways could have given access to the wall walk of such a walled enclosure. It is possible that there was a thickening in the curtain wall on the northern side to accommodate a garderobe. There are examples of tall circular or polygonal towers closely surrounded by a curtain wall or shell keep, as at Shanid, Co. Limerick (Sweetman 1999, 85), and Launceston in Cornwall (Saunders 2006, 15–19).

There is also a possibility that Phase 1 of the tower was never roofed and properly completed when the de-

Pl. 7.2—A reconstruction watercolour of Phase 2 of the castle (Phelim Manning).

cision was taken to build Phase 2 by adding a stair turret and greatly heightening the tower. The fact that no evidence for a Phase 1 roof or parapets survived would support such a theory.

THE BUILDING OF THE TOWER TO ITS PRESENT HEIGHT (PHASE 2)

As argued above, there is a strong possibility that the Phase 2 work was carried out by William Gorm de Lacy soon after 1221, when he had a mandate to build three stone castles in Bréifne, but before 1224, when the castle was besieged by O'Reilly and William Marshal's knights. Phase 2 consisted of the building of the tower to its present height and the addition of the now-missing stair turret (Pl. 7.2). It was undoubtedly a rather strange phase of building because, though doubling the height of the tower, no extra accommodation was added. There is no evidence of window or door openings at this time in the upper part of the tower, apart from the access from the stairs to the parapet level. While it is possible that there could have been second- or third-floor windows

in the missing southern section of the tower, the lack of evidence for doorways giving access from the stair turret to such upper floors is telling. The purpose of the massive beam that spanned the interior at a high level is unknown. The builder of Phase 2 of the tower appears to have been more interested in the imposing appearance of the higher tower than in providing further accommodation. There is ample evidence of low-level or countersunk roofs in keeps/great towers in Ireland and elsewhere in the Norman world (Manning 2002), and the earlier phases of the de Lacy keep at Trim Castle are good examples of this (Sweetman 1998; Hayden 2011, 105–11).

The fact that William Gorm entrusted the safety of important non-combatant female relatives to this castle is an indication that he thought that it would be very difficult to capture. Nevertheless, the combined forces of O'Reilly and the knights dispatched by Marshal to assist him did bring about the surrender of the castle. The fact that Marshal gives details of his noble captives in his letter to the king is an indication of the significance he attached to this event. Having William Gorm de Lacy's mother, the daughter of Rory O'Conor, as his prisoner proved useful in his subsequent peace negotiations with her cousin, the king of Connacht.

There is no documentary evidence as to what happened to the castle after it was taken by O'Reilly. It is not listed among the castles that were returned to the de Lacys when peace was restored in 1225, though Kilmore is on the list. It is possible that Clogh Oughter was returned to the O'Reillys, as Marshal's letter specifically states that O'Reilly had returned to the king's peace and was cooperating closely with his knights in its capture. The O'Reillys had a long tradition of co-operation with the Anglo-Normans, going right back to the siege of Dublin in 1170, and Marshal may have trusted O'Reilly with Clogh Oughter. Whatever long-standing agreement was in place between O'Reilly and the de Lacys quite probably specified de Lacy control of Kilmore and mutual protection against common enemies. Cathal O'Reilly, in attacking and demolishing the castle of Kilmore in 1226 and driving the de Lacys out of East Bréifne, was declaring independence in a daring fashion, against which the de Lacys do not seem to have been in a position to retaliate. William Gorm de Lacy presumably still hankered after the idea of conquering Bréifne and in 1233 led a mixed army of Irish and Anglo-Normans into the territory but was defeated in battle and died soon after.

It is possible that in 1224 Clogh Oughter was granted to O'Rourke, O'Reilly's old overlord under the Gaelic system. This could have been part of a divide-and-conquer strategy, using one Gaelic lord to keep another in check. The traditions recorded in *A genealogical history of the O'Reillys* (Carney 1959) appear to reflect O'Rourke control of Clogh Oughter in the mid-thirteenth century.

CIRCULAR TOWERS OF THE EARLY THIRTEENTH CENTURY

Clogh Oughter is one of a number of large circular towers built by the Normans in Ireland and Britain in the early thirteenth century. Some of these were free-standing great towers within larger castles, as at Pembroke in Wales, Dundrum, Co. Down, and Inchiquin, Co. Cork. Some were on the circuit of a curtain wall, as at Nenagh, Co. Tipperary, and as apparently intended at Clogh Oughter. In other cases a new type of castle was being built at this time with a number of circular towers positioned at the angles, as at Dublin, Kilkenny and Limerick (Manning 2012).

Great towers, sometimes called keeps or donjons, and mural towers of the eleventh century and most of the twelfth century in Britain and France were mostly square or rectangular in plan. The use of circular towers in castles became popular in France during the reign of Philip Augustus (1180–1223), who appears to have favoured this type of plan (Knight 2000, 32). The building of such towers appears to have spread to Ireland and Britain around 1200 (Manning 2012, 226–8). Some of the first to have been built in Ireland are likely to have been the Bermingham Tower of Dublin Castle, originally built soon after 1204 as a single great tower (Manning 1998; 2012; forthcoming),[1] and the lower three storeys of the great tower of Nenagh Castle, which was probably built before 1205 (Leask 1936).

Circular great towers were built in the early thirteenth century by some of the great Norman lords in Ireland, such as Maurice FitzGerald, who is likely to have built Inchiquin, Co. Cork, in the years after 1215 (Manning 2012, 228–9), Theobald Walter I, who is likely to have built or at least started Nenagh before his death in 1205, and Hugh II de Lacy, earl of Ulster, the half-brother of William Gorm de Lacy, who built Dundrum about this time. It is interesting that William Gorm's father-in-law, Llywelyn ab Iorwerth (the Great) of Wales, also built a circular great tower at his castle of Dolbadarn. This tower has a projecting turret (Avent 2004, 30–5), probably not unlike what was formerly attached to the northern side of Clogh Oughter. There is no close dating evidence for Dolbadarn; while a date in the 1230s has been suggested (*ibid.*, 12), an earlier date is also possible. There is another circular tower on a lake island in County Cavan: the tower on Port Island in Lough Macnean at the north-western edge of the county (O'Donovan 1995, 227). Dense undergrowth has made inspection impossible in recent years, but from Davies's (1947, 83) description it may be another early thirteenth-century tower. In this case the tower, which only survived to a height of 1.8m, had a batter and an internal diameter of 6.8m, with walls 1.37m thick. The only openings at ground-floor level were three embrasures with loopholes, suggesting to Davies that the tower must have had a first-floor entrance. This tower might also have been built by William Gorm de Lacy in the early 1220s.

Around 1200 a new type of castle with no single great tower but with circular towers at the angles was being built in France, Britain and Ireland (Knight 1987, 78–9). Kilkenny Castle was built on these lines by

---

[1] For an alternative view see O'Keeffe 2009.

William Marshal I, probably from about 1207 on, while the king's castle at Limerick was also built at this time in this form. Dublin Castle, which was mostly built between 1213 and about 1228, was also of this form, and the pre-existing Bermingham Tower, which appears to have been built soon after 1204 (Manning 1998; 2012; forthcoming), was incorporated into the new plan.

This is the building tradition to which the tower of Clogh Oughter belongs. Such towers were being built either by the king or by major lords in the early thirteenth century in Ireland and Britain. They vary quite a lot in their architectural details and in their diameter and wall thickness (Manning 2012, 227, table 1). Although Clogh Oughter has the greatest internal diameter of any of these towers, many have thicker walls. Nevertheless, only Nenagh and the south tower of Kilkenny have greater external diameters (excluding any batter), while the external diameter of Pembroke is roughly the same as that of Clogh Oughter. It is therefore one of the largest towers of the series in Ireland and Britain.

The original entrance to virtually all of these towers was at a high level (usually the first floor) and would have required an external wooden stair or a forebuilding with stairs for access. Many were subsequently provided with a ground-level entrance for convenience in late medieval or early modern times, as at Clogh Oughter. Some also had one or more subsidiary doorways giving access to curtain walls, as at Nenagh, Dundrum and Clogh Oughter.

The plan of the original openings and the form of head or arch can vary considerably. Some of the towers in Wales, such as Pembroke and Cilgerran, have narrow splayed openings that would have been virtually useless for defence. Many have parallel-sided embrasures with narrow loops or windows at their ends, as at Dundrum, Nenagh, Kilkenny (Murtagh 1993) and the Record Tower at Dublin Castle (Manning 2003). The plan of the embrasures at Clogh Oughter, where the sides initially diverge from the inner face as radii of the circle, is paralleled only at Kiltinan, Co. Tipperary (McNeill 1997, 31, 94, 188–9). Another circular tower with this feature is the Talbot Tower, a thirteenth-century mural tower on the town walls of Kilkenny (Munby and Tyler 2005, 107–9). Some of the towers have semicircular arches over the embrasures, as at Nenagh, Kilkenny and the Record Tower of Dublin Castle. At Clogh Oughter the ground floor has segmental arches over the two surviving embrasures, while at first-floor level the arches appear to have been pointed. The partially surviving head of the eastern first-floor window shows that it was pointed. The use of segmental and pointed arches would

favour a date in the 1220s rather than earlier among towers of this type.

Mostly these towers have either spiral stairs within the thickness of their walls, as at Dundrum, Dublin, Pembroke, Dolbadarn etc., or a curving mural stair, as at Aghadoe, Co. Kerry, and in a related circular tower built by William Marshal I as a lighthouse at Hook Head, Co. Wexford (Colfer 2004, 84–5). Having a projection to at least partly accommodate a spiral stair was the solution applied at Nenagh, Kiltinan, Ardfinnan and Skenfrith in Wales (McNeill 2003a, 99–100). Dolbadarn has a rectangular projection but this was a garderobe tower and there is a spiral stair within the wall of the main tower. Clogh Oughter is unusual in not having a stair within the wall, and even its stair turret was an afterthought built only in Phase 2. It is possible that the stair turret at Clogh Oughter also had a garderobe or garderobes in it. In not having a stone stair Phase 1 of Clogh Oughter is more comparable with some hall-keeps such as Glanworth (Manning 2009a, 14–21) and the great tower at Maynooth (Sweetman 1999, 69).

The use of large timber beams set deeply in the wall to form the first floor is also a feature of many hall-keeps, as again at Glanworth (Manning 2009a, 15, 19). It is also a feature of the circular towers, as demonstrated by McNeill (2003a; 2003b). There are similarities in this regard between Clogh Oughter and the two floors at Dundrum, and close similarities with the second floor at Inchiquin (Hartnett 1945). In other towers offsets were used to hold the floors, as at Nenagh.

No evidence survives as to whether the wall tops of Phase 1 had stone parapets and/or timber hoarding, or as to how it was roofed. Indeed, Phase 1 may never have been completed with a roof and parapets. The height of the tower was almost doubled in Phase 2 but this upper part has no early openings or evidence of early floors. In particular, there is no evidence of doorways leading from the stair turret to a second or third floor. It therefore appears that the Phase 2 roof was countersunk within the tower, which continued to have just a ground floor and a first floor. Most quadrangular great towers in Britain, such as the Tower of London, Hedingham, Dover, Richmond, Newcastle, Norham and Scarborough, originally had countersunk roofs (Booth and Roberts 2000, 23; Goodall 2011, 109–44), and great towers and hall-keeps in Ireland, such as Athenry, Trim, Maynooth and Adare, had similar roofs originally (Manning 2002). There is also evidence that some polygonal and circular towers had countersunk roofs, as at Orford and Conisbrough (Goodall 2011, 126–30, 150–1) and at Dolbadarn (Avent 2004, 30–5). At Clogh Oughter no physical evidence for the nature of the Phase 1 or Phase 2 roof was noted during the project. The water outlet or outlets may have been in the missing southern side or on the northern side where later windows were quarried through the wall. The holes for a large cross-beam at about third-floor level are a puzzle and, while they may be connected in some way with a roof, there are no parallels known to the author for such an arrangement.

Calling Clogh Oughter a castle is itself problematic, as there was not sufficient room on the island for the normal buildings of a castle. Possibly the intention was to make the island larger or there may always have been a land base, maybe where the Culme house later stood to the south in Inishconnell townland.

THE USE OF THE CASTLE FROM THE MID-THIRTEENTH CENTURY TO *c.* 1600

Apart from the tradition of O'Rourke occupation in the mid-thirteenth century, the O'Reillys appear to have held the castle right up to 1600. It is unlikely that it was ever used as a lordly residence, and certainly after the fourteenth century the O'Reilly residential castle was at Tullymongan, dominating the market town of Cavan. The entries in the annals indicate that Clogh Oughter was mostly being used as a prison for rival claimants to the lordship but also played a part in wars between O'Rourke and O'Reilly. Its first appearance in government records since 1224 is in 1601 and 1602 in lists of government forts, being then held for the government by the family of Sir John O'Reilly, in particular Katherine Butler, the widow of his son. Soon afterwards in 1607 it was used by the rebel baron of Delvin and was besieged and captured by Sir Richard Wingfield.

RECONSTRUCTION OF THE TOWER AS A ROYAL FORT/PRISON (PHASE 3)

After its capture in 1607, the government continued to hold Clogh Oughter and Captain Hugh Culme carried out necessary repairs to it. Lord Deputy Chichester intended to use it as a store for munitions and victuals in case there was a rebellion. In 1610 it was leased to Hugh Culme and between then and 1620 some £200 sterling was spent on it to convert it into a prison for Catholic priests. This is undoubtedly the Phase 3 work (Pl. 7.3). As well as providing prison accommodation, there was

an attempt to make the tower more defensible in the age of artillery by demolishing the stair turret and any enclosure walls that survived and by restoring the tower as a plain circular structure. Strong circular towers were useful in artillery defence and circular gun towers have a long history, from the Cow Tower at Norwich, which dates from the late 1390s (Goodall 2011, 420–1), to the coastal defences built by Henry VIII in the early sixteenth century and to the Martello towers built in the first decade of the nineteenth century to oppose Napoleon. Reducing Clogh Oughter to a plain circular tower would have made it into a stronger and more compact defensive unit. It is also possible that the stair turret had come adrift from the circular tower and had to be demolished for safety reasons.

The opening of a new ground-floor doorway was probably more for convenience than defence, though it was supplied with an external iron grill or yett, which could be secured by a chain internally, and probably with a portcullis, as well as having a strong wooden door. These iron grills or yetts are a feature of tower-houses in Ireland, especially those dating from the sixteenth century, but are also found in fortified houses and fortifications of the early seventeenth century (Waterman 1961, pl. XXXI; Manning 2009b, 20–3).

A major aspect of this phase was the building of a dividing wall within the tower, which, as it contained fireplaces, must have extended up to the roof. It would also have made the flooring of the tower simpler, with considerably shorter spans between the cross-wall and the curving walls of the tower. New openings were broken through the tower wall and existing ones adapted to the new floor levels. The heavy timber-framed foundation of the cross-wall is particularly interesting and indicates that they feared differential subsidence of the material under the floor. Their fear was groundless, as the foundation of loose stones on bedrock would not have subsided. A somewhat similar timber-laced foundation was used when rebuilding the north-west tower, subsequently called the Cork Tower, of Dublin Castle after the original fell in 1628. This was uncovered during excavations and the timber was still preserved because it was below the level of the water-table (Lynch and Manning 2001, 187). At Clogh Oughter the former presence of the timber was indicated by voids in the masonry. The use of intramural timbers in this manner is recorded in some medieval castles and has also been noted at Hillsborough Fort, Co. Down, in work of the mid-seventeenth century (Wilcox 1981, 30–1).

Most, if not all, of the stone for building the cross-wall could have been recycled from the old stair turret on the northern side and any other attached walls that

Pl. 7.3—A reconstruction watercolour of Phase 3 of the castle (Phelim Manning).

were demolished as part of this phase of work. The discovery of demolition rubble in Area F would indicate that there was rubble left over from these demolition works even after the cross-wall was built. There can be no certainty as to whether or not the great beams of the original first floor survived up to the seventeenth century and continued to be used in Phase 3, because no part of the cross-wall survived to this height. If they did survive in reasonably good condition, the cross-wall could have incorporated them and been built around them, which would have required only the removal of floorboards that might have been in the way.

The quantity of seventeenth-century roof tiles found shows that the conical roof was covered with these tiles. These were flat peg tiles, not pantiles, and parallels from this period are known from Portumna Castle and elsewhere. There are also records of similar flat tiles being made locally for other buildings constructed in connection with the Plantation of Ulster. The reconstructed tower had five storeys and probably an attic floor. The remains of a fourth-floor window were filled in with masonry during the conservation work. Access between the floors was by wooden stairs,

as stated in Richard Castledine's deposition, but no evidence was seen as to where exactly these were located or how they were constructed. Bricks found were probably used for the chimney-stack and/or for flue linings, and daub found is likely to have come from wattle-and-daub panels in timber-framed partitions.

During this period the Culme family were living in a house on the shore near the castle in Inishconnell townland (see below for discussion on this house). They probably had little reason ever to visit the castle, apart from occasional inspections to check on its state of repair.

THE USE OF THE CASTLE DURING THE 1640S (PHASE 4)

The only significant change that might have been made to the building during this period was the insertion of a ground-floor fireplace in the southern face of the cross-wall. Presumably there was a fireplace at first-floor level in the same wall, and it would have been a relatively simple matter to connect the new fireplace with the older flue. There is no evidence that the tower was used as a prison for priests or for any other active purpose between the completion of the Phase 3 work and the outbreak of rebellion in October 1641. The immediate imprisonment of Arthur Culme was probably its first use in two decades, and the practicalities of using it as a prison might have necessitated a ground-floor fireplace near the entrance for the guards. It is possible, however, that this fireplace was inserted as an afterthought as part of the Phase 3 work, and indeed in 1623 Pynnar recommended that a further £150 be spent on Clogh Oughter (Hunter 2012, 130). In the winter of 1641–2 Bishop Bedell and his fellow prisoners were, it is clear from the accounts, held at first-floor level, from where they could hear reports in Irish of the siege of Drogheda through gaps between the floorboards. They also had a fireplace where they could cook, presumably one of the original fireplaces from Phase 3. Their description of rotten floorboards and a lack of shutters for the windows speaks of neglect and disuse of the building for a couple of decades. Massari's account indicates that Viscount Montgomery of Ards was held on one of the upper floors.

Most of the finds recovered would appear to belong to this period of active use from October 1641 to April 1653. It is unlikely to be a typical household assemblage in that it was only occupied by a garrison and, at times, prisoners, mostly males, who had to do their own cooking, as in an army camp. The utensils were presumably requisitioned as required from the Culme house and there may also have been looted material from other settler houses in the area. Many of the prisoners being held there were of high status, such as Bishop Bedell, Arthur Culme and Richard Castledine, and at a later stage Viscount Montgomery of Ards, and some of the artefacts uncovered, such as the decorated spurs and the fragments of gold lace, reflect this. There were also high-status people on the Irish side staying at the castle in the latter part of this period, such as Philip Mac Hugh O'Reilly.

One of the problems in relation to historical references to Clogh Oughter is to know whether it is the tower on the island or the Culme house on the shore that is intended. For example, when we read that Owen Roe O'Neill died at Clogh Oughter in November 1649, did it happen at the castle or at the house? With no immediate security threat in the vicinity, it is unlikely that a sick and dying man would have been brought with difficulty out to the castle when there was a fine comfortable house on the shore. It is clear from Dean Massari's account that he was accommodated at the house in 1646. The Catholic primate, Hugh O'Reilly, probably also used the house as a residence and for a

council of bishops in 1650 and 1651, though the discovery of half a papal seal in the excavation might indicate that he at least on occasion visited or stayed at the castle itself, especially at that time, when the security of the house could not be guaranteed.

While many of the finds recovered are likely to date from the last few years leading up to the siege of 1653, it is possible that some were either lost or disposed of earlier in the 1640s or could have continued in use from the early 1640s up to the time of the siege. For example, the cooking pots and some of the pottery found could have been used by the prisoners in the winter of 1641–2, and some of the carpenter's tools found, such as the hammers, saw and nails, could have been used by Richard Castledine for making makeshift shutters for the windows while Bishop Bedell was held prisoner there. The faunal remains recovered are indicative of a reasonable diet of beef, mutton, pork, chicken and some fish for the prisoners and the garrison. The remains indicate that hens were probably kept on the island for at least some of this period, both for their meat and for their eggs. With food waste being disposed of both within the tower and around it, the finding of rat bones is not surprising.

THE SIEGE OF 1653

This was a landmark siege in that Clogh Oughter Castle was the last significant outpost in Ireland to surrender to the Cromwellians, almost four years after Cromwell landed with his army in Ireland. The number of fragments of cannon-balls and mortar bombs found is eloquent testimony to the intensity of the bombardment. It is clear from tradition recorded by O'Donovan in the 1830s that the Cromwellians, having transported their artillery along Cromwell's Road, set up their battery in Inishconnell townland, possibly availing of the shelter provided by the Culme house and its associated buildings, gardens, orchards and paddocks. We can no longer assess the damage caused by the bombardment, as it was concentrated on the southern side, the very side that was subsequently demolished. Two cannon-ball strikes were observed in the surviving lower part of the wall, however, and it is clear from these that it would have taken a lot of bombardment to do any serious damage to solid portions of the wall. Openings in the wall would have been another matter, and strikes here would have put personnel inside at serious risk. Even more of a threat to personnel within was the chance of a mortar bomb penetrating the roof, though the odds of achieving that degree of accuracy with a mortar bomb were slim. The discovery of lead shot in the lake close to the castle indicates that the besiegers may have attempted to storm the castle from boats at some point during the siege.

Conditions within the castle as the siege and bombardment progressed must have been harrowing, and the discovery of a horse bone that showed evidence of butchering suggests a dwindling supply of meat. The querns would have been most useful for milling the supplies of grain so that bread could be baked, but the report of 1 March 1653 indicates that most of their corn supply had probably been destroyed by then. The burials tell their own story of furtive interment, probably under cover of darkness in one of the only scraps of ground available around the tower—one individual with a broken leg, another buried prone and possibly partly dismembered, and a woman with a horrific injury to the head. These injuries could have resulted from the bombardment. Burials have been found at other siege sites in Ireland, such as Limerick Castle and Carrickmines, Co. Dublin, both relating to sieges in 1642 (Wiggins 2000, 100–2; Clinton *et al.* 2007).

It is difficult to know how many people would have actually been in the castle during the siege and whether Colonel Philip Mac Hugh O'Reilly was there all the time. Clearly there were many compatriots hiding out in this very difficult terrain around Lough Oughter, and the horses of the officers must have been held somewhere, as there was certainly no possibility of keeping them on the island. The importance of the horses is demonstrated by the discovery of seven spurs, at least two curry-combs, parts of a cheek-piece and horseshoe fragments, as well as the clauses in the surrender terms specifying that the officers could dispose of their horses to their best advantage. It is likely that some of the defenders could come and go to some extent at night-time to the northern, western and eastern shores of the lake even after their main fleet of boats had been destroyed, and certainly during the surrender negotiations it had to be possible for messages to be relayed to other outposts in the area. The surrender terms specifically applied also to 'Colonel Reily [possibly Myles O'Reilly] and the party now with him on the west side of Loughern' and Colonel Hugh Maguire and his regiment in County Fermanagh. With difficulties of communication on both sides, the surrender negotiations may have taken some time to finalise. Quite possibly Philip Mac Hugh O'Reilly and his garrison could have held out longer but, with the rest of the country subdued, further resistance was pointless and they were in no position to turn down the good terms they were offered.

THE SLIGHTING OF THE CASTLE

No documentary reference was found to the slighting of the castle. It makes sense that this would have been done soon after the surrender, and certainly the castle does not figure in the Jacobite/Williamite conflict around 1690 (J.G. Simms 1979). The excavation also indicated that there was no great lapse of time between the bombardment, which would have created a layer of debris consisting of broken cannon-balls and broken masonry, and the main destruction rubble caused by the slighting of the tower. If some decades had intervened between the two events, a humus and sod layer would have developed over the bombardment debris. There was, however, no such layer and the bombardment debris, with its many cannon-ball fragments, blended into the overlying destruction rubble as one layer.

The slighting resulted in the demolition of the entire southern third of the tower. This could have been achieved in different ways: by undermining techniques, by explosives or by a combination of both. The state of the upper outer courses of the surviving base of the wall as found in the excavation seemed to support an explosion. The stones of the outer face were displaced outwards and jutted out over the courses below in a manner that seemed to be the result of the outward force of an explosion. Slighting by explosives would have been a convenient way of using up gunpowder left over at the end of a prolonged campaign. The theatrics and symbolism of badly damaging this ancient fortress and stronghold of the rebels in this way would have further demoralised the defeated local Gaelic population. It is possible that some mining of masonry took place to ensure that the explosion would have the desired effect. The slighting certainly ensured that the building was never to be used again.

THE ARTEFACTS RECOVERED

It is likely that the siege and subsequent destruction of Clogh Oughter created conditions whereby artefacts that would normally have been recycled ended up in destruction rubble or on old surface levels. It is certainly a very rich assemblage of finds, and many individual finds, such as the decorated spurs and the gold and silver cloth, must originally have belonged to high-status individuals.

It is also interesting to have a latest possible date of 1653 for most of the finds, especially those from secure contexts. The bulk of them are in keeping with such a dating but one or two groups of pottery would not have

Pl. 7.4—A print of Castle John, Lough Scur, Co. Leitrim, from Grose's *Antiquities of Ireland* (1791). The Culme house may have looked something like this residence of the Reynolds (Mág Raghnaill) family. The castle on the island in the background is a ruined seventeenth-century square tower, apparently used as a prison.

been dated so early before. While it is possible that some later finds may have trickled down through the rubble, it is also possible that those pottery groups may turn out to be earlier than previously thought.

The discovery of cast-iron cooking pots at this date is interesting and, while it ties in with documentary evidence, these may be some of the earliest examples of cast-iron pots recovered archaeologically in either Ireland or Britain. The possibility that both the cooking pots and the cast-iron fireback were made relatively locally is a reminder of the industrial revolution that took place in Ireland in the early seventeenth century, spearheaded by ruthless entrepreneurs such as the first earl of Cork and Sir Charles Coote.

The richness of the finds generally and the wide variety of imported pottery are reflective of the growth in the market economy in Ireland in the early seventeenth century, even in inland areas such as County Cavan (Canny 2001, 308–401; Gillespie 2007, 60). Such a quantity and variety of finds from this period have been noted also at other castle excavations, such as

Roscrea, Co. Tipperary, and Glanworth, Co. Cork (Manning 2003, 79–87; 2009a, 65–116, 147). The development of the market economy in County Cavan at this period was partly due to the plantation and the associated influx of investment and settlers from Britain, as well as the establishment on a new footing of towns such as Belturbet and Cavan.

THE CULME HOUSE IN INISHCONNELL

Unfortunately there are no historical descriptions of the Culme house and, as with the castle itself, we have no record of the state of the Culme house on the shore after the 1653 siege. Arthur Culme died at the siege of Clonmel in 1650, and his extensive lands in County Cavan, including Clogh Oughter, were restored to the family in the Cromwellian settlement. They did not, however, live at their house on the shore south of Clogh Oughter but rather used Lisnamaine Castle, on their lands north of the lake, as their residence thereafter. We can only guess as to why they made this choice—possibly the house at Clogh Oughter was badly damaged, or perhaps it embodied bad memories because of its association with the rebellion. Whatever the reason, the house at Clogh Oughter was never reoccupied as a high-status residence, and only crumbling remnants, marked as an L-shaped structure on the OS first-edition map, survived by the early nineteenth century.

The geophysical survey of the area around the site of the house (Appendix 1) has thrown light on its shape and size. The footprint is rectangular (some 14m by 12m) with internal divisions and is open to various interpretations. It is possible that the southern part of the rectangle represents a principal rectangular block (some 14.5m by 6m) and that the north-western portion is a kitchen wing (6m by 4m), with the remainder to the north-east being a small open court. The areas of possible burning (Fig. A1.3: G2, G3) might indicate kitchen hearths and/or bread ovens. An early seventeenth-century house of very similar shape and dimensions survives at Killincarrig, Co. Wicklow, where the main block measures 14.3m by 7.6m and the similarly sited wing was a kitchen block (Leask 1961, 246; Grogan and Kilfeather 1997, 192). The house at Killincarrig had two storeys and an attic. The main block would also be of similar dimensions to Castle John on Lough Scur (Gowly townland, Co. Leitrim), a three-storey early seventeenth-century house of the Reynolds family (Pl. 7.4), which measures 14m by 6.25m in internal dimensions (Grose 1791, vol. 2, 91–2; Moore 2003, 213). A second possibility is that the south-eastern section was a tower, as it stands out strongly in the magnetic gradiometer data, with a wing attached to the west and then the kitchen wing at right angles, and the open court completing the rectangle. Another possibility is that the house took up the full rectangle and had two A-framed roofs with a valley between. The ruined house/castle at Newtownstewart, Co. Tyrone, had a similar footprint, being about 13.8m by 14.3m in external dimensions, with a large spine wall dividing it into two rectangular blocks. It had three levels over a basement, an attached circular stair turret and one rectangular corner tower. The surviving west wall has three gables and a star-shaped brick chimney. It was almost complete apart from the roof in 1620 (Meek and Jope 1958, 109–10). A seventeenth-century house of this shape but of smaller size (11m by 10.3m) and with a single gabled roof is at Faugher, Co. Donegal (Lacy 1983, 267–9), while larger houses, with the addition of corner towers, such as at Rathfarnham, Co. Dublin, and Raphoe, Co. Donegal, had double roofs (*ibid.*, 376–9; Craig 1982, 73–4). The

house at Inishconnell could have been somewhere between the size of Faugher and these larger houses but without the corner towers. It could still have been a large house by the standards of the time in Ireland, especially if it had two or three storeys and an attic. It is possible that the house was built of brick, like the house or castle of John Fishe at Lisnamaine, which was 34–36ft square and four storeys high (O'Reilly 1985, 265–6). Davies saw brick fragments on the site in the 1940s but it may be that only parts of the building were of brick. He also saw the foundations of a rectangular building measuring some 8m by 5.4m internally with walls 0.9m thick. Though not neatly tallying with the results of the geophysical survey, this could have been part of the narrow rectangular building hypothesised above.

Maol Mórdha MacHugh O'Reilly's house at Kevit, some 7.5km south of Clogh Oughter, was described in 1622 as 'a strong house of stone and lime, 3 storeys high, 40 foot long and 20 foot broad' (Treadwell 2006, 520). This would be very close in size and shape to the main block in the first suggested plan above and might indicate that Maol Mórdha, who was regarded by the Irish as the head of the family, built his house in imitation of that of Hugh Culme.

The house does not appear to have been particularly defensible and Richard Castledine's deposition refers to the insurgents building a fort nearby to defend the house in 1642. It does not seem to have had a strong bawn but could have had gardens, orchards, paddocks etc. around it. In this regard it is interesting that the preservation of the gardens and orchards belonging to the castles of nearby Croaghan and Keilagh is specifically mentioned in the surrender terms for these two castles in June 1642 (Gilbert 1879–80, vol. 1, 495). Some of the enclosures showing up in the geophysics, even if used later as small fields, could reflect such features around the house. Two of these lines, at the north-east corner (Fig. A1.3: G6 and G10), may indicate the access road or avenue to the house. Other features showing in the geophysical survey may be earlier than the seventeenth century and it is likely that there was a shore base associated with the castle in medieval times. The location of the fort that was being built in 1642 'between the wood and the lough' is unknown. It is possible that it was on the presently wooded ridge above Gubarinn and only a little over 200m west-south-west of the house site. An irregular field on the highest part of the ridge may reflect the footprint of the fort, at least in part. In particular, a pointed projection on its western side is like a bastion, though inspection on the ground revealed that the bank, like this entire field fence, is no larger than a normal field bank.

7.5—A view of Clogh Oughter from the shore to the south in January 2011 during high water levels in the lake and ice around the island. The lake had been frozen over completely two weeks before the photograph was taken.

CLOGH OUGHTER SINCE THE SEVENTEENTH CENTURY

The Culme lands were acquired by the Maxwells of Farnham in 1715 and Clogh Oughter would have been cherished as a picturesque ruin on the estate, as shown in Wynne's drawing (Pl. 2.12), and as a venue for family picnics, as shown in Ashford's painting (Frontispiece). It entered local folklore, as O'Donovan recorded, with the siege being personally associated with Cromwell. As the location of Bishop Bedell's incarceration in 1641–2 and of Owen Roe O'Neill's death in 1649 it has had a symbolic importance for Irish people of all political and religious affiliations since the nineteenth century (Pl. 7.5).

Geophysical survey of the site of the Culme house in Inishconnell

HEATHER GIMSON

INTRODUCTION

Today no traces can be seen of the seventeenth-century house of the Culme family at Inishconnell townland, Co. Cavan. Substantial archaeological remains associated with the house can, however, be seen through the use of subsurface geophysical surveys.

The site of the Culme house was investigated by Earthsound Archaeological Geophysics, using a range of geophysical methodologies, in January 2011. The aim of the survey was to identify possible archaeological remains associated with the house, outbuildings, paddocks and gardens through the use of non-invasive, non-destructive scientific methods. Any remains detected could

then be assessed to determine their likely composition, extent and purpose within the landscape.

THE SURVEY

The surveys were located upon a rectangular grid that was laid out with a Trimble Pro-XRS Differential Global Positioning System. The grid was centred over the location of the house as shown on the Record of Monuments and Places (RMP No. CV020-047) (Fig. A1.1). The survey area was bounded to the north-west by a lakeside fence. The site was covered in short grass with slight patches of waterlogged ground, which was

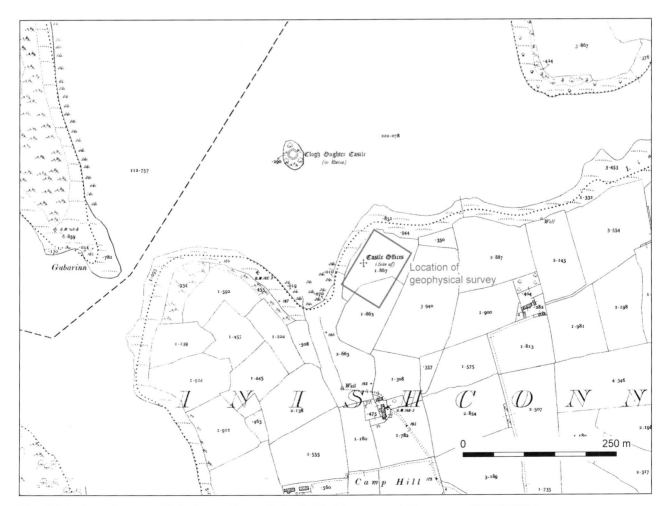

Fig. A1.1—Location map. (© Ordnance Survey Ireland. All rights reserved. Licence no. EN0059212.)

207

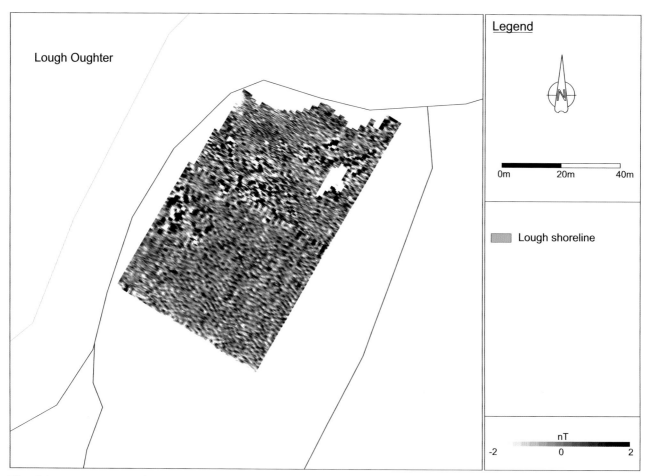

Fig. A1.2—Magnetic gradiometer data.

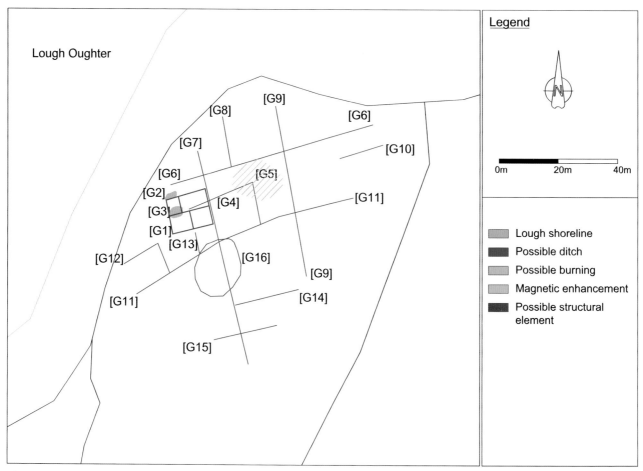

Fig. A1.3—Magnetic gradiometer interpretation.

generally amenable for each of the survey techniques. The survey area was located near the shore of Lough Oughter, with the general topography sloping down to the north-west. There were a large number of linear topographical features visible, indicating possible field boundaries and some depressions indicating the possible presence of archaeology towards the north-western end of the site. The land was generally more waterlogged around the topographically lower areas in the north-western and north-eastern ends of the site. There was also an old hawthorn tree near the north-eastern end of the site which impeded surveying to a small extent in that area.

The survey was conducted upon a bedrock geology consisting of Ballysteen Formation, a dark muddy limestone and shale. This geology gives a weak magnetic contrast for earth-cut features such as pits and ditches when using a fluxgate gradiometer, but the use of multiple geophysical techniques assisted in the detection of a range of possible archaeological features.

The site was assessed using an earth resistance meter, a magnetometer and a magnetic susceptibility meter. The earth resistance survey was selected to identify the masonry remains of the house and outbuildings. The magnetic gradiometer survey was used to identify zones of occupation or possible brick-built features. The magnetic susceptibility survey was selected to determine the presence of occupation layers, gardens and other cultural activities.

The earth resistance survey was undertaken using a Geoscan Research RM15 earth resistance meter, mounted on an articulated quadripole square array, comprising an MSP40 Mobile Sensor Platform. Measurements were taken along parallel traverses at a sampling resolution of 1m x 0.25m.

The magnetic gradiometer survey was undertaken using a Geoscan Research FM256 fluxgate gradiometer mounted on the Mobile Sensor Platform. Measurements were collected along parallel traverses at a sampling resolution of 1m x 0.125m intervals along those lines.

A magnetic susceptibility survey was carried out using a Bartington MS2 Magnetic Susceptibility meter and MS2D search loop interfaced with a Trimble Pro-XRS Differential GPS, at a sampling resolution of 10m x 10m. This technique revealed the presence of two broad trends, which are likely to be associated with cattle movement and agricultural processes rather than archaeology.

Further details on the methodology and processing can be found in the original report in the National Monuments Service Archive (Gimson and Regan 2011).

RESULTS AND DISCUSSION

The anomalies detected within the magnetic gradiometer and earth resistance surveys have been numbered in Figs A1.3 and A1.5 and are described and interpreted below.

Magnetic gradiometer survey

(Figs A1.2 and A1.3)

Anomaly G1 comprises a possible structure. It consists of an outer rectilinear structure, measuring 14m x 11m, and three internal ditches, robber trenches or masonry features, which divide the structure into four distinct but unequal cells or rooms. The north-west cell measures approximately 4m x 6m, the north-east cell is approximately 10m x 6m, the south-west cell is 7.5m x 6m and the south-east cell measures 7m x 6m. This possible structure overlooks Lough Oughter, on a topographically flat portion of the landscape.

It is possible that two areas of potential burning, G2 and G3, are associated with the structure. A former landowner claims that a section of stone was dug out and removed from the approximate northern edge of this structure by previous landowners.

Anomaly G2 comprises one area of possible burning, located close to the shore of Lough Oughter. The shape of the anomaly is roughly rhomboidal, measuring approximately 4m x 2m. This burning may be associated with the possible structure G1 and its destruction (or modern bonfire activity at the site).

Anomaly G3 comprises a second area of possible burning, located to the south of G2, within the confines of the possible structure G1. The anomaly is roughly circular, measuring approximately 4m in diameter. The presence of burnt remains within the confines of the structure suggests that it might be associated with domestic use (such as a hearth), with the destruction of the house or modern bonfire activity.

Anomaly G4 comprises a possible ditch, right-angled in shape, approximately 39m in length. The morphology and parallel orientation to other ditches detected on site suggest that this anomaly is likely to represent a former field system. A former landowner remembers the site being covered in a number of very small fields surrounded by vegetation, which were removed by the previous landowner. The remains of these field systems are visible on site as a series of interconnecting linear depressions.

Anomaly G5 comprises a roughly circular area of magnetic enhancement. The anomaly could be geo-

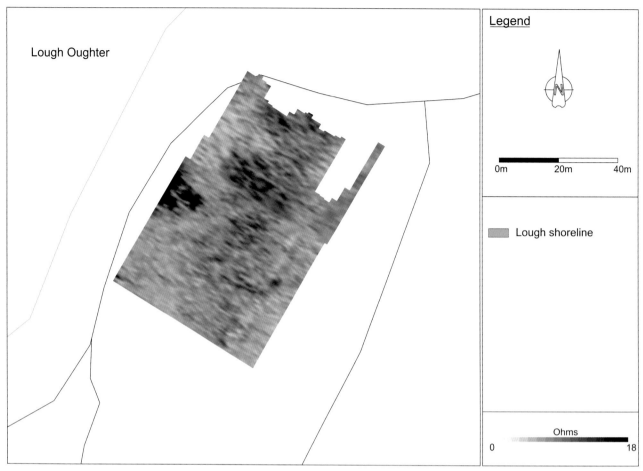

Fig. A1.4—Earth resistance data.

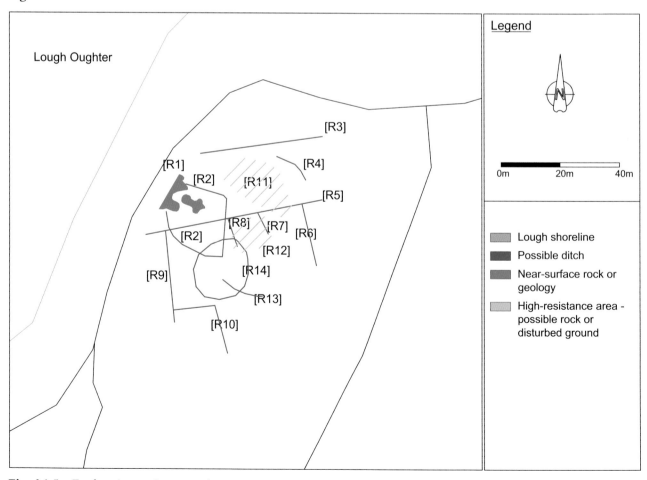

Fig. A1.5—Earth resistance interpretation.

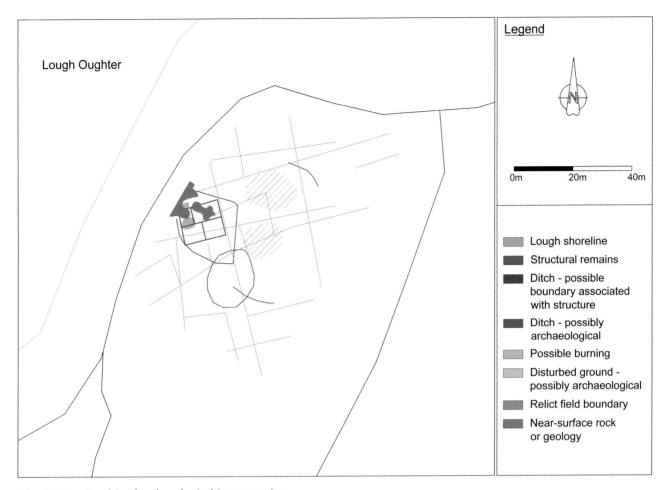

Fig. A1.6—Combined archaeological interpretation.

logical, although its proximity to the possible structure G1 means that there is a distinct possibility that it is archaeological, possibly comprising an area of rubbish or other debris associated with the possible structure. It may also be a result of rubbish or burning associated with agricultural land clearance.

Anomalies G6–G11 comprise possible linear ditches that appear to form a series of parallel and interconnecting relict field boundaries representing part of the relict field system.

Anomaly G12 is a right-angled possible ditch located close to the south-western edge of the survey area. It has a total length of 25m, lies adjacent to anomaly G11 and is roughly aligned to G4. It is possibly associated with the relict field system mentioned above.

Anomalies G13–G15 are linear possible ditches that match the orientation of the relict field system discussed above.

Anomaly G16 comprises a subcircular possible ring-ditch, 18m in diameter. This could be archaeological or geological in origin and may be indicative of archaeological activity that pre-dates the construction of the house.

Earth resistance survey (Figs A1.4 and A1.5)

An area on the north-eastern edge of the site could not be surveyed owing to the presence of a hawthorn tree and waterlogged ground associated with a relict field boundary which runs from this tree.

Anomaly R1 represents two areas of high resistance. The location of these anomalies places them on the downward slope close to the lakeside fence in an area from which the former landowner claimed to have removed stone. The high-resistance responses indicate the presence of near-surface rock (either archaeological or geological) within this area.

Anomaly R2 is a rectilinear possible ditch that may surround the structure detected in the magnetic gradiometer data (G1). The anomaly runs very close to (but respects) the structural trenches, indicating that it might represent a paddock or garden associated with the structure. The anomaly would enclose the topographical high point within the landscape.

Anomaly R3 comprises a possible linear ditch located close to, but not coinciding with, the possible ditch (G6) found in the magnetic gradiometer data. This could be part of a relict field system.

Anomaly R4 comprises an arcing possible ditch measuring 14m in length. This feature could represent a boundary ditch associated with R11, but is more likely to be geological or agricultural.

Anomaly R5 comprises a linear possible ditch, which represents the northern edge of R6–R9 and crosses through the southern part of anomaly R2. Running parallel to the relict field system ditches detected in the magnetic gradiometer data, but not on the same alignment as G11, this anomaly may represent part of the relict field system once present on the site.

Anomalies R6–R10 represent possible ditches that form part of the relict field system detected in both the magnetic gradiometer and earth resistance data.

Anomaly R11 comprises a roughly elliptical area of high resistance that matches the location of G5, an area of magnetic enhancement detected in the magnetic gradiometer data and a zone of enhancement detected in the magnetic susceptibility data. These responses suggested possible burning or disturbance associated perhaps with land clearance. The high resistance of R11 also suggests the presence of compacted earth or stone remains in this area.

Anomaly R12 comprises a roughly circular area of high resistance. It is located just to the south-east of G1 (the possible structure) and at approximately the same place as an area of increased magnetic susceptibility, suggesting that it is associated with habitation remains, land clearance or near-surface stone.

Anomaly R13 is an arcing possible ditch that could be archaeological, geological or agricultural in origin.

Anomaly R14 comprises an oval-shaped possible ring-ditch. The composition and location match those of G16, indicating that it is most likely archaeological in origin, possibly associated with habitation on the site prior to the construction of the structure G1.

CONCLUSION

The geophysical surveys revealed a rich archaeological landscape, as illustrated in the combined archaeological interpretation plot (Fig. A1.6). The surveys detected the presence of a four-celled structure located on a topographical expression affording extensive views of the castle and the surrounding Lough Oughter. The composition of the structure has been revealed by two internal divisions, one of which is off-centre, as well as two areas of possible burning. These are located on the external edge and in the centre of the structure and may be associated with habitation features such as hearths. The burning, if associated with a hearth, could indicate a kitchen or living space. The structure appears to be surrounded by an arcing possible boundary ditch, which does not follow the orientation of the structure but appears to respect it.

Further potential archaeological activity has been shown by an oval feature identified as a possible ditch, which may be suggestive of previous habitation on the site. Two areas of soil disturbance were also revealed, possibly archaeological or associated with land clearance.

Later agricultural activity on the site appears to have greatly affected the area surveyed. A large number of interconnecting linear ditches can be seen across the survey area. These are mostly parallel or perpendicular to one another and appear to form a relict field system consisting of very small paddocks.

The presence of a large number of relict field boundaries, reportedly removed by previous landowners, has, however, severely affected the ability of the geophysical surveys to detect other remains associated with the structure, if indeed they survive. The large number of relict field boundaries and two areas of disturbed soil mean that no outbuildings, paddocks or gardens, other than the boundary ditch, could be detected. It is probable that none ever existed in the area investigated using geophysical surveys. The complicated interconnecting pattern of relict field systems may, however, mask small features and any garden features present.

APPENDIX 2

Underwater investigations of the waters surrounding Clogh Oughter

KARL BRADY

INTRODUCTION

During 2012 the Underwater Archaeology Unit (UAU) carried out a series of underwater archaeological investigations in waters surrounding Clogh Oughter Castle to see whether submerged archaeological remains were present at the site. An initial underwater geophysical survey carried out by Trevor Northage resulted in the discovery of twelve lakebed anomalies of archaeological potential, which were subsequently examined and assessed. The geophysical survey also resulted in the production of a bathymetric chart providing information on the lake's water depth, bottom type, terrain and geology—the first time such a detailed bathymetric chart

has been produced for this part of the Lough Oughter lake system. A systematic dive survey was also carried out around Clogh Oughter Castle to determine whether any submerged archaeological remains were present at the site that were not imaged or identified during the geophysical survey (Pl. A2.1). The outcome of both investigations resulted in the discovery of material relating to the thirteenth-century defence works of the castle or an earlier crannog, the use of boats on the lake during the sixteenth or seventeenth century and artefactual evidence for siege warfare relating to the siege of the castle in 1653. The bathymetric survey also provided a better understanding of the castle's position and setting in the lake.

Pl. A2.1—Divers carrying out metal-detection survey to the north of the castle (Con Manning).

AIMS OF THE SURVEY

The main purpose of the investigations was to ascertain whether any features recorded by Kirker (1890–1) and Davies (1947) were still present at the castle site, including the remains of a crannog, a possible causeway, a possible submerged flagged stone roadway and a wooden palisade. In 1890 Kirker (1890–1, 294–5) noted the presence of a number of small stakes and piles and horizontal timbers around the island's margins, which were visible when lake levels were low. He surmised that the castle was built on an artificial island or crannog, made up of loose stones and brushwood. When drainage of the lake lowered water levels by *c.* 2m between 1849 and 1859 (Lohan 1994, 242–3) the castle island became more exposed and Davies (1947, 83) also noted the presence of these features, describing a series of piles and beams along the north-eastern periphery of the island as defensive outworks or quays. Davies, however, rejected Kirker's theory that the island was an artificial construction, maintaining instead that the island was natural and that the castle was built on a rocky crag.

THE SURVEYS

In order to ascertain whether the previously recorded material survived, a geophysical survey and dive survey were carried out around the island. The geophysical survey covered a large area of the lake and the surrounding shorelines, while the dive survey focused on the waters immediately surrounding the castle and on the twelve geophysical anomalies.

The side-scan sonar and bathymetric surveys were commissioned by the UAU and were carried out by Trevor Northage in April 2012. An area measuring approximately 800m north–south by 800m east–west was surveyed using both side-scan sonar and a single-beam echo-sounder. The side-scan sonar survey was carried out using a Lowrance Structurescan side-imaging sonar system, which can operate at a frequency of 455kHz and 800kHz. This is a new generation of side-scan sonar equipment which is relatively inexpensive to purchase and has the potential to yield high-resolution data. The positional data for the Lowrance HDS were acquired using a DGPS. The equipment was deployed from a small inflatable boat capable of accessing very shallow water (see www.anglingcharts.com for further detail). Good coverage was achieved during the survey, with only a few areas being inaccessible owing to shallow depths and/or navigational hazards. The survey took one day to carry out and resulted in the production of a 2D contour or bathymetric map of the lakebed, as well as indicating twelve geophysical anomalies of archaeological potential (Fig. A2.1).

Three days were spent diving the area around the castle site and the geophysical anomalies. First, a systematic dive survey was carried out around the entire circumference of the island over one day, and this identified a possible logboat, several artefacts and a wattle panel. The twelve geophysical anomalies located during the geophysical survey were then dived over a two-day period and only one of the anomalies turned out to be archaeological, viz. a logboat.

Bathymetric survey

Almost full coverage was achieved of the waters surrounding Clogh Ougher Castle. A detailed 2D bathymetric chart was produced which mapped out the topography and terrain of the lakebed (Fig. A2.1). Overall, the water depth in the lake is relatively shallow but varies depending on seasonality; depths range from 0m up to 7m in the immediate vicinity of the castle. To the north and south of the castle and along the western side of the lake, depths average between 1.5m and 2m. In contrast, directly to the east and west of the island there are two large, deeper pools where the lakebed descends to a maximum depth of 7m. There are slightly shallower pools to the north-east of the castle, apparently scoured out by lake currents. An area of limestone bedrock runs directly northwards from the island for approximately 400m, occasionally breaking the lake surface to form a series of small islets and navigational hazards. The survey confirmed that the base of the island is an outcrop of bedrock (Pl. A2.2), a natural island, which was enhanced and enlarged to facilitate the construction of either a crannog or a later stone castle in the early thirteenth century. There are further shallows and hazards to boating in the lake in the form of a series of small islands to the east-north-east and north-north-east of the castle, which are also formed by limestone bedrock breaking the surface of the water.

Side-scan sonar

The side-scan sonar survey indicated twelve anomalies of archaeological potential and provided detailed imagery on the nature of the lakebed and its terrain. The lakebed is dominated by soft muds and silts interspersed with outcrops of limestone bedrock, from which all of the lake's islands are formed and which define large stretches of the shoreline to the north and west. Areas of gravel are also present around some of the islands and

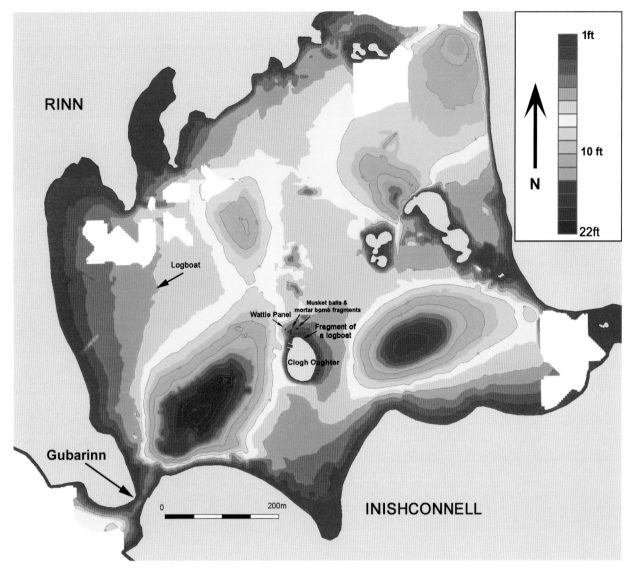

RINN

Logboat

Musket balls &
mortar bomb fragments

Wattle Panel

Fragment of
a logboat

Clogh Oughter

Gubarinn

0   200m

INISHCONNELL

Fig. A2.1—Bathymetric chart of the Clogh Oughter section of the lake, showing water depths and underwater archaeological sites found during the survey. The linear contours are marked at intervals of 2ft between depths of 4ft and 22ft, while the colours change for each foot between depths of 1ft and 10ft, but only for each 2ft between depths of 10ft and 22ft (Trevor Northage).

along parts of the shoreline where the bedrock is exposed and has been subjected to weathering.

The geophysical survey failed to show any crannog remains, wooden palisade or archaeological features that could be directly associated with the island and castle; nor did it locate any features to indicate the presence of further crannog sites in this section of the lake. It did, however, identify what Kirker described as a causeway running underwater from the castle to the northern shore. This feature is entirely natural and represents the ridge of limestone outcrop mentioned above, which forms a series of islets and shallows running in a northerly direction from the castle to the northern shore. Kirker mentions, but discounts as unlikely, a local tradition of a submerged flagged stone roadway on the southern side of the island; this is also a natural feature and can be explained by the natural fracturing of the

Pl. A2.2—Natural fracturing of the limestone bedrock gives the appearance of flagstones purposely laid down around the shoreline of Clogh Oughter (Karl Brady).

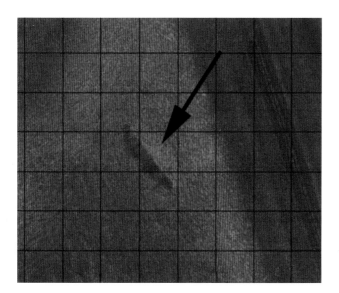

Fig. A2.2—Side-scan sonar image of the remains of a logboat on the lake floor. The logboat does not stand out well against the muddy lakebed owing to its poor condition and because it is partially buried in the silt (Trevor Northage).

a number of others had the potential to be logboats or other archaeological material. Circular searches were carried out at all of the anomalies and all were located except for two (SS2 and SS10) which are more likely to be natural lakebed features. Visibility was generally poor and varied between 0.5m and 1m. In addition, once the bottom or lakebed was disturbed visibility was reduced to near zero, which made for difficult conditions when photographing and drawing underwater. The two wrecks (SS7 and SS9) were dived first and both proved to be modern lake boats or rowing boats, probably lost in the latter half of the twentieth century. Anomalies SS1, SS3, SS4, SS5, SS6, SS8 and SS11 were all modern or natural objects, including anglers' parasols, keep nets, a plastic box, a plastic bag and tree branches.

SS12, however, which was originally considered to be the anomaly with the least archaeological potential based on the side-scan sonar imagery, turned out to be a logboat (Fig. A2.2). It was one of two linear objects identified in the side-scan sonar data, lying 25m apart. They were both initially interpreted as possible logs, tree branches or possibly tree trunks. The most westerly of these anomalies turned out to be a branch of a tree measuring 2m in length, while the more easterly proved to be the remains of a logboat. This highlights the need to take a cautious approach when assessing side-scan sonar anomalies for archaeological purposes.

The logboat is located 245m west-north-west of Clogh Oughter (54 01.184N, 07 27.495W) and 160m

limestone, which gives the appearance of stones laid down side by side or of a pavement. This fracturing is clearly visible at various parts of the lake's shoreline and in the shallows around the castle, and it is entirely understandable how this could be mistaken for a man-made feature, given its pavement-style appearance.

The geophysical anomalies are scattered around the lake; at least two were identified as definite wrecks and

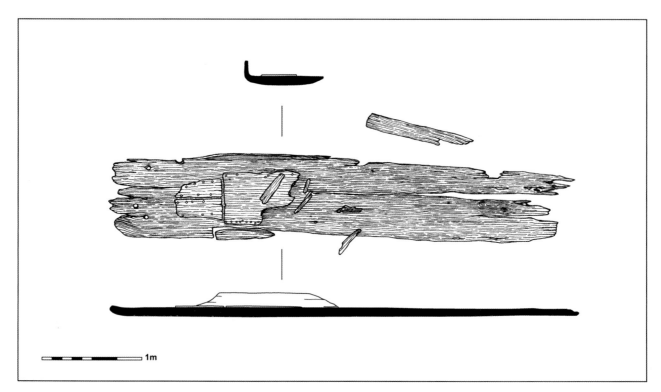

Fig. A2.3—Plan of logboat (Rex Bangerter).

east of the western shoreline of the lough. It lies in approximately 2m of water in an area of soft muddy lakebed (Fig. A2.3). It was left *in situ* and was recorded underwater, although a layer of thick sticky sediments and lake weed covering the boat resulted in extremely poor visibility. The logboat is in poor condition, with both ends missing and only a small portion of one side wall surviving. A number of broken-off pieces of the vessel scattered around the boat would originally have formed part of its floor and side walls. These were left *in situ* and were not disturbed during the survey. The boat is parallel-sided, but as both ends are badly eroded it is difficult to discern which is the bow and which the stern. It has a surviving length of 4.62m and a maximum width of 0.8m. The side wall survives for a length of 1.5m on one side; it has a maximum surviving external height of 0.16m and a maximum thickness of 50mm.

The boat's longitudinal section is flat-bottomed, although one end is slightly rounded and has a slight curve upwards, indicating an original rounded end. In cross-section the boat has a flat internal floor with a slightly curved bottom. The surviving side wall of the boat is almost vertical, which would originally have given the boat a U-shaped cross-section. The base of the boat had a maximum thickness of 70mm.

A number of splits have formed along the long axis of the boat, most of which developed as a result of normal stress and strain while in use. Attempts to repair these splits are evident in the presence of three repair patches near the rounded end, consisting of flat boards held in place by iron nails. The largest repair board measures 0.8m long by 0.5m wide, has a thickness of 5mm and is held in placed by thirteen iron nails. The two smaller boards were placed beside each other at one end of the large board and may represent a second phase of repair. One patch measures 0.47m long by 0.24m wide and is held in place by seven iron nails, while the smallest board measures 0.44m long by 0.2m wide and is also held in place by seven iron nails. These repair patches were intended to deal with the longitudinal split that runs along the boat from the rounded end for 0.5m before running under the repair patches. Another longitudinal split runs from the opposite end for at least 2.66m but does not appear to run under the repair patches. This split may have occurred after the boat had gone out of use. Again, a series of smaller splits at both ends of the boat appear to be due to natural erosion or damage that would have occurred after it was deposited on the lakebed, with the result that the bow and the stern have a jagged and fractured appearance.

The boat was made of oak with a straight grain, which indicates that the tree was of good quality.

Although no sapwood was evident, the presence of two knots at one end indicates that the original tree would not have been much thicker than the present width of the boat. There are no other internal features, apart from three possible thickness gauges on the floor of the boat near one end (thickness gauges are holes drilled into the floor or sides during the construction phase as a guide to determine the remaining thickness of the timber, to ensure that the floor or sides are kept at the requisite thickness). If these features are thickness gauges they have expanded as a result of drying out at some stage, or owing to erosion, as they measure between 40mm and 50mm in diameter, which would be a little bit wide for such gauges. Alternatively, they could be tree knotholes. No tool marks were discernible on the boat. This boat has been radiocarbon-dated to 300 ± 30 BP (Beta-329542) or cal. AD 1490–1600 (cal. BP 460–350) and cal. AD 1610–1650 (cal. BP 340–300), indicating that it was probably constructed sometime in the sixteenth or early seventeenth century and could potentially be one of the logboats mentioned in the contemporary account of the siege of Clogh Oughter in 1653.

Dive survey of the island

A dive survey was carried out around the entire circumference of the island over one day and identified a fragment of a possible logboat, lead shot, fragments of iron mortar bombs and a wattle panel. A wade and metal-detection survey was also carried out using a bathyscope in waters less than 0.75m deep around the island, while deeper water was assessed through a combination of diving and snorkelling. The dive assessment consisted of a systematic survey along a series of marked transects or lanes set 2–5m apart, depending on visibility. These transects acted as guides to the divers in conditions of poor visibility and ensured that full coverage was achieved of the waters around the island. The castle is positioned on a natural rock outcrop or knoll and its shoreline is composed of a combination of gravels, rock paving and soft silts and mud. The waters adjacent to the island are shallow, but towards the south and south-east the water deepens to over 2m within 10m of the shoreline and there are two deep pools over 7m in depth to the east and west of the island. The dive survey did not locate any material of an archaeological nature that could be considered to be part of a wooden palisade or any of the piles and beams on the shoreline described by Kirker and Davies. A wattle panel was, however, discovered approximately 25m to the north-west of the landing stage (54 01 09N, 07 27 19W). It lies in 1.8m of water and appears to be an isolated find rather than part

Pl. A2.3—Underwater photo of the wattle panel barely protruding above the lake sediments, 25m north-west of the island (Karl Brady).

Pl. A2.4—Musket-balls found during dive survey in waters around Clogh Oughter (Con Brogan).

of an *in situ* structure (Pl. A2.3). It is in a very fragile state and was drawn, photographed and recorded *in situ*. It is a rectangular panel, measuring 1.9m by 1.4m. A small sample was taken for dating and wood identification purposes. The panel has been radiocarbon-dated to 790 ± 30 BP or cal. AD 1210–1280 (Beta-329539), placing it firmly in the thirteenth century and around the time the castle was built, *c.* 1220–4. It is unclear what the original function of the wattle may have been, but it could have formed part of a structure or defences relating to the original crannog or the newly built thirteenth-century castle.

Possible logboat

A fragment of a possible logboat was also found on the north-eastern side of the island, lying loose in an area of muddy lakebed, in 0.5m of water. It was temporarily recovered so that it could be recorded and was then returned to its original find-spot, where it was reburied. The fragment is oak, 2.92m in total length with a maximum width of 0.51m. It is a flat piece of wood, badly eroded at both ends and along one of its sides. Neither the bow nor the stern is discernible and neither of the boat's sides survive. There were no other recognisable features present in the boat and no tool marks were present. It is possible that this timber originally formed part of the floor of a logboat, or it could have had some other function connected with the castle or its defences.

Finds

The licensed metal-detection survey of a small area of the waters surrounding the north-western and northern

sides of the castle resulted in the discovery of seven pieces of lead shot (Pl. A2.4) and two fragments of iron mortar bombs. It was decided to discontinue metal-detecting after a short period owing to time constraints and because of the problems associated with recovering and conserving the many finds that could potentially have been discovered. The lead shot were found over a 12m² area in water depths of 0.5–2m and include five pieces that appear to have been intended for use with a musket and one piece (12D0012:01) that was used as 'hail shot'. The smallest piece (12D0012:11) is definitely pistol shot, having a weight to the pound range of 64.80 (see above, pp 146–8, for detailed analysis of the shot found during the underwater survey). All of the lead shot have been fired, with one found on the current shoreline of the island and the remainder found in water just north of the island's shoreline. The distribution of the shot on the northern side of the island indicates that a previously undocumented skirmish took place on this side of the island. It is very unlikely that these shot were fired by the main besiegers who were encamped on the southern shore of the lake, as the effective range of muskets was far less than the 200m+ distance between the castle and that shoreline. This is further backed up by a description of the castle in 1641 as being 'above a musket shot from it to each shore' (Shuckburgh 1902, 189). The evidence would therefore appear to point to an engagement on the northern side of the island between a Parliamentarian raiding party and the besieged inhabitants of the castle, and may represent an unsuccessful Parliamentarian attempt to destroy the Confederates' boats before they were eventually destroyed by the use of a 'fiery floate' in March 1653 (see above, p. 30).

Two fragments of mortar bomb were found 6m apart, suggesting that they may be part of the same bomb. One fragment was found 18m to the north-west of the island in 1.5m of water. It has a curved profile and measures 22.5cm by 16.4cm, with a maximum thickness of 4.6cm. The second fragment was found by metal-detecting 12m to the north-west of the island in 1m of water. It has a curved profile and measures 19cm by 17.2cm, with a maximum thickness of 4.4cm. These finds are undoubtedly associated with the siege of the castle in 1653 and add to the considerable assemblage of mortar bomb fragments (36 possible examples) found during the excavation (see above, pp 144–5). These two fragments were not lifted and were too heavily corroded to yield any definite information regarding their original diameter or calibre. It would appear, however, from the fragmented nature of these finds that they were successfully fired at the castle and exploded in the air or fragmented upon impact against the castle walls.

As previously noted, the causeway and submerged flagged stone roadway proved to be natural, and show natural fracturing of the limestone (see Pl. A2.2). There was no evidence of an earlier crannog at the island and it is likely that the palisade and timbers mentioned by Davies and Kirker have since rotted away or are now covered in sediment. Three possible crannogs in the lough at Derryna (CV020-061) and at Drumany Rahan (CV020-040 and CV020-041) were also dived, but nothing of archaeological significance was found. The dive survey of the lake did not locate any other features, although it is likely that other archaeological material is still present on the lakebed. The dive survey was non-intrusive and the build-up of sediments over the centuries would certainly have buried material. Given the results achieved from the short survey, the archaeological potential of the waters surrounding the castle must still be considered to be high, and further licensed dive survey work in the area would certainly result in more archaeological discoveries.

DISCUSSION

Underwater archaeological investigations carried out in waters surrounding Clogh Oughter Castle resulted in the discovery of twelve geophysical anomalies, one of which turned out to be archaeological, a logboat. Through dive and metal-detection surveys a fragment of a possible logboat, seven pieces of lead shot, fragments of iron mortar bombs and a wattle panel were also discovered. This material is important in creating a fuller understanding of the castle's past and provides tangible links to important phases of the castle's history, such as the siege of the castle in 1653, activity on the site during the thirteenth century and the use of boats on the lake during the sixteenth or seventeenth century. The bathymetric survey also provided a better understanding of the castle's position and setting in the lake and confirmed that the castle was sited on a shallow north/south-running limestone bedrock outcrop, giving it a strategic prominence over boating traffic plying the Lough Oughter lake system. There are deep pools to the east and west of the island, and it is certain that even when lake levels were at their lowest during dry spells before the mid-nineteenth century the castle could not have been accessed by wading from the south or the north.

The archaeological material visible in the past at low water around the island's margins reported by Kirker and Davies, including a palisade, small stakes and piles and horizontal timbers, were not identified during the survey and it is likely that these have rotted away and decayed since they were first noted. Their exposure above the water level when the lake was drained around 150 years ago would have resulted in the timbers drying out and gradually decaying, leading to their eventual destruction. It is probable, however, that some of these timbers survive buried either in the lake sediments or on the island, but only excavation would confirm this. Unfortunately this does not help us to answer the question of whether or not the thirteenth-century castle was built on the original O'Reilly crannog mentioned in several of the sources. For example, in 1220 Walter de Lacy attacked and captured O'Reilly's crannog and 'obtained hostages and great power' (Orpen 1920, 32–3). The dive survey did not locate any remains of this earlier crannog at the site, and neither were a causeway or a flagged road visible at the site. A wattle panel was, however, discovered approximately 25m to the north-west of the present landing stage; this has been dated to the thirteenth century and could indicate that a wattle palisade was erected around the castle when it was first constructed *c.* 1220–4. Alternatively, this panel could have been from an earlier crannog on the site.

The seven pieces of shot and two fragments of mortar bombs are undoubtedly associated with the siege of the castle in 1653 and highlight the archaeological potential for more material relating to this significant event being present in the surrounding waters. Interestingly, the distribution of the fired lead shot on the northern side of the island appears to provide evidence for a previously undocumented skirmish between a Parliamentary raiding party and the defenders of the castle.

Use of logboats on Lough Oughter

The underwater survey found important evidence for the use of boats on the lake during the sixteenth/seventeenth centuries, and this is not surprising considering that waterways were a major focus of human activity and settlement from the earliest times. Lakes were exploited for their abundance of natural resources, including fish, waterfowl and raw materials, such as reeds for basketry, clay for pottery production and carr woodlands (woodlands in swampy or wetland areas dominated by alder and willow), which were exploited for a variety of everyday purposes. Lakes formed an essential part of major routeways and acted as channels of communication, travel and trade. Given the poor and limited road system, the use of boats on rivers and lakes would have been the easiest means of travel in such a water-dominated landscape, linking one community to another.

Lough Oughter is made up of a complex of small, interconnecting lakes interspersed with drumlins, islands, peninsulas, wetlands and narrow channels, and forms the southern part of the Lough Erne complex. It is a relatively shallow lake, covering an area of almost 90km^2, but would have been somewhat larger in antiquity, before it was drained during the mid-nineteenth century. The lake is connected to a number of other watercourses by the River Erne, including Lough Gowna to the south and Lough Erne to the north, making it a strategic section in an important regional waterway, with Clogh Oughter commanding the narrow point at Gubarinn.

The use of boats on Lough Oughter is well attested in the historical sources and in the archaeological record. In 1607 Lord Deputy Chichester highlighted the importance of the water system, stating that Ballyshannon could almost be reached from Lough Oughter by boat 'with a little help over a ford or two' (*CSPI* 1606–8, 336). Small craft or shallow-drafted vessels would have been perfectly suited for navigating shallow waters and could have manoeuvred throughout the lake systems with ease. This is attested by the large number of logboats that have been found to date in the lake, and undoubtedly there are many more to be discovered.

At least 23 logboats have been found in Lough Oughter over the last 150 years, and this represents approximately 5% of the known logboat finds in Ireland. Another twenty logboats, some dating from the Neolithic, have also been found on the Upper and Lower Lough Erne lake systems, which are connected to Lough Oughter by the River Erne. This significant concentration of logboat discoveries in the region illustrates their widespread use over a long period of time

and their importance in the lives of the communities utilising the resources of these waterways (Fry 2000, 123–8, 144). With regard to Lough Oughter, logboats have been found in all parts of the lake: three at Derries Lower, two at Derries Upper, seven at Trinity Island, two at Tirliffin, two at Killygowan, five at Killykeen, one at Rinn (logboat found by the UAU west of Clogh Oughter) and a possible logboat from Clogh Oughter Castle itself (see above). The earliest dated logboat was found in 2012 by the Underwater Archaeology Unit at Derries Upper and has been dated to the tenth century BC. This 12m-long logboat would have been an impressive sight plying the waters of the lake during the Late Bronze Age. The concentrations of boats near sites such as Trinity Island can be explained by the need to service the island community of an important monastic site from the thirteenth century onwards. These communities would have used boats to ferry people and goods to and from the mainland and other parts of the lake, as well as for travel and communication further afield. Fishing and the related use of boats on the lake would have played an important role in the life of the Trinity Island priory because of the monks' need for fish, particularly in Lent and on fast days. The number of logboats recorded from the lake indicates, however, that boats were in widespread use throughout this landscape over several millennia by all levels of society.

One of the earliest historical references to boats on Lough Oughter is from 1231 (*AFM*) and refers to a raid by Donnell O'Donnell, lord of Tirconnell, against O'Reilly, using boats that his party brought with them to plunder Eoinish. Again, in 1272 Lough Oughter was raided by an O'Donnell who carried boats from Lough Erne to Lough Oughter and raided the islands and the surrounding countryside. The majority of references in the annals and state papers refer to the use of boats for raiding and rarely distinguish the type of boat used. Occasionally, however, some sources do specify the use of logboats or cotts, as they were often called in the sources. In 1607 it is recorded that the baron of Delvin, who had just escaped from imprisonment in Dublin Castle, had used 'cottes' to escape from an unsuccessful cattle and sheep raid on Lough Oughter (*CSPI* 1606–8, p. 352). In 1641 the bishop of Kilmore, William Bedell, and his two sons and son-in-law were imprisoned in Clogh Oughter by the O'Reillys. Interestingly, their account of the ordeal states that they were transported to the island 'by a colt (*sic* cott) or trough made of one piece of timber' (Shuckburgh 1902, 190). This undoubtedly was a logboat and could possibly be the logboat found to the west of the castle during the underwater survey, which has been dated to this period.

Logboats are also referred to in contemporary sources relating to the siege of Clogh Oughter in 1653. Colonel Barrow, commander of the Parliamentarian forces besieging the castle, burnt the 'boates or cottes' of the castle using a 'a fiery floate' (Gilbert 1879–80, vol. 3, 371). 'Cotte', 'cot' or 'coite' were contemporary terms used to describe logboats, and it is clear that a number of the castle's logboats were destroyed by fire during the siege. Again, it is possible that the logboat discovered at Rinn (245m to the west of the island) or the fragment of a possible logboat found on the northern shore of the island could have been one of these cotts or logboats mentioned in the account of the siege. The date of the Rinn logboat is roughly contemporaneous with the siege and its close proximity to the castle, along with the fact that it is largely destroyed, would support this argument. No evidence for burning was found on the remains of the boat but its upper works, where the burning would have taken place, are now gone and it is therefore uncertain whether this boat was one of those burnt during the siege. The several attempts that were made to repair and prolong the life of this boat indicate that its owners were forced to patch it up well beyond its normal lifespan, possibly during a time of stress or pressure such as a siege, when the resources to make a new boat would not have been available.

This underwater survey was more of a reconnaissance than an in-depth study of the underwater cultural heritage of the lake and its environs, and even though important new archaeological evidence relating to the 1653 siege has been discovered, the lake itself would be worthy of a more focused project that would give us a deeper understanding of its importance and significance through time.

ACKNOWLEDGEMENTS

The following divers are thanked for their hard work and the contribution they made during the underwater survey: Rex Bangerter, Jimmy Lenehan, Eoghan Kieran, Aisling Collins, Fionnbarr Moore, Chris Corlett and Brian MacAllister. Thanks are also due to Fionnbarr Moore for his comments on an earlier draft of this text, to Rex Bangerter for producing the drawing of the logboat and to Damian Shiels for his report on the military finds recovered during the survey. Trevor Northage is also thanked for carrying out the geophysical surveys in the waters surrounding Clogh Oughter and for the supply of images used in this publication. Finally, I would like to thank Con Manning for requesting the Underwater Archaeology Unit to carry out the underwater survey and for providing many useful insights into the archaeology and history of Clogh Oughter.

APPENDIX 3
XRF analysis of selected artefacts

PAUL MULLARKEY

METHODOLOGY

The analysis was carried out using a Spectro Midex EDXRF (energy dispersive X-ray fluorescence) spectrometer with a molybdenum anode. The diameter of the tube collimator and the measurement spot size is 0.7mm, and the distance from the sample surface varies from 2mm to 5mm. The operating conditions for the X-ray tube were 45kV and 0.6mA at normal air pressure. Sample counting time was 180 seconds livetime. The principal elements analysed were copper, tin, lead, zinc, silver, gold, arsenic, antimony, iron and mercury (Table A3.1).

The components were analysed within the sample chamber and the measurement spot, which is indicated by a laser, was viewed on an adjacent monitor screen, thus allowing for accurate positioning of the sample sites. Owing to the shape and curvature of the spurs, the constrictions of the XRF chamber and the short focal distance to the X-ray source, only limited areas could be analysed. There was no sample preparation, such as polishing or abrasion of the surface, as this would have resulted in unacceptable damage. All the artefacts were recently conserved, however, resulting in relatively clean surfaces. Other factors affecting the results are the surface depletion and enrichment of copper, zinc, silver and lead, owing to corrosion mechanisms during burial. Where possible, three readings were taken from the chosen sites and the mean and standard deviation calculated.

RESULTS AND COMMENT

Owing to the bright yellow colouration of the three brass spurs it was assumed that they were gilt, but the analysis demonstrates that there was no gold present and the appearance may have been due to corrosion/patination mechanisms while buried. Spur E409:811 was damaged along the edge of the arm and revealed a void containing iron fragments and deposits. The damage to the arm was probably due to an iron core that had expanded in volume as a result of corrosion and which then erupted through the brass shell. In addition, there may have been imperfections in the brass through casting flaws or minute perforations, thus allowing ingress of moisture and initiating corrosion. The presence of an iron core may have been simply to save on the amount of brass required for casting the spur.

The presence of silver, gold and mercury on the threads of textile E409:1120 indicate that the thread covering was fabricated from silver, which was then gilt using the mercury amalgam method.

Table A3.1—Summary of results of XRF analysis.

Reg. no.	Component	Alloy	Copper	Tin	Lead	Zinc	Silver	Gold	Arsenic	Antimony	Iron	Mercury	Comments
E409:242	Spur, decorated	Brass	79.89	n.d.	0.58	16.73	0.1	n.d.	0.04	n.d.	0.57		
E409:811	Spur	Brass, ? iron core	80.24	2.4	0.56	14.97	0.11	n.d.	0.05	n.d.	0.72		
E409:304	Spur	Brass	80.97	0.9	0.67	16.02	0.09	n.d.	0.04	n.d.	0.38		
E409:64	Spur, rowel	Iron, arm inlay	0.0259	n.d.	n.d.	n.d.	31.71	n.d.	n.d.	n.d.	65.46		Inlaid strip
E409:64	Spur, rowel	Iron, brass plating	25.76	0.43	0.55	3.76	0.1	n.d.	0.02	0.05	65.84		
E409:104	Spur, inlay	Silver	1.2	n.d.	0.16	n.d.	96.12	0.3	n.d.	n.d.	0.73		
E409:1121	Spur	Iron, silver	0.34	n.d.	0.05	n.d.	92.69	n.d.	n.d.	n.d.	5.05		
E409:479	Strip, openwork	Gunmetal, leaded	75.19	9.18	5.82	7.09	0.12	n.d.	0.17	0.26	1.52		
E409:15	Key	Iron, brass plating	76.73	1.24	0.71	16.7	0.04	n.d.	0.03	n.d.	3.37		
E409:712	Key	Iron, brass plating	80.46	0.91	0.77	6.73	0.07	n.d.	0.04	n.d.	9.86		
E409:316	Watch–case	Iron, brass inlay	75.79	1.58	0.74	15.06	0.09	n.d.	n.d.	n.d.	8.2		
E409: 1119a	Textile, small	Silver	0.09	n.d.	0.08	0.02	96.59	n.d.	n.d.	n.d.	0.2	0.03	Wire over thread
E409: 1119b	Textile, smallest	Silver	0.13	n.d.	0.11	0.01	96.79	n.d.	n.d.	n.d.	0.16	0.05	Wire over thread
E409:1120	Textile, medium	Silver, gilt	2.33	n.d.	1.57	n.d.	90.6	3.18	0.03	n.d.	0.22	0.18	Wire over thread
E409:1120	Textile, large	Silver, gilt	3.2	n.d.	1.64	n.d.	88.33	3.01	0.04	n.d.	0.56	0.25	Wire over thread

Bibliography

Abbreviations

AC = A.M. Freeman (ed.), *The Annals of Connacht* (Dublin, 1970).

AFM = J. O'Donovan (ed.), *Annals of the Kingdom of Ireland by the Four Masters* (7 vols) (Dublin, 1854).

ALC = W.M. Hennessy (ed.), *Annals of Loch Cé* (2 vols) (London, 1871).

AU = W.M. Hennessy and B. MacCarthy (eds), *The Annals of Ulster* (4 vols) (Dublin, 1887–1901).

CSPI = *Calendar of state papers relating to Ireland, 1509–1670* (London, 1860–1912).

DIB = J. McGuire and J. Quinn (eds), *Dictionary of Irish biography from the earliest times to the year 2002* (9 vols) (Cambridge, 2009).

DIL = E.G. Quinn (ed.), *Dictionary of the Irish language* (compact edition) (Dublin, 1983).

DNB = H.C.W. Matthew and B. Harrison (eds), *Oxford dictionary of national biography* (60 vols) (Oxford, 2004).

Irish Fiants = *The Irish Fiants of the Tudor sovereigns, 1521–1603* (4 vols) (Dublin, 1994; reprinted from the Reports of the Deputy Keeper of the Public Records in Ireland, 1875–90).

NAI = National Archives of Ireland.

NLI = National Library of Ireland.

TCD = Trinity College Dublin.

References

Ainsworth, J. 1948 Abstracts of 17th century Irish wills in the prerogative court of Canterbury. *Journal of the Royal Society of Antiquaries of Ireland* **78**, 24–37.

Andrews, J.H. 1974 The maps of the escheated counties of Ulster. *Proceedings of the Royal Irish Academy* **74**C, 133–70.

Anon. 1949 *Souvenir programme of the Owen Roe O'Neill tercentenary commemoration, Cavan Town, Oct. 2nd to Oct. 9th, 1949*. [Cavan.]

Anon. 1960 National Museum of Ireland: archaeological acquisitions in the year 1958. *Journal of the Royal Society of Antiquaries of Ireland* **90**, 1–40.

Anon. 1968 National Museum of Ireland: archaeological acquisitions in the year 1965. *Journal of the Royal Society of Antiquaries of Ireland* **98**, 93–159.

Armstrong, E.C.R. 1917–18 Communication on cheek-pieces of bridle-bits in the museum of the Royal Irish Academy, Dublin. *Proceedings of the Society of Antiquaries of London* **30**, 187–9.

Arnold, J. 1987 *Patterns of fashion*. New York.

Avent, R. 2004 *Dolwyddelan Castle, Dolbadarn Castle, Castell y Bere*. Cardiff.

Bagwell, R. 1909–16 *Ireland under the Stuarts* (3 vols). London.

Barker, A.D. 1980 *Gold lace and embroidery*. Altrincham.

Barker, D. 1986 North Staffordshire post-medieval ceramics—a type series. Part two: Blackware. *Staffordshire Archaeological Studies* (new ser.) **3**, 59–75.

Barnard, T.C. 1975 *Cromwellian Ireland: English government and reform in Ireland 1649–1660*. Oxford.

Barnes, E. 1994 *Congenital defects of the axial skeleton*. Colorado.

Barratt, J. 2000 *Cavaliers: the Royalist army at war, 1642–1646*. Gloucestershire.

Bedell, W. 1685 *Leabhuir na Seintiomna arna ttarruing go gaidhlig tre chúram & dhúthracht an Doctúir Uilliam Bedel, roimhe so Easbug Chille móire a Néirinn*. London.

Bedell, W. 1871 *Life and death of William Bedell* (ed. J.E.B. Mayor). London.

Bernard, N. 1659 *The judgement of the late archbishop of Armagh*. London.

Berry, A.C. and Berry, R.J. 1967 Epigenetic variation in the human cranium. *Journal of Anatomy* **101** (2), 361–79.

Betts, I. and Weinstein, R. 2010 *Tin-glazed tiles from London*. London.

Bickerton, L.M. 2000 *English drinking glasses 1675–1825*. Princes Risborough.

Bickley, F. (ed.) 1947 *Report on the manuscripts of the late Reginald Rawdon Hastings, Esq., of the manor house, Ashby de la Zouch*, vol. IV. London.

Biddle, M. 2005 *Nonsuch Palace: the material culture of a noble Restoration household*. Oxford.

Blackmore, H.L. 1961 *British military firearms 1650–1850*. London.

Blackmore, H.L. 1976 *The armouries of the Tower of London: the ordnance*. London.

Boessneck, J. 1969 Osteological differences between sheep and goat. In D.R. Brothwell and E. Higgs (eds), *Science in archaeology: a survey of progress and research*, 331–58. Bristol.

Booth, K. and Roberts, P. 2000 Recording the keep, Dover Castle. *Château Gaillard* **19**, 21–3.

Bottigheimer, K. 1998 The hagiography of William Bedell. In T.C. Barnard, D. Ó Cróinín and K. Simms (eds), *A miracle of learning: studies in manuscripts and Irish learning: essays in honour of William O'Sullivan*, 201–8. Aldershot.

Boucher, F. 1965 *Histoire du costume*. Paris.

Brady, C.F. 1985 The O'Reillys of East Breifne and the problem of 'Surrender and Regrant'. *Breifne* **6** (23), 233–62.

Brady, C.F. 2004 The end of the O'Reilly lordship, 1584–1610. In D. Edwards (ed.), *Regions and rulers in Ireland, 1100–1650: essays for Kenneth Nicholls*, 174–200. Dublin.

Brazier, J.D. and Franklin, G.L. 1961 *Identification of hardwoods: a microscopic key*. London.

Breathnach, D. 1971 *Bedell and the Irish version of the Old Testament*. Baile Átha Cliath.

Brewer, J.S. and Bullen, W. (eds) 1868 *Calendar of the Carew manuscripts preserved in the archiepiscopal library at Lambeth 1575–1588*. London.

Brothwell, D.R. 1981 *Digging up bones*. London.

Buckley, L.A. 1994 Skeletal report, King John's Castle, Limerick. Unpublished report for Kenneth Wiggins.

Buckley, L.A. 1996 Skeletal report, Francis St., Dublin. Unpublished report for ADS Ltd.

Buckley, L.A. 2001 Bettystown, Co. Meath. Unpublished skeletal report for ADS Ltd.

Buckley, L.A. 2002 The excavation of an Early Christian cemetery at Solar, Co. Antrim. Appendix 2: The human skeletal remains. *Ulster Journal of Archaeology* **61**, 71–82.

Buckley, L.A. 2004 Smithfield, Dublin. Unpublished skeletal report for Margaret Gowen and Co. Ltd.

Buckley, L.A. 2008 St Peter's Church, Aungier Street. Unpublished skeletal report for ADS Ltd.

Buckley, L.A. and McConway, C. 2004 Wee band of brothers. *Archaeology Ireland* **18** (3), 40.

Buckley, L.A., Rouard, O. and Russell, A. 2008 Church Street, Dublin, skeletal report. Unpublished report for ADS Ltd.

Bull, S. 2008 *'The Furie of the Ordnance': artillery in the English Civil Wars*. Woodbridge.

Burnet, G. 1685 *The life of William Bedell, D.D., bishop of Kilmore in Ireland*. London.

Burnet, G. 1736 *The life of William Bedell, D.D., bishop of Kilmore in Ireland*. Dublin.

Byrne, F.J. 1973 *Irish kings and high-kings*. London.

Byrne, M.J. 1903 *Ireland under Elizabeth . . . being a portion of the history of Catholic Ireland by Don Philip O'Sullivan Bear*. Dublin.

Campbell, J.W.P. and Saint, A. 2002 The manufacture and dating of English brickwork 1600–1720. *Archaeological Journal* **159**, 170–93.

Canny, N. 2001 *Making Ireland British, 1580–1650*. Oxford.

Carney, J. 1950 *Poems on the O'Reillys*. Dublin.

Carney, J. 1959 *A genealogical history of the O'Reillys*. Cavan.

Caseldine, C.J. and Hatton, J.A. 1996 Early land clearance and wooden trackway construction in the third and fourth millennia BC at Corlea, Co. Longford. *Proceedings of the Royal Irish Academy* **95**B, 1–9.

Casway, J. 1980 Unpublished letters and papers of Owen Roe O'Neill. *Analecta Hibernica* **29**, 220–48.

Casway, J. 1984 *Owen Roe O'Neill and the struggle for Catholic Ireland*. Philadelphia.

Casway, J. 2006 The Ulster refuge of the northern army. *Breifne* **12** (42), 194–206.

Cherry, J. 2009 The indigenous and colonial urbanization of Cavan town, *c.* 1300–*c.* 1641. In B. Scott (ed.), *Culture and society in early modern Breifne/Cavan*, 85–105. Dublin.

Clark, J. (ed.) 1995 *The medieval horse and its equipment c. 1150–c. 1450*. Medieval Finds from Excavations in London: 5. London.

Clarke, A. 1989 Bishop William Bedell (1571–1642) and the Irish reformation. In C. Brady (ed.), *Worsted in the game: losers in Irish history*, 61–72. Dublin.

Cleary, R.M., Hurley, M.F. and Shee Twohig, E. 1997 *Skiddy's Castle and Christ Church, Cork: excavations 1974–77 by D.C. Twohig*. Cork.

Clinton, M., Fibiger, L. and Shiels, D. 2007 Archaeology of massacre: the Carrickmines mass grave and the siege of March 1642. In D. Edwards, P. Lenihan and C. Tait (eds), *Age of atrocity: violent death and political conflict in Ireland 1547–1650*, 190–203. Dublin.

Clogie, A. 1862 *Speculum Episcoporum, or the apostolic bishop: a brief account of the life and death of the most reverend father in God, Dr William Bedell* (ed. W.W. Wilkins). London.

Clyne, M. 2007 *Kells Priory, Co. Kilkenny: archaeological excavations by T. Fanning and M. Clyne.* Dublin.

Colfer, B. 2004 *The Hook Peninsula, County Wexford.* Cork.

Colgan, J. 1655 *Tractatus de Ioannis Scoti doctoris subtilis theologorumque principis vita, patria, elogiis encomiasticis, scriptis . . .* Antwerp.

Contini, M. 1965 *Fashion from ancient Egypt to the present day.* London.

Cotter, J.L. 1958 *Archaeological excavations at Jamestown, Virginia.* Washington.

Cowgill, J., de Neergaard, M. and Griffiths, N. 1987 *Knives and scabbards.* Medieval Finds from Excavations in London: 1. London.

Cox, M. and Mays, S. 2000 *Human osteology in archaeology and forensic science.* London.

Craig, M. 1982 *The architecture of Ireland from the earliest times to 1880.* London and Dublin.

Croker, T.C. (ed.) 1841 *Narratives illustrative of the contests in Ireland in 1641 and 1690.* London.

Crookshank, A. 1995 A life devoted to landscape painting: William Ashford (*c.* 1746–1824). *Irish Arts Review* **11**, 119–30.

Crookshank, A. and the Knight of Glynn 1994 *The watercolours of Ireland: works on paper in pencil, pastel and paint, c. 1600–1914.* London.

Cunningham, B. 1995 The Anglicisation of East Breifne: the O'Reillys and the emergence of County Cavan. In R. Gillespie (ed.), *Cavan: essays on the history of an Irish county*, 51–72. Blackrock.

Cutler, D. and Gale, R. 2000 *Plants in archaeology: identification manual of artefacts of plant origin from Europe and the Mediterranean.* Westbury and the Royal Botanic Gardens, Kew.

Davies, O. 1942 Contributions to the study of crannogs in south Ulster. *Ulster Journal of Archaeology* (3rd ser.) **5**, 14–30.

Davies, O. 1947 The castles of County Cavan, part 1. *Ulster Journal of Archaeology* (3rd ser.) **10**, 73–100.

Davies, O. and Quinn, D.B. (eds) 1941 The Irish pipe roll of 14 John, 1211–1212. *Ulster Journal of Archaeology* (3rd ser.) **4**, supplement.

Dawson, A. 2010 *English and Irish delftware 1570–1840.* London.

de hÓir, E. 1970 Annála as Breifne. *Breifne* **4** (13), 59–86.

Drury, H.C. 1925 The rushlight and its associates. *Journal of the Royal Society of Antiquaries of Ireland* **55**, 99–111.

Dunlevy, M. 1989 *Dress in Ireland.* London.

Dunlevy, M. 2011 *Pomp and poverty—a history of silk in Ireland.* New Haven and London.

Dunlop, R. 1913 *Ireland under the Commonwealth* (2 vols). Manchester.

Eames, E. and Fanning, T. 1988 *Irish medieval tiles.* Dublin.

Edlin, H.L. 1951 *British plants and their uses.* London.

Edwards, R.D. (ed.) 1938 Letter-book of Sir Arthur Chichester, 1612–1614. *Analecta Hibernica* **8**, 3–177.

Egan, G. 1998 *The medieval household: daily living c. 1150–c. 1450.* London.

Egan, G. 2005 *Material culture in London in the age of transition: Tudor and Stuart period finds c. 1450–c. 1700 from excavations at riverside sites in Southwark.* London.

Egan, G. 2010 *The medieval household: daily living c. 1150–c. 1450.* Woodbridge.

Ellis, B.M. 1995 Spurs and spur fittings. In J. Clark (ed.), *The medieval horse and its equipment c. 1150–c. 1450*, 124–56. Medieval Finds from Excavations in London: 5. London.

Eogan, G. 2012 *Excavations at Knowth, 5. The archaeology of Knowth in the first and second millennia AD.* Dublin.

Faber, G.R. 1938 Dyeing and tanning in classical antiquity. *Ciba Zeitschrift* **9**, 278–312.

Fanning, T. 1976 Excavations at Clontuskert Priory, Co. Galway. *Proceedings of the Royal Irish Academy* **76**C, 97–169.

Fenlon, J. 2003 *Goods and chattels: a survey of early household inventories in Ireland.* Dublin.

Fenlon, J. (ed.) 2012 *Clanricard's castle: Portumna House, Co. Galway.* Dublin.

Ferguson, N. 2012 *Civilization.* London.

Finnegan, M. 1978 Non-metric variation of the infracranial skeleton. *Journal of Anatomy* **125** (1), 23–37.

Foley, C. and Donnelly, C. 2012 *Parke's Castle, Co. Leitrim: archaeology, history and architecture.* Dublin.

Francis, P. 2000 *Irish delftware: an illustrated history.* London.

Fry, M. 2000 *Coití: logboats from Northern Ireland.* Antrim.

Gaimster, D. 1997 *German stoneware 1200–1900.* London.

Giblin, C. 1958 Catalogue of the material of Irish interest in the collection Nunziatura de Fiandra, Vatican Archives: Part 1, Vols 1–50. *Collectanea Hibernica* **1**, 7–134.

Gilbert, J.T. (ed.) 1879–80 *A contemporary history of affairs in Ireland from 1641 to 1653* (3 vols). Dublin.

Gillespie, R. 1995 Faith, family and fortune: the structures of everyday life in early modern Cavan.

In R. Gillespie (ed.), *Cavan: essays on the history of an Irish county*, 99–114. Blackrock.

Gillespie, R. 2007 The end of medieval Roscrea. In G. Cunningham (ed.), *The Roscrea Conference*, 55–60. Roscrea.

Gimson, H. and Regan, D. 2011 Site of 17th-century house, Inishconnell, County Cavan. Earthsound Archaeological Geophysics, unpublished report no. EAG 201.

Goodall, J. 2011 *The English castle 1066–1650*. New Haven and London.

Grant, A. 1975a The animal bones. In B. Cunliffe (ed.), *Excavations at Portchester Castle, Vol. 1: Roman*, 378–408. London.

Grant, A. 1975b Appendix B: The use of tooth wear as a guide to the age of domestic animals. In B. Cunliffe (ed.), *Excavations at Portchester Castle, Vol. 1: Roman*, 437–50. London.

Grant, A. 2005 *North Devon pottery*. Appledore.

Green, C. 1999 *John Dwight's Fulham pottery: excavations 1971–79*. London.

Griffith, M. (ed.) 1966 *Calendar of the Irish patent rolls of James 1st*. Dublin.

Grogan, E. and Kilfeather, A. 1997 *Archaeological inventory of County Wicklow*. Dublin.

Grose, F. 1791 *The antiquities of Ireland* (2 vols). London.

Halpin, A. and Buckley, L.A. 1995 Archaeological excavations at the Dominican Priory, Drogheda, Co. Louth. *Proceedings of the Royal Irish Academy* **95**C, 175–253.

Harbison, P. 2012 *William Burton Conyngham and his Irish circle of antiquarian artists*. New Haven and London.

Hartnett, P.J. 1945 Some Imokilly castles. *Journal of the Cork Historical and Archaeological Society* **50**, 42–53.

Harvey, J. 1972 *Conservation of buildings*. London.

Hather, J.G. 2000 *The identification of the northern European woods. A guide for archaeologists and conservators*. London.

Hayden, A.R. 2011 *Trim Castle, Co. Meath: excavations 1995–8*. Dublin.

Hayes-McCoy, G.A. 1960 Sir John Davies in Cavan in 1606 and 1610. *Breifne* **1** (3), 177–91.

Hayfield, C. 1988 Cowlam deserted village: a case study of post-medieval village desertion. *Post-Medieval Archaeology* **22**, 21–109.

Hegarty, S. (forthcoming) County Cavan's physical geography—the canvas for our cultural imprint. In J. Cherry and B. Scott (eds), *Cavan: history and society*. Dublin.

Hencken, H. O'N. 1942 Ballinderry crannog no. 2. *Proceedings of the Royal Irish Academy* **47**C, 1–76.

Henry, C. 2005 *English Civil War artillery, 1642–51*. Oxford.

Herity, M. (ed.) 2012 *Ordnance Survey Letters: Londonderry, Fermanagh, Armagh–Monaghan, Louth, Cavan–Leitrim*. Dublin.

Hibbert, C. 1968 *Charles I*. London.

Hickson, M. 1884 *Ireland in the seventeenth century or the Irish massacres of 1641–2* (2 vols). London.

Hill, G. 1877 *An historical account of the Plantation of Ulster at the commencement of the seventeenth century, 1608–1620*. Belfast.

Hodgkinson, J. 2010 *British cast-iron firebacks of the 16th to mid-18th centuries*. Crawley.

Horning, A.J. 2001 'Dwelling houses in the old Irish barbarous manner'. Archaeological evidence for Gaelic architecture in an Ulster Plantation village. In P.J. Duffy, D. Edwards and E. FitzPatrick (eds), *Gaelic Ireland. Land, lordship and settlement c. 1250–1650*, 375–96. Dublin.

Hume, I.N. 1969 *A guide to artifacts of Colonial America*. Philadelphia.

Hunter, R.J. 1970 An Ulster plantation town—Virginia. *Breifne* **4** (13), 43–51.

Hunter, R.J. 1973–5 The English undertakers in the plantation of Ulster, 1610–41. *Breifne* **4** (16), 471–99.

Hunter, R.J. 2012 *The Ulster Plantation in the counties of Armagh and Cavan 1608–1641*. Belfast.

Hunter, R.J. and Perceval-Maxwell, M. 1977 The muster roll of *c.* 1630: Co. Cavan. *Breifne* **5** (18), 206–22.

Hurley, M.F. and Sheehan, C.M. 1995 *Excavations at the Dominican priory, St Mary's of the Isle, Crosse's Green, Cork*. Cork.

Hurst, J.G. 1981 Nieder Seltsers mineral-water containers. In P.D. Sweetman, 'Some late seventeenth- to late eighteenth-century finds from Kilkenny Castle'. *Proceedings of the Royal Irish Academy* **81**C, 262–6.

Hurst, J.G., Neal, D.S. and van Beuningen, H.J.E. 1986 *Pottery produced and traded in north-west Europe 1350–1650*. Rotterdam.

Hutton, R. and Reeves, W. 1998 Sieges and fortifications. In J. Kenyon and J. Ohlmeyer (eds), *The civil wars: a military history of England, Scotland and Ireland 1638–1660*, 195–233. Oxford.

Institute of Archaeologists of Ireland 2007 *Environmental sampling guidelines for archaeologists*. Dublin.

Jackson, D. 1975–6 The taking of the earl of Ormond, 1600. *Journal of the Butler Society* **1** (6), 480–6.

Jennings, S. 1981 *Eighteen centuries of pottery from Norwich.* Norwich.

Johnston, R.A. 2011 *All things medieval: an encyclopedia of the medieval world.* Santa Barbara.

Jones, H. 1642 *A relation of the beginnings and proceedings of the rebellion in the County of Cavan, within the province of Ulster in Ireland, from the 23 of October, 1641, until the 15 of June, 1642, whereof hitherto nothing hath been reported . . .* London.

Jones, T.W. (ed.) 1872 *A true relation of the life and death of the right reverend father in God William Bedell, lord bishop of Kilmore in Ireland.* London.

Jope, E.M. 1961 Cornish houses 1400–1700. In E.M. Jope (ed.), *Studies in building history*, 192–222. London.

Kavanagh, J. (ed.) 1936 *Commentarius Rinuccinianus*, vol. 2. Dublin.

Kavanagh, J. (ed.) 1941 *Commentarius Rinuccinianus*, vol. 4. Dublin.

Kearney, H.F. 1953 Richard Boyle, ironmaster. A footnote to Irish economic history. *Journal of the Royal Society of Antiquaries of Ireland* **83**, 156–62.

Kelleher, C. 2011 *La Trinidad Valencera*—1588 Spanish Armada wreck. *Journal of Irish Archaeology* **20**, 123–39.

Kelly, F. 1997 *Early Irish farming: a study based mainly on the law-texts of the 7th and 8th centuries AD.* Dublin.

Kirker, S.R. 1890–1 Cloughoughter Castle, County Cavan. *Journal of the Royal Society of Antiquaries of Ireland* **21**, 294–7.

Knight, J.K. 1987 The road to Harlech: aspects of some early thirteenth-century Welsh castles. In J.R. Kenyon and R. Avent (eds), *Castles in Wales and the Marches*, 75–88. Cardiff.

Knight, J.K. 1993 Excavations at Montgomery Castle, Part II. The finds: metalwork. *Archaeologia Cambrensis* **142**, 182–242.

Knight, J.K. 2000 *The three castles: Grosmont Castle, Skenfrith Castle, White Castle.* Cardiff.

Knusel, C. 2000 Bone adaption and its relationship to physical activity in the past. In M. Cox and S. Mays (eds), *Human osteology in archaeology and forensic science*, 381–401. London.

Lacy, B. 1983 *An archaeological survey of County Donegal.* Lifford.

Lawson, G. 1994 Musical instrument remains from Montgomery Castle, Powys. In J. Knight, 'Excavations at Montgomery Castle, Part III. The finds: other than metalwork'. *Archaeologia Cambrensis* **143**, 196–203.

Leask, H.G. 1936 The buildings. In D.F. Gleeson, 'The castle and manor of Nenagh'. *Journal of the Royal Society of Antiquaries of Ireland* **66**, 263–9.

Leask, H.G. 1941 *Irish castles and castellated houses.* Dundalk.

Leask, H.G. 1961 Early seventeenth-century houses in Ireland. In E.M. Jope (ed.), *Studies in building history*, 243–50. London.

Lenihan, P. 2001 *Confederate Catholics at war, 1641–49.* Cork.

Livingstone, P. 1980 *The Monaghan story.* Enniskillen.

Lloyd, J.E. 1919 Who was Gwenllian de Lacy? *Archaeologia Cambrensis* (6th ser.) **19**, 292–8.

Lohan, R. 1994 *Guide to the archives of the Office of Public Works.* Dublin.

Longfield, A.K. 1929 *Anglo-Irish trade in the sixteenth century.* London.

Lynch, A. 2010 *Tintern Abbey, Co. Wexford: Cistercians and Colcloughs. Excavations 1982–2007.* Dublin.

Lynch, A. and Manning, C. 2001 Excavations at Dublin Castle, 1985–7. In S. Duffy (ed.), *Medieval Dublin II*, 169–204. Dublin.

Mac an Ghallóglaigh, D. 1988 Bréifne and its chieftains (940–1300). *Breifne* **7**, 523–55.

McCafferty, J. 2009 Venice in Cavan: the career of William Bedell, 1572–1642. In B. Scott (ed.), *Culture and society in early modern Breifne/Cavan*, 173–87. Dublin.

McCaughey, T. 2001 *Dr Bedell and Mr King: the making of the Irish Bible.* Dublin.

McCavitt, J. 1998 *Sir Arthur Chichester, lord deputy of Ireland 1605–1616.* Belfast.

McCracken, E. 1957 Charcoal-burning ironworks in seventeenth and eighteenth century Ireland. *Ulster Journal of Archaeology* **20**, 123–38.

McErlean, T. 1983 The Irish townland system of landscape organisation. In T. Reeves-Smyth and F. Hamond (eds), *Landscape archaeology in Ireland*, 315–39. British Archaeological Reports, British Series 116. Oxford.

McNeill, C. 1943 *The Tanner letters.* Dublin.

MacNéill, E. and Hogan, J. (eds) 1931 MS Rawlinson A 237, the Bodleian Library, Oxford. *Analecta Hibernica* **3**, 151–218.

McNeill, T.E. 1997 *Castles in Ireland: feudal power in a Gaelic world.* London.

McNeill, T.E. 2003a Squaring circles: flooring round towers in Wales and Ireland. In J.R. Kenyon and K. O'Conor (eds), *The medieval castle in Ireland and Wales: essays in honour of Jeremy Knight*, 96–106. Dublin.

McNeill, T.E. 2003b Flooring systems in the round towers of Wales and Ireland around 1200. In J.-M. Poisson and J.-J. Schwien (eds), *Le bois dans le château de pierre au Moyen Âge*, 311–19. Besançon.

McSparron, C. 2011 The medieval coarse pottery of Ulster. *Journal of Irish Archaeology* **20**, 101–21.

Maginn, C. 2009 Elizabethan Cavan: the institutions of Tudor government in an Irish county. In B. Scott (ed.), *Culture and society in early modern Breifne/Cavan*, 69–84. Dublin.

Mahaffy, R.P. (ed.) 1912 *Calendar of the state papers relating to Ireland 1601–3*. London.

Manning, C. 1989–90 Clogh Oughter Castle. *Breifne* **8** (1), 20–61.

Manning, C. 1997 The bridge of Finnea and the man who built it. *Archaeology Ireland* **11** (1), 29–33.

Manning, C. 1998 Dublin Castle: the building of a royal castle in Ireland. *Château Gaillard* **18**, 119–22.

Manning, C. 1999 *Clogh Oughter: a medieval island castle in County Cavan*. Archaeology Ireland Heritage Guide No. 7. Bray.

Manning, C. 2002 Low-level roofs in Irish great towers. *Château Gaillard* **20**, 137–40.

Manning, C. 2003 The Record Tower, Dublin Castle. In J.R. Kenyon and K. O'Conor (eds), *The medieval castle in Ireland and Wales*, 72–95. Dublin.

Manning, C. 2009a *The history and archaeology of Glanworth Castle, Co. Cork: excavations 1982–4*. Dublin.

Manning, C. 2009b Irish tower houses. In G. Perbellini (ed.), *Towers and smaller castles: Europa Nostra bulletin* **63**, 19–30.

Manning, C. 2012 Clogh Oughter Castle, Co. Cavan, and thirteenth-century circular towers in Ireland. *Château Gaillard* **25**, 223–32.

Manning, C. (forthcoming) 'But first you are to build a tower': the Bermingham Tower, Dublin Castle. In T. Reeves-Smyth and P. Logue (eds), *Beyond the horizon of memory: a festschrift in honour of Christopher Lynn*.

Mant, R. 1840 *History of the Church of Ireland*. London.

Margey, A. 2009 Surveying and mapping plantation in Cavan, *c.* 1580–1622. In B. Scott (ed.), *Culture and society in early modern Breifne/Cavan*, 106–20. Dublin.

Marshall, K. 1950 Cast bronze cauldrons of medieval type in the Belfast Museum. *Ulster Journal of Archaeology* **13**, 67–75.

Massari, D. 1917 My Irish campaign (parts). *Catholic Bulletin* **7**, 179–82, 246–9.

Medieval Pottery Research Group 1998 *Guide to the classification of medieval ceramic forms.*

Meehan, C.P. 1870 *The fate and fortunes of Hugh O'Neill, Earl of Tyrone, and Rory O'Donnell, Earl of Tyrconnell; their flight from Ireland and death in exile*. Dublin.

Meehan, J. 1906 The arms of the O'Rourkes: a metal casting from County Leitrim seventeenth-century foundries. *Journal of the Royal Society of Antiquaries of Ireland* **36**, 123–42.

Meek, H. and Jope, E.M. 1958 The castle of Newtownstewart, Co. Tyrone. *Ulster Journal of Archaeology* (3rd ser.) **21**, 109–14.

Monck Mason, H.J. 1843 *The life of William Bedell, D.D., lord bishop of Kilmore*. London.

Monk, M., McLaren, F. and Sexton, R. 2004 Burning the biscuit: evidence from the Lisleagh excavations reveals new secrets twenty years on! *Archaeology Ireland* **18** (3), 18–20.

Moody, T.W. (ed.) 1938 Ulster plantation papers 1608–13. *Analecta Hibernica* **8**, 179–297.

Moody, T.W., Martin, F.X. and Byrne, F.J. (eds) 1976 *A new history of Ireland*, vol. 3. Oxford.

Moore, M. 2003 *Archaeological inventory of County Leitrim*. Dublin.

Moorhouse, S. 1971 Finds from Basing House, Hampshire (*c.* 1540–1645): part two. *Post-Medieval Archaeology* **5**, 35–76.

Moorhouse, S. 1988 Documentary evidence for medieval ceramic roofing materials and its archaeological implications: some thoughts. *Medieval Ceramics* **12**, 33–55.

Morgan, H. 2010 True likenesses? The search for authentic portraits of the Great O'Neills. In P. Murray (ed.), *Portraits and people: art in seventeenth-century Ireland*, 22–5. Cork.

Morley, H. 1890 *Ireland under Elizabeth and James the First*. London.

Morrin, J. (ed.) 1862 *Calendar of the patent and close rolls of chancery in Ireland from the 18th to the 45th of Elizabeth*, vol. 2. Dublin.

Morrin, J. (ed.) 1863 *Calendar of the patent and close rolls of chancery in Ireland of the reign of Charles the First, first to eighth years inclusive*, vol. 3. Dublin.

Munby, J. and Tyler, R. 2005 *Kilkenny City walls conservation plan*. Kilkenny.

Murphy, D. 1883 *Cromwell in Ireland*. Dublin.

Murray, P. (ed.) 2010 *Portraits and people: art in seventeenth-century Ireland*. Cork.

Murtagh, B. 1993 The Kilkenny Castle archaeological project 1990–1993: interim report. *Old Kilkenny Review* (new ser.) **4** (5), 1101–17.

Museum of London: The Ceramics and Glass Collection (http://www.museumoflondon.org.uk/ceramics/; accessed 13/06/2011).

Naessens, P. and O'Conor, K. 2012 Pre-Norman fortification in eleventh- and twelfth-century Connacht. *Château Gaillard* **25**, 259–68.

Norman, A.V.B. 1980 *The rapier and small-sword, 1460–1820*. London.

O'Conor, K. 1998 *The archaeology of medieval rural settlement in Ireland*. Dublin.

O'Conor, K., Brady, N., Connon, A. and Fidalgo-Romo, C. 2010 The Rock of Lough Cé, Co. Roscommon. In T. Finan (ed.), *Medieval Lough Cé: history, archaeology and landscape*, 15–40. Dublin.

O'Donovan, E. 2001 Limerick's history through artefacts: discoveries in advance of construction on the bed of the Abbey River. In *Limerick navigation 1999–2001*, 26–31. Limerick.

O'Donovan, E. 2003 Limerick: new discoveries in the old city. *History Ireland* **11** (1), 39–43.

O'Donovan, J. (ed.) 1854 *Annals of the kingdom of Ireland by the Four Masters* (7 vols). Dublin.

O'Donovan, P.F. 1995 *Archaeological inventory of County Cavan*. Dublin.

Ó Floinn, R. 2002 Late medieval Ireland, AD 1150–1550. In P.F. Wallace and R. Ó Floinn (eds), *Treasures of the National Museum of Ireland: Irish antiquities*, 257–300. Dublin.

Ogden, A.R. 2008 Periapical voids in human jaw bones. In M. Brickey and M. Smith (eds), *Proceedings of the Eighth Annual Conference of the British Association for Biological Anthropology and Osteoarchaeology*, 51–6. British Archaeological Reports, International Series 1743. Oxford.

Ohlmeyer, J. 2012 *Making Ireland English: the Irish aristocracy in the seventeenth century*. New Haven and London.

Ohlmeyer, J. and Ó Ciardha, E. (eds) 1998 *The Irish statute staple books, 1596–1687*. Dublin.

O'Keeffe, T. 2009 Dublin Castle's donjon in context. In J. Bradley, A.J. Fletcher and A. Simms (eds), *Dublin in the medieval world: studies in honour of Howard B. Clarke*, 277–94. Dublin.

Ó Mórdha, E. 2002a The Uí Briúin Bréifni genealogies and the origins of Bréifne. *Peritia* **16**, 444–50.

Ó Mórdha, E. 2002b On Loch Uachtair (Lough Oughter, Co. Cavan). *Peritia* **16**, 477–8.

Ó Mórdha, S.P. 1970 Hugh O'Reilly (1581?–1653), a reforming primate. *Breifne* **4** (13), 1–42.

Ó Mórdha, S.P. 1972 Hugh O'Reilly (1581?–1653), a reforming primate (continued). *Breifne* **4** (15), 345–69.

Ó Mórdha, S.P. 1981 The castle of Ballynacargy: some notes on aspects of its history. *The Heart of Breifne* [**4**], 49–61.

Ó Muraíle, N. (ed.) 2007 *Turas na dtaoiseach nUltach as Éirinn: from Ráth Maoláin to Rome*. Rome.

O'Reilly, H. 1985 Lisnamaine Castle. *Breifne* **6** (23), 263–76.

Orpen, G. 1920 *Ireland under the Normans, 1216–1333*. Oxford.

Ortner, D.J. 2003 *Identification of pathological conditions in human skeletal remains* (2nd edn). London.

O'Sullivan, A. 1998 *The archaeology of lake settlement in Ireland*. Dublin.

O'Sullivan, A. 2001 Crannogs in late medieval Gaelic Ireland c. 1350–c. 1650. In P.J. Duffy, D. Edwards and E. FitzPatrick (eds), *Gaelic Ireland. Land, lordship and settlement c. 1250–1650*, 397–417. Dublin.

Parker, C. 1991 The O'Reillys of east Breifne c. 1250–c. 1450. *Breifne* **8** (2), 155–80.

Parker, C. 1995 Cavan: a medieval border area. In R. Gillespie (ed.), *Cavan: essays on the history of an Irish county*, 37–50. Blackrock.

Pearsall, D. 2000 *Palaeoethnobotany: handbook of procedures* (2nd edn). San Diego.

Perceval-Maxwell, M. 1999 *The Scottish migration to Ulster in the reign of James I* (2nd edn). Belfast.

Peterson, H.L. (ed.) 1964 *Encyclopaedia of firearms*. London.

Petrie, G. 1972 An essay on military architecture in Ireland previous to the English invasion. *Proceedings of the Royal Irish Academy* **72**C, 219–69.

Platt, C. and Coleman-Smith, R. 1975 *Excavations in medieval Southampton 1953–1969* (2 vols). Leicester.

Pretsch, S. 1999 *Antico Setificio Fiorentino*. Florence.

Prummel, W. and Frisch, H.J. 1986 A guide to the distinction of species, sex and body size in bones of sheep and goat. *Journal of Archaeological Science* **13**, 567–77.

Rackham, O. 1980 *Ancient woodland: its history, vegetation and uses in England*. London.

Reeves-Smyth, T. 2007 Community to privacy: late Tudor and Jacobean manorial architecture in Ireland, 1560–1640. In A. Horning, R. Ó Baoill, C. Donnelly and P. Logue (eds), *The post-medieval archaeology of Ireland, 1550–1850*, 289–326. Dublin.

Reid, W. 1922 Killykeen and Clogh Oughter. *Breifne Antiquarian Journal* **1** (3), 240–61.

Roberts, K. 2002a *Matchlock musketeer 1588–1688.* Oxford.

Roberts, K. 2002b *Soldiers of the English Civil War: infantry.* Oxford.

Robinson, P. 1979 Vernacular housing in Ulster in the seventeenth century. *Ulster Folklife* **25**, 1–28.

Roulston, W. 2009 The Scots in plantation Cavan, 1610–42. In B. Scott (ed.), *Culture and society in early modern Breifne/Cavan*, 121–46. Dublin.

Russell, C.W. and Prendergast, J.P. (eds) 1874a *Calendar of the state papers relating to Ireland of the reign of James 1, 1606–1608.* London.

Russell, C.W. and Prendergast, J.P. (eds) 1874b *Calendar of the state papers relating to Ireland of the reign of James 1, 1608–1610.* London.

Russell, C.W. and Prendergast, J.P. (eds) 1877 *Calendar of the state papers relating to Ireland of the reign of James 1, 1611–1614.* London.

Russell, C.W. and Prendergast, J.P. (eds) 1880 *Calendar of the state papers relating to Ireland of the reign of James 1, 1615–1625.* London.

Russell, E. 1974 *Excavations on the site of the deserted medieval village of Kettleby Thorpe, Lincolnshire.* Journal of the Scunthorpe Museum Society, Series 3 (Archaeology), No. 2. Scunthorpe.

Rutter, J.A. and Davey, P.J. 1980 Clay pipes from Chester. In P. Davey (ed.), *The archaeology of the clay tobacco pipe III*, 41–272. British Archaeological Reports, British Series 78. Oxford.

Samson, R. 1982 Finds from Urquhart Castle in the National Museum, Edinburgh. *Proceedings of the Society of Antiquaries of Scotland* **112**, 465–76.

Saunders, A. 2006 *Excavations at Launceston Castle, Cornwall.* Leeds.

Schweingruber, F.H. 1978 *Microscopic wood anatomy.* Birmensdorf.

Scott, A.B. and Martin, F.X. (eds) 1979 *Expugnatio Hibernica: the conquest of Ireland.* Dublin.

Scott, B. 2007 *Cavan, 1609–1653: plantation, war and religion.* Dublin.

Scott, B. 2009 Reporting the 1641 rising in Cavan and Leitrim. In B. Scott (ed.), *Culture and society in early modern Breifne/Cavan*, 200–14. Dublin.

Scott, B. 2010 *Farnham: images from the Maxwell Estate, Co. Cavan.* Dublin.

Scott, I. 2001 The military artefacts and horse gear. In M. Biddle, J. Hiller, I. Scott and A. Streeten (eds), *Henry VIII's coastal artillery fort at Camber Castle, Rye, East Sussex*, 189–212. London.

Scully, O.M.B. 1997 Metal artefacts. In M.F. Hurley and O.M.B. Scully, *Late Viking Age and medieval Waterford: excavations 1986–1992*, 438–89. Waterford.

Scully, O.M.B. 2007 The ferrous artefacts. In M. Clyne, *Kells Priory, Co. Kilkenny: archaeological excavations by T. Fanning and M. Clyne*, 353–80. Dublin.

Sexton, R. 1998 Porridge, gruels and breads: the cereal foodstuffs of early medieval Ireland. In M. Monk and J. Sheehan (eds), *Early medieval Munster: archaeology, history and society*, 76–86. Cork.

Shiels, D. 2007 The potential for conflict archaeology in the Republic of Ireland. In T. Pollard and I. Banks (eds), *War and sacrifice: studies in the archaeology of conflict*, 169–87. Leiden.

Shirley, W.W. (ed.) 1862 *Royal and other historical letters illustrative of the reign of Henry III. Vol. 1 (1216–1235).* London.

Shuckburgh, E.S. (ed.) 1902 *Two biographies of William Bedell, bishop of Kilmore.* Cambridge.

Silver, I.A. 1971 The ageing of domestic animals. In D.R. Brothwell and E. Higgs (eds), *Science in archaeology, a survey of progress and research*, 230–68. Bristol.

Simms, J.G. 1979 The Williamite war in South Ulster. *Clogher Record* **10** (1), 155–62.

Simms, K. 1979 The O'Reillys and the kingdom of East Breifne. *Breifne* **5** (19), 305–19.

Simms, K. 2001 A lost tribe—the Clan Murtagh O'Conors. *Journal of the Galway Archaeological and Historical Society* **53**, 1–22.

Smith, B. (ed.) 1996 *The register of Milo Sweteman, archbishop of Armagh 1361–1380.* Dublin.

Stalley, R. (ed.) 1991 *Daniel Grose (c. 1766–1838). The antiquities of Ireland: a supplement to Francis Grose.* Dublin.

Stevenson, J. 1995 A new type of late medieval spectacle frame from the City of London. *London Archaeologist* **7** (12), 321–7.

Straker, E. 1931 *Wealden iron.* London.

Straube, B.A. 2006 'Unfitt for any modern service'? Arms and armour from James Fort. *Post-Medieval Archaeology* **40** (1), 33–61.

Strickland, W.G. 1913 *A dictionary of Irish artists* (2 vols). Dublin and London.

Sutherland, W.J. 1996 *Ecological census techniques: a handbook.* Cambridge.

Sweetman, H.S. (ed.) 1875 *Calendar of the documents relating to Ireland 1171–1251.* London.

Sweetman, P.D. 1998 The development of Trim Castle in the light of recent research. *Château Gaillard* **18**, 223–30.

Sweetman, [P.]D. 1999 *The medieval castles of Ireland.* Cork.

Swift, M. 1999 *Historical maps of Ireland.* London.

Thompson, A., Grew, F. and Schofield, J. 1984 Excavations at Aldgate, 1974. *Post-Medieval Archaeology* **18**, 1–148.

Treadwell, V. (ed.) 2006 *The Irish Commission of 1622: an investigation of the Irish administration, 1615–1622, and its consequences, 1623–1624.* Dublin.

Trevelyan, W.C. and Trevelyan, C.E. (eds) 1872 *Trevelyan papers*, Part III. London.

Tyler, K. and Willmott, H. 2005 *John Baker's late 17th-century glasshouse at Vauxhall.* London.

Veach, C. and Verstraten Veach, F. 2013 William Gorm de Lacy, 'chiefest champion in these parts of Europe'. In S. Duffy (ed.), *Princes, prelates and poets in medieval Ireland: essays in honour of Katherine Simms*, 63–84. Dublin.

Vicars, J. 1897 *Index of the prerogative wills of Ireland, 1536–1810.* Dublin.

Walker, J.C. 1788 *Historical essay on the dress of the ancient and modern Irish.* Dublin.

Walsh, P. 1960 *Irish chiefs and leaders.* Dublin.

Warner, R. 1994 On crannogs and kings (part 1). *Ulster Journal of Archaeology* **57**, 61–9.

Waterman, D.M. 1961 Some Irish seventeenth-century houses and their architectural ancestry. In E.M. Jope (ed.), *Studies in building history*, 251–74. London.

Waterman, D.M. 1971 A marshland habitation site near Larne, Co. Antrim. *Ulster Journal of Archaeology* **34**, 65–76.

Webb, J. 1981 *Buckles identified.* Hutton.

Went, A.E.J. 1957 The pike in Ireland. *Irish Naturalists' Journal* **12** (7), 177–82.

Wheeler, E.A., Bass, P. and Gasson, P.E. 1989 IAWA list of microscopic features for hardwood identification. *IAWA Bulletin* **10** (3), 219–332. Leiden.

Whitehead, R. 1996 *Buckles, 1250–1800.* Chelmsford.

Wiggins, K. 2000 *Anatomy of a siege: King John's Castle, Limerick, 1642.* Bray.

Wightman, W.E. 1966 *The Lacy family in England and Normandy 1066–1194.* Oxford.

Wilcox, R.P. 1981 *Timber and iron reinforcement in early buildings.* London.

Wilde, W. 1861 *A descriptive catalogue of the antiquities of animal materials and bronze in the museum of the Royal Irish Academy.* Dublin.

Williams, N. 1986 *I bprionta i leabhar: na Protastúin agus prós na Gaeilge 1567–1724.* Baile Átha Cliath.

Willmott, H. 2002 *Early post-medieval vessel glass in England c. 1500–1670.* York.

Wincott Heckett, E. 2012 Gold metal thread lace. In T. Bolger and L. Hegarty, 'Archaeological excavations at Castle Donovan, County Cork'. *Journal of the Cork Historical and Archaeological Society* **117**, 73–5.

Wincott Heckett, E. (forthcoming a) The textiles from Dublin Castle.

Wincott Heckett, E. (forthcoming b) The textiles. In *Excavations at South Main Street, Cork.*

Wood, H. (ed.) 1933 *The Chronicle of Ireland 1584–1608 by Sir James Perrott.* Dublin.

Wren, J. 1987 Crested ridge-tiles from medieval towns in Leinster, 1200–1500 AD. Unpublished MA thesis, University College Dublin.

Wren, J. 2004 Roof, floor and wall tiles. In E. Fitzpatrick, M. O'Brien and P. Walsh (eds), *Archaeological investigations in Galway City, 1987–1998*, 452–9. Dublin.

Wren, J. 2011 Ceramic roof tiles. In A. Hayden, *Trim Castle, Co. Meath: excavations 1995–8*, 379–84. Dublin.

Wren, J. (forthcoming a) The roof tiles. In A. Hayden, 'Excavations at the Cornmarket, Dublin'.

Wren, J. (forthcoming b) Clay building materials. In T. Petervary, 'Excavations at Cross Street, Athenry'.

Wren, J. (forthcoming c) Clay building materials. In A. Quinn, 'Excavations at Boyle Abbey, Co. Roscommon'.

Wren, J. (forthcoming d) Roof tiles and kiln material. In C. Walsh, 'Excavations at Hanbury Lane, Dublin'.